ECONOMICS OF EUROPEAN INTEGRATION

ECONOMICS OF EUROPEAN INTEGRATION

Edited by

TIBOR PALÁNKAI
Budapest University of Economic Sciences and Public Administration

1828

AKADÉMIAI KIADÓ, BUDAPEST

This book is published with the financial assistance of the Office of Higher Education Programmes (FPI)

ISBN 963 05 7990 1

Published by Akadémiai Kiadó
H-1519 Budapest, P. O. Box 245

Printed in Hungary

CONTENTS

A. INTRODUCTION INTO THE ECONOMICS OF GLOBAL AND REGIONAL INTEGRATION 11

I. The global world economy and integration 13
1. Global economics or megaeconomics 13
2. Transnational companies and global integration processes 14

II. Main schools of international integration theories 22
1. The genesis of integration theories 22
2. The content of integration 27
2.1. Division of labour theories and transactionalists 28
2.2. Interdependence and integration 32
3. Basic forms and institutions of integration 37
3.1. Basic forms of integration 37
3.2. Liberal integration theories 39
3.3. Institutionalism and integration 42
3.4. Federalism contra intergovernmentalism 44
4. Regulation (policies) and governance of integration processes 48
4.1. Integration and regulation 48
4.2. From functionalism to neofunctionalism 52
4.3. Multi-level governance 56
4.4. What sort of future European Union? 61
5. Some possible theoretical interpretations of international integration 65

III. Integration maturity – membership criteria 72
1. Theoretical approaches 72
2. Market economy criteria of integration 82
3. Developmental and structural (competitiveness) requirements 89
4. Macroeconomic stability and stabilization 99
5. Convergence (real or financial) 107
6. Financing and financeability 110
7. Social cohesion and integration 116
8. The political criteria for membership 118
9. Maturity for membership – institutions and law harmonization 127
10. Some methodological questions 131

IV. The economics of market integration 137
1. 'Classical' customs union theories: market advantages and disadvantages 137
1.1. Mechanisms of integration effects in customs union theories 137
1.2. Analysis in a supply and demand model 141
1.3. The customs union and the abolition of quantitative restrictions 146
1.4. Factors influencing gains and losses 148
2. "Dynamic" concepts in customs union theory 150
3. Some macroeffects of the customs union 154
4. Critical observations on the advantageousness of customs union integration 156
5. The theoretical frameworks of the common market 159
5.1. Comparative advantages and factors of production 159
5.2. Relative factor prices and comparative advantages on global markets 162
5.3. Comparative advantages and international factor flows 165
5.4. The theoretical foundations of the common market 170
6. The customs union – the common market – the single internal market 175
7. Measuring the effects of integration 177

B. THE PROCESSES OF EUROPEAN INTEGRATION 183

I. From the customs union to the single European market by Á. Kengyel and T. Palánkai 185
1. The program of the single European market 185
1.1. Dismantling the physical barriers 186
1.2. Removal of technical barriers 187
1.3. The single market and tax harmonization (removal of fiscal barriers) 192
2. Some effects of the 1992 single European market 195
3. The state of the single market and further tasks 199
3.1. Further integration of markets 200
3.2. Improvement of the business environment 201
3.3. Satisfying citizens' needs 202
3.4. Preparation for enlargement 202

II. Economic and Monetary Union 204
1. The beginnings of monetary integration in Europe 204
1.1. First experiments in monetary integration 204
1.2. The European Monetary System – EMS 206
1.3. The EMS and "external" monetarism 210
2. Economic and Monetary Union – EMU in EU 214
2.1. The theoretical bases of economic and monetary union 214
2.2. The Maastricht decisions about EMU 219
2.3. The performance of the euro and the euro-zone economies 225
2.4. Structural problems and the need for reforms in the EU 232
2.5. Structural reforms and the euro 238
3. The economics of monetary integration 242
3.1. The costs and benefits of monetary integration 242
3.2. Economic and monetary union – integration maturity 246
3.3. Market economy requirements for monetary integration 247
3.4. 'Asymmetric shocks' – convergence – financiability – cohesion 253

4. EMU and economic policy coordination – institutional criteria ... 258
4.1. First experiences of coordination of monetary policy and economic policy ... 263
4.2. The euro and international monetary coordination ... 268
5. EMU and the CEE candidates ... 276

III. The budget of the European Union ... 291
1. The characteristics of the EU budget ... 291
1.1. Principles and characteristics of budget financing ... 293
1.2. The economic policy functions of the EU budget ... 297
1.3. Principles of program financing ... 300
2. The main directions of reform of the common budget ... 301
3. The common budget and EMU ... 308
4. Fiscal federalism ... 312

IV. Structural policy roles and directions by Á. Kengyel and T. Palánkai ... 317
1. Industrial policy ... 320
1.1. The development and aims of industrial policy ... 321
1.2. Sectoral policies ... 323
1.2.1. The steel industry ... 324
1.2.2. Shipbuilding ... 326
1.2.3. The textile and clothing industry ... 327
1.2.4. Aircraft manufacture ... 328
1.2.5. Information technology sectors ... 329
1.2.6. Telecommunications ... 331
2. The Common Agricultural Policy ... 332
2.1. The reasons for the development of the Common Agricultural Policy ... 332
2.2. The regulation and operation of the Common Agricultural Policy ... 334
3. Research and development policy ... 338
3.1. The necessity for a common R&D policy ... 339
3.2. The development and regulation of R&D policy ... 341
3.3. The new R&D framework program and the European Research Area ... 345
4. Community energy policy ... 346
4.1. The energy situation of the member countries ... 347
4.2. The main directions of Community energy policy ... 349

V. The EU's regional policy by Á. KENGYEL 355
1. The necessity of an active regional policy 356
2. Regional development differences in the EU economy 359
3. Components of the EU's regional policy 362
4. Expenditure on subsidies 365
5. The effects of subsidies in helping countries catch up 367
6. The EU's Eastern enlargement and regional policy 370

VI. The integration performance of the EU countries by Á. KENGYEL and T. PALÁNKAI 376
1. Integration in trade and production 377
2. The flow of factors and the integration processes 382
3. The development of microintegration processes 386

VII. The member countries' macroeconomic performance by Á. KENGYEL and T. PALÁNKAI 392
1. Pattern of economic development 392
1.1. The 'golden age' of economic development 394
1.2. The European economy in crisis 395
1.3. The restoration of economic stability 397
1.4. New tendencies and efforts in the 1990s 399

VIII. The EU's foreign trade relations by M. BATÓ and T. PALÁNKAI .. 403
1. The frameworks of trade relations 403
2. The common commercial policies 406
3. Types of EU trade relations 407
3.1. Non-discriminatory systems 407
3.2. Preferential systems 408
3.3. Free trade systems 410
3.4. Relations with EFTA and the European Economic Area 412
3.5. Discriminatory systems 415
4. Associations with former colonies 417
4.1. The main measures of the Lomé Conventions 419
4.2. The Cotonou Agreement 422

IX. Central and Eastern Europe and the European Union 427
1. Association agreements between Central and Eastern Europe and the European Union 427
1.1. From 'east-west' relations to association 427

1.2. The main elements and new features of the Europe Agreements ... 431
1.3. The results of the Europe Agreements ... 433
1.4. The deficiencies of the association agreements ... 438
2. Sub-regional cooperation and integration ... 442
3. Central and Eastern Europe on the way to full membership ... 446
3.1. The start of negotiations on full membership (antecedents and conditions) ... 446
3.2. The new members' "fitness" (maturity) for integration ... 450
4. The EU's 'receptiveness' (absorption capacities) and its interests... 453

A.

INTRODUCTION INTO THE ECONOMICS OF GLOBAL AND REGIONAL INTEGRATION

I.

THE GLOBAL WORLD ECONOMY AND INTEGRATION

1. GLOBAL ECONOMICS OR MEGAECONOMICS

The globalization of the world economy and the processes of integration are developments of historical importance in our time. In the past decades they have caused radical changes in the conditions of economic activity and production, and the possibilities of consumption. The development of national economies has entered a new stage. The content of the traditional economic categories and the laws of operation and the mechanisms of the economy have changed.

The world economy must be understood and handled as an organic unit. Global economics (or megaeconomics) seeks to describe it. The changes in the globalized world economy can no longer be analyzed on the basis of the traditional categories of international economics. These have to be revised in a number of places, while in others completely new approaches are required.

Some people talk about a "Copernican revolution" in connection with the changes that took place in the world economy by the beginning of the 1990s (INOTAI 1989). The process can best be characterized in terms of interdependence, the globalization of resources and markets, the expansion of transnational cooperation on the part of companies, and attempts at global governance of world economic relations. With the new world economy structures broad new channels have opened up for the improvement of efficiency and prosperity. Levels of development are closely and mutually dependent on integration into the global world economy.

It is mainly since the 1970s and 1980s that we have witnessed the emergence of global world economic structures based on the accelerating process of internationalization. Globalization is extending to every area of social and economic life, to both micro- and macroprocesses. The international division of labour is becoming more complex. In addition to movement of goods the international trade in services is growing rapidly, and these are linked to large-scale, intensive production-factor flows.

The other very significant process is the formation of regional economic integrations. The idea of regional unification is not a new one, but it has begun to be implemented only in the last few decades. A particularly high level of international integration has been achieved by the European Union, in which on the basis of intensive economic interconnection and interdependence certain elements of political union are now gradually being established.

Regional integration does not run counter to the globalizing trend, but is developing in conjunction with it and with reciprocal effects. So I regard as integration on the micro level the transnationalization of company structures, which is linked at macro level with regional and global integration. There are many arguments in favour of differentiating the megaeconomic level, but I still prefer to think in terms of the micro and macro levels, examining them in world economy dimensions (at micro level, for example, the individual producer's possibilities of securing global advantage, or at macro level, the world economic interrelations of growth). The reason is simple: in my opinion, the "megalevel" cannot be analyzed without the micro and macro approach. The main theme of this study is an analysis of the nature, laws and effect mechanisms of these processes and of their economic and social consequences (advantages and disadvantages).

2. TRANSNATIONAL COMPANIES AND GLOBAL INTEGRATION PROCESSES

In the global world economy an important part is played by transnational company systems, in the framework of which new possibilities have opened up for exploiting the advantages to be gained from international cooperation, through direct foreign capital investments, joint ventures, subcontracting and franchising.

Particularly since the 1960s, in the developed countries there has been rapid and significant expansion of the transnational company division of labour. In the arena of today's world economy a transnational company, with its internal and external cooperational and business relations, is a modern producing and commercial organization that is in close connection with the demands of present-day technical and social progress, and which strives globally to optimize its resources and activities. Global company structures are developing organically from the cooperation of the developed countries, while their relations with certain areas of the world economy (e.g. developing countries) are less intensive and contradictory. I think of the transnational company as a comprehensive, general category, in which the various forms of multinational or "international" company are concrete manifestations of the transnational company.

The transnational company integrates and optimizes in a comprehensive way the process of re-production. The research and development capacities of the developed countries are chiefly concentrated in the hands of the transnational companies, and they have profited the most from the accelerated product-innovation and technical modernization of recent decades. Companies that manoeuvre and do business on a global scale are best able to minimize costs and achieve rational, global allocation and use of resources and factors of production (capital, technology, labour, etc.). In today's world economy the advantages and efficiency gains of direct international cooperation in research and development, production and sales ("transnational competitive advantage") can to a large extent be exploited in the global division of labour. The world market tends directly to recognize as standard the cost conditions of globally organized and optimized production, and this results in qualitative changes in the price-formation processes.

The transfer of production capacity from one country to another is accelerating very markedly, especially in cases when the technology is easily movable, the fixed cost of buildings is not too high, and a skilled workforce is available. The big global companies set up alternative suppliers, which they promptly dispense with in a slump or for other reasons or transfer to other countries. This is particularly typical in the case of easily-assembled electronic goods (screwdriver plants), for example. In 1984, when dumping duties were levied by the EU on Japanese electronic typewriters, about 700,000 units were imported from Japan. By 1988 that many were being assembled inside the EU, and the number imported from Japan had fallen to 35,000, or 1/20 of the former figure. In the same year the Japanese were reprimanded on the basis of the "screw-driver rules", and were forced to accept that the typewriters must consist of at least 40% non-Japanese parts. One direction of the reaction has been that end-producers are following parts manufacturers in transferring production capacity abroad. On the other hand, transnational companies, in collaboration with the local supply industries, can contribute to the industrial development of the country in question.

The dumping procedures relating to local content no longer fall within the traditional GATT regulations, according to which dumping duties can be levied only at the "border". The difficulty with the prescriptions referring to local content is that a copier contains more than 1,000 components, and to objectively determine their origin is a very complicated task. It is in producers' interest to procure cheap components, and this in certain cases becomes a source of trade policy conflicts.

An important development concerning transnational companies is their "internalization" of international relations. This means that the international division of labour is becoming to a greater extent internal to the company. This applies mainly to an increasing proportion of the earlier traditional commodity relations. According to estimates, roughly one-third of international trade is carried on within companies, and direct cooperation between companies is even more widespread. Transnational company structures internalize research and development in particular, direct cooperation in production (component outsourcing) and the infrastructure. The most modern technology on the market tends not to be for sale, but flows within companies with increased intensity, on the international level as well. It is estimated that more than one-third to one-half of international technology transfers take place within companies, and they are increasingly being "sucked out" of the traditional market frameworks.

Particularly among the developed countries specialization is becoming more and more "intrasectoral", resulting in strong convergence of the structure of export and import ("intrasectoral trade"). In many areas within the same commodity group significant, dynamically expanding trade is taking place, partly owing to cooperation in the areas of components and processes, and partly reflecting efforts to satisfy consumer requirements in a more differentiated way. On the other hand, we are witnessing the emergence of new forms of cooperation (e.g. cooperative relations in computer-organized production). International production has become an important characteristic of economic structures (*World Investment Report* 1993).

Internalized relations are becoming linked to monopoly market phenomena and this is having an impact on price formation processes as well. Within companies there is widespread use of so-called transfer prices, which among other things makes possible hidden international flows and redistribution of revenues. Thus the advantages in terms of efficiency of the division of labour are gained and distributed within the company. Meanwhile externally monopoly prices are set for these products and services (high prices for components or services), which in some cases can severely restrict possibilities of competition on the part of producers outside the transnational company spheres.

The transnational company division of labour is playing a major role in the globalization of national markets. An organic relationship has developed between trade and capital flows, and the transnational companies are also the chief vehicles of technology flows.

In recent decades the increased opening up of certain countries to external trade has been achieved mainly by transnational companies. It is increasingly characteristic of the developed countries that "import competition" takes place directly in the internal market. According to estimates, this is the way the greater proportion of American industrial products come face to face with their foreign competitors even on the domestic market.

Capital flows are many times greater than the trade in goods and services. The capital markets represent the main sphere of global integration. One of the main characteristics of the global world economy in the 1980s was the enormous, rapid flow of capital. On a daily basis, in that period cross-border capital movements were about 20 times bigger than trade flows (DEANNE and THOMSEN 1988). The foreign direct investments have become major components of world economy, and they represent a qualitatively new structure of international economic relations.

In these circumstances trends in interest rates depend not on the decisions of governments but on the behaviour of foreign capital. This applies to the USA as well. After the stock market crash of 1987 the drop in Japanese private capital investments directly affected the American bond market, and played a large part in raising interest rates.

The traditional economic categories such as, for example, the real trade balance of a given country require re-evaluation. The complete picture of global integration and competitiveness includes not only import and export but also the turnover of foreign-owned companies, which in the given case acts as a substitute for import or export. If we calculate again the transactions between American and foreign-owned companies both in the USA and abroad, then in 1986 the country's total "sales abroad" amounted to $1,145 bn while "purchases abroad" totalled $1,088 bn. The "real" surplus was thus $57 bn, while formally the American trade balance showed a $144 bn deficit.

The economic effect of exchange rates is changing. In connection with the export-stimulating effect of devaluation there have long been reservations, and it was considered effective only in the short-term. Now the situation is very different. In conditions of mutual interconnectedness devaluation does not improve the exporter's competitiveness; in fact, in some cases it can reduce it, while also having inflationary effects. With high import inputs devaluation causes production costs to rise faster than its export-competitiveness-improving effect can be exploited. Import prices go directly into export prices.

The basic interrelations of monetarism are also being re-evaluated. Clearly, with the enormous volume of international financial transactions the indices relating to money in circulation are completely illusory. Since the 1980s "external monetarism" has been gaining ground: it places the emphasis on exchange rate stability. Exchange-rate movements, rather than money in circulation, have come to determine inflation.

Since the 1970s the global infrastructure of the international division of labour has been taking shape (transcontinental transportation systems, and space communications), with far-reaching consequences from the point of view of production costs and competitiveness. The infrastructural costs of international cooperation, thanks to developments in communications technology and transportation, have decreased significantly. This has been a decisive development particularly as regards modern "global" company organization and management, and cooperation in component supply. By the 1980s the infrastructure of international company integrations showed qualitative improvement, and the new technology of the coming years promises further rapid development (construction of company satellite systems, etc.).

Resources and the infrastructure are often evaluated directly in an international context. The traditional relationship of domestic and world market prices has been reversed. In the case of a considerable proportion of products the world market price traditionally sums up and derives from domestic costs and prices. In the case of global resources and factors, the price appears directly as the world market price (e.g. oil prices, or transportation tariffs), and domestic prices derive from world market prices.

With globalization, the possibility of *global externalia* has to be taken more and more seriously. The "external costs" of environmental pollution are steadily growing. At present these are not included in any form in the price formation process, but sooner or later it will be unavoidable.

World economic processes cannot be dealt with in isolation. In the last few decades, revolutionary changes have taken place in the whole socio-economic structure. Undoubtedly in this a major part was played by the technological revolution that after World War II renewed the whole structure of technology, from basic materials to automated production systems. This process accelerated from the 1970s on, with microelectronics, biotechnology and robotics, resulting in completely new means of production and techniques of organization, management and communication (computerization). Perhaps it is no exaggeration to say that after the breakthrough to agriculture (the "first transformation", 5,000 years ago), then the development of mechanized large-scale industry (the so-called "industrial revolution", about 200 years ago), today we are at another big turning-point in human history, based on computers. The spread of the Internet is often compared in importance to the discovery of America.

All this has made possible unprecedented growth in productivity and efficiency, as well as real incomes.

Within the domestic economy the sphere of influence of the market has widened, and private ownership has spread. The process of socialization has reached a higher level, and real life has refuted MARX's assumption that this is irreconcilable with private "appropriation".

In the political sphere, in every area we have witnessed extensive democratization. One decisive development was the fall of the Iron Curtain, bringing to an end the period of a confrontational bipolar world. With the disappearance of artificial confrontation, the unity of the world economy can be raised to a higher level, and the obstacles to real globalization can be removed. The global world economy also means that traditional bilateralism will be replaced more and more by multilateralism, and instead of being confrontational, the multipolar world economy has a better chance of becoming cooperational. Since the Gulf War there has been much talk of the "new world order", but to this day we are unable to say what this means. Globalization is not a linear process, and it gives rise to countless contradictions and tensions. The past decade has provided ample proof of this; it is another question to what extent globalization has caused the conflicts, and what part was played in them by ethnic, religious and other aspects of civilization. At the beginning of the third millennium, particularly after September 11 of 2001, undoubtedly one of the key issues is the defeating of international terrorism. It is also clear that for this, military means are inadequate. Greater attention must be paid to the negative effects of globalism, and tensions can be reduced only if wider and wider strata enjoy the "blessings" of globalism.

The above-mentioned processes gradually developed and accumulated over the past few decades, but their effects erupted explosively only in the 1980s. The result was constrained radical adaptation and structural change in every sector of the world economy. Simplifying things a little, the process was finally responsible for the collapse of the socialist systems of Central and Eastern Europe. A genuine, quiet and perhaps peaceful revolution has been taking place at the turn of the millennium. Whether it will remain peaceful, what it is costing and where it is going, are questions that cannot be answered yet in the first few years of the third millennium.

For Hungary's economy and society, internal transformation was just as vital and significant a task as (re)integration into the world economy. The fact that we lagged behind in the world economy, and from the 1970s onwards faced the increasing danger of being relatively marginalized, was due not just to internal anomalies in the system but chiefly to our lack of organic links to the world economy. Not only did the closed and bureaucratic foreign trade system deprive us of the enormous advantages of the globalizing world economy and international division of labour, but the Soviet type of system of cooperation (COMECON) meant increasing disadvantages and direct losses. According to a World Bank study our level of development could be one-third higher if we had followed the example of the Western countries (*New York Times*, January 2, 1990). This is clearly a modest estimate, if we compare the development and present situation of Czechoslovakia and Denmark, or Hungary and Finland.

Under central planning, only inorganic and bureaucratic "integration" with the world economy was possible, thus depriving us of many of the advantages of the international division of labour. Between 1938 and 1989, Hungary suffered 50% in terms of trade loss, and its share of world exports fell from 0.65% to 0.29% (*Világgazdaság*, December 23, 1992).

Connecting up with the globalizing world economy, therefore, is in our fundamental interest. Historically and geopolitically we belong directly to Europe, and the EU is the developed centre of attraction with which we hope to be linked in order to catch up. Integration into the EU is a historic challenge and opportunity for the whole of Central and Eastern Europe, in fact, by means of which we now have a good chance of breaking out of our centuries-old peripheral situation. Europe, for us, is *a modernization anchor*. If Northern and, as it appears, Southern Europe has successfully clung to it and taken the risk, then there is no reason why the East should not succeed. Our global and regional integration is not automatic, however, and does not automatically guarantee its beneficial effects. Stringent adaptation and preparation will be necessary, which may be painful and involve considerable sacrifices and costs. Hungarian society must accept this, because it is worth it! It may be that the fruits will be fully enjoyed only by the next generation, but we have a great responsibility to make them ripen as fast as possible, and to facilitate the process. And we cannot afford to fail! The stakes are too high now. It is not simply a case of losing time, at worst: if we fail, we jeopardize our future. The alternative is to relapse into new totalitarian systems. And this is in no one's interest.

REFERENCES

DEANNE, J. and THOMSEN, S. (1988) *Capital Flows and International Economic Relations: The Explosion of Foreign Direct Capital Investment among the G–5.* Royal Institute of International Affairs, London.

GILL, S. and LAW, D. (1989) *The Global Political Economy (Perspectives, Problems and Policies).* The John Hopkins University Press, Baltimore.

INOTAI, A. (1989) *A működő tőke a világgazdaságban* (Foreign Direct Capital Investments in the World Economy). KJK, Budapest.

World Investment Report 1993, Transnational Corporations and Integrated Production. U.N., New York, 1993.

II.

MAIN SCHOOLS OF INTERNATIONAL INTEGRATION THEORIES

1. THE GENESIS OF INTEGRATION THEORIES

It was only in the last half-century that international integration became the subject of research by social scientists. Economics and political science really began to deal seriously with the question only after World War II. Interest in it subsequently became extraordinarily intense, and on the basis of research many theoretical schools soon appeared, and enough literature on integration to fill libraries. The intensification of efforts at European integration, the many integration experiments and the groupings achieved (the EU, EFTA, NAFTA, ASEAN, and at least several dozen more could be listed) gave an especially strong impetus to research.

Integration research is not without theoretical antecedents. The conceptual foundations of the theory of international economic integration can be traced all the way back to the classics (ADAM SMITH and DAVID RICARDO). Concrete theoretical and methodological interpretations of them, and the techniques of analysis employed are based mainly on neoclassical and welfare international economics, which examined the benefits to be gained from international trade. Analysis of the international integration processes became general in international economics and world economics only in the period after World War II was similar in the political sciences. Functionalism and institutionalism were underpinned by extensive theoretical literature, and carried out many analyses, which even in the inter-war period had relevant things to say from the point of view of later integration attempts (federalism or functionalism).

From the 1950s, customs union theories are regarded as the basis of the economics literature on international integration. The first basic works appeared in 1950, when three studies dealing with the advantages and disadvantages of customs union (by JACOB VINER, MAURICE BYÉ and HERBERT GIERSCH, respectively) appeared more or less simultaneously. Of these, JACOB VINER is regarded in the international literature as the father of customs union theory. Customs unions existed earlier; from the beginning of the 19th century to the period of World War II more than a dozen of them were formed. Among them one of the most important was the German Zollverein set up in 1834, the effects of which were analyzed by such famous economists as J. R. MCCULLOCH and FRIEDRICH LIST. Nevertheless, the first, most comprehensive analysis, which also weighed the advantages and disadvantages, was undoubtedly that carried out by VINER. His theoretical conclusions have been debated and further developed, but even today his basic premises represent the backbone of customs union and international integration theory. VINER's "static" allocationary efficiency analyses, based on the theory of comparative advantage, were later made dynamic, and within the framework of the so-called "new" integration economics the emphasis shifted to the advantages of economies of scale, product differentiation and the effects of competition (J. BRANDER, E. HELPMAN and P. KRUGMAN). In the political science field neo-functionalism, federalism and the analyses relating to intergovernmentalism are recognized as the main theoretical currents with regard to attempts at European integration.

Marxist theory started to deal with the question from the early 1960s, in connection with the integration of Western Europe, and at first it regarded the process as a phenomenon of the capitalist economy. Many theoretical analyses and works appeared, but it was only at the end of the 1960s that it became officially accepted that integration is a general world economic process and had to be treated as an "objective law" in the economy of the so-called socialist countries as well. The notion of socialist international integration was officially accepted, and after the publication of the "Comprehensive Programme" of Socialist Integration by the CMEA in 1971, a great number of studies on the topic were published.

Despite the "novelty" of integration theory it must be remembered that the idea of European union and within this, for example, a "United States of Europe" was by no means new. From the 16th century the idea of uniting Europe, and efforts aimed at this, had occupied the minds of many of the continent's great thinkers (ERASMUS of ROTTERDAM, JAN AMOS COMENIUS, WILLIAM PENN, FRANÇOIS-MARIE VOLTAIRE, CHARLES-LOUIS DE SECONDAT MONTESQUIEU and IMMANUEL KANT), and kept on reappearing among the aims of Europe's bourgeouis revolutions. From the 19th century the plan of a United States of Europe, parallel with the strengthening of national and labour movements, and often equally in harmony with them, was proclaimed from the most diverse political platforms, and the arguments cut across party-political boundaries (CLAUDE-HENRI DE SAINT-SIMON, VICTOR HUGO, GIUSEPPE MAZZINI, and on the side of the Communist Movement the name of LENIN can be mentioned).

Between the two world wars the Pan-Europe movement had a great influence on all kinds of political trends, and concrete proposals were put forward. These stemmed from the lessons of World War I, and the desire to prevent another war in the future. From this period the book by RICHARD COUDENHOVE-KALERGI, "Pan-Europa", which was first published in 1923, has to be mentioned among the first. His vision was a united Europe built on federal structures. One of his most influential followers was ARISTIDE BRIAND, the French foreign minister, who embodied these ideas in practical proposals in 1930 in his famous "Memorandum on the Organization of a Regime of European Federal Union". The Pan-Europe concept also influenced the Hungarian intelligentsia between the two world wars. Nazism tried to mask its attempts at conquest with the slogan of "the New Europe", but after the outbreak of World War II the idea of a democratic European union was authentically represented, again from widely differing platforms, by the resistance movements. From this period special mention must be made of the 1941 Ventotene Declaration entitled "For a free and united Europe", formulated by the antifascists exiled to the island of Ventotene, headed by ALTIERO SPINELLI.

At the end of World War II the question of a European union arose with renewed force, and in contrast to earlier periods the integration initiatives of the leading European politicians (WINSTON CHURCHILL, JEAN MONNET, ROBERT SCHUMAN, KONRAD ADENAUER and ALCIDE DE GASPERI) did not merely attract attention but began from the 1950s to achieve practical results (by creation of Montanunio, the Council of Europe, and, more importantly, the European Communities and European Union). The coherent theoretical basis and directions of integration, and within it, European integration, thus gradually took shape.

The integration attempts of recent decades drew the attention not only of economists and political scientists but also of academics in many other fields, and on this basis many theoretical trends and schools of integration theory have emerged. The subject of integration involves legal, sociological, historical and cultural research. In connection with integration,

"European studies", as a new field of scholarship, is increasingly characterized by a multidisciplinary approach (combining history, economics, law, sociology, political science and culture).

Integration is conceived as a *complex* process, which embraces the *different fields of social life.* NYE, for example, distinguishes between *economic, political and social integration* (NYE 1968). "Economic integration would constitute high trade; social integration would include the unification of masses, special groups or elites; political integration would encompass a wide array of phenomena, including more decisions on the international level, international bureaucracies, and attitudinal similarity among nations" (SULLIVAN 1976: 215).

In spite of the considerable amount of literature and analysis, there are those who *deny the existence of integration theory.* They argue that integration analyses represent only a part of the major theoretical trends (neo-functionalism, international economics), and that there is no justification for treating integration theory as an independent discipline. D. J. PUCHALA is a typical representative of such sceptical views about the meaning and future of integration theory, which, according to him, may be a "rather long but not very prominent footnote in the intellectual history of twentieth century social science" (PUCHALA 1984: 198). One should acknowledge, there is only one example of fully-developed integration, the European Union, available to us ("N = 1"), whereas any valid analysis and generalization can draw relevant and scientifically well-founded conclusions only from a large number of manifestations. The establishment of laws requires the study of a large number of "cases".

The uniqueness of the EU cannot be denied, but at the same time it is not true that it is the only form of regional integration. In the present world economy there are several dozen free trade associations or customs unions in operation (NAFTA, ASEAN, CEFTA, CARICOM, etc.), and although these mostly represent rudimentary forms of regional integration, their importance should not be underestimated, and they make it possible to analyze certain processes (e.g. the advantages of liberalization, and the problems arising from differences in development levels). In fact, with the introduction of the euro internal EU relations are now of a "domestic economy" nature, and can thus be analyzed using traditional macroeconomic methods, particularly related to federal states. Indeed, in practice it is increasingly necessary that they should be analyzed in this way. The forms of integration are organic parts of the global world economy structure, and their effects on the world economy are by no means negligible. The extreme complexity of the EU integration provides an opportunity for serious scientific research and analysis, and many parallels to the various processes (regional inequalities or leveling, development towards federalism, multi-level governance, etc.) can be found in other regions as well. "European integration may well be a totally unique enterprise without either historical precedent or contemporary parallel, but it is a ready source for comparative study" (ROSAMOND 2000: 197). "The EU may constitute nothing less than the emergence of the first truly post-modern international political form" (RUGGIE 1998: 173).

Despite the theoretical analyses and extensive research, it would be difficult to give a comprehensively valid and generally acceptable definition of international integration. "It is clear that quite a lot of work in contemporary EU studies operates in a climate of relative theoretical eclecticism" (ROSAMOND 2000: 101). As it is noted, "however, for an overall picture of the multifaceted integration process one needs to adopt eclecticism" (VERDUN 2002: 28). This "eclecticism" and the undeniable confusion are well formulated in the following summary: "Having welcomed the new millennium, and after nearly five decades of uninterrupted theorizing about European Integration, international scholarship is still puzzled as to what exactly the EU is or may come to resemble in the future. Today, both 'process theories' of international integration, such as functionalism, neo-functionalism and transactionalism, and others that focus on alternative integration outcomes, such as federalism and confederalism, find it difficult to grasp the distinctive nature of the European polity and its complex and increasingly overlapping governance structures. The same can be said of those theoretical perspectives that were advanced during the 1970s, such as international regimes, interdependence and concordance systems, or even of recent theoretical insights drawn from the likes of consociationalism, liberal intergovernmentalism, new institutionalism and multi-level governance, to mention but a few" (CHRYSSOCHOOU 2001: 1). Nevertheless it is possible for us to formulate the many *interpretations* of integration, and this, apart from revealing the variedness of theory, may be particularly useful if intelligent, practical conclusions can be drawn from it to guide policy and action. More than this we cannot undertake in this study.

We can define integration as a *state* or as a *process*, as a *fact* or as an *aim to be achieved*. In the Marxist literature, integration as a *fact-concept* fell victim, in the work of several writers, to ideological and propaganda considerations, which gave rise to many distortions. The postulated future –

victory in "peaceful competition", communism – became confused more and more with reality, and this led practical politics into a trap. From the most varied theoretical and political platforms integration is treated as an *aim-* or *requirement-concept,* and this finds expression in the program of many integration organizations.

In general, integration theories focus on *five important dimensions* of the process:

- the *content* (or essence) of integration processes;
- the *organizational forms and institutions* of integration;
- *regulation (policies) and governance* of integration;
- the *advantages and disadvantages* of integration (*cost-benefit* analysis); and finally
- the problems of *integration maturity* (capacities or capabilities for integration).

For pragmatic reasons, for a long time the literature on integration attached particular importance to the forms of integration, and to cost-benefit analysis. In connection with "eastward" expansion, from the 1990s the question of integration maturity appeared on the agenda. With the development and increasing complexity of the integration process it became more and more necessary to solve the questions of governance. Regarding the content, forms and effect mechanisms of the integration processes a number of theoretical schools have emerged, each emphasizing a different aspect of integration; together, they provide a comprehensive picture and ultimately they express the evolution of the process in all its complexity.

2. THE CONTENT OF INTEGRATION

A general semantic interpretation of integration itself presents no special difficulty. Expressed in the most general way, integration is a process of unification, the merging of parts into a whole, becoming a unit, fitting together, melting into one another, linking up. It can be understood as the cooperation of parts, the harmonization of their operation, their reciprocal influence and their becoming interconnected. According to F. PERROUX, "integration is the uniting of two or more economic units into a certain whole" (PERROUX 1954: 419). The integration is a process, which leads to larger communities (MARJOLIN 1953: 41). Integration in the general sense is the adaptation and interweaving of parts in a higher whole (PREDÖHL and JÜRGENSEN 1961: 371).

In philosophical terms, integration can be defined as a general concept, which in fact can be applied both to nature and to society. It is possible to see integration (and disintegration) as a general law of nature and of society. The philosophical interpretation of integration phenomena in nature, the living world (cell metabolism or the organization of cells into living organisms) or in mathematics (addition, finding the common denominator, integrations) is not the subject of this study.

2.1. DIVISION OF LABOUR THEORIES AND TRANSACTIONALISTS

The content of integration can be approached from several directions. Interpretation of the content of economic integration can perhaps best be linked to *theories of the division of labour*. From the 1970s approaches from this aspect were particularly characteristic of the integration literature of the East European countries, which sought to deduce the phenomenon of integration from the evolution of the international division of labour. The essence of these analyses was that they *separated the simple transactions or "cooperation" and contrasted them with "integration", and interpreted the latter as a new quality.* This approach to integration was typical of many other theoretical schools as well. Defined generally, integration is nothing else but "the most advanced type of cooperation" (HARTOG 1963: 165).

The relation between the division of labour and integration can be expressed in several dimensions. On the one hand, integration can be approached through cooperation, or *a certain"intensity"* of transactions, which can be interpreted both quantitatively and qualitatively. BEN ROSAMOND characterizes some of the international integration organizations, like the ECSC or EEC, as involving "quite intensive international cooperation among the group of countries" (ROSAMOND 2000: 10). "An important criterion of integration is a certain fairly significant intensity of relations between producers of goods in the different domestic economies. Of course there is no recipe for the exact percentage of products, in relation to exports or the volume of national income, that must be traded within the community for the intensity of transactions to reach the critical level. Anyway, if in the course of development the turnover between the members of a group of countries becomes a significant volume by a considerable percentage compared with the national income of the individual countries or end-users, and from the re-production point of view important products play a significant part in the composition of the goods, we can regard the criterion as satisfactory" (KOZMA 1970: 62–63). In such an approach, for measuring the state and development of integration we can in practice use many statistical indices.

Clearly, integration between countries is hardly conceivable without economic relations. A precondition of integration, therefore, is *a certain intensity or quantitative densification of the international division of labour,* which beyond a certain point results in *a new quality.* In comparison with KOZMA, the Pole ZBIGNIEW KAMECKI, referring to the conditions for integration, describes them more broadly: "Their reciprocal economic turnover must be fairly big in relation to the total volume of their output. This in turn presupposes the existence of a sufficiently highly-developed infrastructure, which makes possible mass exchange of goods between these countries. Appropriate political and economic measures (e.g. removal of customs duties and quantitative and currency restrictions, etc.) constitute the other condition" (KAMECKI 1972: 15). We shall return to the question of mutual dependencies of the division of labour and integration, as a new quality, when we deal with the question of interdependence.

Furthermore, international integration means that "relations between national economies take on an increasingly firm, lasting and long-term character, deriving from the developing structure of international relations and the division of labour. The lasting, long-term nature of relations is guaranteed by a system of bilateral and multilateral agreements between companies and economic organizations" (MAKSZIMOVA 1975: 120). The notion of integration as *"lasting" and "long-term"* cooperation recurs in the works of other authors as well.

According to others, integration can be seen as *an organized or institutionalized division of labour.*

We can define integration as *a process embracing various forms and areas of the international division of labour. Integration is a comprehensive form of international cooperation* that extends to *the whole re-production process and the system of international relations* (trade, the flow of capital and labour, technical relations, macroregulation, etc.). "The national economy, as a basic macroeconomic unit for the production, distribution and use of assets is a determinate system. The social re-production process today still consists basically in re-production of domestic products. The national economy provides the framework in which, through the system of economic forms, the proportions of re-production and equilibrium of economic activities are achieved. From this point of view, the national economy embodies the determinate complexity of social production. International economic integration unites the national re-production processes and increases their reciprocal dependence" (PALÁNKAI 1989: 18–19). Thus internationally *microintegration* takes place within the framework of transnational corporations and company relations. The *macrointegration* process can be defined through the various degrees of commercial and economic groupings.

Integration, then, from the economic point of view can be defined as *an intensive, lasting and long-term, organized and institutionalized division of labour embracing the whole re-production process.*

The *economic theories of integration* emphasize that the international division of labour, through specialization and cooperation, is accompanied by an increase in efficiency. According to division of labour theories, *enhancement of efficiency and prosperity* is the general, fundamental motivating factor in integration. But it must be emphasized that precise assessment of the advantages and disadvantages is a political question as well. The "fair distribution" of these or the "just retour" was from the outset an accepted basic principle in the EC, and in certain cases decisively influenced the formation of public opinion (e.g. in connection with decisions to join).

Political science concepts of integration have differing approaches with regard to its purpose and value. According to many schools of political science, international integration assists in the handling and solving of conflicts, arguments, tensions and clashes of interest. Integration means a process, when conflicts are solved without application of force (LINDBERG 1963). After the war, "starting from the ruins, it was imperative to develop new conceptions and more grandiose ideas that would make any future civil war between European brother nations impossible" (KITZINGER 1963).

Among the different schools, first we have to mention *transactionalism*, which shares several common or similar aspects of interest and approach with division of labour theories of integration. In dealing with conflicts and tensions, as the condition and basic objective of integration, transactionalism conceives integration in a very broad sense as the formation of *"security community"*. The *transactionalist or communication theories* can be associated directly with the works of KARL DEUTSCH. "Thus, international integration is defined as being about the achievement of security within a region or among a group of states. Successful integration is about the radical reduction in the likelihood of states using violent means to resolve their differences. The definition of 'security community' was bound up with the conception of integration. 'Security communities' were groups of people that had become 'integrated'. Further, integration was defined as 'attainment, within a territory, of a sense of a security community' and of institutions and practices strong enough and widespread enough to assure a long-time, dependable expectation of 'peaceful change' among its population" (DEUTSCH et al. 1957: 5). Consequently, integration assumes community feeling, solidarity, political and social cohesion, and what is equally important, a corresponding institutional system, which can be world-wide (UN) or regional (EC/EU).

The transactionalists, in many respects similarly to division of labour theories, also put great emphasis on *intensity of relations and cooperation as the lever* for building a security community and consequently for integration. "The guiding hypothesis of transactionalist work on integration was that a sense of community *among* the states would be a function of the level of communication *between* the states. The route to international Gemeinschaft was the establishment of a network of mutual transactions. The more interaction that existed between state *a* and state *b*, the greater the reciprocal importance (or 'mutual relevance') of *a* and *b* to one another. Perceptions that the interaction is beneficial will promote feelings of trust between *a* and *b*. With trust would come further interaction" (DEUTSCH 1964: 69).

The sources of conflict are dealt with by the so-called *distance theories*, which are linked on many points to transactionalist and communicational theories. According to these, conflicts and rivalries (wars and disputes) can be attributed to divergences, differences, absence of similarity, which may be rooted in the economy (differences in levels of development and incomes) or culture (traditions, religion, etc.) According to followers of this trend in political science, "hostility between men would cease if we were all alike. Wars, this argument runs, are prompted by dissimilarities between men and the conflict of interests, fears, and jealousies arising from those dissimilarities" (SULLIVAN 1976: 208). "International systems that are integrated are going to be – on the whole – more peaceful" (Ibid. 209). Thus integration is an economic and social "rapprochement" which in certain areas eliminates "distances". The equalizing of levels of development therefore features as a criterion of integration. From this point of view, the intensity of communication and cooperation is of crucial importance; in fact, "integration is very often defined as high communication or transactions. Hence, as we will find, especially in studies of Western Europe, the level of integration is seen to be directly correlated with levels of transactions" (SULLIVAN 1976: 214). The parallels are obvious, and we can take these formulations as generalizations of what was said in terms of economic integration by division of labour theories.

2.2. INTERDEPENDENCE AND INTEGRATION

From the point of view of defining the content of integration we attach special importance to *interdependence*. The development of mutual dependence is closely related to the development of the division of labour, particularly the international division of labour that has characterized recent decades. We can say that eventually a certain intensity of international cooperation leads to the internal *development of interdependence and ultimately to its increase.*

In one of the first quantitative formulations, a "rough measure of the economic relationship is given by the ratio of their imports and exports of goods and services to their gross domestic product" (SALVATORE 1993: 3). K. DEUTSCH proposes a similar approach, measuring interdependence by means of simple quantitative proportions: "How large a proportion does the foreign trade of a country represent as compared to its total economic activities, as indicated by its gross national product? In general, then the larger the proportion of the transactions between any two actors (which may be states or groups of states), the greater we can expect to be the weight of their interdependence" (DEUTSCH 1978: 261).

In a broader and more general approach, interdependence can be interpreted as a state or process when the position of agents becomes mutually dependent and their actions mutually determined. "There are many other crucial ways in which nations are interdependent, so that economic events and policies in one nation significantly affect other nations (and vice versa). For example, if the United States stimulates its economy, part of the increased demand for goods and services by its citizens spills into import, which stimulates the economies of other nations that export those commodities. On the other hand, an increase in the United States' budget deficit is likely to raise interest rates in the United

States and attract funds (capital) from abroad. This inflow of funds to the United States increases the international value of the dollar, which in turn stimulates import and discourages U.S. exports. This then leads to a trade deficit, which dampens economic activity in the United States and stimulates economic activity abroad. Finally, trade negotiations that reduce trade barriers across nations may lead to an increase in the exports of high technology goods (such as computers) and thus to an increase in employment and wages in those industries in the United States, but it may also increase imports of shoes and textiles, thereby reducing employment and wages in those industries in the United States. Thus, we see how government policies directed towards purely domestic problems can have significant international repercussions" (Ibid. 5–6). We can see that these effects greatly depend on the size of the related countries.

In summary, interdependence can be defined as *a new quality of international relations,* when as a result of the expansion of cooperation, at a certain point the position of countries changes significantly toward each other, and their policies and actions become mutually dependent. The question remains, what is that critical point? What is the level of intensity when simple relations acquire a new quality, and lead to interdependence among nations? This question was asked earlier in relation to integration as "intensive" cooperation. It might help us if we set a *minimum dependency threshold,* beyond which one can say that economic relations place countries in an interdependent position. This threshold is assumed to be somewhere around 10%, which can be interpreted as meaning that if the proportion of foreign trade of a country in its GDP goes above that level, then the given country has become dependent on foreign trade.[1] In the 1950s, the relation of world trade (export and import) to aggregate world GDP was around 5–6%. In recent times this share has increased to around 20%. One can take this as *an indicator of the emergence of a state of global interdependence,* which has developed in the last half-century. Of course, this holds only as a generalization, because relations were structured very unevenly and in very asymmetric ways (one-sided dependencies). Some countries (small and less developed) were for a long time highly dependent on foreign economic relations, while in the case of countries like the USA, Japan, China or the former Soviet Union the share

[1] Similarly if for example the share of one oil supplier is more than 10% of the oil import of a country, then that country is dependent on the given source. This threshold has been used as an indicator of dependence in cases of energy policy decisions of the International Energy Agency, and of course of the EC/EU.

of foreign trade in GDP was only a few (3–5) percent in the 1950s. It was an important new development in the process of globalization that by the 1970s the share of foreign trade in the GDP of these countries had increased to around or beyond that "magic" 10%. If we add the massive foreign capital inflow from the 1970s to the American economy, then one can no longer consider it an "isolated" economy; its global dependence has greatly increased.

Theorizing about interdependence started as long ago as the 1950s and 1960s, but in international relations interdependence became a core concept only during the 1970s.[2] "In common parlance, *dependence* means a state of being determined or significantly affected by external forces. *Interdependence,* most simply defined, means *mutual* dependence. Interdependence in world politics refers to situations characterized by reciprocal effects among countries or among actors in different countries. These effects often result from international transactions – flows of money, goods, people and messages across international boundaries. Such transactions have increased dramatically since World War II. Yet this interconnectedness is not the same as interdependence. The effects of transactions on interdependence will depend on the constraints, or costs, associated with them. Where there are reciprocal, although not necessarily symmetrical, costly effects of transactions, there is interdependence. Where transactions do not have significant costly effects, there is simply interconnectedness" (KEOHANE and NYE 1977: 8–9).

Introducing the notion of *sensitivity and vulnerability* makes possible further distinctions, which are important qualitative properties of the process. "In the case of two nation-states, we must ask about the *sensitivity* of each country to any diminution or disruption of their mutual transaction flow. How badly needed were the goods and services which had been obtained from the partner country? How easily could substitutes be obtained for them, or other sources of supply be found and used, and at what costs? Obviously, this sensitivity varies with the economic, technological and political structure of the state concerned, and with the type of transactions cut back or interrupted" (DEUTSCH 1978: 262). GILPIN stresses the necessity to distinguish 'sensitivity' and 'vulnerability' interdependence. "This latter term refers to the possibilities of political exploitation of market interdependencies" (GILPIN 2001: 82).

[2] The term"interdependence" was earlier mentioned in the "Communist Manifesto" of MARX and ENGELS, published in 1848.

Hungary's economics literature soon began to pay attention to the qualitative changes that took place in the world economy from the 1970s onwards. On questions such as globalization and 'global problems', world economy dependence relations and thus mutual dependence, or transnational companies and integration, studies by many writers (JÓZSEF BOGNÁR, BÉLA KÁDÁR, TIBOR PALÁNKAI, MIHÁLY SIMAI, TAMÁS SZENTES and others) were published. "By the 1970s the historical process of *internationalization* had entered a qualitatively new phase. The process is characterized by the development of interdependence, the spread of transnational companies, and the intensification of global problems" (PALÁNKAI 1986: 33).

In the Hungarian literature, interdependence is defined from the outset as a comprehensive process and phenomenon. "The literal interpretation of 'interdependence' and its sphere of problems is extremely many-sided. In the first place it means that the life and existence of states are in many respects interwoven with the consequences of the life and existence of other states. As a result, they can achieve their aims only by taking into account the existence and influence of the other countries, in both the political and the economic sphere" (SIMAI 1985: 102).

Simai distinguishes between 'isolated mutual effects' (accidental, marginal partner relations), 'intensive mutual effects' (long-lasting, many-layered relations with significant political and economic effects) and the concept of *"interdependence and comprehensive interdependence"*, which is "not just an economic category but a political one as well, and cannot be narrowed down to changes in the importance of economic cooperation between states". Relations of interdependence in the economic sphere "mean that the flow of goods, services, capital and labour, and international financial relations affect not only the growth of national income but also its distribution. In the interdependent international structural system economic relations between states are based on a certain level of community of interest. This at first helps to stabilize inter-state relations. Interests and as a result inter-state relations naturally change over time. But the consequences of the breaking-off of relations between the countries that belong to the system are many, and the costs are high. Comprehensive interdependence means that in this phase, relations between states are particularly many-channeled. This includes informal relations among the ruling elite, and intimate connections among the non-governing elite" (SIMAI and GÁL 2000: 79–80).

Interdependence and integration were related from the beginning, and in some respects they are often considered as very similar and close concepts. "*Integration,* then, is a relationship among units in which they are mutually interdependent and jointly produce system properties which they would separately lack. Sometimes, however, the word 'integration' is also used to describe the *integrative process* by which such a relationship or state of affairs among formerly separate units is attained. In politics, integration is a relationship in which the behaviour of such political actors, units or components is modified from what it otherwise would be. An integrated system is *cohesive* to the extent that it can withstand stress and strain, support disequilibria, and resist disruption" (DEUTSCH 1978: 198–199).

The development of interdependence can therefore be taken as an indicator and measure of global or regional integration. In fact, the intra-trade of the EC countries was only about 6–7% of their aggregate GDP in the 1950s before they signed the Treaty of Rome. By 1973 this proportion had increased to around 12%, which indicates a real development and turning-point in terms of their regional integration. Not by chance, many felt that integration reached the "point of no-return". These indicators well demonstrate both the state and the process of integration.

HIRST and THOMSON consider it important to introduce a third concept, *openness,* in addition to interdependence and integration, and they also indicate the close and mutual relationship of these. "By the term 'autonomy' we mean the ability of the authorities in a national economy to determine their own economic policy and implement that policy. This is obviously a matter of degree. Autonomy is closely linked to 'openness', 'interdependence' and 'integration'. Openness implies the degree to which national economies are subject to the actions of economic agents located outside their borders and the extent to which their own economic agents are oriented towards external economic activity. This in turn is linked to the degree of interdependence of the economic system in which these agents operate. Thus interdependence expresses the systemic links between all economic activity within a system or regime. Integration is the process by which interdependence is established" (HIRST and THOMSON 1999: 281). Consequently, the position of countries in a regional integration can greatly differ according to their size and level of development (openness).

"Interdependence, however, does not always lead to integration. The word 'interdependence' suggests a two-way process. Among states or other international actors, it reminds us that this relationship is mutual – what happens to actor *A* makes a difference to *B*, but what happens to *B* also makes a difference to *A*. Beyond this, however, the word 'interdependence' seems to suggest that these two effects somehow should be equal, and this is by no means necessarily the case. The more unequal and one-sided the flow of influence and power, the more have people in the poorer and weaker countries been inclined to speak of 'imperialism' and 'dependency'" (DEUTSCH 1978: 263).

To sum up, it can be stated that in this connection integration means that through interdependence the given countries' development, equilibrium conditions, economic stability and performance are determined by their relations with their community partners. The process becomes organized into regional institutions, but globally too is organized and served by an increasing number of institutions. The world economy is an independent organic system, which with the globalization of the last few decades can increasingly be seen as an integrating structure. Integration, therefore, is cooperation between the individual elements of a system in which the stability and internal equilibrium of the system is maintained, or even by means of which it is achieved. Accordingly, integration improves the performance and competitiveness of the group of countries and stabilizes their economy and their social and political relations. Interdependence is the most important feature of the content of integration.

3. BASIC FORMS AND INSTITUTIONS OF INTEGRATION

3.1. BASIC FORMS OF INTEGRATION

Integration can be implemented in the form of various commercial and economic groupings or institutions. These can be regional free trade blocs, which apply collective protectionism or discrimination against outsiders, or various sorts of organization in which economic policies are integrated. On the basis of the work by BÉLA BALASSA, considered a classic of the literature on integration (BALASSA 1961), the *following main forms* can be distinguished:

– *The free trade area.* Within the area trade is liberalized by the reduction of customs tariffs and quotas, and with outsiders every member country applies separate customs tariffs and quotas. To counter exploitation of national differences in customs tariffs, certification of origin (rule of origin) is demanded. For certifying the country of origin of goods, determination of local content is important.

– *The customs union.* Within the area foreign trade is liberalized, but with outsiders common customs tariffs (but not necessarily quotas) and ultimately joint foreign trade policies are applied. To ensure that there are no obstacles to competition, a common competition policy is essential. If the customs union is complete, extending to every sector of the economy, then other common policies (like a joint agricultural policy) may be also required.

– *The common market.* This is more than a customs union, in that within the area there is not only free movement of goods and services but also a free flow of factors of production (capital and labour). (While one example of a free trade area is EFTA, the EC exemplifies the customs union and the common market.) Common market measures can also be based on free trade agreements (e.g. the European Economic Area, involving the EU and EFTA).

– *The single market.* This represents complete liberalization, 'internal market' conditions, with the removal not just of customs tariffs and quantitative restrictions but of all restrictions of a 'non-tariffs' nature. This was implemented in the EU in 1992, and now extends to the elimination of 'physical' barriers (border formalities), 'technical' ones (standards, specifications, etc.) and fiscal ones (tax harmonization). (This was not included in BALASSA's list.) The unified market presupposes wide-ranging harmonization of economic regulations (laws) and economic policies.

– In *economic union,* not only has market integration taken place, but integration of economic policies is also implemented, in the form of the unification and harmonization of economic policy, which in its final phase can lead to unification of domestic economic policies at community level (community, 'common' or union policies). In the EU many elements of economic union have been brought into being (CAP). The economic union supposes the introduction of a common or 'single' currency, which leads to monetary union. Economic and monetary union is the most highly developed form of economic integration, and apart from a common currency requires common monetary policy and a central bank. Economic and monetary union presupposes unified market integration and in many respects follows from it (complete capital market liberalization and a single currency).

– *Political union.* This involves the gradual transfer to community level of power and legislative authority (parliament, government, jurisprudence, etc.). It assumes the establishment of a 'supranational authority', which can take decisions that are binding on all the member nation states.

Each form represents higher and more 'developed' levels of integration. On the basis of various considerations we can draw dividing lines between them, but one of the most relevant courses open to us is to distinguish between *forms of market integration* and forms requiring closer *economic policy integration* and ultimately political integration. So-called *liberal concepts* can be regarded as the basis of market integration forms, which we can define as ranging from the free trade area to the unified internal market. Certain rudimentary elements of economic policy cooperation, as we have mentioned, are already present in the customs union, and these become especially important in the single market (law harmonization). Comprehensive integration of economic policies is represented by economic and monetary union. We shall examine the theoretical background of these in more detail when we come to deal with questions of regulation and governance.

The following diagram indicates the calendar of the process and state of European integration, taking into account the coming Eastern enlargements:

CEE		EC/EU
1991–2000	Free trade area	
–	Customs union	1958–68
–	Common market	1958–68
Upon entry to EU 2004–	Single Market	1992
From 2006–2008 (earliest)	EMU	1990–2002
?	Political union	?

3.2. LIBERAL INTEGRATION THEORIES

One of the dominant trends of international integration theory is represented by the *liberal or neo-liberal schools.* The liberal theory of integration rests on the premises of classical economics, the principles of unlimited free competition and free trade. According to them, integration is possible where free movement of goods and services and factors of production exists and there is unlimited free competition (ARON 1953). So for the liberals integration is necessarily accompanied by free trade and obviously also by freedom in the sphere of payments.

Since integration is identified with free trade, many consider that historically, every free trade system can be regarded as integration. Röpke goes so far to say, that if anything deserves the notion of international integration then that is the world economy, which existed prior to 1914 (Röpke 1959: 225).

It cannot be uncritically accepted that in the pre-1914 period the world economy based on free trade was more highly integrated, and that that situation should now be restored, as the liberals assert. Free trade, which did in fact represent considerable volume, applied mainly to Great Britain's sphere of interest, but included also elements of protectionism. It was the latter that characterized most of the countries of the world.

There were problems with "integration" in connection with world economic linkage and the incorporation of national economies into international trade. In both relational and structural terms (in product structure) this showed huge inequalities and with regard to the most highly developed countries was based on relatively primitive sectoral specialization. Export was poorly diversified, and this was typical of even the developed countries right up to the end of the 19th century. Complexity of the division of labour, as a precondition of integration, can also be taken to mean that trade embraces the widest possible range of sectors, and intra-sectoral trade becomes dominant. Trade relations between the EU countries is increasingly characterized by intra-sectoral cooperation (product specialization). The structure of the earlier international division of labour was very different from this. As far as "intra-industry trade in similar products" is concerned, "indeed, much of the increase in intra-block trade in manufactures that took place following the establishment of the EC took that form and it has become a major component of trade in manufactures" (Robson 1998: 82).

Several aspects of the liberal concept of integration must be highlighted. One is that, according to the schools of economics, integration is achieved through the 'four freedoms', the *"free" and "intensive" flow of goods, services and the factors of production*. Integration is identified with freedom of flow and movement by the so-called *communication and cooperation schools* as well. They extend the free flow requirement to every area of social and economic life, not just economic cooperation (free trade and flow of production factors) but to social, political and cultural relations as well (tourism, television viewing, correspondence, etc.). They measure "intensity" by means of many indicators (B. Hughes, J. Schwarz, P. McGowan, etc.). Integration can be characterized by "the growing proportion of cross-boundary trade, mail correspondence, travel, university attendance" (DEUTSCH 1978: 236).

The integrated area is a market economy structure that automatically evolves on the basis of *competition mechanisms*. "The fundamental significance of economic integration is the increase of actual and potential competition" (PELKMANS 1997: 3). "The newer analyses of gains from trade liberalization and regional market integration, while not excluding the operation and importance of comparative advantages based on factor endowments for certain factors, do in fact focus on situations in which the gains from trade stem purely from increased competition in the presence of scale economies and product differentiation, rather than from comparative advantage as such" (ROBSON 1998: 83).

As RÖPKE emphasizes, integration is nothing else than a strict "community of markets and prices" (Ibid. 21). In this approach, integration is defined as *price equalization*, which for factors of production takes place through market mechanisms. It must be added that while with market liberalization product prices really can become equalized, this is not the situation with factors of production. Particularly the equalization of wages and that of interest rates obey quite different laws and mechanisms. The liberals set out from "the individual", whether producer or consumer; that is, their approach is of a micro nature.

Integration theories examine equalization and unification on the macro level as well. In this concept, integration means *the approximation to each other of levels of economic development* and the gradual disappearance of differences. In a certain sense factor-price equalization implicitly presupposes that behind it there is equalization of productivity levels, which in turn implies similar levels of development. Development level equalization features in the founding charter of the EU and of the other integration organizations, as a general political aim and priority.

As a condition or concomitant of the movement of goods and factors, "internal market" type of relations are formed among the "units" in question. Integration "in the economic policy sense is the unification of several state territories into a single economic area, in which relations similar to those of the internal market exist" (PREDÖHL and JÜRGENSEN 1961). In the Hungarian literature a similar approach is used by SÁNDOR AUSCH in interpreting integration. "By integration we mean a close interconnection and division of labour developed within national frameworks between economic units or countries or between different regions within an empire, which manifests itself in intensive flows of products and factors of production that bear determinate qualitative marks. Integration when it takes place between independent or to a certain extent independent nation states has a historical tendency to create conditions similar to domestic economic relations in the cooperation between different areas belonging to a region" (AUSCH 1969: 15).

Integration, as an "intensive flow" of goods and factors of production, or as "close division of labour" can obviously change the internal structure of the economies in question and their qualitative characteristics. The liberals do not deal very seriously with this, apart from equalization. The above concepts of integration identify the interlinking of national markets with actually becoming homogeneous or equal. Liberal theories can best be interpreted with reference to the free trade area, customs union, common market and single market.

The chief advantage of market integration is *that it is accompanied by an increase in efficiency and welfare.* "Market competition can be expected to lead to lower prices for similar products and services, greater qualitative variety and wider choice in the integrated area, and provides general encouragement to change. Product design, ways of providing services, production and distribution systems and many other aspects become actual or potential objects of challenge" (AUSCH 1969: 3). The profits and losses arising from integration, its benefits and costs, are dealt with in detail by the various liberal schools. The advantages and disadvantages have most successfully been quantified by the customs union theories.

3.3. INSTITUTIONALISM AND INTEGRATION

One debated aspect of international economic integration is to what extent it is necessary to distinguish between the real process of integration and the institutional forms. It is a fact that integration is a structured process, and various institutions promote cooperation and interweaving. The schools of theory that focus their analysis on institutions and questions of organization are generally described as *institutionalist.* "International economic integration, often termed regionalism, may be defined as the institutional combination of separate national economies into larger economic blocs or communities" (ROBSON 1998: 1).

The concept of institutionalists is very simple: "institutions matter" inasmuch as "political struggles are mediated by prevailing institutional arrangements". New institutional theory treats institutions as instruments capable of producing determinate policy and of shaping "the pattern of political behaviour", thus going beyond the formal organs of government to include "standard operating procedures, so-called soft-law, norms and conventions of behaviour" (Bulmer 1993: 355).

Institutions are an important framework for any social activity; they represent a certain "institutional architecture"; they set the norms and rules of the "game"; they provide the necessary policy instruments and procedures and are usually associated with conventions, symbols, and "cultures". "Rather than being simple and passive vessels within which politics occurs, institutions provide contexts where actors can conduct a relatively higher proportion of positive-sum bargains. Institutions offer 'information-rich' venues where transparency prevails and where trust is high. They act as intervening variables between actor preferences and policy outputs" (Rosamond 2000: 114).

Clive Archer takes a similar approach, when associating the scene of integration processes with a marketplace. "To return to the metaphor of the marketplace, it can be seen that international organizations can indeed play the role of instruments for those who bargain in this place – as servants carrying messages; changing money to order; or acting as bodyguards. They can also be likened to that part of the marketplace where the occupants meet to discuss, trade and settle disputes – the forum. Finally, they may also be given the likeness of a participant in the marketplace, perhaps as powerful and as able to mould events as some of the other traders and customers" (Archer 1992: 159).

William Wallace defines integration as "the creation and maintenance of intense and diversified patterns of interaction among previously autonomous units" (Wallace 1996: 9). But he does not consider institutions unconditionally necessary. Wallace makes a distinction between "formal" and "informal" integration. "The former consists of outcomes (institutions, policies, legislative change) that have occurred as a consequence of deliberate action. The other lacks formal, authoritative intervention" (Wallace 1996: 13).

The heavy institutionalization associated with the early communities was particularly emphasized (Rosamond 2000: 10) or, to put it differently, *integration* can be defined as *institutionalized cooperation*. Such organizational forms as the free trade area or economic union can serve as general frameworks, which are supported by other functional and political institutions.

The institutionalists approach integration mainly from the political side (they can be regarded as chiefly political science schools), and they link economic integration with political integration. According to the institutionalists, political integration consists in a transfer of power (decision-making, legislation, governance and implementation) from the national level to international (or community) institutions. According to ETZIONI, the criterion of integration is the existence of "central executive organs" and "common centers of identification" (ETZIONI 1965). In addition to national parliaments, governments and other power institutions there is therefore an increasing need for community institutions for legislation and governance, and competences and power are gradually shifting to that level.

There is disagreement, of course, among the various representatives of this approach concerning the degree and pace of the shift.

The institutionalist integration theories are closely related, in fact, comprising several schools or trends, depending on how they see the relations between the new integration institutions and the national states (intergovernmentalism, federalism, confederalism, consociation, etc.).

3.4. FEDERALISM CONTRA INTERGOVERNMENTALISM

The *federalists* favour supranational, effective community power structures and institutions (HAAS, PINDER, MONTANI, etc.). Federalism has acquired increasing political influence in the EU countries, and has exerted effective pressure in the direction of political union. The majority of federalists support worldwide political integration (world government). The main aim of "Eurofederalists" is the creation of the United States of Europe.

The idea of federalism has a long history, in fact one of the longest in the history of discussions related to a new international order, and contains several tendencies. "The first draws on the legacy of ideas associated with IMMANUEL KANT, who advocated an expanding federation as the most appropriate constitutional safeguard against the threat of war. The second draws on those elements of democratic theory concerned with devising ways of ensuring efficient governance within a democratic framework so that authority is supplied as closely as possible to the people. The third strand is the scholarly contemplation of federalizing tendencies and processes" (ROSAMOND 2000: 25).

One of the outstanding proponents writes that federalists "point out that the national states have lost their proper rights since they cannot guarantee the political and economic safety of their citizens. They also insist that European union should be brought about by the European populations, and not by diplomats, by directly electing a European constituent assembly" (SPINELLI 1972: 68).

"Federalism most commonly describes political systems in which there is a division of authority between central and regional or state government. The federalist project involves achieving appropriate balances between different, rival levels of authority on the one hand, and between efficiency and democracy on the other" (ROSAMOND 2000: 24, 26). "The virtue of a federal system, it is claimed, is that unlike other types of supranational state, it is designed as a framework in which such 'centralizing' principles as security, order, authority, administrative rationality, constitutionalism and unity can be reconciled with the 'decentralizing' values of liberty, local autonomy, representation, pluralism, flexibility and diversity" (PENTLAND 1973: 157).

For these reasons, federalism is particularly preferred by some small states. They feel that their interests can be better represented in a legally framed setup than in intergovernmental structures, where the informal decision-making processes favour the larger states. Concerning the next IGC it is noted that "an intergovernmental outcome" would mean "an arrangement where decisions are mainly taken outside the current institutional framework. The system would not be transparent and not necessarily democratic and efficient. It could also potentially lead to a blockage of decision-making and a *directoire* of large states" (STUBB 2002: 13).

PINDER advocates what he calls 'neo-federalism' as "a way of combining theoretical reflection upon and policy advice about the trajectory of Communities. Neo-federalism is built around the idea that a federal settlement continues to be a rational solution in light of both the problems faced by European states and the quasi-federal solutions already in existence. Contrary to 'classical' federalism, which placed too great emphasis on the convening of a powerful European representative assembly with the power to design a constitution for the United States of Europe, PINDER is more attentive to the power of countervailing forces and, thus, more aware of the need to follow incrementalist strategies to spur on unifying forces and to lend legitimacy to protofederalist institutions." (Reference by ROSAMOND 2000: 103 on PINDER 1991.)

The first backlash against federalism took place in the mid-1960s. CHARLES DE GAULLE's "empty chair" action was the culmination. There was a certain reassertion of nationalist sentiment among the European political elite. Emphasis was placed on national interests, and the centrality of member-state governments prevailed over emerging community institutions. It was asserted that states should be regarded as primary actors in the integration process. Some felt that intergovernmentalism had triumphed over supranationalism.

After the completion of customs union and the common market by 1968, from the end of the 1960s European integration seemed to acquire new impetus. In 1967, DE GAULLE's obstruction was abolished by the Luxembourg compromise, and by formulating the European Communities (the European Commission was created by merging the High Authority of Montanunion and the Commission of the European Economic Community and Euratom) the institutional setup was somewhat strengthened. In 1969, a plan for economic and monetary union was proposed, and it was foreseen that it could be implemented by 1980. Based on the Werner Plan, the first steps were taken from January 1, 1971, and clearly had wide political implications, including creating a sort of political union. Although the plan for a European Union (the Tindemans Report) was published in 1976, as a result of the economic crises of the 1970s (the collapse of the international monetary system based on Bretton Woods, and the waves of oil crises), the EMU project and consequently political union had to be abandoned. The crisis seriously hit the economies of the member states, and under these circumstances the countries preferred national solutions. It not only negatively affected any community action, but even disrupted some of the formerly developed cooperations. During the crisis, even the share of intra-trade among the member countries stagnated. Concerning the role and future of integration an attitude of "euro-scepticism" and "euro-sclerosis" prevailed.

The change came only from the 1980s (after 1983), when the European economy started to consolidate, economic growth accelerated (compared to 5% in the 1960s, however, only to around 3% per year), inflation moderated (from the crisis level of around 12% to 4–5% on average), and unemployment stopped rising (but remained around 10%). The integration process regained its dynamism, both in terms of the real economy (growth of trade and company integration), and also in terms of the launching of new integration projects. In this respect, undoubtedly the most important was the program of the Single European Market (adopted in 1987 with a 1992 deadline), and soon afterwards the plan for economic and monetary union (the Delors Plan) was published in 1989. As particularly the single market program promised substantial gains, "eurosclerosis" turned to "euro-optimism" (some even spoke about "europhoria"), and political and public support for integration greatly increased.

The integration projects were accompanied by important institutional changes, and the Treaties of Rome were modified and developed in several waves (the Single European Act, the Maastricht Treaty of European Union, then the Amsterdam and Nice Treaties). No one denies that the scope and competence of the European institutions have been widened, but theorists and politicians remain deeply divided as to how far the changes have affected the character of these institutions.

Many maintain that in spite of the ups and downs of the integration processes, the intergovernmentalist character of European institutions and decision-making prevailed, and there has not been any breakthrough toward supranational federal structures. The predominant direction of integration was liberalization (the single market), and even the positive integration measures were subordinated to the aim of the perfect functioning of that liberalized market. Monetary union, to a large extent, followed from the single market project, and the transfer of monetary policy to union level has not yet changed this trend. At the same time, the national states were successful in maintaining their primacy in strategic decisions. The theory which tries to describe these types of developments is called *liberal inter-governmentalism,* and ANDREW MORAVCSIK (1995) is considered one of its main proponents. This is a model of a two-level game to explain European integration consisting of a liberal theory of national preference formation and an intergovernmentalist account of strategic bargaining between states (ROSAMOND 2000: 136). MORAVCSIK, for his part, by developing a state-centric theory of liberal intergovernmentalism, describes the Union as a regime that makes inter-state bargaining more efficient, whilst enhancing the role of national leaders (MORAVCSIK 1993: 507).

While in general the federalists were strongly criticized and attacked, no one could, however, deny that the European Communities and later particularly the European Union amounted to something more, and probably much more, than a simple international institution, even if not yet a supranational, classical federal structure. Several new concepts were developed which tried to formulate that specific, unique and in many respects "in-between" character of the institutional setup of European integration.

Donald Puchala (1972) advocated an alternative to the former theory of EU integration by introducing the notion of a "concordance system". "A concordance system was a complex entity where nation-states remained important and were still probably primary actors, but where arenas of political action operated at several levels (subnational, national, transnational and supranational) and where levels of influence varied from issue area to issue area. A concordance system was also a forum for positive-sum interaction and for development of mutual understanding" (Rosamond 2000: 89). It can be defined as "such a system of 'cooperatively interacting states' based on the harmonization of the actors' interests and on mutually beneficial interactions. The role of the nation-state remains central in the integration process but at the same time the institutions of the larger system possess their own organizational and operational logic" (Chryssochoou 2001: 85).

Murray Forsyth (1981) defined the EU as a confederation – a voluntary association of states with common interests in building larger markets. Institutionalization is necessary to ensure the stability and longevity of the system (Rosamond 2000: 148). Forsyth notes, however, that although we cannot speak about the Community as a federal state, "this does not prevent it from being a federal union, that is to say a permanent linking together of states to form a corporate entity with a distinct boundary *vis-à-vis* the outside world, and possessed of two coexisting structures of government" (Forsyth 1996: 40).

The notion of the EU as a "consociation" is mainly associated with the work of Paul Taylor (1993). As a result of integration, the EC/EU can be defined as a European or "pluralist regional *polity*", which can be "best captured by the term 'confederal consociation'," and can be conceptualized as a "highly interactive system of mutual governance" (Chryssochoou 2001: 2).

4. REGULATION (POLICIES) AND GOVERNANCE OF INTEGRATION PROCESSES

4.1. INTEGRATION AND REGULATION

From the outset, the liberal concepts of integration were criticized from several directions. What the critics chiefly objected to was that their premises did not correspond to reality (perfect competition, free trade, interference-free market conditions), and that free market mechanisms are not capable of creating integration in the sense in which it is understood by the liberals. One main trend of criticisms of the liberal theories is that they overlook the importance of *regulation of the economy*. They approach integration *from the side of economic policies* and their attention is directed mainly towards economic union, as a form of integration.

Free trade did not bring the developed countries and the former colonial territories closer together but rather increased the gulf between them. It would be difficult to prove that in colonial times on the basis of free trade (which did not always come about), equalization of the costs of factors of production was achieved between the colony and the mother country. The critics of liberals object that on a free market basis integrational equalization cannot even be accomplished within a given country, as regional problems (e.g. southern Italy, etc.) prove. "Economic integration, as a notion, obviously cannot be defined, if we link it to classical free-market economics."..."It was assumed that every national economy became wholly integrated, given the internal conditions, as if it were a perfect market. This was of course an unrealistic assumption: only a few countries – and those only in the last two generations – have gradually reached a state that we can reasonably call national integration. These more perfectly integrated economies, however, are not of the market type" (MYRDAL 1972: 92–93).

Regulatory theories do not deny the importance of the market and of liberalization, but they emphasize that present-day economies are no longer based on free-market mechanisms in the 19th-century sense, but that economic life is *influenced, regulated and directed by the state*. According to regulatory theories, in addition to the market, "economic policies" have to be integrated, which on the international level enables international economic policies to be unified, harmonized, and in certain cases implemented in a collective, community manner. Thus international integration means state regulation and intervention is carried out at international (community) level.

The most important representative of integration theories related to regulation is JAN TINBERGEN, a Nobel Prize-winning Dutch economist. According to TINBERGEN: "Integration may be said to be the creation of the most desirable structure of the international economy, removing artificial hindrances to its optimum operation and deliberately introducing all the desirable elements of coordination and unification. The problem of integration, therefore, forms part of a more general problem, namely that of the *optimum economic policy*" (TINBERGEN 1965: 57).

So in TINBERGEN's conception, integration is an "optimal economic structure" which on the one hand removes "artificial hindrances" to market optimalization, and on the other hand helps to form the "optimum economic policy". The latter can be understood partly as optimum economic regulation and partly as a rational structure of institutional and mechanism elements (the "totality of institutions", import duties, the "currency regulation system", etc.). Thus international integration means that economic optima are not attainable within national frameworks but require the development of international institutions, mechanisms and regulation. "Policy optimalization" refers to the fact that "ultimately, international economic integration has to be viewed as a state and process for enabling its participants to achieve a variety of common goals more effectively by joint or integrated action than they could by unilateral measures" (ROBSON 1998: 6).

The difference between liberalization, the removal of "artificial barriers", and the integration of economic policies is expressed by JAN TINBERGEN through the introduction of the concept of *negative and positive integration*. "It appears useful to make a distinction between *negative and positive* integration. By the former we mean measures consisting of the abolition of a number of impediments to the proper operation of an integrated area. By the latter we mean the creation of new institutions and their instruments or modification of existing instruments" (TINBERGEN 1965: 76). Thus "negative" integration is simply liberalization, whereas "positive integration" is institution-building, that is, partly the development of new institutions and mechanisms, and partly the modification of existing mechanisms. JOHN PINDER has a different approach in applying the distinction between negative and positive integration. In his view, the objectives are either the elimination of discrimination or maximalization of welfare (PINDER 1969).

In today's modern economies the market and the state (social) macro-regulatory systems form an organic whole. In classical capitalism spontaneous competition among a large number of producers was typical. In present-day market economies producers are capable of a high and increasing degree of organization in their relations with each other and with the consumer. Modern computer technics and electronic communications take computerized organization of production "outside the factory gates", and with modern methods of market planning and organization new possibilities are opening up for assessing and satisfying consumer demand. Microelectronics and computer technics are increasingly making it possible for production to order to gain ground in broad segments of the traditional consumer market (on the basis of flexible manufacturing systems), and global infrastructures (communications and transportation systems) create widespread opportunities for international cooperation.

Self-regulating market mechanisms are becoming mixed with elements of social macroregulation. It must be noted that from many points of view I consider it more appropriate to use the term "social" instead of "state". This is not only because the state has to be interpreted broadly, and in regulation besides the central government or parliament local, municipal authorities play a part, but also because in the functioning of the present-day economy non-state social and political organizations (consumer protection, environment protection, trade union and professional lobbies, etc.) exert a decisive influence. Not only must macroregulation provide normal, legal frameworks for the operation of the market, but state intervention is essential for balanced economic growth, employment, the maintenance of internal and external equilibrium and the provision of a large proportion of basic public services. This is expressed by the "eco-social market economy" model accepted and promoted by many European political parties; it means that the optimum relationship between the market and social and environmental considerations has got to be found.

The role of the state was emphasized particularly in relation to the former socialist countries and the developing countries. There they sometimes talked about integration with reference to planning or development. "Such synchronizing actions are necessary, for example, for influencing the distribution of income among countries. Structural change and economic development are really in the common interest of both developed and developing countries alike; this is an area that must be totally subjected to state planning, and therefore demands positive international treatment" (SANNWALD and STOHLER 1958: 35).

From the point of view of regulatory theories GIANDOMENICO MAJONE made important contributions; he considers the EU as more and more an instance of a "regulatory state", or at least one which is on the way to becoming such an entity. According to him, the regulatory state "may be less of a state in the traditional sense than a web of networks of national and supranational regulatory institutions held together by shared values and objectives, and by a common style of policy-making." (Regulation can be defined as addressing problems of market imperfection and failure.) (MAJONE 1996: 276.) At the same time, it must be stressed that while regulation at regional level (at least in the case of the EC/EU) has progressed somewhat, this is not the case in global dimensions. These theories are closely linked to institutionalism and governance.

It is a central assumption of liberal and division-of-labour theory concepts of integration that on the basis of free-market mechanisms resources are more rationally allocated, efficiency improves, and finally the maximum common good is achieved. As a result of integration, therefore, not only is a bigger market area formed, where competition can more freely develop, but greater opportunities are created for the more efficient use of resources and the optimum division of labour. The question of advantages and disadvantages turns up again in the regulatory theories as well, only according to them "optimization" of economic policies must contribute to these.

4.2. FROM FUNCTIONALISM TO NEOFUNCTIONALISM

For the functionalist integration theories the most important question is the appropriateness and effectiveness of regulation. The *functionalist* schools place the emphasis directly on better functioning of the integration system, and on the improvement of its functioning. According to the functionalists, the nation state is increasingly incapable of fulfilling its basic social, economic and political tasks. Therefore more and more shared aims and functions should be delegated to the more efficient integration organizations, which are able to implement these more perfectly. The functions may be economic, political, social, infrastructural or military. In these spheres they can represent more efficient solutions to "tasks" like economic growth or the acceleration of technological progress, development of infrastructures at international level (construction of a community road network or communications system), equalization of development levels or in fact greater military security. Representatives of functionalist theory emerge mainly from political science trends (D. MITRANY, etc.) but for example the Polish Z. NOWAK regards himself as principally an economic functionalist.

The functionalists are aware that shifts in the exercising of functions presuppose institutional changes. "The functionalists constitute the most explicit and articulate section of a large body of conventional wisdom about international organization. Briefly, these ideas reflect a near-consensus that the modern technology of communication, industry and warfare, as well as the growth of economic, ecological and social problems on a regional or global scale, present irresistible pressure toward international cooperation and ultimate political unity. This consensus supplies the chief rationale for a large number of international organizations such as the Specialized Agencies and Regional Commissions of the United Nations and the proliferation of technical and economic organizations in Western Europe" (PENTLAND 1973: 66–67).

Functionalists and federalists often seem to be on the same platform inasmuch as they aim in the long run at supranational institutions. "The theory of *functionalism* in international relations is based on the hope that more and more common tasks will be delegated to such specific functional organizations and that each of these organizations will become in time *supranational;* that is, superior to its member governments in power and authority. In this way, says this theory, the world's nations will gradually become integrated into a single community within which war will be impossible" (DEUTSCH 1978: 208).

Although the functionalists' logic leads to supranational institutions, most of them leave the final objectives vague. "At the core of this agenda is the prioritization of human needs or public welfare, as opposed to, say, the sanctity of the nation-state or the celebration of any particular ideological credo. Indeed, functionalists tend to express considerable nervousness about the capabilities of nation-states to fulfil human needs. It follows that human beings need to be both rational about what their needs are and creative with respect to the construction of authoritative institutions that can perform the *functions* assigned to them. Human needs change over time and vary across the place. This means that the design of institutional solutions has to be open-minded and flexible" (ROSAMOND 2000: 33–34). According to MITRANY "form flows from function", that is, the institutional forms derive from given functions. As he points out: "The nature of each function tells precisely the range of jurisdiction and the powers needed for its effective performance" (MITRANY, Working Peace System; quoted by CHRYSSOCHOOU 2001: 58). "Integration need not necessarily be equated with the actual formation of an international body" (SULLIVAN 1976: 210). As communication theories stress, a high level of communication and transaction may lead to more integration than the concluding of formal agreements.

"For many intellectuals and politicians of the first part of the twentieth century, the civilized mind needed to turn itself to the avoidance of war. So, federalists contemplated the ways in which states could engineer some sort of mutual constitutional settlements that involved the delegation of power upwards to a higher form of government, thereby securing peace. Functionalists, on the other hand, chastised the nation-state as an irrational and value-laden concept. For them, the task was to secure the most efficient method of ministering to the real needs of people. Often – perhaps predominantly – human welfare could be best served on a post-national, post-territorial basis" (ROSAMOND 2000: 1–2).

Functionalists, like federalists, consider democratic political support important also from the point of view of the successful operation of institutions. "The simple proposition underlying functionalist theories of integration is that men's loyalties focus naturally on those institutions which gratify their basic material and social needs" (PENTLAND 1973: 85).

The so-called *neofunctionalists* (E. B. HAAS and LEON LINDBERG) emphasize prosperity, internal peace and external security, the role of national political elites, and in contrast to the global view, the possibility of regional integration. The functionalists were originally in favour of universal peace and were against regional integration. MITRANY, in fact, rejected European integration. "Functionalism was primarily a theory of *post-territorial* governance, whereas neofunctionalism was an early theory of *regionalism*. Indeed, there did appear to be real signs from the early 1960s that regional integration was developing into a world-wide trend" (ROSAMOND 2000: 69).

"For many, 'integration theory' and 'neofunctionalism' are virtual synonyms. It might even be described as the 'authorized version' of European integration. Neofunctionalism acquired the status of an ideology in Brussels" (CHRYSSOCHOOU 2000: 54). "Neofunctionalism (in its early manifestations at least) might be thought of as an attempt to theorize the strategies of funding elites of post-war European unity" (ROSAMOND 2000: 50–51). The need for the creation of purposeful (supranational) institutions was particularly emphasized. "This view sees neofunctionalist integration theory as a vehicle for lending legitimacy to the project of creating a federal Europe via integration of national economies" (ROSAMOND 2000: 8).

One of the most controversial ideas of the neofunctionalists is the notion of "spillover". "Perhaps the most important concept in the neofunctionalist armoury was the idea of "spillover", which was used to depict the mechanisms supposedly driving processes of regional integration. The creation and deepening of integration in one sector would create pressures for further economic integration within and beyond that sector, and greater authoritative capacity at the European level" (ROSAMOND 2000: 59–60).

LINDBERG defined spillover as "a situation in which a given action, related to a specific goal, creates a situation in which the original goal can be assured only by taking further action, which in turn creates a further condition and a need for more action, and so forth" (LINDBERG 1963: 10). According to JAMES CAPORASO: "Spillover is commonly thought of as a process whereby integrative activity in one societal sector leads to integrative activity in other related sectors" (CAPORASO 1970: 365). A certain parallel can be found with the determinism of Marxist theories, which assumed that "development of productive forces" (technologies) enforces corresponding changes in the superstructure (institutions). Integration was conceived of as an "objective law" of socio-economic development by most of the East European Marxists.

The theory of spillover was questioned primarily by intergovernmentalists. The latter sharply criticized the notion of any automatism or functional dynamism which would drive integration processes. Instead they emphasized the importance of national interests, and the primary role of national actors. As opposed to the neofunctionalists, intergovernmentalist theorists also denied the need for supranational institutions. "The resultant conversation between neofunctionalists and governmentalists is usually presented as the main ongoing schism in the integration theory literature since the mid-1960s. In many ways they present stark alternatives. In terms of identifying key actors, intergovernmentalists emphasize the centrality of national executives, whereas neofunctionalists point to supranational institutions such as the Commission as well as national and transnational interest organizations. Neofunctionalism is a theory of change and transformation, whereas intergovernmentalists emphasize international politics as usual, albeit under novel conditions" (ROSAMOND 2000: 2).

The arguments of neofunctionalists were reinforced by the new developments of the 1980s, particularly the launching of the program of the single European market, and then the amendment of the Single European Act. "The SEA was hailed by many observers at the time as opening up new horizons for positive integration. Neofunctionalism was in fact the only theory that could place, if not justify, such claims in a dynamic perspective, linking institutional reform, albeit of a limited nature, to the expansive logic of community action" (CHRYSSOCHOOU 2001: 93). At the same time, opponents argued that these developments did not change the character of the Community, inasmuch as they "have followed the same pattern: the joint exercise of the authority by state executives has not led, either gradually or automatically, to the erosion of sovereign statehood, but rather has strengthened the capacity of states to promote and in the long run secure a fair share of their interests within the general system, whilst preserving an area of autonomous domestic jurisdiction crucial to their identity as states" (CHRYSSOCHOOU 2001: 94). The liberal intergovernmentalist arguments are repeated in this context as well.

The 1990s, however, brought a new turn in the history of European integration, and one could hardly deny that national sovereignty was affected. The most important development was the amendment of the Treaty of European Union in 1992, which "clearly marked the passage of the community's evolution 'from policy to polity'" (CHRYSSOCHOOU 2001: 96). Although the member states did not consider abandoning their devotion to national sovereignty, "there was evidence that the TEU brought the new structures closer to being considered as a political system in its own right, with significant capacity for governance. Under the new paradigm, 'polity' referred to a system of institutionalized shared rule whose governance structures were capable of producing authoritative political decisions over a given population and of allocating values in the society. The characterization of the Union as an 'emerging polity', compound yet easily identifiable as a collectivity, makes it possible to contemplate the idea replacing the rather deterministic concept of 'integration' – for it is usually associated with 'a sense of *directionality*' – with that of 'polity-formation': the making of a large-scale system of mutual governance without the formal legal or constitutional attributes of competence embedded in classical state structures" (CHRYSSOCHOOU 2001: 96–97).

4.3. MULTI-LEVEL GOVERNANCE

Functionalism, like federalism, was a branch of the broad movement that sought to theorize "the conditions for ending human conflict" and give "prescriptions for future human governance" (ROSAMOND 2000: 32). LINDBERG and SCHEINGOLD are considered major proponents of multi-level human governance. The main role of theory can be "to reveal ways of improving the conditions of human governance. The latter may be defined as the art of organizing the production of knowledge about the constitution of human activity. By theorizing is meant the systematic study of the conditions, structure and evolution of that constitution, by means of explicating, interpreting, understanding and, where possible, predicting individual, small- or large-scale social action" (CHRYSSOCHOOU 2001: 6).

As HOOGHE defines multi-level governance: "it amounts to a multi-layer polity, where there is no centre of accumulated authority, but where changing combinations of supranational, national and subnational governments engage in collaboration" (HOOGHE 1995: 176).

Multi-level governance is a product of the integrating world economy, which with growing interdependence, both regionally and globally, is a response to new challenges and needs in controlling and managing complex processes and harmonizing interests within a multi-actor system. "The point of departure for this multi-level governance (MLG) approach is the existence of overlapping competencies among multiple levels of governments and the interaction of political actors across those levels. States are not an exclusive link between domestic politics and intergovernmental bargaining in the EU. Instead of the two-level game assumptions adopted by state-centrists, MLG theorists posit a set of overarching, multi-level policy networks. The structure of political control is variable, not constant, across policy areas" (MARKS, NIELSEN et al. 1996: 41). "If anything, MLG is an attempt to depict *complexity* as the principal feature of the EU's policy system and its emphasis on variability, unpredictability and multi-actorness tends to set adherents of this approach in opposition to the contemporary intergovernmentalists" (ROSAMOND 2000: 111).

In my opinion, multi-level governance, in fact, means the emergence of a new structure, where the constitutional foundations of sovereignty may remain largely unchanged, leaving national member states as basic entities, but at the same time, it challenges the functional or operational autonomy of states by sharing decisions, and pursuing certain policies in a shared way. In fact, it means a "search for more effective and cost-reducing means of organizing, structuring and executing collective policy programmes that nevertheless remain crucial for the political viability of the constituent units" (CHRYSSOCHOOU 2001: 111). In other words, while power and power sharing remain basically of intergovernmental character even on the longer run, along the line of the principle of subsidiarity, the Union level of governance takes growingly supranational pattern. That might be the major field of creeping supranationalism, supported by the pressure of increasing efficiency of the governance in general. Policy developments and reforms already tend to that direction.

Compared to intergovernmentalism, multi-level governance brings in a third dimension into the operational structure of the Union, namely domestic, local or sub-regional interests and actors. WALLACE calls this process "post-sovereign", leading to further power-sharing, or a "post-modern approximation to political reality" (CHRYSSOCHOOU). "The Union is thus conceived of as a multi-level system of governance composed of interlocked arenas for political contest, where direct links are established among actors in diverse political spaces and political domains, where political control is diffuse (often leading to 'second-best' policy outcomes)" (CHRYSSOCHOOU 2001: 107).

Globalization often appears in the literature as a form of external 'regulatory shock' that forces a policy response from within the EU (ROSAMOND 2000: 182). "European integration can be seen as a distinct West European effort to contain the consequences of globalization" (WALLACE 1996: 16). In fact, it should be added that as integration extends more and more to global dimensions (globalization), that creates its own issues and needs (global governance). "Global governance is in fact a part of a multi-level governance system which will retain this forum of states while making room for the growing number of important non-state actors in the world's economy and politics" (SIMAI 2001: 105).

From the point of view of European governance it means that it has to take on certain global roles, while on the other hand it is a certain dimension of global governance. The EU and European governance can be a model for the whole world, partly for other regional integrations, and partly in global directions, even if we cannot expect any significant move toward any sort of global institution with federal aspirations in the foreseeable future. It is clear also that the roles and scope of European governance will and should be much wider and more complex than they can be on a global level. "There were two big political science issues here: the relationship between economics and politics, and the future of the nation-state as a viable and desirable method of organizing human affairs in advanced societies. While the nascent European Communities offered the ideal empirical laboratory for the pursuit of the issues, the ambitions of most of these theorists stretched well beyond Europe. Perhaps the experiment of the six original member-states could be shown to be part of a trend that would come to affect other parts of the world. Perhaps, therefore, universal dynamics of regional integration could be revealed. Perhaps theorists could lead creative policy-makers into the design of rational institutions to secure better forms of governance in a modern, interdependent world" (ROSAMOND 2000: 1).

Governance, even on a global level, should not be limited to securing peace and preventing future tensions or conflicts. "The future tasks of global governance, however, cannot be confined to the anticipation and management of risks. In this era of interdependence and interactivity, with information highways crisscrossing the globe, qualitatively new solutions must be found to problems in an increasing number of areas. States, which are likely to remain the key members of the global society, will have to harmonize their actions in a broad range of areas and extend their cooperation if they are to enjoy the beneficial consequences of their interactions" (SIMAI 1994: 354). It is clear that as globalization extends to broad fields of social life, new real governance issues arise, particularly in dealing with problems of the world economy.

The European Commission published a White Paper on future reform of "European Governance" in July 2001. The main objective of the white paper is to reform and improve the governance system of the Union by the creation of greater coherence among the different policies of the Union, increase the efficiency of these policies, and bring them closer to the citizens. It expresses a certain urgency concerning the reform of governance, which should go ahead without waiting for the probably cumbersome process of modification of treaties and the institutional changes.

The Commission determines five principles of "good governance", which must guide the reforms concerning the improvement of the decision-making and executive system of the Union. These are: *openness* (more open operation of institutions, and more active communication toward public opinion), *participation* (inclusion of the citizen, the different organizations, etc. in the decisions and actions), *accountability* (greater transparency and responsibility), *efficiency* (in terms of both setting objectives and implementation) and *coherence* (relevant definition of objectives, and better coordination among policies). These five principles are strengthened and supplemented by two traditional concepts, *proportionality and subsidiarity*. The chosen measures should be proportional to objectives, and the level of action (regional, national or union) should be appropriately chosen.

It is clear that there are two main concerns of "European governance", namely more *"democratic governance"* and *increased efficiency of that governance*. The democratization of the institutions and operation of the Union is one of the central issues of the coming IGC (and consequently of the

Convention). "Democratic governance" implies improving citizen participation in Union affairs, including a greater role for civil society. Delimitation of competencies should also be an important objective, creating a structure where the allocation of scopes and responsibilities is more transparent and enables citizens to hold the given level politically accountable. Many propose increasing the role of national parliaments in the EU policy process, although it needs clarification what their role should be, and how this could contribute to the elimination of the democracy deficit of the Union. The reform of institutions and their operation is an important part of this democratization process. The increase and clarification of the role of the Commission as an executive body and that of the European parliament as the legislative power are crucial (although controversial) questions from the point of view of creating a real democratic governance structure in the European Union.

"Good governance" and efficient governance are also controversial issues, and depending on their levels they have to fulfil different conditions, requirements and expectations. "The concept of governance has been debated widely in recent years. It is certainly not management, even though it may imply managerial tasks. It is not about 'governing' countries or even less the world. It is often understood as the guidance provided to participants or actors within a system for the coordination of different functions. The quality of governance and the characteristics of 'good governance' have been formulated by the IMF and laid down as the crucial postulate of the development process. The Managing Director of the IMF defined good governance thus: 'governments must be accountable and participatory; laws must be transparent, non-essential regulations eliminated and competence and impartiality ensured'. These are of course important postulates but they fail to specify the crucial responsibility of governments for the welfare of the people and the state of the country. This definition, moreover, is insufficient in the national framework" (SIMAI 2001: 104). We should add that the same applies to "European governance". The EU's distinct property of having broad fields of common policies, and institutions with extended competencies, needs broad cooperation and coordination, unprecedented in any other international organization. This is particularly the case with the proper and efficient operation of economic and monetary union.

The efficiency of governance, particularly with enlargement, is becoming one of the primary aspects, and the success and stability of the Union may greatly depend on whether the Union is able to build a "system conducive to positive-sum governance" (CHRYSSOCHOOU 2001: 86). A Union with 25 members (soon probably 27–28 members) can operate efficiently only if the objectives are clearly defined, the competencies are properly delimited, and coordinated measures can secure the achievement of the common objectives and interests.

4.4. WHAT SORT OF FUTURE EUROPEAN UNION?

In the future, with enlargement, a new European Union will emerge with not only almost double the number of member states (this could soon be the case) but with qualitatively new challenges, necessarily new rules of operation and with much greater diversity in every aspect of economic and political life. If we take the present commitments (for the Balkans) the EU may find itself in a process of continuous enlargement lasting for decades, and ending up with around 35–40 members. (In 20 years, the membership of 6–7 Balkan countries, besides that of Norway, Switzerland and Iceland, can be foreseen.)

In order to avoid dilution of the integration process, a reversion to being a simple free trade area, and failure to achieve the aim of a real united Europe, *several important elements of the development of the integration process* should be strongly stressed.

First of all, *the maintenance of the process of deepening* is essential, in order to continue *strengthening the "Centre"*, which sets and holds the pattern and is able to maintain the pattern in spite of the growing number of members; the Centre, which is able to absorb new members without weakening or giving up its identity. This "centre" or "hard core" would not be just a political alliance of a small number of these countries, but rather *a broader political and economic structure,* following the traditional European social, cultural and moral values, which would comprise probably most of the present members (and could gradually be strengthened by new members). "Enforced cooperation" offers a proper framework, but it should be open to all, including the newly admitted countries. It should not create "second-class" members.

This structure should be composed of several elements, some of which are of particular importance. To simplify, a strong centre assumes:

1. *Stable and functioning democratic structures,* which are based on the broad support of the citizens of the European Union in terms of gradual integration measures, and which correspond also to the aspiration of candidates for consolidation of their new-born democracy.

2. *Credible and functioning security systems* should be created with the direct participation of the candidate countries. If conflicts and tensions in the East seriously threaten the security of the Centre, on the other hand, it is common sense that a stable and secure CEE is a precondition of pan-European security. Full commitment to and responsibility for the security of the whole continent is of the utmost importance.

3. *Efficiently functioning institutional structures,* which require further progress with institutional reforms in the EU, and also broad institutional adjustment on the part of candidate countries.

4. *Continued increasing of the efficiency of policies,* which assumes progress in ongoing policy reforms, particularly in such fields as the CAP or budgetary policies. Successful implementation and functioning of EMU will demand improved policy coordination. *A stable euro* will probably be one of the most important integrating factors for the Union.

5. *Prospering and globally more and more competitive economies,* together with enlargement, should contribute massively to improving Europe's competitiveness. Prosperity in the Eastern part could give a boost to the whole European economy, and enhance the global competitiveness of European companies. On the other hand, a crisis in their economies could have negative effects on the general development and global position of the Union's economy as well. The Union took historic decisions in March 2000 at the Lisbon Council, when matching the performance of global competitors and meeting the challenges of globalization and the new economy were considered. Eastern enlargement is important from the point of view of not only the candidates' chances of catching up, but also the improvement of the global competitiveness of Europe.

6. From the point of view of increasing the economic and social strength of the whole Union, a *continuous process of internal and external convergence* is an important requirement. The process of external convergence among the European countries is probably *one of the most important developments in European history in the last half-century.* And integration has played an undeniable role in the process. The spectacular convergence of the northern, the western and the southern periphery towards the "centre" has been one of the main attractions of that European integration. Finland, a few decades ago a poor country, has become one of the richest countries on the continent, and Ireland, Portugal and Spain have spectacularly caught up in the last few decades. Internal social convergence has become one of the most important factors of social cohesion and of the success of the integration process in the last decades of history of the EU.

What sort of European Union can we foresee with about 35–40 members? Conventional logic may conclude that a great number of countries can integrate and efficiently operate only in a federal type of structure. But how far would federal solutions be accepted, and would they be accepted more readily by the future 25 or 35 countries than by the present 15 members? The answer remains uncertain. Some new members may be more in favour of federalism for certain reasons than many of the present members. Some others may be hesitant to accept such a prospect. There are several among the new candidates which recently quitted one federation (the Soviet Union, or Yugoslavia), and have achieved national statehood, which they never enjoyed, or only for a short time, in the past. Of course, the Soviet Union does not compare with the EU, but the attachment to newly-gained "independence" may be strong enough to make some candidates wary of hurrying into a new federal structure.

But while a constitutional federation is not a viable prospect in the short run, *an operational or functional integration in a framework of multi-level governance* could be highly desirable and even a necessary alternative. Taking into account, however, that except Poland and Romania the other ten candidates are small countries, for them sub-regional or local-level governance has a totally different meaning than for Spain and Germany, or even for Italy and France. For them, probably, *an inter-regional level of governance* could be much more relevant, taking into account the traditions and rationality of close cross-border economic, political and human relations, based on historically long existing regions with geographic, cultural or ethnic similarities or identities. Such cross-border inter-regional cooperation has already started formally (e.g. among the West Hungarian and the neighbouring counties) or informally, and they could be institutionalized and integrated into the new emerging system of multi-level governance among the EU members.

The question remains, what sort of European Union is emerging and what might this new entity be? The great number of theories of the last decade do not even help in analysis of the past development of European integration, not to speak about the future. From 2001, a broad discussion started about "the future of Europe", related to the Convention and the next Intergovernmental Conference. This might clarify several issues, but the process toward "closer union" will probably remain contradictory and lengthy. All parties agree, however, that the European Union is a unique, special, complex entity without precedent in the past. As far as the future is concerned, "the Union remains an integrative venture whose final destination is yet to become discernible" (CHRYSSOCHOOU 2001: 16). It is still a sort of halfway house between federal and confederal structures, a "partial polity" or "part-formed political system", a "betweenness" which is still in a "grey area" between the national and the supranational state. "The Union remains an unresolved social scientific puzzle with an 'open *finalité politique*'" (CHRYSSOCHOOU 2001: 15, WESSELS 1997: 12). It is a "baffling mixture" of federal and intergovernmental properties (BELLAMY and CASTIGLIONE 1999: 11), and "the most complex polity that human agency has ever devised" (SCHMITTER 1966: 25–40).

The terminological confusion is well represented by the following summing-up of the results of the theoretical literature: "Other terms to be found in the *acquis academic* as means of conceptualizing the political and/or constitutional physiognomy of the Union include: proto-federation, confederance, concordance system, network governance, quasi-state, *Staatenverbund,* meta-state, market polity, managed *Gesellschaft,* nascent *Gemeinschaft,* regional regime, federated republic, sympolity, confederal consociation, and so on" (CHRYSSOCHOOU 2001: 23).

"Theorizing [about] European integration has so far impelled many promising theoretical departures but has managed to achieve only a few concrete theoretical arrivals. At a time when the Union remains much of an unspecified entity with an open-ended political *telos,* its dynamism is caught between federalist aspirations to become a more congruent polity and a modified type of intergovernmentalism which confirms the centrality of states in managing the regional arrangements. The overall conclusion to be drawn is that, despite its continued political and constitutional evolution, and gradual accretion of substantive policy competences, the Union has not developed the attributes of a sovereign entity. It has, however, evolved into a fully-fledged political system whose proper conceptualization is to be found outside pre-existing statist categories, despite the rather paradoxical fact, at least from a realist state-centric perspective, that it does share a multitude of state-like characteristics. It is precisely this dialectical union of integrative and autonomy forces operating at the same time across distinct but interdependent policy domains and levels of governmental and societal action that constitutes the fundamental stability of the Union. All the above contribute to an understanding of the Union as a compound polity best captured by the term 'confederal consociation': a consensual form of polity that has achieved a level of integration that is comparable to many plurinational federal polities, without however threatening in any fundamental way the sovereignty of its component states. Instead, the common management and joint exercise of separate sovereignties have acquired a new qualitative dynamic, assisted by an accommodationist process of political co-determination" (CHRYSSOCHOOU 2001: 192).

5. SOME POSSIBLE THEORETICAL INTERPRETATIONS OF INTERNATIONAL INTEGRATION

Obviously, the various schools of integration theory approach the process of unification, and mutual adaptation from different sides and with differing emphases. It would be difficult to say which of these are important and correct. In fact, taken together they constitute the integration theory of our time. "The fable of the elephant and the wise men, about the ineffectiveness of theories, applies not only to integration theories but to virtually all the social and natural sciences. Though it is true that the theories examined contain only a grain of truth, and cannot provide a comprehensive explanation of the integration process, still they have advanced knowledge, contributed to an understanding of the European political processes and above all have created a body of concepts with the help of which rational debate can be conducted concerning the European processes; that is, they have laid the foundations of Europe's integration policy culture" (KENDE 1995: 96).

The various theoretical schools and trends call attention to the important interconnections of integration theory, and enable us to formulate some general questions. It is not really possible to give a single definition of integration, especially if we examine it on the international level, but on certain questions we can with relative confidence adopt a position.

1. Integration is a *historical process,* which cannot be limited to the unification or interconnection of national economies. A tendency to unite and become interwoven can be traced throughout the whole of human history, from the coming together of tribes in old times to the globalizing world economy of our age. The modern nation states of Europe, in the course of the recent history of the continent, evolved basically from the uniting of cities, principalities or provinces. Integration to form a nation is a complex process, and has taken place in very varied ways in different regions of the world (Brazil, the USA, India, etc.); and this applies to integration on the international level, too.

On an international scale, integration appears to have been taking place in recent decades within organized, institutional frameworks. One of the most important peculiarities of international integration at present is that it can be defined as *the voluntary, comprehensive economic and political linkage of sovereign states and national economies.* So it has nothing in common with the 'imperial' integration of earlier times, based on conquest and colonization. In Hungary, for instance, there is substantial literature dealing with integration issues relating to the Austro–Hungarian monarchy, the 'disintegration' following its dissolution, and the consequences of this. Today's efforts at integration have completely new foundations and conditions, though historical experiences can provide useful lessons (BEREND 1968).

2. International integration is regarded by most of the theoretical school as a *multi-level process*. In relation to international economic integration I make a distinction between the concepts of micro- and macroeconomic integration.

Microintegration is a process that takes place between individual actors in re-production, in the form of international production, sales, market, technical and development cooperations or joint ventures. Macrointegration is a process of unification involving the whole of society, which takes place between national economies as units. The national economy is ultimately the integration of individual producers and traders, which can be understood as the interlinking of the re-production processes. It is characteristic of the world economy today that company, national, regional and global integration processes are going on parallel with one another; they have reciprocal effects and are interlayered in a comprehensive manner.

The economy and economic relations *build from below,* and the laws of their operation always take effect through the activity of the individual (producer, consumer, entrepreneur, taxpayer, etc.) Their attitudes, behaviour and actions are motivated by interest. From their situation, relations, thinking and aspirations emerge a society's sociology, its political complexion and ultimately its economic efficiency. I therefore see the *individual as the chief actor* in society and the economy, their point of departure and motivating force, and integration is basically about how and in what frameworks the individual's socio-economic activity and life is organized.

3. Integration can be thought of *as a process and as a state*. In the "static" sense, "economic integration" can be seen as a situation in which the national elements of a larger economy are no longer divided by economic boundaries but function together as a unit. As BÉLA BALASSA points out the integration as a process covers those measures, which aim at elimi-

nating discrimination among the economic units belonging to different national states (BALASSA 1962).

4. Integration is *an organic process,* which evolves from the rational activity of economic actors and the more efficient operation of the economy. Many think that to regard integration as unification is a superficial and quantitative approach. *Qualitatively the tendency to integration is the formation of more highly developed communities or organisms of a higher order and increasing efficiency and effectiveness.* In the economic sense this means that increasingly finer and more complex specialization and cooperation on the part of the individual producer and consumer take place, and their social activities are organized into increasingly efficient organisms from the level of direct production (the microeconomic sphere) to that of the national economy or world economy (the macro- or megaeconomic sphere). We can call this the organic conception of integration.

Integration is a comprehensive process, which embraces every area of social, economic, political and cultural life, including individual human relations and macrosocial relations.

5. International integration is *a democratic process.* This is especially important from the point of view of understanding "voluntarism" of integration units. Integration, as unification and interconnection, ultimately leads to the weakening of the given national economy and limitation of its sovereignty. At the same time, the nation, particularly in recent history, has proved to be a community to which the attachment of individuals and societies is very strong. This is demonstrated by the bloody ethnic and national wars in Eastern Europe at the end of the 20th century. Therefore very powerful considerations, constraints or "gains" are necessary, to induce a nation state to give up voluntarily even part of its sovereignty.

Democracy is a value concept which is accepted by broad masses, and which in the last few decades has become closely associated with the concept and process of European integration. "Economic integration is a value-laden concept. As a consequence, its achievement is desirable. But the unity of any culture means there is a relatively high degree of community of interest, and consequently vagueness is kept within bounds. In this book we have linked the concept of 'economic integration' with old ideas of western civilization such as freedom and equality, and particularly with equality of economic opportunity. In developed countries the tendency of development is for these ideas to be given increasing emphasis, and they are being implemented more and more within national frameworks" (MYRDAL 1972: 87, 89, 90). In Europe the idea of integration has from the outset been supported by political parties and broad strata of public opinion. In recent decades, on the basis of the progress and success of EU integration the gradual unification of Europe has become a popular, attractive prospect all over the continent.

REFERENCES

ARCHER, C. (1992) *International Organizations* (Second Edition). Routledge, London and New York.

ARON, R. (1953) *Problems of European Integration.* Lloyds Bank. *Review,* April.

AUSCH, S. (1969) *A KGST-együttműködés helyzete, mechanizmusa, távlatai* (State, mechanisms and perspectives of CMEA cooperation). KJK, Budapest.

BALASSA, B. (1961) *The Theory of Economic Integration.* Irwin, Homewood, Illinois.

BALASSA, B. (1962) *The Theory of Economic Integration.* London.

BELLAMY, R. and CASTIGLIONE, D. (1999) Democracy, Sovereignty and the Constitution of the European Union: The Republican Alternative to Liberalism. EurCit Working Papers, no. 1.

BEREND, T. I. (1968) 'Birodalmi integráció' az Osztrák–Magyar Monarchia keretében. A közép- és kelet-európai gazdasági integráció kérdéséhez (Imperial Integration in the Framework of Austro–Hungarian Monarchy. Questions of Central and Eastern European Integration). *Közgazdasági Szemle,* nos. 3 and 5.

BULMER, S. (1993) Governance of European Union: A New Institutionalist Approach. *Journal of Public Policy,* 13, no. 4.

CAPORASO, J. A. (1970) Encapsulated Integrative Pattern vs. Spillover: the Case of Transport Integration in the European Economic Community. *International Studies Quarterly,* 14 December.

CHRYSSOCHOOU, D. N. (2001) *Theorizing European Integration.* SAGE Publications, London.

DEUTSCH, K. W. et al. (1957) Political Community and the North Atlantic Area: International Organization in the Light of Historical Experience. Princeton University Press, Princeton, NJ.

DEUTSCH, K. W. (1964) Communication Theory and Political Integration. In P. E. JACOB and J. V. TOSCANO (eds): *The Integration of Political Communities.* J. P. Lippincott and Co., Philadelphia.

DEUTSCH, K. W. (1978) *The Analysis of International Relations* (Second Edition). Harvard University, Prentice Hall, Inc., Englewood Cliffs, New Jersey.

ETZIONI, A. (1965) *Political Unification.* New York.

FORSYTH, M. (1981) *Union of States. The Theory and Practice of Confederation.* Leicester University Press, Leicester.

FORSYTH, M. (1996) Political Theory of Federalism: The Relevance of Classical Approaches. In HESSE and WRIGHT (eds): *Federalizing Europe?*

GILPIN, P. (2001) *Global Political Economy.* Princeton University Press, Princeton.

HARTOG, F. (1963) European Economic Integration. A Realistic Concept. *Weltwirtschaftliches Archiv,* Vol. 2.

HIRST, P. and THOMSON, G. (1999) *Globalization in Question*. Polity Press.

HOOGHE, L. (1995) Subnational Mobilisation in the European Union. In J. HAYWARD (ed.): *The Crisis of Representation in Europe*. Frank Cass, London.

KAMECKI, Z. (1972) A gazdasági integráció fogalmának kérdéséhez (To the Question of Economic Integration) (in Russian). Lecture given at an international symposium in Moscow on 'Integration Processes'.

KEGLEY, W. and WITTKOPF, E. (eds): *The Global Agenda: Issues and Perspectives*. Random House, New York.

KENDE, T. (1995) Integrációs elméletek (Integration Theories). In KENDE, T. (ed.): *Európai közjog és politika* (European Public Law and Politics). Osiris–Századvég, Budapest.

KEOHANE, R. O. and NYE, J. S. (1977) *Power and Independence. World Politics in Transition*. Little, Brown and Company, Boston–Toronto.

KINDLEBERGER, C. P. (1966) European Integration and the International Corporation. *Columbia Journal of World Business*, Vol. 1. No. 1. 1966.

KITZINGER, U. W. (1963) *The Politics and Economics of European Integration: Britain, Europe and the United States*. Praeger, New York–London.

KOZMA, F. (1970) *A "két Európa" gazdasági kapcsolatai és a szocialista nemzetközi együttműködés*. (Economic Relations of "Two Europe" and the Socialist International Cooperation). Kossuth–KJK, Budapest.

LINDBERG, L. N. (1963) *The Political Dynamics of European Economic Integration*. Stanford University Press–Oxford University Press, Stanford, California–London.

LINDBERG, L. N. (1993) *The Political Dynamics of European Economic Integration*. Stanford University Press, Stanford.

MAJONE, G. (1996) A European Regulatory State? In J. RICHARDSON (ed.): *European Union: Power and Policy-Making*. Routledge, London.

MAKSZIMOVA, M. M. (1975) *A tőkés integráció alapvető problémái*. Kossuth Könyvkiadó, Budapest.

MARJOLIN, R. (1953) *Europe and the United States in the World Economy*. Duke University Press, Durham, N. C.

MARKS, G., NIELSEN, F. et al. (1996) 'Competencies, Cracks and Conflicts: Regional Mobilization in the European Union. In G. MARKS et al.: *Governance in the European Union*. SAGE, London.

MOLLE, W. (1990) *The Economics of European Integration*. Dartmouth, Aldershot.

MORAVCSIK, A. (1993) Preferences and Power in the European Community: a Liberal Intergovernmentalist Approach. *Journal of Common Market Studies*, 31, No. 4. 1993.

MORAVCSIK, A. (1995) Liberal Intergovernmentalism and Integration: A Rejoinder'. *Journal of Common Market Studies*, 33 (4).

MYRDAL, G. (1972) *Érték a társadalomtudományban* (Value in the Social Sciences). KJK, Budapest.

NYE, J. S. (1968) Comparative Regional Integration: Concept and Measurement. *International Orgatnization*, 22 (4).

PALÁNKAI, T. (1986) *A fejlett tőkés országok világgazdasági alkalmazkodása* (World Economic Adjustment of Developed Capitalist Countries). KJK, Budapest.

PALÁNKAI, T. (1989) A nemzetközi integráció elméleti kérdései (Theoretical Questions of International Integration), pp.11–58. KOLLÁR, Z. and PALÁNKAI, T. (eds): *Integrációs rendszerek a világgazdaságban* (Integration Systems in the World Economy). KJK, Budapest.

PELKMANS, J. (1997) *European Integration. Methods and Economic Analysis.* Longman, Heerlen. Open University of the Netherlands.

PENTLAND, C. (1973) International Theory and European Integration. The Free Press (Macmillan) New York.

PERROUX, F. (1954) *L'Europe sans rivages.* Paris.

PINDER, J. (1969) *Problems of European Integration.* (Ed. G. R. DENTON.) Weinfeld and Nicolson, London.

PINDER, J. (1991) *European Community: The Building of a Union.* Oxford University Press, Oxford.

PREDÖHL, A. and JÜRGENSEN, H. (1961) Europäische Integration. In: *Handbuch der Sozialwissenschaften.* Bd. 1.

PUCHALA, D. J. (1972) Of Blind Men, Elephants and Integration. *Journal of Common Market Studies,* 10.

PUCHALA, D. J. (1984) The Integration Theorists and the Study of International Relations. In C. W. KEGLEY and E. WITTKOPF (eds): *The Global Agenda: Issues and Perspectives.* Random House, New York.

ROBSON, P. (1998) *The Economics of International Integration.* (Fourth Edition.) Routledge, London and New York.

ROSAMOND, B. (2000) *Theories of European Integration.* Macmillan Press Ltd., London.

RÖPKE, W. (1959) *International Order and Economic Integration.* Dordrecht.

RUGGIE, J. (1998) *Constructing the World Polity: Essays on International Institutionalization.* Routledge, London.

SALVATORE, D. (1993) *International Economics.* Macmillan Publishing Company, New York.

SANNWALD, R. and STOHLER, J. (1958) *Wirtschaftliche Integration. Theoretische Voraussetzungen und Folgen eines Europäischen Zusammenschlusses.* Kyklos Verlag, Basel.

SCHMITTER, P. C. (1996) Some Alternative Futures for the European Polity and their Implications for European Public Polity. In MENY et al. (eds): *Adjusting to Europe: The Impacts of the European Union on National Institutions and Polities.* Routledge, London and New York.

SIMAI, M. (1985) *Hatalom – technika – világgazdaság.* (Power – Technology – World Economy). KJK, Budapest.

SIMAI, M. (1994) *The Future of Global Governance.* United States Institute of Peace Press, Washington, D.C.

SIMAI, M. and GÁL, P. (2000) *Új trendek és stratégiák a világgazdaságban* (New Trends and Strategies in the World Economy). Akadémiai Kiadó, Budapest.

SIMAI, M. (2001) The Uncertain Fate of Nations. World Affairs *(Journal of International Issues),* Vol. V. No. 1.

SPINELLI, A. (1972) The Growth of the European Movement since the Second World War. In M. HODGES (ed.): *European Integration.* Penguin, Harmondsworth.

STUBB, A. (2002) Debating the Future of the EU: from Laeken to IGC 2004, pp. 5–16. In *From Union to Constitution? Debating the Future of the EU. Collegium,* College of Europe, Bruges. No. 23: Spring.

SULLIVAN, M. P. (1976) *International Relations. Theories and Evidence.* Prentice Hall, Inc., Englewood Cliffs, University of Arizona, New Jersey.

TAYLOR, P. (1993) *International Organization in the Modern World: Regional and the Global Process.* Pinter, London.

TINBERGEN, J. (1965) *International Economic Integration.* Elsevier, Amsterdam.

WALLACE, H. (1996) Politics and Policy in the European Union: the Challenge of Governance. In H. and W. WALLACE (eds): *Policy-Making in the European Union.* Oxford University Press, Oxford.

VERDUN, A. (2002) *Merging Neofunctionalism and Intergovernmentalism: Lessons from EMU.* In A. VERDUN (ed.): The Euro. Rowman & Littlefield Publishers, Lanham.

WESSELS, W. (1997) *The Amsterdam Treaty in View of Fusion Theory.* Paper presented to the British International Studies Association, University of Leeds, 15–17 December.

III.

INTEGRATION MATURITY – MEMBERSHIP CRITERIA

1. THEORETICAL APPROACHES

Since the establishment of GATT (the General Agreement on Tariffs and Trade) in 1948, 214 regional trade agreements had been concluded in the world economy by 2000. Of these, only 134 were in force in 2000. This means that a large proportion of them failed; either they stopped their activity or they were disbanded. This applied particularly to the first wave of regionalism, which owing to the great political and economic changes of the past decades (the world economic crisis in the 1980s, the collapse of the Soviet bloc) mostly faded away. The *second wave of regionalism,* beginning from the 1990s, seems much more successful, inasmuch as it "has possibly been precipitated by increasing international economic interdependence and advances in communication" (JONES 2001: 28). Only since 1995, 90 such new regional trade arrangements (from free trade area to common market) have been created.

Obviously, in the high "failure rate", the role of several concrete economic and political factors can be traced and identified. The great number of failures, however, may indicate that some more general and fundamental causes should also be taken into account. Consequently the question arises, how the general conditions were secured, and whether the given countries were prepared for even the primary and simple forms of regional integration. The answer is probably not, but it cannot be confirmed without deeper analysis of the circumstances. Or, to put it differently, one can simply ask how far these countries were *mature and ready for that integration.*

Every integration organization can set certain membership conditions or criteria for those who wish to join it. Most of these are obvious (they follow from geographical proximity or political orientation) or general enough not to be exclusive. The Treaty of Rome prescribed for membership of the European Community only that the country in question should be 'European' and 'democratic'. This has caused uncertainty regarding its geographical boundaries (e.g. in the case of Turkey), but it was sufficiently general to offer as widely as possible the opportunity to join. In other cases the social and political orientation of the countries (e.g. those of COMECON) was decisive.

With the advance of integration it can be assumed that the preparedness of potential participants for integration, their 'maturity' with regard to integration, progressively increases in importance. This is indicated by the development of the European Communities, in which, as they progressed from a simple customs union and common market towards a single market and economic union, this question became more and more prominent. In connection with economic and monetary union, formal accession criteria for would-be participants were set in Maastricht.

In relation to the earlier stages of market integration (free trade agreements, customs union, common market) in the EC the question of readiness for integration could at the outset be left out of consideration for many reasons.

– There was no need to examine integration-maturity criteria, because especially in the initial period the countries joining were basically similar in their economic development level and structure. On the basis of their given level of development the participating countries qualified as mature for integration.

– In subsequent enlargements, political considerations were given priority to such an extent that the determination of economic membership criteria did not even feature on the agenda. Since in the given world political situation the accession of the three Mediterranean countries in the 1980s was basically a political question, it took place on the basis of political considerations. It must be added that historically the Copenhagen criteria were also the outcome of a political bargain: when in 1992 against EU opposition the countries of the Eastern bloc were seeking to gain acceptance for the possibility of their accession, it was by setting 'criteria' that the EU tried to reach a compromise. Whether in fact they formulated the membership criteria in a relevant way became clear only later.

– Consideration of the question of integration maturity and in this connection examination of the membership criteria was always determined by the extent to which wider membership or community interests were involved. The question has arisen more and more unavoidably in connection with the increasingly close forms of integration, and the program of economic and monetary union has shown that at this level integration maturity cannot be left out of consideration.

In the EC/EU *concrete accession criteria* were first formulated *in 1991 in relation to the transition to economic and monetary union.* The so-called Maastricht convergence criteria set an important requirement of monetary integration, when as a condition of membership of EMU on the part of member countries, specific and well-defined indicators of monetary and fiscal stability were examined.

Maastricht convergence criteria:
They are applied from the beginning, but at the third stage the countries must be suitable. (The single currency is envisaged as non-inflationary, like the DM.)

1. Price stability measured by the consumer price index. The annual inflation rates of member countries must not diverge by more than 1.5% from the average of the three best-performing countries.
2. Stable monetary positions. Budgetary deficits have to be kept under 3% of GDP and the national debt under 60% of GDP.
3. Convergence of interest rates. Long-term nominal interest rates should not diverge from the average of the three best-performing countries by more than 2%.
4. Stable national currencies. No devaluation against the national currency of any other member country allowed for two years.

It was an important new development in economic union, or 'positive integration', that participation in it on the part of member countries or those interested was now by no means automatic: *certain conditions must be fulfilled*. Market liberalization was not without consequences, but these were mostly unilateral and asymmetric (the less developed, weaker partner could lose more) and the retroactive effects were not manifested in a direct manner. With economic union the situation is different. The reciprocal effects are heightened and become direct. The less developed partner's economic difficulties (budget deficit or regional inequalities) have repercussions on the economy of the more developed, and can destabilize it (e.g. by triggering inflation) in more direct ways. The decision to join in an economic union is one that fundamentally affects the institutional and political structure of the country in question. In this connection *maturity or readiness for integration* is an issue that has to be examined.

For new candidates for admission, the EC/EU accession criteria were first determined in connection with 'Eastern enlargements'. The so-called *Copenhagen criteria* were approved in June 1993, and form the basis for assessing the preparedness of applicant countries.

The Copenhagen criteria:

– stability of institutions, guaranteeing democracy (rule of law, human rights, respect for and protection of minorities);
– a functioning market economy;
– capacity to cope with competitive pressure and market forces within the Union;
– ability to take on the obligations of membership, including adherence to the aims of political, economic and monetary union;
– the Union's capacity to absorb new members.

Taking into account the complexity of preparation and of the preparedness of countries for participating in regional integration arrangements, however, we feel that a distinction should be made between:

– fulfilment of membership (accession) criteria and
– integration maturity.

Integration maturity is defined as the capacity or ability to maximally exploit the advantages offered by given integration forms, and at the same time to minimize the costs and disadvantages. Integration maturity can be measured by the balance of the costs and benefits of integration. A country is mature for integration if it is able to turn its membership into a positive-sum game, that is, integration is advantageous for it. Integration maturity can be analyzed for the different basic forms of integration from the free trade area to economic union. Assessment of integration maturity concentrates not only on the conditions and requirements of participation in integration, but also on its outcome and the consequences of that integration.

Membership criteria in a broad sense refer to the conditions and requirements set (usually formally and officially) as conditions of participation in an integration arrangement. In case of the EU, it means a complete acceptance and adoption of "acquis communautaire". The *accession criteria* are narrower, and refer to some concrete integration organization (e.g. in our case we are looking at the question in relation to the EU), and they (e.g. the Copenhagen ones) *formulate narrowly only the conditions for becoming a member.*

– The Maastricht criteria (1991) for joining EMU.
– The Copenhagen criteria (1993) for Central and East European (CEE) candidates.

Thus *accession criteria* refer to some concrete integration organization (e.g. in our case we are looking at the question in relation to the EU), and they (e.g. the Copenhagen ones) *formulate narrowly only the conditions for becoming a member*. Membership criteria mean conditions that have to be fulfilled at the time of joining, naturally depending on what stage integration has reached in the given organization. Greece and Portugal joined an EC still modeled on the common market, but new members now join a single market on entering, and want to (in fact, have to) match up to the requirements of economic and monetary union. The *more specific membership criteria are officially defined* (Maastricht and Copenhagen), and their fulfilment, formally and in reality, is a condition of membership.

The two are closely interdependent, since accession criteria seek to express integration maturity, as they do in reality, but in a narrower sense. Accession criteria rather formulate the minimum requirements for admission to take place, while the question of maturity goes beyond this, and in general examines the conditions for successful and effective integration. Accession criteria approach integration maturity, readiness for integration, in a detailed way, and mostly from certain aspects only, while in the case of integration maturity these interrelations have to be analyzed in their entirety and complexity.

In integration economics integration maturity was not formerly dealt with comprehensively and in detail. An exception to this is the literature analyzing the integration of developing countries, which from the outset drew attention to the problems, for example in free trade areas or common markets, arising from wide developmental and structural differences.

In analyzing integration maturity we can rely on various analyses carried out in macroeconomics, integration economics, political sciences, sociology and European studies. Accession criteria are concrete, but particularly for interpreting the Copenhagen criteria we have no proper guide. With regard to their maturity and readiness for membership the candidate countries are regularly surveyed by the EU Commission and other organs (Regular Reports; the European Parliament) of course chiefly from the point of view of fulfilment of the membership criteria. These do not provide a more serious theoretical and methodological foundation for integration maturity. Their system of criteria and methods of analysis are not yet clear, and provide only a loose framework for evaluation that takes place on political grounds.

In some cases the parameters relating to fulfilment of certain criteria have been precisely worked out (e.g. the Maastricht convergence criteria), while in other cases the parameters required for analysis and evaluation are sketchy, inconsistent, highly debatable, or simply non-existent. This can often be attributed to the rough nature of methods of analysis; in other cases it reflects a certain deliberate intention, making it possible to treat the conditions flexibly, or to accelerate or even delay and hinder the integration process. An effort to be flexible can be detected in connection with both EMU and eastward enlargement.

Examination of integration maturity is necessary and timely not only in connection with entry. And it is not only the case that apart from full membership it arises in connection with participation in certain phases of integration (EMU membership), but in practice the maintenance of integration capabilities is always a condition of later exploitation of the advantages of membership. The situation with the accession criteria is somewhat different. Examination of these loses its importance after admission, since there is no question of expelling any member country for non-fulfilment. It is another question with membership criteria as certain conditions can be examined later (e.g. those of monetary union and the Stability Pact), and in connection with these sanctions can be applied. The admission of new members may set requirements for the member countries themselves and for the Union as a whole. We can refer to the criterion set for itself by the EU (absorption capacity), which from many aspects we can analyze according to the logic of the membership criteria.

The 'accession' criteria were defined in the EU as an official requirement as well (Maastricht and Copenhagen). These are demanded of countries seeking admission, at the time of entry. Broader membership criteria have to be fulfilled by them from within, as participants (single market measures, or the Stability Pact). On other membership conditions there is complete agreement among integration theories (e.g. the possibility of 'asymmetric shocks' in connection with participation in EMU), yet formally these are not examined. With regard to EMU, naturally, the question of integration maturity is much broader and more complex than the examination of monetary convergence. Officially only the latter was formulated, mainly because in connection with monetary union absolute priority was given to a sound, non-inflationary single currency.

Examination of questions of integration maturity became particularly timely in relation to full membership for the CEE countries. Considering the huge differences in development and the number of these countries, enlargement will have far-reaching consequences for the development of the whole Union. On the other hand, preparation for membership, the state of preparation and analysis of the effects of membership can provide important information for the negotiations and in general for policy makers and public opinion. Hungary, for instance, has committed itself to asking the opinion of its citizens on EU accession in a referendum. It is essential that every citizen be enabled to form a realistic picture of this, and that in making the decision the long-term interest not just of individuals but of the whole country be taken into account.

Both, accession criteria and integration maturity can be analyzed in *three main dimensions:*

– economic criteria;
– political criteria; and
– institutional criteria.

This applies to the Copenhagen and the Maastricht criteria, but we can structure the analysis of integration maturity also along these lines.

1. Economic criteria. For new members, the Copenhagen and other official decisions set three major requirements:

– a "functioning market economy";
– the "capacity to cope with competitive pressure and market forces within the Union";
– stabilization of economies.

The Maastricht criteria are all basically of an economic character.

In the economic context, membership criteria and integration maturity cannot be separated; in fact, they overlap. But the fulfilment of accession criteria can be (and in practice, is) judged according to narrower parameters (Country Reports), while *the "functioning market economy"* is a broader and more complex notion and in fact it should be considered *the main factor in integration maturity*. The "mobility of factors of production" or "flexible factor markets" as conditions of the smooth operation of a monetary union (optimal currency area) are nothing else than an extended interpretation of the concept of a "functioning market economy". Competitive capacities are important conditions of monetary union as well, even if in the Maastricht criteria de facto they are restricted to the requirement of exchange rate stability. Monetary union assumes a certain convergence of development levels and economic structures (able to cope with "asymmetric shocks"), but in many respects the question arises even at the lower stages of integration. Most of the parameters set in Maastricht refer to the stability and stabilization of participating economies, although they are formally limited to only the monetary and fiscal aspects of the process. They stress monetary and fiscal "convergence", but avoidance of asymmetric shocks requires convergence in a broader structural sense. Stability of monetary union cannot be achieved without economic policy coordination, and budgetary transfers among the participating countries (extension of the theory of the "optimal currency area" by G. M. A. MacDaugall and P. R. Allen) could be necessary to cope with social and regional tensions. A normally-functioning economy cannot be imagined without social stability. Successful integration presupposes social integration and cohesion; social and political support for the integration process is of the utmost importance.

Taking into account the above considerations, in an integration economics approach, in relation to the different basic forms of integration the following *basic criteria of integration maturity* could be formulated:

- a market economy ("functioning");
- structural and development competitiveness;
- macrostability and stabilization;
- convergence (real or financial convergence);
- financing or financeability;
- social integration and social cohesion.

These criteria are partly general frameworks for the normal operation of given integration forms; partly they express the conditions of the success of the given integration. The economic criteria will be more broadly analyzed, inasmuch as the advantages of enlargement depend to a large extent on economic circumstances, and they are important from the point of view of the welfare of the whole society. As we can see, only the first three are concretely formulated as membership criteria, but even in their case, we take a broader analytical approach.

2. *Political criteria*. Although the Treaty of Rome concerning potential members refers to certain political conditions (democracy, and belonging to "Europe"), the first formal political criteria for membership (accession)were set for CEE candidates only in 1993 in Copenhagen ("stability of institutions, guaranteeing democracy; rule of law; human rights; respect for and protection of minorities"), and then in 1995 in Madrid. Lately political criteria have been set (in fact, codified) for member countries (Amsterdam and Nice Treaties). Consequently, candidates and members must meet the following requirements:

– a *state* of democracy (1957, Rome);
– *"stability"* of democracy and institutions (1993, Copenhagen);
– *"functioning"* democratic institutions (1995, Madrid);
– *compliance* with democratic principles (1997, Amsterdam; 2000, Nice).

The first three are basically accession criteria, while Amsterdam and Nice decisions are typically membership criteria.

In political dimensions, membership criteria and integration maturity cannot be separated. In fact, as they relate to given institutions and a given stage of integration, they can be considered only as *concrete membership criteria.* Of course, the question of democracy can be analyzed in general theoretical terms, and general political conditions of integration can be interpreted as questions of integration maturity (democracy and efficiently functioning market economy). In this respect, there are possibilities for a more general analysis than just looking at criteria, which are taken into account upon entry to the given integration. But the focus is on meeting concrete membership criteria relating to European Union membership.

3. *Institutional criteria*. Institutional criteria can be analyzed in a very broad sense, and they are applied right from the beginning as *membership criteria*. In fact, as they relate to concrete institutions, they cannot be anything other than membership criteria. As countries join a given integration form (a free trade area or common market) and the related institutions, there is no choice other than to comply with the generally agreed rules. As integration progresses, new institutional criteria can be set

(EMU; independence of the central bank), and meeting them is important from the point of view of the successful operation and development of integration. We imply economic policies as institutional membership criteria, although *the efficiency of economic policies* raises the question of broader properties of integration capacities. As far as the Copenhagen accession criteria are concerned (the "ability to take on the obligations of membership, including adherence to the aims of political, economic and monetary union"), they can be divided into the following main obligations:

- acceptance and adoption of "acquis communautaire";
- commitment to EMU;
- commitment to "political union".

Integration maturity, and in some respects membership criteria, should be analyzed and judged not only in the case of enlargements and in relation to new members, but should apply also to full members. Continuous *"maintenance" of integration maturity* is unavoidable, in order to *exploit the advantages of integration*. Most of the membership criteria are met to a great extent from inside (in the internal market), and compliance with the *acquis communautaire* requires continuous adaptation. Enlargements mean a need for adjustment in broad fields for the member countries also. This was recognized in relation to Eastern enlargement, and in fact in Copenhagen the EU noted the importance of its own ability to receive the new entrants (the "Union's capacity to absorb new members"). These requirements were not specified in detail, but the main directions and fields of necessary "reforms" were broadly identified and accepted. In these terms, the necessity of the following measures should be particularly stressed:

- CAP reform;
- budgetary reform;
- completion of EMU;
- institutional reforms.

The first three are in practice "economic criteria", while the "institutional reforms" are necessary to accommodate 10–13 or more new members.

2. MARKET ECONOMY CRITERIA OF INTEGRATION

A *normally functioning* market economy is a starting condition in relation to every form of integration. The whole theoretical and analytical system of integration economics is based on this assumption. In the framework of the various forms it is regional free trade and economic policy barriers to these are removed by liberalization. Only with the proper functioning of market mechanisms can the advantages of internal free trade be exploited. As an official membership criterion the question (of a functioning market economy) arose only in connection with the admission of the CEE countries, but this did not mean that it was not relevant earlier. It is obvious that this question receives varying emphasis at the different stages of integration, and in the closer forms of integration (such as EMU) it cannot be avoided even in the case of the most highly developed countries. It is another question, that the requirement of a functioning market economy (flexible markets and prices for factors of production) was not formulated in the EMU as a membership criterion, but only analyzed in informal theoretical discussions.

Six countries of the EEC fulfilled this requirement as highly developed market economies, and in this regard no real doubts have since arisen, even with the admission of the Mediterranean countries. (In contrast to the Eastward enlargements, Greece, Portugal and Spain "merely" joined a common market.) But at least basically they fulfilled the requirement, since we know there is no such thing as a "perfectly" functioning market economy. It must be added that their fulfilment of it was far from complete and automatic. It is no accident that the customs union and common market are accompanied from the outset by stringent supervision and regulation of competition, and internally *competition policy had to be raised to community level,* this being associated later with wide-ranging law harmonization to ensure freedom and equality in trade. Thus to achieve a "functioning market economy" many measures are applied. In the case of the EC countries, in the given circumstances it was sufficient that this be done after membership was gained.

Similarly, adaptation with regard to *the internal market* went on "from inside" and "afterwards" from the beginning of the 1990s. The single European market is formally a further step towards the common market and is a more highly developed form of integration. Anyway, it brings up more intensively the question of the normal functioning of the market. At the same time, in terms of content it is simply the actual realization of the common market. The common market, too, has as its aims the four freedoms, but it chiefly concentrates on the removal of normative barriers. The 1992 program of the *single European market* seeks systematically to eliminate all the real obstacles in the way of the "four freedoms", and ultimately *extends and in practice creates the conditions for a really "functioning market economy".*

It is important to point out the similarity, in terms of their theoretical approach, between the optimum currency zone and the Copenhagen membership criteria. The *optimum currency zone* also involves *the requirement of a "functioning market economy",* at most concretely *with reference to the "factor markets".* Since the establishment of a single market is a starting condition of EMU, in this case a "functioning market economy" as a criterion is understood in a much wider sense. "In the economic sense a country's EU maturity can ultimately be conceived as its ability to fit smoothly into the single market" (RÁCZ 2000: 812). It can also be said that *"a functioning market economy" is one of the most general and most important criteria for integration, which at a given level of integration is a condition of being able to exploit adequately the advantages of integration.*

In the case of Eastward enlargement, with regard to the membership criteria a new situation arose, in that the question of integration maturity could not be handled automatically and without more serious analysis. At the beginning of the 1990s (Copenhagen – 1993) the CEE countries were still in a transitional situation, and in Copenhagen the membership criterion basically stressed nothing else than that the transition from a centrally-planned to a market economy must be completed. In relation to Central and Eastern Europe, on the one hand the introduction of the condition of a *"functioning market economy"* was in practice an attempt to formulate *a certain desirable minimum transformation* for these countries, while on the other hand it referred to the requirement of participation in the single market.

From the point of view of maturity for membership, one important question is *proper interpretation, identification and in the given case, measurement of* a market economy's *ability to function.* It was obvious that merely to legislate for market economy institutions was not sufficient to ensure that the candidate countries actually fulfilled the maturity requirements.

The ability of a market economy to function is a natural requirement at every level of the economy. "Ability to function" presupposes the free movement, without artificial barriers, of market participants and prices. The main actors in an economy, in a given economic situation and economic policy environment respond appropriately and rationally to the influences of the market. Company profit becomes profit in the true sense of the word, a measure of the company's contribution to the efficiency of the whole economy. The creation of a market economy demands the use of policies, institutions and economic policy instruments that are in harmony with the functioning of the market, and attempt to harmonize the broader interests of society, taking these all into account. In circumstances of globalization, particularly in small, open economies all this applies in relation to external markets as well.

A general approach to the *"functioning market economy"* is possible, which simply takes account of the general parameters of the market accepted by economics, and analyzes the state of these with respect to a given country. In connection with regional integrations it is especially important to examine to what extent the given country meets, or more precisely is capable of meeting the requirements of the given basic form of integration, whether it be a free trade area, customs union, common market, single market or economic and monetary union.

We shall attempt in what follows to formulate and summarize in general, from the integration maturity point of view, the *parameters of a "functioning" market economy,* regardless of the requirements of any given basic form of integration.

– Comprehensive liberalization of prices (wages, interest rates, exchange rates, etc.). Transparency and flexibility of prices.

– Freedom of market actors; free entry to and exit from the market. There are no obstacles to mobility of factors of production.

– Competitive market structures (competition, which prevents prices from remaining for long substantially higher than costs; pressure for innovation and increased efficiency; elimination of monopolies; a great number of market actors; freedom of choice).

– Company performance dependent on profit (agents under severe constraint to cover their current expenditure out of the receipts from their sales, and make a profit on them).

– Elimination of state support and subsidies.

– Liberalization of foreign trade; abolition of state control and monopolies; non-discriminative policies.

– Convertibility of national currencies (mainly on current account).

– Creation of real money and capital markets (reform of the banking system; development of financial services compatible with developed money markets; stock exchange; other forms of non-banking institutions and activities).

– Money as a vehicle of coordination.

– Dominance of the private sector (privatization in countries undergoing transformation).

– Restructuring of companies (corporate finances, marketing, management).

– Market-conformity of state regulation (taxation, monetary policies, "positive" structural policies; "integration conformity" is something more).

– Transparency of regulation (simple and accountable legislation, lack of corruption).

– Efficient "eco-social market economy" (separation of social policies from efficient functioning of the market; recognition of the need for protection of the environment).

Naturally, the requirements receive varying degrees of emphasis in relation to the different basic forms of integration. In a separate chapter we shall deal with economic and monetary union, from the point of view of both integration maturity and membership criteria.

In the countries undergoing transformation the creation of a market economy is a special objective, in itself ultimately one of the most important strategic aims of the transformation (affecting and being affected by privatization). According to JOSEPH VAN BRABANT, the success of the new market economy basically depends on how the various economic activities, as agents of social and economic policy, have changed in respect of their efficiency, productivity and way of working. Eight factors are listed, every one of which is important from the point of view of transition to a market economy and ultimately of integration maturity. These eight factors are the following (VAN BRABANT 1990: 65–83):

1. The essence of creating market economy conditions is the creation of an economic environment that supports self-financing and self-management on the part of companies. The success of companies depends on how they run their business. The internal and external conditions of company cooperation help in breaking down a monopoly situation.

2. In addition to company independence, central macroeconomic policy motivates the individual economic agents to optimize their activities from the point of view of society. This involves the creation of a system of ministries and the implementation of an orthodox budgetary and monetary system, and certain central prices and wages policies.

3. The introduction and development of a real, genuine wholesale trade system.

4. Market prices determine the efficient allocation of resources.

5. Through development of the banking system, prudent commercial banks that show responsibility in their financial decisions are established. They carry out lending on the basis of companies' actual financial results and not as a result of central government intervention or pressure.

6. The relation between the productivity of labour and the remuneration of labour becomes closer. In general it is true that labour productivity should have greater influence on the development of companies' labour policy.

7. The weight of state ownership is considerably reduced. Through various forms of privatization, private ownership becomes dominant.

8. The opportunities latent in foreign trade relations must be more effectively exploited, including widespread use of direct methods of bringing in capital through trade and joint ventures with foreign companies.

From the point of view of the integration of the CEE countries into the world economy, obviously apart from examination of their integration maturity the immediate, top-priority task is fulfilment of the membership criteria. In direct connection with the latter a key question is the state and progress of their transformation, and the extent to which they meet the criteria of the "functioning market economy" formulated in Copenhagen. In the professional literature dealing with this transformation, surveys soon appeared analyzing the viability of their markets (EBRD Transition Reports; World Bank, *World Development Report* 1996). For the interpretation of market conditions several systems of analysis and indices were designed to measure and demonstrate the degree and level of development of market maturity. These, together with the relatively meager EU literature on membership maturity, and the country reports, are from this point of view also very useful.

Among the internationally "registered" systems of indices of market transformation and maturity, the most important are the annual analyses of transformation carried out since 1994 by the European Bank for Reconstruction and Development (EBRD). In our judgment, from these, on the basis of the bank's system of comparison, appropriate conclusions can be drawn about membership maturity. The theoretical assumptions underlying the bank's statistical comparisons set out from the premise that *the countries undergoing transformation* want to evolve from centrally-planned countries into developed countries, with all the concomitant system elements. In the comparisons it is directly assumed that transformation is *a process of approximation,* in which in the macro-, micro- and international economic policies of the CEE countries more and more similarities appear, in the system of aims and means, to those characteristic of the economic policies of present-day developed industrial countries. Theoretically, of course, it can justly be asked *on what theoretical grounds* these countries can be expected to be comparable with the developed European countries in particular. Can it not be assumed that in addition to general market economy characteristics they possess a number of special market features? And if this can be assumed, to what extent do these special features determine their general market economy characteristics? In our opinion, the fact that these countries want to join the EU integration was from the outset the justification for this comparison. Accession itself demands a definite degree of convergence, and this is expressed in the membership criteria.

The *Transition Reports* published since 1994 by the EBRD analyze and compare 24 countries in transition on the basis of uniform indices. These countries are the following: Albania, Azerbaijan, Byelorussia, Bosnia–Herzegovina, Bulgaria, Croatia, the Czech Republic, Estonia, Georgia, Kazakhstan, Kyrgyzia, the former Republic of Yugoslavia, Macedonia, Latvia, Poland, Lithuania, Hungary, Moldavia, Russia, Armenia, Romania, Slovakia, Slovenia, Tajikistan, Turkmenistan, Ukraine and Uzbekhistan.

The EBRD's analyses are based on the following set of indices:

- large-scale privatization (extending to sectors);
- small-scale privatization;
- foreign trade and exchange rate system;
- degree of price liberalization;
- change in structure of companies;
- functioning of financial institutions:
- competition policy;
- banking reform and interest rate liberalization;
- functioning of securities market and non-bank financial institutions;

– progress in establishing the legal framework of transition (since 1995);
– infrastructural progress (since 1998);
– indices of the social maturity of transition.

In connection with the various parameters the *Transition Report* analyzes the state and progress of transition using a 4-point scale marking system. In a given area a mark of 1 means an absence of transitional reforms; 2 means barely acceptable progress; 3 represents satisfactory progress, while 4 indicates the attainment of a level similar to that of the developed market economies. The "scores" gained on the basis of these relatively comprehensive analyses and measures not only act as good indicators of market transformation and functionality, but also provide guidance for investors and for the economic policies of the countries seeking admission. On the basis of the calculations the state and progress of transition and the rank order of the various countries can be measured with relative accuracy. Similar parameters have been used by the World Bank as well, but in its case the fulfilment of the transition program is measured in percentage terms.

Analyses of transition, together with the EU's Annual Country Reports, conclude that the candidate countries of Eastern Europe, including Hungary, *by the end of the 1990s satisfied the "functioning market economy" requirement*. In Hungary privatization has more or less been completed, and the main market economy elements have been harmonized with the chief parameters characteristic of the developed countries. Apart from the Central European countries this also applies to the Baltic states, while among the candidates those most at a disadvantage are Bulgaria and Romania. On the whole, the disadvantages of the other countries in the region (the ex-members of the former Soviet Union and Yugoslavia) are more serious, although countries like Croatia may quickly catch up.

It is a more difficult question, drawing conclusions from integration maturity. Reliable information about it will be available only later, after membership is achieved. At the same time, the effects of the European Agreements based on free trade association so far indicate that these countries are capable of exploiting the advantages of market integration, and for them they have been entirely favourable. From the point of view of opening up the market, full membership (complete integration into the single internal market) does not mean a dramatically new situation (the market for industrial products has been liberalized), and as far as opening it in new areas (agriculture, services) is concerned, the balance of advantages and disadvantages there too may be positive. At the same time, integration maturity must be extended to economic and monetary union, since the new members will wish to join this as well, after a relatively brief transition period (2–4 years).

3. DEVELOPMENTAL AND STRUCTURAL (COMPETITIVENESS) REQUIREMENTS

Developmental and structural requirements and criteria were from the outset in the focus of attention even in connection with *the free trade areas,* the loosest and simplest form of market integration (especially in relation to attempts at integration by developing countries), and regarding the "more highly developed basic forms" this is even more the case.

Even in the choice of the appropriate form of market integration, structural considerations must be weighed. It is generally agreed that the free trade area can be recommended particularly in the case of differing economic structures of a complementary nature. In the case of similar or competitive structures, the customs union is more appropriate. The role of customs tariffs is different depending on whether they are designed to protect domestic production or, in the absence of domestic production, chiefly to tax consumption. This is expressed by distinguishing between protective and restrictive (consumption-regulating) customs duties. The free trade area, by permitting differences in national customs tariffs, suits the varying interests arising from different economic structures. In the case of similar economic structures, the customs union is recommended, since in this way the administrative costs arising from differences in national customs tariffs (determination and certification of origin and local content) can be saved.

Thus it is no accident that in the choice of the EEC (1958) and EFTA (1959) these considerations were detectable from the beginning. The very similar economic structures of the Six justified a customs union, and this was also supported by their aspirations to achieve political integration. In the case of EFTA there were differences between the economic structures, although on the basis of their economic structure countries like Great Britain, Denmark and Sweden could easily have been members of the customs union represented by the EEC. Their decision to form a free trade area was determined by political considerations. For various reasons they did not want any restriction of their sovereignty. So the choice of the free trade area or the customs union rationally follows from the economic structures, but may diverge from this for political reasons.

From both the free trade area and the customs union the *common market*, or liberalization of the mobility of factors of production, logically follows. On an open, free market, exploiting economies of scale and responding to the pressure of competition demands the availability of factors at the lowest possible cost, and ultimately optimum allocation of resources. Free flow of factors within the area ensures this, since it adjusts factor prices towards their marginal productivity, and helps to clear market bottlenecks. It was not by chance that in the EEC the customs union was simultaneously supplemented with the common market, which in practice was established by 1968.

A common market program was not directly linked to EFTA, but there was no particular need for it. In fact, the OECD framework ensured the free flow of capital there too by the end of the 1960s, and it was not necessary to free the movement of labour. In the case of Great Britain the required external manpower resources were amply provided by the Commonwealth, while among the Scandinavian countries this was in practice implemented within the framework of NORDEC. Anyway, "external" countries represented the necessary sources of manpower, and it must be added that in the case of the EEC also this was the situation. In the EEC, apart from absorbing southern Italy's regional unemployment, most of the labour came from "outside" (Turkey, Yugoslavia, the Maghreb countries, or from Greece and Portugal, which later became members).

Differences in levels of development demand thorough evaluation. Every market integration which opens countries' markets to each other, within the framework of any kind of free trade bloc or grouping, raises the question of *development differences:* more precisely, *different levels of costs and competitiveness* among the various sectors and companies. A free market is expected at microlevel to increase efficiency, partly through the exploitation of economies of scale, partly as a result of the beneficial effect of competition in reduction of costs and better satisfaction of consumers' needs. In competition, producers that can deliver more modern products at lower cost come to the fore, while the less efficient, if they cannot adapt, are squeezed out of the market.

Bigger differences in development, for example in the case of *market integration between less developed and industrially highly developed countries,* can give rise to serious problems *at macrolevel*. The free trade area is not equally favourable for more developed and for less developed countries. In the case of the latter, owing to increasingly sharp competition large numbers of producers may go bankrupt or lose their markets, with the result that the less developed countries' balance of trade and payments may be severely impaired, with all the attendant negative consequences for domestic employment, the budget, and ultimately economic growth. The situation is similar with the dynamic approach, since producers in the more developed countries are better endowed to adapt to the new competitive situation, to mobilize capital resources, to adopt more modern technologies and to finance rationalization. Producers in less developed countries may simply be incapable of adapting.

In extreme cases these negative consequences can appear as absolute losses, as a result of which either the free trade solution has to be abandoned, or the asymmetries must be built into the trade liberalization. These asymmetries may be temporary (e.g. in the case of the European Agreements), or long-lasting (as, for example, in the case of the Lomé Convention, where in contrast to complete liberalization on the part of the EU, the ACP countries were required in return only to apply the "most-favoured-nation" principle. All this reflects the fact that the partners were not mature for integration).

In the case of more moderate development differences the effects of free trade, as a positive-sum game, can be *beneficial for almost every partner*, though because of the differences in development *the distribution of the benefits will not be equal.*

This is the situation in the case of the European Agreements based on the free trade model. In this case, moderately developed (CEE) countries entered into market integration with the industrially developed (EU) countries. There is no doubt that this partnership had many important advantages for the CEE countries' economies, contributing to strong growth in exports, which provided a proper basis for "export-led" growth, improved levels of employment and efficiency, and assisted structural modernization. After the association agreements came into force, a sizeable deficit developed in the balance of trade between the EU and these countries (compared with more or less balanced trade based on the socialist "planned economy"), which indicates that the balance of advantages is tipped in favour of the EU. It is another question whether these advantages have been less significant in relation to the EU's economy and foreign trade (at present it represents 13% of their foreign trade) than the more modest benefits from the point of view of the CEE countries' economy (2/3 of their trade is with EU countries). Hungary succeeded in reversing the deterioration of its balance of trade after 1997 as a result of very substantial foreign capital investments.

In comparison with the earlier enlargements, *Eastward enlargement* raises most acutely the problem of development and structural differences. In some of the candidate countries agriculture has considerable weight, and in several sectors competitiveness is poor. The need to respond to the "pressure of competition" was seen particularly in 1993 as a very real cause for anxiety. The fear, which in 1993 was to a certain extent justified, was expressed that full membership could have in given cases serious, even catastrophic consequences for the economy of the candidate countries, and this was not in the interest of either side.

Similarly to the concrete parameters of the "functioning market economy", those of "response to competitive pressure" were not defined in more detail by the EU, thereby leaving ample scope for interpretation. In our opinion the EU has defined *competitiveness* only indirectly and in a restricted sense *as a criterion for membership.* At the same time, competitiveness *must be regarded as an important indicator of integration maturity* (perhaps one of the most important), and therefore we must discuss it in this spirit. Unquestionably the candidate countries cannot exploit the advantages of integration unless they possess a company structure capable of holding its own in market competition. This may mean products, or it may mean standing up to competition in terms of costs, quality and innovation. Competitiveness is thus a fundamental interest, since otherwise the competition will sweep most of the candidate countries' companies out of the market.

Competitiveness basically determines the situation of a given country or region's producers and, most important, its possibilities as regards exploitation of the advantages of integration. A lack of competitiveness can have serious negative consequences for the integration, and as we mentioned in connection with development differences, some solution has to be found: either integration, that is, participation in the integration organization or grouping, must be abandoned, or suitable mechanisms must be built in to compensate for disadvantages and losses.

Analysis of competitiveness and assessment of its situation is essential from the point of view of working out the structural policy of a given country or region. At union level, for instance, competitiveness was the focus of attention when in 1993 the Council took its decisions, approving the document entitled "Growth, competitiveness, employment", and in 2000, in Lisbon, with respect to implementation of the e-Europe program. Competitiveness is an equally relevant question in relation to both global and regional integration of a country or group of countries.

The question arises, *how can competitiveness be interpreted, and how can it be measured?* Competitiveness is a complex indicator, therefore interpreting it and expressing it in figures is extremely problematic, and it is not easy to identify it in connection with integration maturity. There are some who say it can be interpreted only on the microlevel (level of costs, quality of products, etc.), while at macrolevel we do not know how to handle it. As one CEPS study states: "Direct analogy among firms and the competitiveness of countries is completely incorrect" (CEPS Newsletter, Summer 1994: 1).

With reference to Hungary's competitiveness, at the BUESPA multidimensional, comprehensive analyses have been carried out under the direction of ATTILA CHIKÁN, and mention must also be made of the similar publications and data produced by the ITDH. In examining our integration maturity many of the data and interrelations in these are very useful.

ATTILA CHIKÁN defines competitiveness in both micro- and macroeconomic contexts. On the micro level: "We may consider enterprises competitive if they are able to transform available resources into a profit flow while complying with the social values of the environment in which they operate and if they are able to perceive and manage external and internal changes that influence their long-run operation in order to maintain their profitability, ensuring long-term survival" (CHIKÁN et al. 2002: 26). On macro level: "The competitiveness of a national economy is the ability of a nation to create, produce, distribute and provide products and services that meet the requirements of international trade so that in the process the return on its own factors of production increases." (Ibid. 25).

We shall not deal with the debate about the concept of competitiveness, or the problems of measuring it. For analyzing the theme it is sufficient if we simply refer to certain international calculations. For measuring competitiveness and establishing the rank order of countries the various research institutes and consulting firms make use of several dozen parameters, from which they derive the so-called "competition or competitiveness index". The competition index of the World Economic Forum uses 155 indices, while the IMD uses 290 indices for 47 countries (World Competitiveness Yearbook. IMD).

From the point of view of integration maturity, however, it is necessary to analyze competitiveness in a comprehensive way; we shall focus on the most important parameters for this. On the basis of these we can draw conclusions not only about a given country's competitiveness but also about the development of its position in the world economy.

Some parameters are particularly worth examining:

– levels of development (per capita GDP, and relative to EU average);

– relative levels of costs and quality of products;

– levels (absolute and relative) of productivity and its growth in relation to real wages;

– R&D expenditures (level, growth, relation to GDP and per capita);

– innovation, introduction of new products and technologies;

– general characteristics of economic structure, share, level of development, productivity and efficiency of services ("postindustrial character");

– position of high-tech sectors (growth, share in GDP, in export and import, balance of trade, and technological balance of payments);

– share of "sensitive products" (agriculture, steel, textiles, chemicals) in foreign trade;

– intra-sector trade, trade balances, structural pattern of foreign trade;

– exchange rate stability;

– development of terms of trade;

– state and development of capital market, availability of venture capital;

– state of labour market (mobility of labour force, flexibility of wages, and level of unemployment);

– comparative wage cost advantages (wage and productivity levels);

– state of human capital (education and training – expenditures in GDP, educational level of the population, etc.);

– use of communication and information techniques in every day life (internet, electronic trade, banking and public services);

– state and development of the infrastructure (both physical and human).

As regards the circumstances of "response to the pressure of competition" as a criterion for membership, the EU does not define it clearly and unambiguously. At the same time, a few aspects are particularly emphasized by the EU, and these turn up whenever fulfilment of the membership criteria is examined.

– The Copenhagen competition criterion definitely implies that the country seeking admission is capable of adopting the EU's *rules on com-*

petition and its competition policy (acquis communautaires). This presupposes not just their application in law (which is formulated in the association agreements, and in the White Book), but also the ability of the given country in the long-term to meet the standards of competitiveness. It is vital to create new institutions and regulatory systems that are in harmony with and conform to the institutional frameworks and competition regulation systems of the EU member countries.

– Competitiveness is closely and mutually dependent on stable macroeconomic policy conditions, especially budgetary and monetary policies. A proper harmony is absolutely essential from the point of view of creating *competition-friendly economic policy and a stable economic environment.*

– There is thus a need for consistent industrial, trade and subsidy policies that will ensure the development of healthy competition in the economy.

– From the point of view of competitiveness, the level of development of the factor markets has an important role, in relation to both capital and labour. The EU's competitive disadvantage relative to the US is most noticeable in connection with this.

– In the EU literature and documents the manifestation and demonstration of competitiveness is linked strongly with *exchange rate development.*

The question of *exchange-rate stability* is one that we shall have to deal with separately. The development of its exchange rate really does in many respects express a given country's competitiveness in a comprehensive and synthetic way. A deteriorating balance of trade reflects weak competitiveness, while a trade surplus indicates that the economy is competitive. Then the balance of trade and payments has a large-scale effect on the development of the exchange rate. Exchange rate development and exchange rate policy are important conditions of entry and competition for external countries, but are also an important factor in price stability. Clearly, if over a long period a country is incapable of responding to the pressure of external competition, this can be a serious source of disturbance from the point of view of the normal development of trade, and the economy may become subject to constant, unmanageable inflationary pressure.

Exchange-rate stability comes to the fore especially in connection with EMU membership. It is no accident that the Maastricht criteria include the requirement that the given country should be capable of maintaining its currency exchange rate unaltered for two years. So the requirement of competitiveness turns up again among the convergence criteria, even if indirectly. And it is not by chance that the EU documents, the country reports and other analyses from the point of view of readiness for membership pay so much attention to foreign trade equilibrium, inflation and exchange rate policy.

It is another question, to what extent the balance of payments and the exchange rate can accurately express competitiveness. Doubts arise in connection with the balance of trade, since apart from competitiveness it can be affected by structural and trade policy factors that have little to do with competitiveness (e.g. world market price movements, or protectionist measures on the part of partner countries). The development of exchange rates is determined by many external world market processes (e.g. oil price explosions). So the problem is on the one hand that exchange rate is dependent on many other external factors, and on the other hand that with regard to internal relations within the EU it turns out that most of the member countries do not fulfil this requirement. In internal trade predominantly Germany is capable of maintaining a long-term active balance, while on account of their long-lasting and sizeable deficits the majority of the countries are simply not competitive on the Union market. While in Hungary the transnational sector entirely fulfils the competitiveness criteria for membership, in certain sectors (e.g. agriculture) membership could have serious negative market effects.

In the case of the balance of payments and the exchange rate, the relationship is very questionable and uncertain. The latter is directly determined by international movements of capital and money, and we know that only a small fraction of these are connected with trade flows. This is wholly confirmed by the balance of payments figures for the last few decades; indeed, they show that the relationship between the balance of payments and the exchange rate has also weakened. In the case of Hungary, in the last ten years the real exchange rate of the forint has mostly moved upwards, while the balance of trade and payments showed a relatively substantial deficit.

Regarding fulfilment of the condition of "responding to the pressure of competition", the EU documents and country reports raise many questions. Among these, we can highlight the following:

– The macroeconomic stability and institutional infrastructure necessary for sustainable growth.

– Development of intellectual and physical capital, the situation of education and re-training. Successful reallocation of human capital to the rapidly-growing export sectors.

– A high level of investments, which have led to significant gains in productivity.

– Attraction of operating capital investments, which have proved to be the main means of transformation.

– Significant efforts to develop the infrastructure. Successful involvement of foreign resources in the modernization of the communications and banking sectors. Mobilization of state resources for road-building, support for small and medium-sized enterprises, house-building, research and development, and information technology.

– Reduction of the general level of taxation; reduction of budgetary expenditure; fiscal stability.

– Development of the labour market; reform of social security and reduction of its burdens.

Association has already caused most of the candidate countries to face competitive disadvantages. With full membership the possibilities for protecting themselves will be reduced, but there will be better chances of compensation. As a result of foreign capital investments their competitiveness has improved spectacularly, and this applies to all the candidate countries where an inflow of capital has begun. The competitiveness of certain sectors remains problematic. Within the framework of a comprehensive structural policy it has to be considered which sectors, on the basis of the principles of an efficient, rational division of labour are doomed to inevitable demise and which, with appropriate support, can be kept alive.

Hungary's integration maturity in terms of competitiveness has improved in recent years. In the World Economic Forum's competitiveness rankings for 2001 Hungary is in 26th place (in 2000 we ranked 32nd), and it is first in the region. In establishment of a knowledge-based economy, among the OECD countries the Financial Times in a study put Hungary in 6th place, which is particularly encouraging from the point of view of its future competitiveness (*Financial Times*, October 29, 2001).

With regard to the competitiveness of Hungarian goods, *the level of productivity and its relative development* (comparative advantages) are important, as are *the relatively good quality and low cost of our human capital, and* formally the fact that *labour is under-priced* is a source of comparative advantage. The competitiveness of Hungarian goods consists in these interrelations, and makes analysis possible. As the ITDH study entitled 'Competitiveness 2000' states, productivity calculated on the basis of output per worker employed in manufacturing industry rose by 2000 to 2.2 times its 1991 level. In contrast, real wages rose only moderately. On this basis the competitiveness and comparative wage-cost advantages of Hungarian industry grew considerably (*Napi Világgazdaság,* July 27, 2001). These significant wage-cost advantages characterize the whole region. While the average level of productivity of the candidate countries amounts to about 2/5 of that of the EU (Hungary's is nearly 3/5 of it), on a basis of purchasing parity, average monthly wages in manufacturing industry in the EU are 7–12 times higher than the corresponding figures for the CEE countries seeking admission in the first round. According to data published by the Economic Intelligence Unit, in the rankings for electronic maturity (use of the Internet, e-commerce, etc.) Hungary occupies the 28th place (the US heads the list), and in the region only the Czech Republic is slightly ahead of it (*Napi Világgazdaság,* May 10, 2001).

As is stated in the report issued by the Hungarian EU Enlargement Business Council and discussed by Parliament's Integration Committee, the Hungarian business sphere is capable of holding its own in market competition after accession to the Union (*Világgazdaság,* October 11, 2001). According to the 2001 Country Report, Hungary is close to being able to withstand the pressure of Union competition. As Finance Minister MIHÁLY VARGA declared, "The Hungarian government disputes this view, because according to the government and the finance ministry the Hungarian economy is already fit to compete with the EU member states" (*Magyar Hírlap,* January 2, 2002).

Competitiveness is an important component of EU membership for the candidate countries, which largely determines the balance of advantages and disadvantages. At the same time, enlargement is extremely important for the EU as well, and it must be particularly emphasized that one main benefit of enlargement will be that the Union's competitiveness in global markets is likely to improve significantly. "The fact is that the Eastward enlargement of the EU has the potential to radically alter the basis of competitiveness in Europe, in the sense that it can make Europe a much more 'attractive place to do business'. Whether Western and Eastern firms are able to take advantage of trade liberalization to foster a dynamic process of regional integration in which differentials are made complementary will have far-reaching consequences for 'European Competitiveness' as defined above" (PELLEGRIN 2001: 2, quoting also STRANGE 1998). Enlargement may contribute to the implementation of the Lisbon aims, according to which the EU should by 2010 become the most competitive region in global markets.

4. MACROECONOMIC STABILITY AND STABILIZATION

There is no doubt that economic stability is an important factor in integration maturity. It is an important factor from the point of view of the normal functioning of the market, and consequently from the point of view of the ability to exploit the advantages of any market integration. Of course, macroeconomic stability and integration are mutually dependent, therefore while it is one of the preconditions of successful integration, at the same time it is also an indicator of the success of that integration. There has been lengthy, chicken-and-egg discussion about the performance of the economies of the EC countries, particularly in the 1960s, when no one could decide which was more important: rapid economic growth promoting smooth and rapid trade integration, or dynamic intra-trade, which was then supposedly one of the main factors in that rapid economic growth. "The causality between trade and growth is arguably not just one-way, as is usually implied. The rapid elimination of intra-EEC tariffs and quantitative restrictions between 1958 and 1968 was made possible because of the favourable macroeconomic environment, characterized by high rates of growth and low employment. Increased exposure to international trade brings with it adjustment costs for both labour and capital. They are much more easily absorbed in times of rapid growth, thus minimizing the resistance from potential losers. This points to a possible virtuous circle: the favourable macroeconomic environment of the late 1950s and the 1960s, attributable to a combination of different factors, created the conditions which permitted the signing of the Treaty of Rome and the successful implementation of its trade provisions. Liberalization then led to more trade and this, in turn, contributed to the remarkable growth rates of this period" (TSOUKALIS 1993: 28–29).

It is, however, a more complicated question, how we can define and then measure the stability or stabilization process of an economy. This is particularly important, because for the CEE candidates stabilization is one of the fundamental questions relating to their integration maturity, and in fact also an expectation concerning their EU membership.

After the collapse of the centrally-planned systems, which culminated in rapidly worsening macroeconomic performance in the late 1980s, these countries as a result of their stabilization and the restructuring of their economies had to go through a "transformation crisis", which in 20th-century economic history was matched only by the Great Depression of 1929–33, and was accompanied by further serious deterioration of their economic performance. In Hungary between 1988 and 1993 20% of GDP was lost, former full employment changed to 12% unemployment, and in 1991 inflation peaked at 38%. Gradual stabilization started in 1994, but in terms of GDP Hungary was able to return to the level of 1989 only by the year 2000. With roughly 7% inflation and a budget deficit of more than 3% in 2001, the process of stabilization has not yet been completed. With diverging performance indices, the same pattern characterizes the other countries of the region.

One important question is how to measure stabilization, and particularly what sort of benchmarks should be used in order to evaluate the process of stabilization. In this respect there are several possibilities, and one can choose depending on what sort of priorities are set in terms of the process of that stabilization. In general, it is difficult to find any absolute standards or parameters upon which one can state that a country shows *a state of "stability" or represents the optimal process of stabilization*. The benchmarks are rather relative, assessing stability in relation to certain considerations. Some feel that using these parameters one can calculate a certain "stability or stabilization index".

– *"Optimal" or favourable macroperformance* is based on an ideal rate of economic growth, inflation, unemployment, budget balance and balance of payments. Of course, this is a highly vague and relative notion. It probably can or should be interpreted only on a case-by-case basis. Economic performance, and consequently "stability", is dependent on several factors (level of development, structure, innovation capacities, world economy position, etc.). In the case of economic growth, the "output gap" can be examined, which is the difference between "potential" and "actual" growth rates (OECD Economic Outlook, November 2001, No. 70). Economic growth may be related to the "trend line" of the country (theory of GY. JÁNOSSY) and 3% growth may be highly unsatisfactory from the point of view of one country, while in the case of another, 2% growth may be an "optimal" or very favourable rate. Unemployment can be related to the "natural rate" of the given country, while inflation can be satisfactory if it falls within the 2–3.5% range of "desirable inflation".

In general, one can assume that a state of equilibrium is needed for a balanced budget or balance in international payments, but even that may not be an absolute requirement. In rapidly modernizing and restructuring countries there is a high probability of budgetary or external imbalances, but formally it would be mistaken to consider that as an indicator of instability. Indicators of "good performance" and "stability", therefore, should be carefully and concretely analysed. In certain cases, it is absolute performance which counts; in other cases, a trend of improvement may be enough to justify acknowledging stability.

– *Achievement of "sustainable growth"* (which should not be confused with "sustainable development", which means economic prosperity compatible with maintaining or even improving the state of the environment) (SURÁNYI 2001: 1–106). This is particularly relevant for Hungary, which from the beginning of the 1970s was coping with a "stop-go cycle", resulting in more than 20 years of stagnation. Economic growth was incompatible with the equilibrium of the economy, and higher growth rates (for example, after 1987 and 1993) led to large budget and balance of payments deficits, and consequently to a substantial increase in indebtedness. The restrictions imposed for the sake of equilibrium resulted in slow growth, and the Hungarian economy was able to get out of this vicious circle only after 1997, in fact, as a result of drastic stabilization measures (the BOKROS package), and successful restructuring of the economy. After 1997, the Hungarian economy took a sustainable growth path, and relatively rapid growth (about 4.5%) seems to be maintainable without any serious deterioration of the external and internal balances. Some other countries had similar problems.

– One can consider the *reverse Phillips curve* as one indicator of stability or stabilization of the economy. The Phillips curve shows that there is a certain trade-off between inflation and unemployment: the one can be improved only at the expense of the other. Historical experience suggests that this *does not apply to stable and structurally competitive economies*. In the case of a serious crisis both may worsen, while on the other hand in the case of successful stabilization both can be improved (this has been the case since 1995 in Hungary). Discussions of the NAIRU (the "non-accelerating inflation rate of unemployment") should be mentioned; this is defined as an unemployment rate above which demand can be stimulated without the danger of increasing inflation. This rate may be structurally determined. In structurally "stable" economies it is very low; in fact, full employment can be combined with non-inflation.

EU-related performance pattern of economies:

1. The performance of the EC countries can be taken as a benchmark, considering the period of the "golden age" (from the early 1950s, when post-war reconstruction ended, till the early 1970s, the beginning of the world economic crisis, particularly after 1971–73). In this period, economic growth was about 5%, inflation in most countries (particularly before 1968) was 2–3%, unemployment non-existent (around 2%), and budget deficits were only around 0.5% of GDP. Of course there were great differences in the economic development of different countries, but the above averages can rightly be considered as benchmarks of "good performance".

2. We can compare our performance to the average of the present EU economies. The problem is that growth rates are relatively low (2.5–3%), while unemployment rates are high, even in international terms (at least, compared to the US and Japan). Taking into account the need for possible convergence, the CEE candidates have to produce at least a 1.5–2% "growth surplus" in order to catch up some time in the future.

3. We can take the best-performing EU countries as benchmarks. The difficulty is that those that produce relatively high growth have to cope with higher inflation, while the low inflation countries are characterized by slow growth and high unemployment.

4. Comparisons can be made between the performances of countries of more or less similar levels of development. In case of CEE, Greece or Portugal.

5. One can rely on the Maastricht criteria combined with the terms of the Stability Pact (about 2% inflation, a 0–3% budget deficit and less than 60% debt in terms of GDP). But these refer only to monetary and fiscal performance, and although the "stability" of candidate countries' economies will be considered along these lines, they do not correspond to the expectations and possibilities of these countries (high growth rates with somewhat higher inflation).

The pattern of the process of stabilization of the CEE (candidate) countries shows quite a controversial and contradictory picture for the period following the years 1989–90. What was common, however, was that the gradual deterioration of the performance of centrally-planned economies culminated by the end of the 1980s, and the collapse of the Soviet system was followed by a so-called "transformation crisis" (a term introduced by JÁNOS KORNAI), which particularly in 1991–93 was characterized by an unprecedented recession. (A similar fall in production happened only during the "Great Depression" of 1929–33, but was not repeated after the war, either globally or in any other region of the world economy.) The depth of the 1990s crisis, however, differed greatly from one country to another, and so did the subsequent recovery, which started in 1994.

Table 1. Decline and growth of GDP

Country	Transformation crisis (in the period 1989–93) Decrease in GDP as %	Post-transformation crisis		GDP growth 1998–2001 as %
		Years	Decrease in GDP as %	
Slovakia	about 20	none		2.9
Hungary	about 20	none		4.5
Poland	about 20	none		3.5
Slovenia	about 20	none		4.1
Croatia	about 25	none		2.5
Czech Republic	about 20	1997–99	4	1.2
Latvia	above 50	none		4.9
Lithuania	above 50	1999	4	2.7
Estonia	about 35	1999	1	4.2
Romania	about 40	1997–99	13	0.3
Bulgaria	about 45	1996–97	17	4.1

1. Most of the countries suffered from stagnation of their economies from the 1970s, and many had negative growth from the second half of the 1980s. This was one of the factors in the collapse of the political system in these countries.

2. The Central European countries, relatively to the others, were "only moderately" hit by the transformation recession, and they turned to recovery after 1993–4. The recovery was based on the opening and expansion of the EU (and other) markets (export-led growth), an inflow of foreign direct investments, and the acceleration of the restructuring of these economies (some of them, at least). These countries reached their pre-transformation-crisis (1989–90) level by around 2000, and now they are on the way to catching up with the EU countries. Other countries are lagging behind.

3. In recent years, most of the CEE candidates produced about 4–4.5% annual growth in GDP, which is about 2% above EU growth. The slower-growing countries, at least in growth years, also match the above ceiling. Catching up, however, will take decades (10–30 years), depending on the level of development of the given countries.

4. In the second half of the 1990s, some countries suffered a new recession (a post-transformation crisis), due to slow and contradictory transformation and stabilization policies, slow and delayed restructuring of their economies, and delayed or postponed privatization. The hesitant privatization of commercial banks caused particular problems, and bad loans re-emerged from time to time. This applied particularly to Romania and Bulgaria, but the character of the problems was the same in the case of the Czech Republic. These countries were particularly sensitive to external shocks, and both the Yugoslav (Bulgaria) and the Russian crisis had strong effects on the neighbouring countries. In the case of the Baltic countries, the Russian crisis caused a mini-recession in the years 1997–99.

Table 2. Unemployment in CEE

Country	Peak year (1990–95)	Level of unemployment as %	Unemployed as % of labour force in 2001
Czech Republic	1994	6.0	8.4
Hungary	1992	12.4	5.7
Slovenia	1994	15.0	6.5
Romania	1994	15.0	9.0
Slovakia	1994	17.0	18.3
Poland	1994	16.5	16.2
Bulgaria	1993	16.4	17.5
Estonia	1995	9.7	12.6
Lithuania	1995	7.3	17.0
Latvia	1995	6.6	7.8

1. Unemployment was a relatively new phenomenon in the region. Before 1989, unemployment was unknown in CEE, except in the former Yugoslavia (Slovenia 3%).

2. As a result of the transformation crisis, unemployment increased in all these countries till 1992–95.

3. Unemployment levels reached about 15–17% in most of these countries. That was one of the costs of transformation. Exceptions were the Czech Republic, Hungary and Latvia.

4. There are diverging performances after 1994–95. Only some CE countries (Hungary, Slovenia and Romania) managed to bring down their unemployment, while in the others in the early 2000s it still remains an acute problem.

5. High unemployment is one of the constraints of enlargement.

Table 3. Coping with high and diverging inflation

Country	Period	Peak year inflation as %	Inflation in 2001 as %
Czech Republic		1991 (58)	4.7
Slovakia		1991 (58)	7.3
Hungary		1991 (35)	9.2
Countries with hyper-inflation:			
Poland	1989–90	1990 (585)	5.5
Slovenia	1989–90	1989 (550)	8.4
Romania	1991–93	1993 (258)	34.5
	1997	(155)	
Bulgaria	1991–94	1991 (480)	7.4
	1997	(1082)	
Estonia	1991–92	1992 (1076)	5.8
Latvia	1991–92	1992 (951)	2.5
Lithuania	1991–92	1992 (1021)	1.3

Note:

"Hyper-inflation" (three-digit or more).
"Moderate inflation" (12–18%) (by 2001, all except Romania).
"Desirable inflation" (2–3.5%) (by 2001, Lithuania and Latvia).

1. Inflation did not exist in most of CEE, except the reform countries (Yugoslavia, Poland and Hungary).

2. Most of the countries had to cope with hyper-inflation, particularly during the transformation crisis. Hyper-inflation was avoided during this period only in the Czech Republic, Hungary and Slovakia. Hyper-inflation re-emerged later in slowly transforming and stabilizing countries (Bulgaria and Romania). Bulgaria is successfully dealing with inflation with the help of a currency board, while Romania has remained a high-inflation country.

3. Most of the CEE countries, including Bulgaria, had brought inflation down below 10% by the early 2000s, but it proved difficult to suppress their inflation to the "desirable" level.

4. The Baltic countries (plus the Czech Republic and Bulgaria for 1999) have managed to bring inflation down near or to the "desirable"level in recent years. The Phillips curve seems to be validated for the Baltics (and Bulgaria), where low inflation is achieved at the expense of high unemployment. In Hungary and Slovenia the opposite is the case: these countries produce a reverse Phillips curve.

To sum up, the CEE countries have produced diverging performance in terms of the stabilization of their economies. CE countries have achieved the best progress. In the last few years, they have started catching up with the EU economies. Others have not yet reached their pre-transition levels, and it will take a longer time to close the gap between them and the developed EU countries. Probably it will take several years till they stabilize in terms of inflation, and unemployment seems to be an acute problem in most of these countries. As far as the Maastricht criteria are concerned, these countries have more problems with the monetary criteria (bringing down inflation) than with the fiscal criteria, but the latter may prove difficult as well.

The candidates for admission are not expected to meet the Maastricht convergence criteria; even the member countries have to fulfil them only by the beginning of the third phase of EMU. As the Commission stated in "Agenda 2000", the convergence criteria "will be key points of reference from the point of view of stabilization-oriented macroeconomic policy, and when the time comes the new member states will also have to maintain compliance with them" (Agenda 2000, The opinion of European Commission on Hungary's Application to EU Membership. Integration Secretariat of Foreign Ministry of Hungary. 1997: 41). The macroeconomic stability requirements were set in the Association Agreements. These countries have to fulfil approximately the regulations that apply to the member countries: independence of the central bank, economic policy coordination, abandonment of every form of direct financing of the budget by the national bank, and adherence to the "Stability and Growth Pact". The above reference can be interpreted to mean that with regard to the more important macroeconomic indices a certain minimum performance in terms of "stabilization or stability" must by all means be achieved.

From the point of view of analysing and measuring stability, probably more than one method should be used. This particularly applies to the specific situation of the transforming CEE countries following 1989–90. Below we show an attempt by one Hungarian research institution to measure and aggregate the stabilization process in this country.

Table 4. "Integration maturity" (stability) index
(ECOSTAT – Institute of Economic Analysis and Information – Budapest)

Parameters (for 1999)	Hungary's performance relative to EU as %
Per capita GDP (PPP) relative to Greece	81
GDP growth rate	100
Growth of personal consumption	100
Growth of gross accumulation	100
Growth of industrial production	100
Growth of retail trade	100
Rate of unemployment	100
Inflation	50
Return on securities	50
Balance of trade	25
Budget deficit as % of GDP	50
Indebtedness as % of GDP	75
Aggregate index	77.6

Benchmarking: 100% better than EU average
75% better than some of the members and improving
50% worse than EU average, but improving
25% worse than EU average, and worsening

Note: In the case of comparison of real data, the index is 101.5%.

Source: Bővülő Európa (Expanding Europe), 2000. No. 1., March.

5. CONVERGENCE (REAL OR FINANCIAL)

Convergence, both in real and in monetary and fiscal terms (monetary union), is desirable, and in a certain sense, a necessary condition of efficient and successful integration. In general, however, there is only a loose relation between levels of development and maturity for integration. Equalized levels are not demanded, but in the case of large differences (industrial and developing countries) the benefits may be unequally distributed. The ideal case is more or less similar levels, and integration programs usually set equalization as a desirable (politically declared) objective (EC/EU documents). In the case of large differences, in integration-type agreements (associations based on free trade) compensation could be provided by

– asymmetric liberalization;
– financial aid (compensation);
– technical and other types of assistance.

These may counterbalance distortions and one-sided advantages, and they can make integration (at least the signing of any type of trade arrangement) mutually acceptable.

When six countries signed the Treaty of Rome, their levels of development and economic structure were very similar, and differences were limited to some regions only (basically to southern Italy). Later, with successive enlargements, differences in levels of development increased, and this particularly applied to the entry of the Mediterranean countries. Their backwardness was fairly substantial (they were about 40–45% below the Community average), but with varying success they managed to accelerate their economic development, and in little more than one decade they were able to achieve impressive convergence with the developed part of the Union.

Eastern enlargement creates a totally different and new situation. The differences in levels of development are much greater (ranging from a 20–30% lag to about 60–70% on average), and the difference between the two extremes (Bulgaria on the one hand, and Denmark on the other) is of a magnitude of nearly 500%. At the same time, the levels of development of the most developed new candidates and the less developed members are very close, in fact, identical. This means that the Eastern candidates represent a highly diverse group, not only in terms of economic and social development but also concerning their historical and cultural traditions. With Eastern enlargement, the population of the less developed members (with incomes below the present average) will increase by 77%.

At the beginning, the large differences were only partly recognized by the CEE associations. The Europe Agreements meant a symmetrical free trade arrangement, but the grace period was secured only for the process of liberalization. Financial aid was given under PHARE. Large deficits accumulated, but most of the countries have been able to cope with them, and even turn them around (Hungary has had a trade surplus with the EU since 1997). In spite of the above problems, association has proved to be a "positive-sum game" for both partners.

Closer forms of integration (EMU) are more sensible from the point of view of real convergence. EMU may aggravate (regional) differences, and among other things, budget (cohesion) transfers may be needed to com-

Table 5. Per capita GDP of candidate countries (purchasing power parities)

Member countries as % of EU average in 2000		Candidate countries as % of EU average in 2000	
Greece	67	Cyprus	82
Portugal	76	Slovenia	71
Spain	83	Czech Republic	58
Italy	100	Malta	53
France	100	Hungary	52
Finland	102	Slovakia	48
Sweden	103	Poland	39
United Kingdom	103	Estonia	37
Germany	106	Lithuania	29
Austria	107	Latvia	29
Belgium	111	Turkey	29
Netherlands	115	Romania	27
Ireland	117	Bulgaria	24
Denmark	117		
EU average	100	CEE average	32

Source: Eurostat.

pensate. Monetary and fiscal convergence (the Maastricht criteria) are preconditions of stable monetary union, particularly from the point of view of price stability.

In the past few years most of the candidate countries have achieved 4–4.5% economic growth. This represents a growth surplus of about 1.5–2% compared with the growth of the EU countries' economies. This roughly 2% growth surplus is the minimum needed to enable the 'periphery' to close up to the 'centre' in the foreseeable future (10–30 years). This does not mean attaining the level of the most highly developed countries, but at least approaching the average (the level of entitlement to structural funds is between 75% and 90% compared with the Union average). So far only a few countries can be said to have begun to catch up.

On the basis of the development achieved in recent years, some people dispute the extent to which we can speak of a 'catching-up effect'; perhaps it is simply a case of the relatively accelerated growth that generally characterizes a period of 'reconstruction'. Some, on the basis of the theory of the periodicity of reconstruction, think that transition drastically re-evaluated and reformulated the general *trends* of development of these countries. That is, GDP growth in excess of the West European average will continue until it reaches the imaginary trend level "that expresses the society's productivity potential". Or we can say *"the limit of the possibilities of production"*, if we want to apply a microeconomic concept. As LÁSZLÓ ANDOR emphasizes: "This is not yet growth that will enable us to catch up, since it will allow us merely to reach our own former level, not the Western average" (ANDOR et al. 2000: 91). The coming years will prove whether in the region the catching-up effect can be achieved. In this a decisive part will be played by the region's ability to attract private capital investment, by the size and efficient use of the expected EU transfers, and by economic policy factors on both sides.

6. FINANCING AND FINANCEABILITY

The approximation to one another of economic development levels and economic structures involves serious development requirements. This demands financing. Similarly, the unequal distribution of trade advantages raises the *question of compensation* of weaker members and losers. Tensions and disturbances due to differences in growth are not in the interest of the more developed partners either, therefore in the various kinds of integration grouping *solidarity and compensation* were from the very outset on the agenda in some way. Since most integration organizations *proclaimed the achievement of equality as a political commitment,* the question could not be ignored. The instruments of convergence can be of a commercial and financial nature.

Since there were no substantial structural and developmental differences among the six founding countries of the EEC, at the beginning there was no need to discuss financing criteria. More precisely, to the extent that such differences existed, and they did, attempts were made to *compensate* for them. This was the aim of the introduction in the 1960s of the common agricultural policy, which sought to compensate France and Italy, with their predominantly agricultural structure, in comparison with heavily industrialized Germany. In practice this compensation began simultaneously with the creation of the customs union and the common market, and in view of the relative backwardness of agriculture in the above-mentioned countries, *internal agricultural free trade* (the common market) was supplemented by *relatively large income transfers* and strong protectionism externally.

It is another question, whether in the case of greater differences in development, *financing criteria* can be considered in connection with free trade agreements or with the customs union as well. Later, as a result of enlargement, this is precisely what happened, when with increasing differences in development the question of regional subsidies came to the fore. Such subsidies were earlier received mainly by southern Italy, but with further enlargements they had to be extended. The creation of the European Regional Development Fund from 1975 was partly due to the accession of Ireland and the UK, which brought more backward areas into the Community. With Mediterranean enlargement the problem became more marked. The *single market,* and later *economic and monetary union,* have tended to increase the need for regional compensation.

With Eastward enlargement, as a result of which the diversity of the future Union will increase significantly, with regard to both economic development levels and structures the question of *financing and financeability* is one of the critical enlargement issues. Naturally, financeability is basically a question of integration maturity, and one of its important indicators.

– Availability of domestic sources of capital. To what extent is the given economy able to produce resources for its own development and for expanded re-production? This among other things raises the question of the interdependence of national capital accumulation and efficiency. With outdated economic structures and loss-making sectors, internal possibilities for saving are reduced.

– The existence of functioning capital markets capable of mobilizing internal and external resources (in centrally-planned economies there was a significant amount of irrational thesauration) and rational allocation of resources. To what extent is the economy capable of minimizing capital losses (devaluation of savings resulting from high inflation, freezing of resources through thesauration, prestige consumption, capital flight abroad)?

– The state of the economies of the candidate countries, their ability to achieve and maintain budgetary equilibrium, while financing the costs relating to accession.

– The capital-absorption capacity of the given country, with regard to both external private capital investments (the existence of skilled manpower, and the necessary infrastructure), and reception of budgetary transfers.

At the same time, financing ability features rather as a membership criterion on the EU's part, and is formulated not concretely but indirectly in the Copenhagen criteria (in relation to the "absorption capacity" of the Union). It is not a question of whether the EU is capable of financing Eastward enlargement, but rather how much willingness there is, politically, to do it, on the part of governments and especially taxpayers. The planned budget transfers of 0.10–0.15% of GDP are of marginal dimensions, and particularly in view of their considerable degree of recycling they would not really be a burden on the economies of the present member countries but rather could have positive effects.

Thus financing serves the purposes of both *convergence and economic stability*. As regards external resources, the ability of CEE countries to catch up in terms of development is of course basically dependent on foreign private capital investment. We can assume that integration will be accompanied by improved allocation of resources.

For meeting membership criteria, and on the whole for successful integration, the candidate countries *need resources* for several reasons:

– The basic requirement is to improve and safeguard the competitiveness of their economy. In the case of CEE candidates, the modernization and restructuring of the economy is based to a large extent on foreign private investments, and therefore the encouraging of these plays a major role. Of course, local private and state sources are equally important.

– Development of the infrastructure for integration. This is where substantial Union resources can be expected, but on the whole the bulk of the burden falls on the candidates (beyond co-financing, nationally initiated and implemented projects).

– Building institutions, meeting requirements (environment) harmonization of laws and regulations.

– Compensation for losses. There is no doubt that EU membership entails costs, and some sectors suffer losses. That is normal, and it is part of the restructuring process, in fact, expected from integration. In other cases, losses should be at least partly compensated for. This is particularly the case with agriculture, where for example Hungary has potential natural comparative advantages, but owing to the present level of competitiveness they cannot be fully exploited. In a rational agricultural division of labour in Europe, CEE agriculture has its place, but only after a transitional period of catching up. This is not automatically guaranteed by CAP membership, even if the best deals can be achieved in the early stages.

– Financing Community budgetary obligations. Although "financing" is based overwhelmingly on private, market sources (private investments, financial markets), the role of state (national and EU) budgets is also important. In this respect, we have to depart from the basic functions of national or federal budgets. It must be noted that the EU budget fulfils all of these functions, even if it has several special features.

– Financing (buying) public goods and services. This is one of the major roles of national budgets, particularly in terms of volume of expenditure (financing education, public health, national security, etc.). The EU budget plays this role only in a limited way, partly owing to its volume, and partly because of the functions assigned to it.

– Financing of investments in infrastructure development, and programs undertaken in the public interest. A great proportion of structural funds is allocated for these purposes (Trans-European Networks).

– Regulation by mobilization of financial resources (this includes tax incentives and compensation for losses). In the EU budget CAP transfers are typical examples.

– Redistribution of incomes. Basically it means transfers from the rich to the poor. "Solidarity" and "cohesion" are the most important principles related to the Structural Funds.

Financing or financeability is one of the major problems of integration maturity, and of attainment of EU membership by CEE candidate countries. The difficulties start with the capital market or investment rating of these countries, and for some of them this makes any financing relatively expensive. In the worst cases, this rating may divert any meaningful investment; so far this has been the case with several candidate countries. The major constraints, however, relate to budgetary spheres, and in fact *budgets are the major constraints on Eastern enlargement*. These apply equally to the budgets of candidates and member countries, and not least to the Community budget as well.

Constraints characteristic of the candidate countries' budgets originate from both their past inheritance and their future requirements, mostly related to their EU membership:

– Although the budgetary positions of candidate countries differ, many of them have inherited heavy indebtedness, which has been aggravated by the substantial costs of transformation and stabilization. In countries where transformation has been sluggish or delayed, these costs have accumulated, and in many countries the relatively favourable budgetary positions of the early 1990s have gradually deteriorated. These costs were usually compensated for mostly from privatization revenues, but as this process has come to an end, these sources have become exhausted.

– Central planning paid limited attention to comprehensive development of the infrastructure and protection of the environment. Backwardness should be diminished, and the requirements of prospective EU membership must be met. As has been pointed out, these are only partly financed from Union funds.

– Institution-building and harmonization cost a lot, and they are only partly supported from "pre-accession funds".

– Although subsidies have been substantially reduced (to OECD level in most countries), in certain sectors, in conformity with EU regulations, there is a need for compensation for losses.

The candidate countries are committed to joining EMU and the eurozone soon, which creates further pressures on their budget (meeting the Maastricht criteria, or even the expectations of the Stability Pact). "Pre-accession funds" (ISPA, SAPARD and PHARE) give support for preparation, but they are modest, particularly in terms of the real needs of these countries.

Constraints on EU members' budget are equally problematic. This is one of the most important bottlenecks in the enlargement process, where the meeting of the membership criteria remains for the most part in question.

– In the last ten years, national budgets have been seriously constrained by meeting the Maastricht criteria and the demands of the Stability Pact in terms of EMU requirements. Even if most countries performed well, and impressive progress was made toward balanced budgets, that process involved drastic measures in many countries. These measures were accompanied by social and political tensions, and in some countries, owing to the world economic recession of 2001, meeting the requirements of the Stability Pact became questionable.

– Most of the countries face pressures for "structural reforms", which on the revenue side assume cuts in taxes and social security contributions, while on the expenditure side, cuts in public (social) services (pensions or health services) are difficult to implement.
– In some countries, the public (political) pressures for cutting tax burdens are particularly strong, and they are often generated by the election promises made by competing parties.

There is no doubt that sooner or later the EU budget should be reformed. In view of enlargement, its volume, structure and financing should all be changed and adjusted to the needs of the normal functioning of the Union. Major constraints are:

– Lack of political acceptance (both by governments and, what is more important, by the population) of any expansion of the budget (beyond the 1.27% ceiling), even if rational considerations support it, and it would be justified on social and political grounds. Support of convergence in an emerging Union with huge, formerly unknown differences is in the interest of the whole Union and of every member, because if these differences were to remain or even increase it would inherently threaten the Union with instability.
– Reform of the budget in terms of revenues would also be needed. After 1988, the principle of "own resources" was de facto given up, which led to the marked politicization of transfers. A return to the principle might help in de-politicization. New "own resources" may be considered, when the Union is financed not by states but by its citizens.
– Reform of expenditure raises political tensions, particularly on the part of former beneficiaries from structural funds, and also on the part of the net contributors.
– Compared with national budgets, which are characterized by a certain automatic redistribution from the rich to the poor, the EU budget is still inherently non-cohesive (so far the net financing position has been only loosely correlated to levels of development). A return to "own resources" might be accompanied by enhancement of the cohesive character of the budget. CEE candidates could expect a net beneficiary position.

Although it is heavily constrained, Eastern enlargement is financeable. Efforts and reforms are needed, however, particularly in the area of budgets and on both sides. Long-delayed structural reforms should be accelerated, and *budgetary discipline* is due more than ever on both sides. If this is achieved, it may be one of the most important dividends of the whole enlargement.

7. SOCIAL COHESION AND INTEGRATION

Social integration and cohesion are an organic part of integration maturity; the success of integration ultimately depends in large measure on the extent to which the whole society shares in the benefits of integration, on the distribution of these benefits, and on the acceptability of integration to broad strata of society. Social integration and cohesion are a condition of social support for integration. The EU has not directly formulated social criteria for membership, but in the areas of economic and especially political criteria, social aspects arise in several connections.

KÁROLY LÓRÁNT, a senior researcher at Ecostat, describes social cohesion as "the most important factor in catching up". "The cohesion or solidarity of society, which is determined by many contributory factors such as, for instance, differences in income, opportunities for social mobility, the behaviour of the political elites who set an example and determine values, etc., is the result of the reciprocal effects of these. In this regard – although we do not really have any objective measure – in the judgment of experts the situation in this country is rather unfavourable. Because of the frequent changes of direction in economic policy, conflict among the political elites, wide differences in income and low social mobility, social cohesion is weak, and this significantly hinders exploitation of external opportunities for catching up" (LÓRÁNT 2001: 11).

Examination of the social and sociological aspects has been particularly emphasized in various candidate countries, for example Poland. Polish researchers draw attention to the *need to broaden social support for accession*. In the *"top-down"* process they see the role of government and party policy as important *(social dialogue and the promotion of integration)* (HAUSNER 1998: 139–140). Examination of the situation of the interest representation structure and interest groups affected by the integration process calls attention to deficiencies that may later represent serious obstacles to social acceptance of integration. In relation to strengthening social support, Polish experts note that employers' and trade union associations, which have close links to the parliamentary parties and government institutions, chiefly use their interest-promoting power for the purpose of redistribution of central budget funds; the importance of these organizations usually depends on the position of their representatives in the governing parties, and workers' organizations are left out of the process of negotiation with the state (HAUSNER 1998: 140).

The clientist and corporative tendencies described by the Polish author have considerable effect on the behaviour of interest groups toward European integration.

– Employers' and employees' organizations by means of their interest-promoting power support the government's efforts and strengthen its negotiating position.

– These organizations, by joining in the accession negotiations, have a better understanding of the real chances associated with accession.

– They help in finding the best solutions to complex problems.

– They contribute to reducing the contradictions and internal tensions arising from accession.

An important part of the government's organizational basis for EU integration is continual improvement of institutionalized cooperation in partnership with economic and social interest-representing organizations; such cooperation, if social acceptance of the negative effects of accession can be attained in time, could decisively influence the outcome of the referendum on accession.

Progress in social integration and cohesion, according to the various EU documents, includes the promotion of civil organizations and interest-representation; the development of social dialogue; the situation of social conflicts and potential; social policy and the raising of peripheral social strata; promotion of interest-representation for minorities; the social integration of gypsies; and social movements in favour of and opposed to the EU. On the basis of the EU Country Reports, defined parameters are available in relation to the human rights and minority rights aspects of integration maturity.

With respect to analysis of the economic, social and cultural processes connected with accession to the Union, we share the opinion of the Polish experts (HAUSNER and MARODY 1998: 157) that the membership requirements are related to social and cultural characteristics which, with the help of various reciprocal social effects (e.g. approximation of social indicators to the EU average, implementation of social policy themes) contribute to strengthening a candidate country's capacity for integration – including adequate social integration of EU norms.

8. THE POLITICAL CRITERIA FOR MEMBERSHIP

The *political criteria* in a wider perspective are linked to political integration, and this is especially the case if the integration grouping commits itself to *political union*. In practice this can be said of only the EC/EU among the roughly 130 regional integration organizations that exist in the world. In connection with the looser forms of integration, political criteria are generally not set. Political expectations and conditions may emerge in relation to even the free trade area or customs union, but these are limited and tend to be of a legal or institutional nature. Since political integration is bound up with specific organizations, it is worth mentioning *membership criteria* here.

This does not mean that *political integration-maturity has no meaning*. On the contrary, its general political implications can in many respects be very well formulated. Political criteria can be important even with regard to the looser forms of market integration, chiefly from the point of view of the normal development of economic relations. Anti-market or anti-democratic political systems (e.g. the East European socialist countries before 1989) can seriously endanger the functioning of the market (in terms of efficiency, interestedness, consumer choice) or entrepreneurial freedom (through the danger of nationalization), therefore closer integration with them is not possible. In some cases "political conditionality" and the determination of "political criteria" to this end (for example, in the event of association) mean no more than the enforcement of behaviour that conforms to international norms (e.g. regarding human rights and minority rights), in harmony with the expectations of international public opinion. In particular cases the setting of political conditions is simply a means of ensuring proper use of subsidies granted.

In the case of political integration (political union), clearly there is more to it. These emerging communities are organized in accordance with *a system of defined political, economic and social values,* acceptance of which is expected of every participant. On the other hand, the given integration organization presumably operates a widening range of *joint policies and institutions,* and it is in the interest of the community that these be *democratic in nature and effective*. Anti-democratic behaviour and development on the part of one member of the integration community can endanger the whole community's security and stability, and even the community itself. At the same time, political and social value systems and aspirations are inseparable from a given community; they depend on its historical and cultural traditions, its level of development, its economic and social relations, and the variedness of its component parts. So we come back to the point that general states of integration maturity always refer only to a specific grouping and therefore should rather be treated as membership criteria. The success of these attempts at integration largely depends on the extent to which they achieve the optimum combination of democratic content and effective operational forms of institution. Well-defined political criteria for membership are thus in the basic interest of the community or union.

In the EC, in the initial phase of integration, the political conditions of membership were formulated only in a limited and general way, though as integration proceeded they were gradually expended. According to the Treaty of Rome "democratic" and "European" countries can be members of the Community. Though the latter condition appears to be a geographical one, in content and essence it is basically of political significance. There is much talk of Europe's "democratic values" or "democratic heritage", but these have not been concretely defined, particularly not in connection with membership. At the same time, these questions have always received a lot of attention, and especially with the Mediterranean enlargements the strengthening of democracy was a fundamental expectation. Later ones confirmed this; the EU proved to be an "anchor" from the point of view of democratic development. It is worth mentioning, however, that in the case of earlier admissions, in practice *only political criteria* were set for applicants. After the Single European Act (then from Maastricht to Nice) political and mainly legal and institutional criteria played an increasingly important role.

In connection with Eastward enlargement it was no accident that the political conditions were expanded, though more concrete definition of them did not take place. On the basis of the Copenhagen criteria and the various discussions and declarations that followed, the expectations can be divided into three major groups.

1. *The state of democracy.* In relation to this the main principles have already been formulated in the association agreements, and in practice for membership a complete, consistent *political transformation* is required: a commitment to pluralist democracy, the rule of law, human rights, basic political, economic and cultural freedoms, minority rights, a multi-party system, free and democratic elections, media freedom, a market economy and the principle of social justice. With reference to Hungary the country

reports mention particularly breaches of the law in connection with gypsies and foreign refugees.

2. *Stability* of democracy and its institutions. It is not by chance that "stability" of democracy is emphasized. The transformation of Eastern Europe proves that the creation of formal democratic frameworks is not enough; far from all of these countries have developed democracies that function in a stable manner. The EU does not concretely define the parameters of "stability"; we can deduce them mainly on the basis of the problems mentioned in the country reports. The literature of political sciences also deals with the stability of democracy. Stability of *democracy and its institutions* is linked to the settling of disputes and solving of problems of a political nature within a parliamentary and democratic framework; to the balance of power among political parties, a parliamentary consensus ensuring the governability of the country, and the maintenance of legal security and public security.

3. The *functioning* of democratic *institutions*. There has been particular emphasis on this since the 1995 Madrid summit. *Effective functioning of democratic institutions* refers to the proper functioning – according to the principles of democracy – of legislators, the executive authority and the justice system, the acceptance and application in practice of law harmonization, the taking of action against corruption, further development of legal security and public security, and finally the implementation of social and economic processes to enhance the country's prosperity.

The *Regular Reports* published by the EU Commission assist in defining more concretely the political conditions for joining the EU. The Commission first outlined in its 1997 annual report, published in the framework of Agenda 2000, the accession conditions for the candidate countries. The Commission's reports evaluate fulfilment of the political criteria *on the basis of a uniform schema*. They *widened the parameters of the criteria and their fullfilment* compared with the earlier ones, and added *new elements*.

In terms of content the Country Reports distinguish two groups, which cover the most important concepts listed with regard to the conditions of Union membership:

1. *Democracy and the rule of law*, which include
   - the parliament and the structure and operation of the legislature;
   - the structure and operation of the executive authority;
   - the structure and operation of the law courts.

2. *Protection of human rights and minorities,* which includes
   - civil and political rights;
   - economic, social and cultural rights;
   - rights of minorities and protection of minorities.

A central requirement formulated in Agenda 2000 and the Luxembourg decisions was the adoption of the whole body of Community law, which the candidate countries had to complete during the period of accession negotiations. The decisions taken at the Luxembourg summit indicate the importance of the *interrelation between differentiation and the implementation of the political criteria* (Agenda 2000, 1997: 1–2).

Interpretation of the political criteria for membership was more concretely expressed in the Accession Partnership document signed in 1998, and the National Program of Adoption of the Acquis Communautaire, where through definition of short- and medium-term priorities and catching-up programs a working hypothesis was established for the implementation of the conditions of accession (Accession Partnership Hungary. European Commission, 1998).

In Poland in March 1998 a catalogue was compiled which enabled further expansion of the range of political conditions for membership. In connection with "Poland's integrative capacity" 5 aspects of the political system were examined, which contained the following elements (JEZIORANSKI 1998: 101).

Integrative capacity and linkage of the political system:

- constitutional order;
- functioning party system;
- interest representation;
- organization of the state sphere;
- organizational basis of government integration policy.

In the Polish approach, emphasis is placed on the close relationship between the EU *integration process and constitutionalization.* In 1997 changes in the 1952 constitution were approved by the Sejm; the new constitution had not come into force by the time the first Commission report was published, but the EU did not regard this as a negative factor in its evaluation of the conditions relating to constitutionality.

In connection with integration and a functioning party system, party-political behaviour with regard to EU membership is particularly highlighted. The compilers of the catalogue mentioned above sought an answer to the question what sort of political, economic, social, legal, etc. approach the Polish parliament adopted in their programs relating to accession to the Union. With regard to integration two striking concepts could be distinguished. One urged *joining as soon as possible* (rapid closure of accession negotiations); the other aimed at *securing the most favourable entry conditions possible* (e.g. long-term protection of agriculture and certain branches of industry, large-scale subsidies from the Structural Fund), and allowed for lengthier accession negotiations. Within the party-political dimension, public support for integration was linked with the opinion of the parties' electoral base about EU membership, which expressed *the responsible nature of the parties' role in society's acceptance of integration. Support for government and party policy in management of the process of European integration* indicates the degree of commitment to EU integration of that government and political elite, party-political attitudes to integration, Euroscepticism, or the emergence of political movements opposed to the EU.

The problematic area of the *development of public administration,* which also features in the Commission's report, can be included under the heading of organization of the competencies of the state. Modernization of the system of public administration, as in the case of Hungary, has come up against many obstacles which hinder fulfilment of the accession conditions. Within the politically-oriented catalogue of "integrative capacities", the new territorial units created as part of Poland's reform of public administration (gmina, powiat, voivodina) were examined from the point of view of the existing barriers to the development of a system of administration conforming to EU expectations.

In recent years many political organizations and research institutes have undertaken to analyze the process of political transformation and democratization in the CEE countries, and in some cases have even attempted to measure the process by statistical and mathematical methods. It is characteristic of these efforts that they have mainly sought to determine the state of transformation, and it has not been their direct aim to adopt a position with regard to integration maturity in connection with EU membership or anything else. Most of these surveys did not attempt a complete evaluation of the political transformation and democratization, but concentrated on certain parameters. Since political conditionality is becoming increasingly a feature of the policy of other international organizations as well, these analyses are also very useful in EU membership surveys.

The study published by the international research group of the Bertelsmann Foundation is (perhaps) one of the initiatives that undertook to further refine the "filter" of the Copenhagen criteria on the basis of analysis of the various candidate countries. The research group compiled a list relating to so-called integrative capacity, and catalogued integration maturity in six dimensions (Bertelsmann Foundation, 1995: 10):

- the state of political reform process;
- government institutions;
- party systems;
- interest groups;
- social organizations;
- system of media, media policies;
- reform of structures of public administration.

Then these questions are examined from points of view of legal, political, economic and social aspects, with an emphasis on the problems related to the association to the EU.

This catalogue of criteria refers particularly to aspects of the transformation process, and this "filter" could be further refined, but as it is, it defines important aspects and criteria of maturity for membership, analysis of which may lead to useful conclusions.

In the comprehensive study of Poland's EU integration policy published in March 1998 by the *Friedrich Ebert Stiftung,* the authors identified as the main reason for differentiation between the Luxembourg Six and the other candidate countries their varying degree of implementation of the political and institutional requirements of EU membership. This work presents a detailed analysis of the legal, political and social dimensions of the conditions of Poland's accession (JEZIORANSKI 1998: 151). In 2000 KAREN HENDERSON published her study on Slovakia's economic, political and social transformation, in which the aspects she examined included conclusions referring to EU accession conditions and regarding the stability and functioning of democratic institutions (HENDERSON 2000: 38).

The EBRD in its annual Transition Reports examines the political transition mainly from the point of view of institutional development and achievements. The situation is similar with the World Bank studies dealing with the transformation of Central and Eastern Europe. These are very useful for examining membership maturity as well. The majority of the analyses are of an economic nature; they touch on politics when analyzing social conditions (chiefly income differentiation and reform of the welfare system), and the efficiency of institutional systems.

Freedom House is one organization that tries to measure political, economic and civil liberty in the transition countries by means of relatively many and comprehensive parameters. In the "Nations in Transit" Report it analyzes relatively concretely the progress or stagnation of democratic and economic reforms in 28 countries in transition. Each report is divided into nine main chapters.

The *political processes section:* in connection with elections it examines how free and properly regulated they were and what development has taken place in the multi-party system and the participation of citizens in the political processes.

The *civil society section* evaluates the development of non-governmental organizations, the legal and political environment in which they operate, their organizational capacities and financial viability, and the participation of interest groups in the political processes.

The *independent media section* examines the legal framework and actual state of press freedom, including harassment of journalists and their editorial independence, the development of a financially viable private press, and citizens' access to the Internet.

The *government and public services section* focuses on the actual power of the legislative organs, on decentralization, the election, responsibilities and functioning of local authorities, and the transparency of the legislative and the executive power.

The *rule of law section* assesses constitutional reform, protection of human rights, reform of criminal law, the independence of courts and the justice system, and the implementation of minority rights.

The *corruption section* deals with the detection of corruption in the state apparatus, the business interests of leading politicians, transparency of financial transactions and business interests, and initiatives and measures to combat corruption.

The researchers use a wide variety of sources in compiling their data: these include research data provided by non-government organizations, articles from local newspapers and journals, analytical reports by multilateral credit institutions, and data published by governments. Freedom House assesses every section in relation to the 28 countries, and on this basis makes comparisons among the sections and the countries. The countries are ranked on a scale ranging from 1 to 7, 1 representing the most significant progress, while 7 means the poorest results. The higher the number, the worse the evaluation (Freedom House, 1998).

For Freedom House surveys directed at showing the interrelations of democracy, economic reforms and economic development are particularly important. According to these, democracy is not in itself important for society, but it plays a key part from the point of view of economic prosperity, reforms and convergence. The analyses dealing with the candidate countries show close correlation in this respect. Good results in stabilizing and developing their economies (in preparing for integration) were achieved by the countries that had made most progress in developing democracy, and *vice versa*.

It is a new development in the history of European integration that the *political criteria for membership* have become part of community law, and *fulfilment of them is demanded of the* member countries as well. The Amsterdam and Nice Treaties were the first attempts to deal with the extreme populist political forces, opposed to European democratic values, that were gaining power in EU member states, and to implement measures against them. *Following the principles of democracy* thereby became in practice an *internal membership criterion*.

In contrast to the Council of Europe, in the EU agreements there is no mention of the possibility of excluding a member state. At the same time, Articles 6 and 7 of the Amsterdam Treaty for the first time create the possibility of applying sanctions against any member countries that violate European democratic norms. When it was formulated in 1997, it was prompted by the possibility of what might happen if as a result of Eastward enlargement of the EU, politicians with no regard for human rights were to gain entry to the Brussels body.

In the Amsterdam Treaty, Article 6 affirms that "the Union is founded on the principle of liberty, democracy, respect for human rights and fundamental freedoms, and the rule of law, principles which are common to the Member States". These principles should be respected, and as is stated in Article 7 (1), the Council "may determine the existence of a serious and persistent breach by a Member State" of these principles under the conditions that it is "meeting in the composition of the Heads of State or Government and acting by unanimity on a proposal by one third of the Member States or by the Commission and after obtaining the assent of the European Parliament" and also "after inviting the government of the Member State in question to submit its observation".

Then Article 7 (2) fixes the possibilities of sanctioning, "where such a determination has been made, the Council, acting by a qualified majority, may decide to suspend certain of the rights deriving from the application of this Treaty to the Member State in question, including the voting rights of the representative of the government of that Member State in the Council. In doing so, the Council shall take into account the possible consequences of such a suspension on the rights and obligations of natural and legal persons. The obligations of the Member State in question under this Treaty shall in any case continue to be binding on that State." Article 7 continues: "The Council, acting by a qualified majority, may decide subsequently to vary or revoke measures taken under paragraph 2 in response to changes in the situation which led to their being imposed."

As far as Article 7 of the Amsterdam Treaty is concerned, important changes were made by the Treaty of Nice. A new paragraph 1 was added, which states: "in a reasoned proposal by one third of the Member States, by the European Parliament or by the Commission, the Council, acting by a majority of four fifths of its members after obtaining the assent of the European Parliament, may determine that there is a clear risk of a serious breach by a Member State of principles mentioned in Article 6 (1), and address appropriate recommendations to that State. Before making such determination, the Council shall hear the Member State in question and, acting in accordance with the same procedure, may call on independent persons to submit within a reasonable time limit a report on the situation in the Member State in question. The Council shall regularly verify that the grounds on which determination was made continue to apply" (Official Journal of the European Communities, 10. 03. 2001: C80/6).

The EU's sanctions mechanisms remain available, but with the modification of Article 7 in reality an "early warning system" was established. With this modification the Council succeeded in finding a balance between sufficient flexibility of response to such challenges and certain procedural guarantees that allow the country in question the chance to be heard on the given matter. The country in question can ask the European Court to examine whether the procedural regulations have been observed; the Court must give a judgment on this within a month from the date of the Council's decision. In this way for the first time in the EU's history a guarantee was put in place, pointing out the procedure to be followed if in any member state extremist, populist forces that threaten European values and human rights come to power.

The shift of power that took place in Austria in 2000 represented a caesura in the history both of Austria and of the EU. The coming to power of Austria's extreme right-wing, populist Freedom Party (FPÖ) together with the conservative People's Party (VPÖ) led to measures unprecedented in the development of the EU. Applying the provisions of the Amsterdam Treaty, the EU for the first time intervened in the internal politics of a member country and questioned that member country's legally elected government's conformity to the political values of the EU. This was followed by the imposition of sanctions by the governments of the other 14 member countries. The situation was made more complicated by the circumstance that prior to the elections the leader of the Freedom Party had indeed made many statements incompatible with European values and human rights, but the program of the coalition government formed by the People's Party and the Freedom Party was in harmony with these values and rights. At the same time, the sanctions ordered by the EU were incapable of preventing the Freedom Party from taking power. The sanctions were imposed before the EU had a chance to observe how the EU-compliant government program was being implemented in practice.

After the Nice Treaty of 2000, the result of the May 2001 elections in Italy again raised the question of the EU's relations with right-wing populists and the Italian coalition government including members of the anti-EU Northern League. The EU did not consider comparison with Austria to be justified, and the member countries saw no reason to take steps against the Rome government.

The question has rightly been asked, whether with the development of European integration the sphere of sovereignty in domestic policy is vanishing. Has the globalization of human and political rights relativized the principle of non-intervention and subsidiarity in the EU? With sanctions, is a new community law coming into being? Here too, the answers to these questions lie in the future.

9. MATURITY FOR MEMBERSHIP – INSTITUTIONS AND LAW HARMONIZATION

Understandably, the institutional criteria apply to specific institutions, and must therefore be treated basically as *criteria for membership*. *Institutional aspects*, at the same time, are extremely important *from the point of view of integration maturity* also. The institutional frameworks provide the forms for implementation of the integration process, and largely determine the effectiveness of integration policies and measures. As integration deepens, particularly with progress towards economic and monetary union the importance of institutional conditions and criteria increases.

In the adoption of the forms of integration we can examine the various degrees of EU integration and the level of their implementation. EU integration may progress from the customs union, the common market, the single market and economic and monetary union right through to political union. By the mid-1990s the EU had more or less completed the establishment of a single internal market and with the 1999–2002 introduction of the single currency the same happened concerning the economic and monetary union.

Compared with the free trade area, the customs union can be regarded as a "real" form of integration. The customs union is therefore a "higher" form of integration, because it presupposes joint policies that involve the surrender of a certain degree of sovereignty:

– for the normal functioning of a customs union, *common competition policy* is needed;

– the logical consequence of common external customs tariffs is the *raising of foreign trade policy to community level;*

– the customs union makes it desirable to stabilize exchange rates, which from the outset has involved a certain *coordination of monetary policy*, and which has gradually led (e.g. through the EMS) towards monetary union.

This means that in a customs union the member countries in several areas – and it must be added, very important ones – partially or completely *surrender their national sovereignty* and transfer it to community level. In a certain sense this is the first important step towards "political" integration. So in this context the customs union, compared with the free trade area, is truly a "more highly developed" and closer form of integration. *With the customs union, therefore, certain elements of economic policy and institutional criteria* are present.

The process becomes more complete with the single internal market. In contrast to the customs union and common market, the core of which is liberalization (negative integration), the single market is widely based on unification and harmonization (positive integration); that is, the role of the acquis communautaire and the linking institutions expands. Fulfilment of the criteria takes place gradually, "from inside".

In fact, "membership criteria" could realistically have been brought up in connection with the association agreements, especially since for the long-term the European Agreements adjusted the association to the single internal market. In this case the EU is satisfied if development of a market economy takes place in the meantime, and has allowed within the association framework a grace period for liberalization (but only a few years), whereas it has rigorously insisted on harmonization of the laws referring to competition and the related commercial and economic laws.

When association took place, competitive disadvantages were very evident, but those were in practice not really taken into consideration, to such an extent that the European Agreements omitted, at least in its classical forms, the financial support accorded in other association agreements to less developed countries. Financial assistance is channelled through PHARE; the amounts are fairly modest, and were originally intended (1989) as support for transition. In other association arrangements the basis of earlier financial support, though not explicitly, was to provide a certain compensation for trade disadvantages, or to counterbalance unfair advantages. The PHARE priorities changed only later, adjusting to some extent to the integration problems and aspirations of the countries concerned.

In connection with Eastward enlargement, among membership criteria institutional questions receive particular attention. When we examine the institutional criteria, in practice we start with the progress of integration. On the one hand we look at the state of adoption of the various forms of integration (institutions and mechanisms). On the other hand, we try to assess fulfilment of the obligations and tasks arising from the Copenhagen criteria ("fulfilment of the obligations involved in membership and acceptance of the aim of political, economic and monetary union") and from other EU decrees and references (the Madrid summit, and the Country Reports). That is, in assessing readiness and "maturity" we can do no more than analyze concretely the state of development of integration institutions, adaptation to these, and the state of law harmonization and the application of laws. Adoption of the "acquis communautaire" is unquestioned, a fundamental condition of acceptance for membership.

On the basis of the Copenhagen criteria and other decisions, from the institutional point of view the EU in practice expects the following from the candidate countries:

– adoption of the "acquis communautaire";
– harmonization of their institutional and legal systems;
– genuine application of the EU legal system; implementation of the laws in everyday practice;
– development of the system of public administration, its integrative capacity and efficiency;
– acceptance of EMU;
– the undertaking of a commitment to "political union".

With regard to EMU and political union the EU expects merely a preliminary commitment on the part of the candidate countries. In practice it does not assume they will join these immediately after entry; indeed, as far as EMU is concerned, they simply do not consider it desirable that the new members should join it at once.

Apart from law harmonization, the EU pays particular attention to the *actual functioning of the institutional system and the practical implementation of the laws adopted*. According to many, the 1995 Council meeting in Madrid defined as a new criterion for membership the candidates' "adjustment of their administrative structures". In evaluating preparedness, the surveys (for example, the Country Reports) pay particular attention to this. Clearly, the reason is that this is the area in which problems tend to arise. As the Kopint-Datorg material prepared for the comparison of the Country Reports states, "the question of public administration capacity has become a central theme of the negotiation process" (Kopint-Datorg and MEH. II., 2000: 42). Thus according to the Commission, in the final phase of negotiations "particular attention is paid to the ability of the candidates for membership to apply the substance of EU law in practice, and to whether and in what form they possess the institutions necessary for this" (*Világgazdaság*, July 30, 2001).

The Country Reports analyze in detail the candidates' progress in institutional preparation for membership, but they cannot be said to have a systematized set of criteria. Nevertheless on the basis of the problems mentioned in the Country Reports these can be summarized:

– the establishment, development and appropriate functioning of institutions for applying the acquis;
– determination and definition of the necessary competencies and tasks;
– development of the infrastructural background for these institutions (Schengen, customs administration, border control, etc.);

– professional level and qualifications of civil servants; their ability to apply community law; level of language skills, etc.;

– The functioning of the justice and internal affairs organization;

– in the area of cohesion, the ability to absorb community resources; organizations for administering community resources;

– supervision of state subsidies; observance of public procurement regulations;

– enforcement of competition law; critical areas for liberalization (telecommunications, energy supply, etc.);

– standardization; development and operation of a system of quality certification; consumer protection;

– the situation of intellectual property law; industrial legal security and data security;

– safety at work; health protection.

Fulfilment of the institutional criteria for membership was considered treated as an important factor in the selection of candidate countries and the closing of membership negotiations. Later, particularly after Laken, when the 10 country big enlargement was decided, the institutional matters as accession criteria were more flexibly considered. Laggings behind in this field could not be obstacles of enlargement, and that was demonstrated by decisions of Copenhagen in December of 2002. The full taking over and adoption of the "acquis communautaire" as membership criteria should be, however, completely fulfilled partly till 2004, and then partly from inside.

10. SOME METHODOLOGICAL QUESTIONS

In connection with the evaluation and measurement of integration maturity many questions and anxieties can be mentioned. The first decisive question is the choice of *the right parameters*. To what extent do given parameters really express maturity? Which are the absolutely essential ones, and which merely shade the picture in? What amount of analysis is needed to give us a realistic picture of integration maturity, and how can we avoid including examination of parameters that are not important, and may actually distort the overall picture? Apart from the simple membership criteria, how can the real components and parameters of integration maturity be identified, and a proper picture be created from these and their internal interrelations? What sorts of indicators can be used to express concrete parameters in the various areas, and to what extent and by what means can they be underpinned with statistical data and expressed in numbers? The methods of measurement are often disputable; *how can methodological problems be handled?*

Secondly, difficulties arise in connection with the precise *measurement of certain processes*. From the point of view of numerical expression, the task is relatively simple in relation to the parameters for which the relevant statistical data are available, or on the basis of the available statistical data the appropriate data can be calculated (e.g. GDP growth, inflation or the budget and trade balance). In other cases, in order to express the facts numerically surveys are needed, which can be carried out by sociological and politological methods or public opinion research. Difficulties may arise when because of the contexts the real processes and effects cannot be detected. Processes must be approached in all their complexity, but this makes measurement extremely difficult. With regard to the fulfilment of criteria the examination of *the time factor* and of *comparability* deserves special attention.

In some areas and with some parameters it is possible to make use of certain means of classification or ranking. For instance, the 4-level classification applied by the EBRD seems very useful. This 4-level classification enables assignment to these categories: (1) unsatisfactory; (2) barely acceptable; (3) progressing satisfactorily; (4) performing well. A score of 4 or thereabouts, for example, can be taken to indicate maturity for membership or integration. Division into four categories permits sufficient differentiation and presumably such evaluation and ranking is feasible. A larger number of categories would permit finer differentiation, but at the same time it is not certain that the actual ranking can be reliably established. Such a method is worth applying in the examination of fulfilment of the political, institutional and legal parameters.

In other cases the well-tried polling method used by the EBRD and elsewhere can be used. If a large enough number of respondents are questioned, we can presumably obtain realistic averages. The main point is the group to be polled (experts, academics, politicians or the general public). It can be important to define this. Media (press) analysis is another method that can be used.

In several areas the possibilities of numerical expression, even by indirect methods, are relatively limited. There are many factors, such as *expectations and effects relating to political considerations and interests,* where *fulfilment can hardly be measured,* and especially not with precision. Political science can indeed supply parameters for "soundness of democratic institutions" (a Copenhagen criterion), but their expression in numerical terms comes up against difficulties.

In certain areas even *economic factors, and especially considerations, cannot be exactly measured*. Some time ago a survey showed that the Hungarian population was prepared for EU membership and that more than 60% demand it because they expect great things from the possibilities of free movement of labour. (It must be noted in parentheses that precisely this expectation will not be immediately fulfilled.) For individuals, greater scope for business activity, whether as employees or as entrepreneurs, and the expanded frontiers of economic freedom promised even by the single internal market represent a challenge and attraction that powerfully influence their opinion and behaviour. Surveys show that when from time to time the people in member countries have said yes to integration, this consideration has always played an important part. The situation is similar with the common currency, where both positive and negative viewpoints are strongly represented. Concrete measurement would be impossible either at individual or country level. Yet these are very important, for instance from the point of view of assessing support for integration. It must be added that the classification method, if used with sufficient care, can be applied in these cases, too.

Thirdly, theoretical and methodological problems arise even more markedly in connection with the *aggregation* of analytical results and certain parameters. It is on the basis of aggregations that comparisons and rankings are drawn up.

There are several possible methods of aggregation, and it can be done in several stages:

– calculations are carried out relating to the different components of integration maturity, and aggregated in this respect. This can clearly be done with regard to the functioning market economy, stabilization or real economic convergence, and with a country's approximation to levels of development;

– an aggregate index can be worked out, summarizing fulfilment of the economic criteria of integration maturity. All the elements, with varying weight and by various methods, can be taken into account;

– the working out of a comprehensive index for integration maturity, where in some way the political and institutional criteria are also taken into consideration, cannot be ruled out, but because of the methodological problems and the politically sensitive nature of the question it needs rather careful handling.

In relation to maturity for membership, a demand for *concrete measurement and ranking in terms of preparedness for membership* may justly arise. This may serve as orientation for the candidate country and provide important information for the receiving institutions. The importance of ranking increases particularly if admission takes place on the basis of a true assessment of progress in preparation and "maturity", and if the group of countries admitted is quite small. In relation to the EU this is a real dilemma.

While there is no doubt that in some areas the situation of individual countries and their maturity for membership or integration can be compared, and a certain relative, meaningful ranking is possible, any comprehensive, numerically expressed rank order may be accompanied by numerous question marks and dangers. In some cases in a particular area rankings can be compiled on the basis of percentages or points scored, but these can be manipulated and are open to question in terms of both content and methodology. The choice weights of averaging can be especially problematic.

In our opinion it is a problem that needs to be considered, since there are no significant differences among the CEE candidate countries as regards preparedness and maturity for membership, especially in the first group, and in fact 10 candidates (leaving out Bulgaria and Romania) are mature for membership, through our choice of weighting methods and proportions we could presumably produce any ranking we wanted. And at the same time the most diverse weighting methods can all equally well be supported by a list of well-founded and plausible principles. A good example of this is the "convergence index" of the EBRD, the Deutsche Bank and the Raiffeisen Bank respectively, where rank orderings of Slovenia, Hungary and the Czech Republic were established on the basis of differences of tenths of a percentage point (between 69.4% and 70.3%). On the one hand this is well within the margin of error; on the other hand, by means of only slight "corrections" in the weighting or calculations they could be radically altered. Apart from political considerations, presumably this explains official reluctance to draw up such rankings, or to evaluate enlargement 'rounds' on the basis of them.

A separate question that must be emphasized is that while *in their fulfilment of the membership criteria there can be scarcely any meaningful difference among the ten*, with regard to *a deeper analysis of integration maturity* we would obtain *a more differentiated picture*. Whereas the 10 countries fulfil the membership criteria more or less equally, we would find more significant differences in terms of integration maturity.

At the same time the question arises, *for what purpose* aggregation and the preparation of rankings on that basis are carried out. Such analyses and rank lists (of market liberalization, competitiveness, transparency, corruption, efficiency of institutions, etc.) are carried out by many institutions, research institutes, consultancy firms, and international organizations, chiefly to provide investment advice, *orientation for investors*. For companies and organizations it is important to be able to judge the relative risks and probable costs of their investments. Such analyses can guide transnational companies, money market investors and international institutions (e.g. the World Bank, or the OECD). The related calculations, and the results and methods of these calculations, are very useful for analyzing both membership and integration maturity.

Analyses and surveys of membership and integration maturity can serve *economic policy aims*. In this case the analyses can provide guidance for governments and international organizations.

– Such analyses help in the identification and effective implementation of economic policy priorities and economic policy trends.

– The processes and effects can be significantly influenced by good or bad economic policies.

– In given areas exposure of deficiencies can draw attention to what needs to be done.

– Fulfilment of the various criteria and the development of the parameters are policy-dependent: preparation and fulfilment of requirements can be speeded up by good policies. Economic policy can contribute to improving integration maturity.

The extent to which it is possible to exploit fully the advantages of integration and optimize the costs ultimately *depends on actual maturity for integration.* Therefore it is not a matter of indifference how capable a country is of underpinning it by means of appropriate economic policy measures.

In relation to integration maturity the aims also determine the priorities and methods of analysis. Aggregation and the drawing up of rank lists, when choices have to be made between countries, are particularly important to decision-makers and investors. Analyses for economic policy purposes tend to emphasize precise definition and measurement (numerical expression) of parameters, and for them aggregation is less important. Indeed, in given cases disaggregation, the breaking down of processes, is much more necessary, since only in this way can diagnosis and therapy be determined. In our own analyses we give priority to economic-policy-oriented approaches.

REFERENCES

ANDOR, L.–GALLÓ, B.–HEGYI, GY. (2000) *Tíz év után... Három írás a rendszerváltásról s annak szükséges korrekciójáról* (After 10 years. Three Papers on System Change and its Necessary Correction). Napvilág Kiadó, Budapest.

BLAHO, A.–KISS, J.–LŐRINCNÉ ISTVÁNFFY, H.–MAGAS, I.–PALÁNKAI, T. (ed.) *Integráció-érettség mérése* (Measuring Integration Maturity). Research program led by Prof. TIBOR PALÁNKAI of Budapest University of Economic Sciences and Public Administration, European Studies and Education Center, supported by the Prime Minister's Office of Hungary.

CHIKÁN, A.–CZAKÓ, E.–ZOLTAY-PAPRIKA, Z. (2002) *National Competitiveness in Global Economy: The Case of Hungary.* Akadémiai Kiadó, Budapest.

Epiascope, No. 2001/1: 23. (http://www.eipa.nl.)

European Competitiveness: That Bad a Record? CEPS Newsletter, Summer 1994.

HAUSNER, J. and MIROSLAWA LARODY (1998) Opportunities for and Barriers to Social Change. In: *Accession or Integration?*

HENDERSON, K. (2000) Slovakia's image abroad. Slovak Foreign Policy Affairs. Spring. Bratislava.

JEZIORANSKI, T. (1998) *Accession or Integration? Poland's Road to the European Integration.* EU Monitoring II. Friedrich Ebert Stiftung, Warsaw.

JONES, R. A. (2001) *The Politics and Economics of the European Union.* An Introductory Text. Edward Elgar, Cheltenham, UK.

Kopint-Datorg and MEH. II. (2000) Az EU Bizottság által készített ország-vélemények összehasonlító elemzése. (Comparative analysis of the country reports prepared by the EU Commission.)

LÓRÁNT, K. *Üzleti 7.* November 6, 2001.

PELLEGRIN, J. (2001) The Political Economy of Competitiveness in an Enlarged Europe. UNU/INTECH. Palgrave, Maastricht.

RÁCZ, M. (2000) Magyarország EU-érettségéről a gazdasági makromutatók alapján (Hungary's EU-maturity on the basis of economic macro-indices.). *Magyar Tudomány,* No. 7.

STRANGE, S. (1998) Who are EU – Ambiguities in the Concept of Competitiveness. *Journal of Common Market Studies,* 36 (1).

SURÁNYI, S. (2001) *Források, népesedés a globális gazdaságban* (Resources and population growth in the global economy). AULA Kiadó, Budapest.

TSOUKALIS, L. (1993) *The New European Economy.* Oxford University Press, Oxford.

VAN BRABANT, J. (1990) *Remaking Eastern Europe – on the Political Economy of Transition.* Kluwer Academic Publishers, Dordrecht, London.

WERNER, WEIDENFELD (eds) (1995) *Central and Eastern Europe on the Way into the European Union. Problems and Prospects. Strategies for Europe.* Bertelsmann Foundation. Publishers: Gütersloh.

World Development Report (1996). *From plan to market.* World Bank, Washington, D.C.

IV.

THE ECONOMICS OF MARKET INTEGRATION

1. 'CLASSICAL' CUSTOMS UNION THEORIES: MARKET ADVANTAGES AND DISADVANTAGES

1.1. MECHANISMS OF INTEGRATION EFFECTS IN CUSTOMS UNION THEORIES

The first comprehensive assessment of the advantages and disadvantages of regional integration took place within the framework of customs union theories. The customs union, as a trade grouping, makes it possible to analyse and expand the regional implications of the international division of labour. The customs union *aims at complete internal free trade, while applying common external tariffs in foreign trade, and a common trade policy.* Compared with universal free trade it is often regarded as a *'second best' strategy*, which though it achieves regional free trade among the partners, nevertheless represents joint protectionism with regard to countries outside the union.

In connection with the customs union, JACOB VINER in his study, which has become a classic of the integration literature, makes a distinction between the effects of *trade creation* and *trade diversion* (VINER 1950). We shall interpret these first in an example with simplified figures, then in supply-and-demand and welfare models for a country.

We can analyse the effects of trade creation and trade diversion quantitatively in a constructed example as follows:

Country	Production costs of product (in any currency unit, e.g. euros)	
	x	*y*
A	450	200
B	400	230
C	300	300
Tariff (as %)	50	50

In the case of product *x* (which could be a ton of steel), at the given levels of costs and tariffs with the exception of country *A* the other two countries' producers enjoy an absolutely protected market. The producers in country *C*, even after paying the 50% customs tariff, can export their steel to country *A* for 450 units (300 units production costs +150 units tariff), which is as much as the production cost of the steel manufactured in country *A*. We can assume that country *C* is thus present on the country *A* market as a supplier. In the case of product *y* (which could be a ton of cement), the 50% tariff means absolute protection for all three countries' producers, that is, each other's markets are inaccessible to them. The situation changes, if countries *A* and *B* form a customs union and abolish tariffs between them. In the case of product *x*, country *B*'s producers can now enter the country *A* market duty-free at a cost level of 400 units, and can squeeze out the more efficient and cheaper but 'external' country *C* producers, who still pay the 50% tariff. Country *A*'s steel import is thus 'diverted' from country *C* to country *B*, which is a negative development, because the union favours the expansion of the higher-cost producers. Country *A*'s consumers benefit by 50 units, since they acquire imported steel more cheaply (for 400 units instead of 450 units), yet through the trade diversion country *A* as a whole nevertheless loses 100 units, because 150 units of customs tariffs are lost to the budget.

The situation is different in the case of product y (a ton of cement, say), where we can observe trade creation. While before the customs union there was no trade, now country *A*'s producers with their production costs of 200 units can squeeze the less efficient country *B* producers out of the market. Thus the customs union 'creates trade' between new partners, and enables the cheaper cement industry of country *A* to expand. Country *B*'s consumers gain 30 units, but without any loss of customs duty.

Thus trade creation is regarded as *the positive effect of customs union*. This is because, as a result of the abolition of tariffs, within the union less efficient domestic producers with higher production costs are no longer protected. Production and consumption is reorganized in favour of the new external community partners with the lowest costs. Thus *new trade is created* between the partner countries, *since costly domestic production is now replaced by imports from the other countries.*

In comparison with this, trade diversion is a negative process and represents a loss. Prior to the customs union, at a given level of tariffs – in the absence of relative discrimination – on a given country's market theoretically all external producers could be assumed to have an equal chance. In these circumstances any competitors can gain an advantage only by lowering their level of costs.

The situation changes if within the given zone a group of countries form a customs union. Reciprocal tariff reduction puts the new partner countries in a more favourable position in each other's markets, even to the extent that the latter are able to squeeze out former cheaper suppliers from non-member countries. Thus trade diversion takes place, which means that import is transferred from lower-cost external countries to less efficient new partners. So while trade creation means replacement of domestic products by cheaper imported ones, *trade diversion involves replacement of a cheaper source of import by another, costlier one.* The overall effect of the customs union is given by the *balance of the two.*

Viner's original analysis concentrated on interpreting trade creation and diversion, and it identified gains and losses mainly from a theoretical point of view. JAMES MEADE was the first to attempt a comprehensive *quantification of all the effects of a customs union* (MEADE 1956).

MEADE pointed out that in analysing the advantages to be gained from a customs union, not only the volume of trade created and diverted but also cost savings per unit of product must be taken into account. He observed that though it is directly possible, as a result of customs union, for the volume of trade diverted to be greater than the volume of trade created, customs union as a whole is profitable. The reason for this is that the cost savings associated with trade creation are great enough to counterbalance the losses due to trade diversion.

In quantifying the effects of customs union, MEADE introduced the distinction between the so-called *production and consumption effects.* The consumption effects of customs union were analysed by R. G. LIPSEY, in his examination of the structure of consumption.

One early critical observation relating to VINER's theory was that it presupposed inflexible demand, or zero price elasticity, while supply-side flexibility was regarded by him as infinite. The introduction of price flexibility, and the further development of customs union theory in view of it, is associated with the name of MEADE. The original example quoted by Meade was based on the fact that with the abolition of the 100% Belgian–Dutch tariffs, import was diverted from cheaper German steel to the more expensive steel made in Belgium. But these (trade creation and trade diversion) were only the production effects of customs union.

The consumption effects must also be distinguished. In fact, the consumer gets steel more cheaply than before. This means income-savings, and enables him to increase his consumption. So if we take into account that demand is flexible, then the expansion of the partner country's steel export results not only in trade creation and diversion but in an increase in consumption. MEADE calls this kind of import growth *trade expansion,* and the opposite kind of development in a negative direction as a result of income reduction he calls *trade contraction*.

Thus assessment of the advantages and drawbacks of customs union can be made more accurate by taking the consumption effects into account. The supplementary consumption effect and the gains from it may be great enough in themselves to counterbalance the negative production effects of trade diversion. In order to calculate this it is necessary to quantify the consumption effects. The amount of gain may be determined by multiplying the difference in prices before and after the union by the supplementary volume of import expanded as a result of the consumption effect. This must be added to the gain resulting from trade creation.

The consumption effect and the import growth arising from it can also come about through substitution of other products. It is not certain that consumption of the same product will increase as a result of income-savings from changing over to cheaper import. Demand may be inflexible, and therefore the consumer may use his surplus income to increase his purchases of other products. This is in fact a change in the structure of consumption. Import may thus increase in such a way that neither domestic production nor import from other countries is replaced.

Customs union theories examine the advantages and disadvantages deriving from trade creation and trade diversion using a comparative approach. At the same time, they do not clearly separate the micro- and macrolevels, so that analysis of the effects and consequences often mixes them up.

In the customs union theories the macroapproach – in line with the universal free trade approach – examines the gains and losses not just in national economy dimensions (according to countries) but considering the global world economy (JACOB VINER'S 'whole world'). It follows logically from all this that the classical customs union theories cannot really be regarded as believers in customs union integration though it often appears so, to judge from the literature on integration. *In contrast to universal free trade, every customs union necessarily involves a lesser or greater degree of trade diversion and represents sub-optimal utilization of resources.*

1.2. ANALYSIS IN A SUPPLY AND DEMAND MODEL

We can model trade creation and diversion with the help of the supply and demand curves. In this model we interpret gains and losses for one product and one country. The big advantage of such an analysis is that we are able to express separately and compare at micro- and macrolevel the short-term static effects of union. We examine the processes (production, consumption, trade and income distribution) from the point of view of the consumer, the producer, and the state. In addition to trade creation and diversion we quantify trade expansion and contraction as well, that is, the change in the trend of consumption resulting from lower prices.

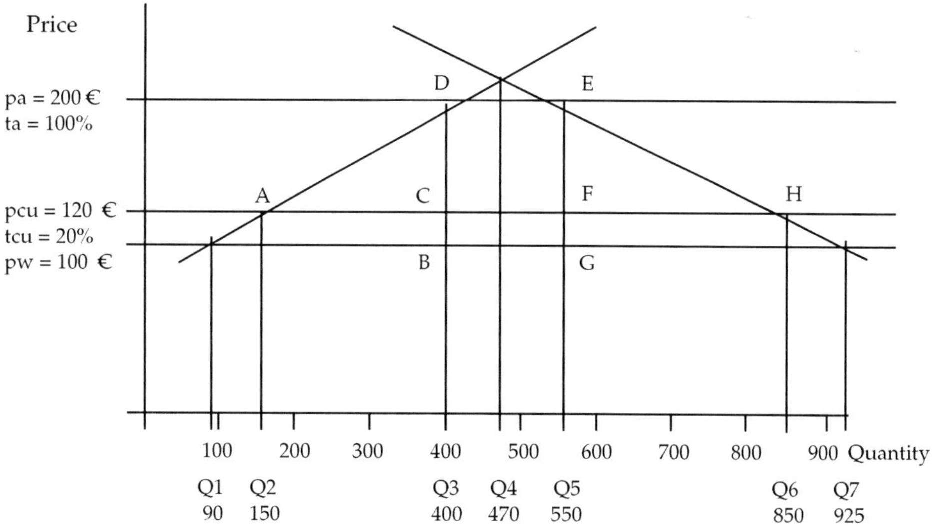

Figure 1. Country A

We examine the effects on trade, production, consumption and distribution, following the formation of the customs union, *for product x* (1000 tons of steel) *in country A*. The world market price for the product (pw) is 100€. Before the customs union the customs tariff (ta) was 100%, which means that the internal market price (pa) of product *x* is 200€ (pw + ta = pa).

A large proportion of the country's producers are far from efficient, as is shown by the fact that the supply and demand curves intersect above a price level of 220€. According to our diagram (Q4) this is equivalent to the production and consumption of 470 thousand tons of steel. For such a market price, obviously complete self-sufficiency would be necessary, which could be enforced by tariffs of about 120%, or quantitative quotas. A policy of self-sufficiency, because of the high degree of protectionism, is directly beneficial to domestic producers, but it is accompanied by inefficient allocation and utilization of production factors. Consumers have to pay high price for the product.

The other extreme would be the possibility of free trade, with which only a small proportion (about 20%) of the domestic producers would remain in the market (Q1, amounting to about 90 thousand tons). By comparison the consumer would gain, because he could buy about 925 thousand tons of steel (Q7), which means that in contrast to the self-sufficiency economic policy alternative, almost twice the amount of consumption would be possible at half the price. Most of what was consumed (Q7–Q1, that is, 925–90 = 835 thousand tons) would be imported.

Prior to the customs union, at a price of 200€ (pa) the country's producers are able to sell about 400 thousand tons of steel (Q3) on the domestic market. At this price, consumer demand is for about 550 tons of steel (Q5). Understandably, the difference between the two, about 150 thousand tons of steel (Q5–Q3 = Mxa), is imported from the world market.

Following the creation of the customs union the situation changes. We examine the effects on country *A*, but we assume that several countries are involved in the union. The union equilibrium price (pcu) is not necessarily derived from the aggregate demand and supply, and the import requirement and export supply induced by the customs union do not necessarily cover one another (the union is not self-sufficient). The countries belonging to the customs union set the common external tariff (tcu) at 20%, as a result of which the price within the union stabilises at around 120€ (pcu = pw+tcu). Clearly it cannot rise any higher than this, otherwise it would be squeezed out by the cheaper world market suppliers, while the union's producers have no interest in a lower price. We examine the effects on production, consumption and (state) revenues from tariffs.

From the diagram it can clearly be seen that in country *A* as a result of the customs union 250 thousand tons' worth of trade creation (Tc) has taken place (Q3–Q2), that is, the more expensive domestic production has been replaced by cheaper import from union partners. We can obtain the cost savings from the area of the ACD triangle or from the formula (Q3–Q2) × (pa–pcu) : 2 = Tc, which is equivalent to (250 × 80 × 0.5) or 10 million €. While the consumer gains by this, at the same time factors of production become available for more efficient utilization. A further consumption gain (trade expansion–Te) is the 300-thousand-ton increase in trade (Te = (Q6–Q5), which is equal to the area of triangle FHE, or (Q6–Q7) × (pa–pcu), that is (300 × 80 × 0.5), or 12 million €.

Another significant consumption gain is the fact that after the formation of the customs union there is no longer a 100% tariff on the 150 thousand tons formerly imported (Q5–Q3), and the consumer can buy it at a price of 120 €. The (150 × 80) or 12 million € consumer saving (Cs) (the CFED quadrangle) or (Q5–Q3) × (pa–pcu) = Cs on the other hand means an equivalent loss of budget revenue for the state. Similarly, a customs revenue loss is caused by the diversion of former import from the world market in favour of less efficient union suppliers (the BGFC quadrangle). This 3 million € trade diversion (Td = (Q5–Q3) × (pcu–pw) or 20 × 150 enriches other union suppliers, while the state budget of country *A* loses 15 million € altogether (the BGED quadrangle) in customs revenues.

With the given price and cost conditions the consumer undoubtedly benefits the most from country *A*'s entry into the customs union. He can now buy a ton of steel for 120 € instead of 200 € before the customs union, which means a saving of (Q5 × (pa–pcu) = 550 × 80) or 44 million € on consumption of 550 thousand tons. Add to this the 300-thousand-ton expansion of consumption (trade expansion) –(Q6–Q5) with further savings of 12 million € (Q6–Q5) × (pa–pcu), which brings the total consumer gain to 56 million €.

In addition to the state, country *A*'s producers are also considerable losers. While for reasons of efficiency they are obliged to reduce production by 250 thousand tons (Q3–Q2), their total price losses amount to 22 million €. This is the difference between the price reduction on the 400 thousand tons of former production (Q3 × (pa–pcu)= 400 × 80) and the cost-saving or trade creation (Q3–Q2)×(pa–pcu):2 = 250×80×0.5, that is, the difference between 32 and 10 million €. This loss to producers appears as a gain for the consumer, and forms part of his total savings.

At macrolevel trade creation and expansion appear as gains for country *A*, while trade diversion represents a loss (Tc+Te–Td). In our present example (12+20–3) is equivalent to 19 million €. This means that according to our example, for country *A*, while significant redistribution of the gains takes place among producers, the state and consumers, entering the customs union is advantageous overall.

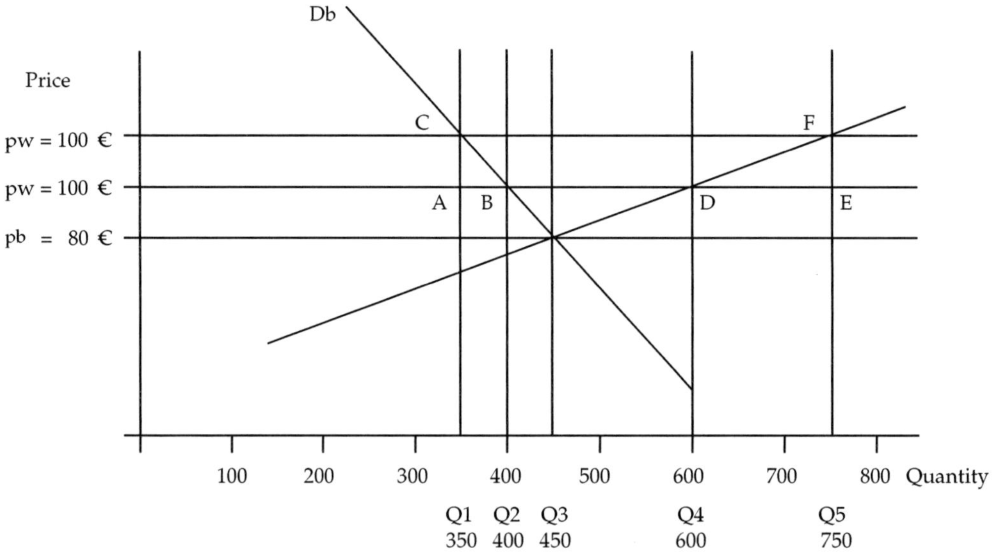

Figure 2. Country B

In *Figure 2* we examine *country B*, as the other member of the customs union, with regard to *product x* (again, 1000 tons of steel).

Here too, the world market price is 100 euros a ton, but the domestic producers make steel very efficiently, with the result that the country is a net exporter. The demand and supply curves would intersect at 80€, but the producers are able to adjust the price on the domestic market to the world market price, since as long as the domestic equilibrium price (pb) is lower than the world market price (pw), export is preferred to selling on the domestic market. This means that the producers continue to make a comparative profit in both markets.

Before the customs union, at a price of 100€ there is demand on the domestic market for 400 thousand tons (Q2), which, if the quality is the same, is presumably satisfied by the local producers. Add to this 200 thousand tons of export supply (Q4–Q2), whereby the country is able to utilize production capacity of 600 thousand tons. With the given cost conditions the country does not need any kind of protection; indeed, at macrolevel even with free trade negative effects on prosperity appear. At the world market price instead of the domestic equilibrium price (pb), consumption (i.e. trade) shrinks by (Q3–Q2) × (pw–pb):2 = 50 × 20 × 0.5 = 500 thousand €, while for producers there is a possibility of negative trade creation by expansion of export by (Q4–Q3) × (pw–pb):2 = 150 × 20 × 0.5 = 1500 thousand €. We can interpret the latter as the expansion of higher-cost production, that is, less efficient utilization of factors of production.

After the creation of the customs union the production and consumption effects alter. The domestic price rises to 120 €, which means that consumer demand has to be reduced by 50 thousand tons (Q2–Q1), involving a loss of (Q2–Q1) × (pcu–pw):2, or 50 × 20:2 = 0.5 million € (the area of triangle ABC). So the customs union causes *trade contraction.*

On the production side the fact that the higher-cost producers also gain access to the market means a loss of efficiency, since on the union market in the new price conditions sales could be increased by 150 thousand tons (Q5–Q4), whereby production capacity could be expanded. The aggregate effect (Q5–Q4) × (pcu–pw):2, or 150 × 20:2 is equal to 1.5 million €. Factors are tied down which might have been more efficiently utilized in other fields. In view of the above, this is *negative trade creation.*

In the given cost conditions, in country *B* the customs union is extremely favourable at microlevel for producers, since with the 20% price increase they can gain considerable surplus income. According to our example the producers' profit is Q5 × (pcu–pw) = 750 × 20 = 15 million €, from which the total loss of 1.5 million € resulting from negative trade creation, or in other words increased costs, can be subtracted, giving 13.5 million €.

By contrast, in the customs union the consumer loses out. This loss is due to the price increase [Q1 × (pcu–pw) or 350 × 20 = 7 million €], and the contraction of consumption (i.e. trade) (0.5 million €), thus equal to 7.5 million € altogether. The higher price forced on the consumer means surplus profit for the producer, while the producer compensates for the contraction of consumption (trade contraction in the internal market) by increasing export.

In the case of country *B* there is no loss of customs revenue, since the goods were not imported either before or after the union.

Adding up the microlevel advantages and disadvantages, it turns out that country *B* also gains net advantage from the customs union. The difference between the 13.5 million € net price earnings and the 7.5 million € consumer loss (6 million €) is a considerable sum. Nevertheless, on the basis of a macrolevel analysis of efficiency and prosperity, the customs union is disadvantageous for country *B* as a whole. There is no positive trade creation (or even trade diversion) to compensate for the trade contraction (0.5 million €) and the negative trade creation (1.5 million €). For country *B* the macrobalance of the customs union is thus a 2 million € loss in efficiency and prosperity.

Analysis using the demand and supply curves therefore offers the possibility for a given product of separating the effects on various microactors (the producer, the consumer and the state) and assessing the macrogains and losses in comparison with these. At microlevel some actors may achieve sizeable profits from customs union, yet at macrolevel the country may become either a winner or a loser. *This significant redistribution of gains and losses* can cause political and social problems, which obviously have to be dealt with.

It would be possible to continue the examples for the given product with different levels of costs and prices, and of tariff reductions. So far we have examined one product. Linking in the division of labour, the processes have to be aggregated for 'n' products, and the macroanalysis has to be extended to the balance of trade and payments, and the terms of trade.

1.3. THE CUSTOMS UNION AND THE ABOLITION OF QUANTITATIVE RESTRICTIONS

According to international trade theories the removal of quantitative restrictions (QR) is accompanied by practically *the same effects of increasing prosperity* as the abolition of customs tariffs. In the demand and supply model we examined above it can be assumed that in the case of country *A* compared with the world market price (pw) the domestic market price (pa) at a given level is simply enforced by means of quantitative restrictions, the actual effect of which is thus equal to that of the tariffs (ta) in our example. *The main difference*, however, is that in this case *the state loses out on the revenue from tariffs*, which in the case of our example above amounted to 100 € per ton, and we can obtain the total from the area of the quadrangle BGED (15 million €). Voluntary export restraint (VER) has a similar effect.

As regards the achievement of profit from higher prices, in the case of quantitative restrictions there are two possibilities: it is pocketed either by the domestic importing company or by the foreign supplier. The government can prevent the latter by auctioning import licences. In the case of voluntary export restraint, on the other hand, in the absence of special measures it is probable that the foreign supplier will compensate himself for import restrictions by increasing his price earnings. In this way governments face worse than if they apply tariffs, yet for several reasons they may be obliged to take such measures. On the one hand it may be that competition on the market is imperfect, or both supply and demand may react inflexibly to prices. Partners are often forced by GATT (WTO) prescriptions to make use of VER.

In the framework of the customs union removal of quantitative restrictions always has a positive effect. Abolition of quantitative restrictions or quotas by partner countries creates trade and promotes trade expansion just as abolition of tariffs does. In accordance with our example relating to country *A*, this is equal to (Q3–Q2) (250 thousand tons) and (Q6–Q5) (300 thousand tons). If import formerly came from the new partner country (country *B*, say) then clearly country *B*'s producers derive profit from the trade creation and expansion, and there is no question of trade diversion. Similarly, trade diversion does not take place if quantitative restrictions applied to third countries are maintained, but not changed.

Customs union by liberalizing trade in the given zone is a step forward in the direction of obtaining and exploiting comparative advantages. It reduces the most important elements of protectionism (tariffs and quotas) but by no means completely eliminates them. As 'economic policy borders', subventions, taxes and exchange rates can be the subject of further liberalization.

The customs union also reduces structural protectionism by removing quantitative restrictions and especially by doing away with restrictive tariffs, but from the points of view of product quality through the various prescriptions it leaves a wide range of means of protection untouched. In the physical sense the customs union also facilitates the movement of goods, and by reducing customs bureaucracy makes possible further savings in costs, labour and time. Complete liberalization is represented by the so-called single internal market (in the EU since 1993).

1.4. FACTORS INFLUENCING GAINS AND LOSSES

The customs union is regarded as a halfway house between universal free trade and protectionism. Therefore, according to integration theories, whether in the case of a given group of countries a customs union is desirable or not can be decided by comparing trade creation and trade diversion or trade expansion and contraction. If trade creation (and expansion) predominate, then customs union is good, and if trade diversion (and contraction) do, then customs union means a loss overall both for the member countries and for the 'whole world'.

According to customs union theories, in the case of a given group of countries whether trade creation or trade diversion predominates, and to what extent, *depends on several factors.*

1. On the one hand, *the higher the tariffs that are abolished* between the partners, the greater will be the advantages resulting from customs union. Since a high tariff level generally protects lower efficiency, the more producers are left unprotected, the greater the likelihood that efficiency will improve. From this notion it logically follows that *the lower the tariff level of the new partners with regard to external countries,* or the lower the common external tariff level is set, the more beneficial the overall effects of the customs union will be. In these circumstances the number of protected, inefficient producers and sectors in the union will be smaller, as a result of which there is less possibility of trade diversion. From the point of view of maximization of efficiency it is also desirable that on a reciprocal basis the lowest possible tariffs should be applied in export markets outside the union. Lower tariffs on these could contribute to export expansion by efficient producers in the union.

In his analysis of the effects of tariff reduction within a customs union, J. VINER makes a distinction between *protective tariffs and restrictive tariffs.* By means of protective tariffs the various countries provide protection for the domestic economy (modification of comparative advantages). By contrast, restrictive tariffs have effects only on consumption. We can speak of these mainly in connection with products where domestic production for some reason is not possible at all or would be extremely costly (structural advantages or disadvantages) (e.g. in Hungary, production of tropical fruit). Through the abolition of restrictive tariffs, import of such products becomes possible. If the products were not formerly consumed in the country in question, then the new import can only be regarded as trade expansion, and there can be no question of trade diversion, even if the partner country has higher production costs than other countries outside the union. Through reduction or removal of external tariffs, naturally the consumer gains in prosperity.

2. *The larger the economic area and size of a customs union,* the greater are the advantages deriving from it.[1] Analysis of the effects of trade creation and trade diversion ultimately rests on the assumptions of the neoclassical theories of foreign trade. In accordance with these, the ideal state of the world economy is universal free trade; in the event of its implementation there is no trade diversion, thus it embodies the maximum efficiency. With general free trade, in accordance with their comparative advantages all countries can specialize in whatever has the most favourable conditions of production. The world 'as a whole' can thus at the same cost achieve maximum performance in terms of output and real income.

In contrast, the smaller the size of a customs union, the greater the scale of trade diversion, and if from this point of view losses predominate, then it is better for the countries in question to abandon the idea of customs union. (These questions arose, for instance, in connection with the Benelux customs union and later also with the Central American Common Market.)

Some theories relating to customs union question whether there is a direct correlation between the advantages and the size of a customs union. DUNCAN and RÖPKE, for example, are of the opinion that a large union is less desirable, since in that case self-sufficiency is more likely and there is a danger of protectionist economic policy being pursued. A smaller customs union (this applies to smaller countries as well) is better suited to division of labour with external countries, and therefore is likely to apply more moderate trade restrictions. Such tendencies can be clearly shown by comparing the tariff levels and trade policies of the industrially developed countries, large and small.

3. In any examination of the effects of the customs union, *transportation costs* must not be left out of consideration. Increased trade presupposes an efficient transport system both in the physical sense and in terms of

[1] Economists disagree about the economic size of a country or union. In interpreting it, the size of the population, the volume of GNP and national income per capita must certainly be taken into account. The concept can be extended and refined by including many further indices of potential and development.

cost levels. This is especially important in a big customs union, where transport costs can be considerable. Assuming identical cost levels, as a result of customs union nearer external suppliers can be in a less favourable situation than more distant partners. It we add transport costs to production costs, then it is a matter of trade diversion. In a given case with supplementary transport costs equal to the earlier tariff the consumer does not lose out, but the country and the national budget do, to the extent of the tariffs lost. As a result of all this, a customs union among adjacent countries is considered the most advisable.

Transport costs can be understood in a wide sense. Thus we can include not just the other costs arising from 'distance' (e.g. communications), but additional expenditure due to differences in culture, law and civilization (costs of language and regulatory differences, additional advertising costs, etc.).

4. The advantages to be gained from a customs union depend on the *economic structures* of the participating countries. According to the classical theories, the more competitive the 'rival' structures of the countries forming the union are with each other, the greater the benefit. From the point of view of gains, the ideal situation is if before the union the maximum range of products was produced in every country, and if the maximum differences existed in the production costs of the various products, that is, the number of 'overlapping' protected goods or sectors was as big as possible.

Therefore it is best if consumers' comparative cost savings are as big as possible, and if trade creation extends to as many products as possible. From the point of view of maximizing gains, it is particularly good if on the different countries within the union the conditions for production of some goods are extremely favourable and therefore their production costs are low. The 'rival' and 'parallel' capacities developed only because of protectionism, and as a result of the creation of the customs union a rational division of labour can emerge which brings significant gains in efficiency and prosperity.

2. "DYNAMIC" CONCEPTS IN CUSTOMS UNION THEORY

One basic *critical objection* put forward against the classical customs union theories is that they are 'static', that is, they assume that *the level of costs of the producers concerned remains unchanged*. So they regard the zone's sources of supply as given, and according to them with customs union all that happens is that consumption and demand, depending on trade creation or diversion, are rearranged in favour of the more efficient or the less efficient suppliers. In my opinion, the classical customs union theories are static also because they do not take account of the structural effects either, for instance product innovation. I entirely agree with WILLEM MOLLE, according to whom instead of 'dynamic effects' it would be more appropriate to speak about 'restructuring effects' (MOLLE 1994: 99).

On the basis of the criticism and repudiation of the classical assumptions about constant costs, a completely new trend later developed in customs union theory. According to the static theories, higher real incomes can only derive from income saving through trade creation. Critics maintain that this approach is narrow, since so-called dynamic advantages also stem from customs union.

In contrast to the static concepts with their analysis restricted to efficiency of allocation, the dynamic theories take a far broader approach to the sources of increased efficiency. According to them, in the framework of the customs union the *dynamic effects* can be attributed particularly to *exploitation of the advantages of economies of scale, more intense competition, and more powerful constraints towards technical development*. It can be added that indeed every source of comparative structural advantage must be taken into account. Frequently the label 'dynamic' is justified on the grounds that all these advantages *add up to more rapid economic growth.* There is extensive literature dealing with the dynamic concept of the customs union (TIBOR SCITOVSKY, PAUL ROSENSSTEIN RODAN, RAGNAR NURSKE, MARCUS FLEMMING, BÉLA BALASSA, etc.) and it includes several different schools.

The dynamic theories, then, *repudiate the assumption of constant cost levels.* According to them, a given producer does not simply step aside in favour of the more efficient one. He concentrates his resources in the interest of larger production scales, uses more modern technology under the pressure of competition, and manages his business more rationally, thereby becoming more efficient himself.

Dynamic advantages may derive partly from *savings due to economies of scale.* In the restricted framework of national markets it is increasingly difficult for individual companies in a given sector to develop even the minimum optimal scale of production: large-scale optimal production series require extensive markets. In big markets, therefore, there are better possibilities of more efficient utilization of resources.

According to the dynamic theories the savings to be gained from large-scale production *can be exploited even in a small customs union*, and it is precisely these that can counterbalance the presumed negative effects of trade diversion.

Of course, the relation between large-scale production and the bigger market cannot be said to be absolute, and is disputed by many. On the one hand it is difficult to determine exactly what we mean by the optimal scale of production. The optimal volume of production may require widely varying production capacities in different sectors and for different products. On the other hand, the optimal scale of production itself depends on the market. With suitably flexible demand, in many cases the higher productivity and reduced costs achieved by increasing the scale of production are enough in themselves to expand the market.

Tariffs and their effects on the scale of production are not unidirectional either. In a given case the tariffs to be paid on external markets may actually encourage exploitation of the advantages of economies of scale, since they may be greater than the tariff costs, and access to the external markets may thus be gained. According to some, rather than tariffs, factors such as knowledge of the external markets or fear of the risks associated with political and economic restrictions may be much more important. In the customs union the possibility of these is really much less.

At microlevel *many concrete advantages* can be derived from *larger company and plant size.* Big companies are in a better position with regard to expansion of production, and the development and application of new technology. This requires substantial investment and concentration of financial resources. Bigger companies obtain loans more easily and at better rates of interest for investment, and their possibilities of self-financing are also better. In most sectors it is mainly the big, capital-intensive companies that are able to maintain the significant research and development potential that is now indispensable. In global world market competition continuous product modernization and the introduction of new products are vitally important. This may demand rapid and flexible expansion or reorganization of research, for which large sums of money are needed. Research involves the acceptance of risk, and the stakes are often high. The market security of a large company is greater, since it is more capable of diversifying its output. A large company's market bargaining position may be better (this does not necessarily mean a monopoly position), and it is better at marketing. It more easily undertakes export market risks and can more easily enter into dialogue with both its own and the receiving country's government.

At the same time it must be emphasized that in a given case the advantages of the large company may be relative, and in some respects they are by no means obvious. *Small firms* are often capable of more flexible adaptation, can operate at lower costs, and may be more strongly motivated to operate efficiently. Mass-production may justify large-scale companies, while small and medium-sized firms may be better suited to the manufacture of special products. We shall not embark on more detailed discussion of the advantages of economies of scale.

According to the dynamic theories, the other most important advantage of the customs union is *the intensification of competition*. The importance of the customs union therefore consists in the fact that it loosens the closed nature of national markets, increases the number of market participants and can break up monopolistic structures and positions. It can be assumed that protectionism in the domestic market favours monopolies and monopolistic behaviour (high costs, neglect of technical development and quality, indifference to the needs of consumers, enforcement of monopolistic prices, etc.). With the lowering of tariffs competition becomes keener on the expanded markets, and the possibility of monopolistic collusion is reduced. On the bigger markets a larger number of efficient companies can now 'make a living', and since for companies the guaranteed nature of the market has decreased, 'more aggressive business behaviour' may predominate, and access may be easier for new producers.

According to the dynamic theories, increased competition and growth in the number of rival producers contending for market share releases forces that *result in a significant improvement in efficiency*. These mean competitive pressure towards cost-cutting, better quality, research and development, technical development and the perfecting of technologies, and generally more efficient operation. While the larger dimensions of the markets and of companies provide a framework and opportunity for cutting costs, the intensification of competition releases the expansive forces that make it necessary actually to utilize them. *So size and competitive advantage are closely linked by reciprocal effects,* and only together can they produce their maximum profit within a customs union.

The dynamic concepts provide a broader and more accurate analysis of the advantages to be gained from a regional international division of labour. By repudiating the assumption of constant costs (which RICAR-

DO's theory also made 'static'), *they make analysis dynamic from the aspect of comparative advantages as well.* In the union, after the reduction of tariffs the static comparative advantages obtainable from the earlier national differences in costs may in fact rapidly disappear in conditions of intense competition, and subsequently in the long-term comparative gains can only be achieved from the factors postulated by the dynamic theory.

The dynamic theory increases the effects of the customs union from the point of view of structural comparative advantages as well. As a result of competition, quality improves and consumer choice widens. Producers in the partner countries can gain structural comparative advantages by faster product innovation and structure modification. The effect of the customs union on innovation and the introduction of new products is often called the 'launching effect'.

The dynamic effects, according to this school of theory, are *not at all unfavourable from the point of view of outsiders;* on the contrary, thanks to the growth and efficiency caused by the customs union incomes rise, and this can mean increased demand for foreign goods as well. This is referred to as the income effect of the customs union, or 'external trade creation'.

According to the dynamic theories, the advantages of the customs union, apart from increasing efficiency, may be much greater than they seem on the basis of static analysis. In their view, comparison of trade creation and diversion, and of production and consumption effects, is no longer enough, since the dynamic gains far outweigh the disadvantages of trade-diversion. While the classical theory was never clearly in favour of regional market integration, *the dynamic benefits represent the chief arguments of the believers in regional integration.*

3. SOME MACROEFFECTS OF THE CUSTOMS UNION

In analyzing the production and especially the consumption effects, customs union theories contributed to deepening the comparative analysis. At the same time, they mostly aggregate microeffects at macrolevel, and *the internal contradictions between the two levels are largely ignored.*

According to both the 'static' and the 'dynamic' concepts, customs union has *growth effects*. They examine the effects of customs union from the point of view of the increase in 'real output' and in the 'total real incomes' of society, since customs union through price reductions ultimately results in an increase in real incomes and resources. As a result of customs union efficiency improves; because of lower costs real incomes rise, making more available for increasing consumption and accumulation. On the basis of the above effects, it can be assumed that employment increases.

Among the various aspects of macroperformance the dynamic theory devotes particular attention to economic growth. In that view, the dynamic effects ultimately add up to faster economic growth. It is assumed that the effect of employment is beneficial, and competitiveness compared with external countries also improves.

According to customs union theories, in competitive structures the gains in welfare attributable to *greater consumer satisfaction* because of increased choice may be important. Cheaper imports resulting from customs union have an *anti-inflationary effect.* On the other hand the customs union theories assume in practice *stable, even fixed exchange rates* in the interest of unhindered trade and the complete removal of restrictions. Stable exchange rates can best be maintained with relatively stable price levels; with rapid and differentiated inflation, serious tensions may arise. Stable exchange rates nevertheless have a moderating effect on the inflation process.

The theories do not pay enough attention, however, to the effects on external equilibrium. Though they indicate the potential problems of equilibrium with the desirability of many overlapping sectors, they do not expect greater deterioration of the trade balances.

For countries joining together in a customs union, they simply set conditions such as that their global economic structures should in fact be similar, their general levels of development should be equal, and divergences between them should consist merely in mutually counterbalancing differences in the cost levels of individual products. But later practical experience, even among countries with relatively similar levels of development, proves that equilibrium disturbances (trade balance equilibrium) can become acute over a long period.

Through its effect on relative import and export prices, the customs union influences a given country's *terms of trade*. Through the customs union's effect on the terms of trade, the redistribution of advantages and disadvantages is expressed. The customs union's effects on the terms of trade were pointed out by J. VINER, but MUNDELL dealt with them in greater detail (MUNDELL 1964).

The terms of trade effects may be multidirectional. Since the new partners' export prices may rise because of discriminatory tariff reductions, in respect of both the tariff-reducing countries and third countries, as a result of customs union, the partner countries' terms of trade may improve. But the tariff-reducing countries' terms of trade may also improve, since import prices may fall. As the ultimate result of a series of discriminatory tariff reductions, every member state may improve its terms of trade with external countries. The members of the customs union can also achieve better terms of trade by taking collective action to gain better bargaining positions for themselves. Here we shall not deal with the world economy role of transnational companies and its interrelation with the development of terms of trade.

The costs of adjustment to the structure change associated with customs union may be severe. They may contribute to great differences between the macroadvantages and disadvantages for individual countries, even though overall they largely counterbalance each other. This is why the question of 'just return' and the search for compensatory solutions are important. The solution may be a mechanism with an asymmetric effect (liberalization) or a direct financial transfer. The asymmetric liberalization construction applied in the course of the Central European partnerships are based on similar considerations, while at the same time financial transfers are largely absent.

4. CRITICAL OBSERVATIONS ON THE ADVANTAGEOUSNESS OF CUSTOMS UNION INTEGRATION

In the debates, *many criticisms* have been leveled against the customs union theories.

1. One fundamental objection refers to *the postulated market structures.* The present-day market structure and operation in the developed countries is very different from that postulated by customs union theories. On the basis of their free trade approach they construct their analyses on a market characterized by 'free and perfect competition', where many equally strong participants confront each other, there is free access for new products, and prices are determined basically by competition. In addition to free movement of goods and services they assume complete and unlimited currency convertibility, and regard tariffs as decisive factors from the point of view of price trends and distortion of competition.

Today as well, competition is the most important characteristic of the market. In a large proportion of the economic branches numerous small and medium-sized producers operate, and over a wide field they are in competition with one another. Nevertheless, in the majority of sectors a few big companies are dominant, and they are able to determine the conditions of competition to a great extent. This *predominantly oligopolistic situation* is a far cry from the free and perfect competition assumed by the liberals. In some sectors the dominance of the big companies is so great that they can dictate prices, quality and supply conditions. The transfer prices used by transnational companies represent artificial price-setting. The operation of market forces in an oligopolistic manner is influenced by the activity of the state.

On the basis of the oligopolistic market structures many question the assumptions of the dynamic theories. Intensification of competition does not necessarily and inevitably follow from the creation of a customs union. In some sectors the small number of producers continues to permit *monopolistic agreements*, and where producers are few, theoretically it is precisely the intensification of competition that prompts oligopolistic collusion. In sectors where in the countries forming the customs union a handful of companies dominated earlier as well, the expanded market can only strengthen the position of these at the expense of weaker ones. In the framework of the customs union the more competitive participants can increase their advantage, while with the loss of protection smaller competitors simply go to the wall. The end result of increased competition can be monopolization of the market in certain areas. Instead of a 'cold shower' to shake up inefficient producers, as a result of monopolization the 'Turkish bath' effects may in fact intensify (PAUL STREETEN).

Many have drawn attention to the fact that efforts to secure the advantages of scale economies and the intensification of competition are mutually contradictory. As the scale of production increases, the process of concentration and centralization intensifies, which strengthens the tendency towards monopolization. In recent decades reality has shown that these reservations are relevant, but the postulated competition mechanisms have proved much stronger, and the efficiency effects have been powerfully manifested.

2. Many question the validity of the free trade approach of customs union theories *from the point of view of development and foreign trade policies.* In his original study J. VINER himself underlined that analysis of trade creation and diversion is confined to the system of free trade theories. In

his view also, believers in protectionism may have a different opinion about the gains and losses. In the case of a given country, in certain periods rapid development of weak domestic industry, improvement of industrial efficiency and structural modernization may in fact highlight the need for protection. And in this tariffs can play a very important part. Many critics make the point that tariffs do not merely have a protective role, but are a means whereby the state seeks to achieve aims relating to growth, structure improvement, equilibrium, income distribution, and even non-economic aims. The legitimacy of protecting new, infant industries is recognized by international trade agreements (e.g. GATT), and temporarily it took place in the case of the European Agreements as well.

3. Many point out that in a customs union among countries *where the economic structures are one-sided or complementary,* the advantages postulated by the classical theories can only be minimal. Among these countries the number of 'rival' sectors is small, and particularly if they are raw-materials-producing or agricultural countries, there is relatively little possibility of further specialization on the basis of their differing production conditions. In such circumstances there is nothing that can be given up, or if it were, it would jeopardize the existence and stability of the whole national economy. These aspects arise especially in connection with integration involving developing countries. At the same time, these objections hold good only from the point of view of static comparative analysis, and the situation is different with regard to structural comparative advantages. Tariff reduction means cost savings for the consumer, and in the wider market competition may favour innovation. If it is combined with an appropriate development policy, a customs union may be beneficial for developing countries, since the negative effects can be counterbalanced.

4. Great difficulties can be caused by *differences in development levels.* In the case of these, with the help of the spontaneous market mechnisms released in the customs union framework reorganization in favour of the 'more efficient' producers may easily be accompanied by all too unidirectional 'trade creation'. This would derive mainly from the wide range of structural comparative disadvantages, but equilibrium is not guaranteed on the basis of the direct cost advantages either, since even slight technical or qualitative disadvantages may be decisive. Customs union deprives the less developed of the ability to counterbalance their structural comparative disadvantages with protective measures, and thus they may face serious trade and balance of payments deficits. Moreover, customs union in itself does not guarantee that development opportunities will

not be blocked even more than under national market protection, or that the fundamental aims of economic policy (employment, price stability) will not become unattainable. Thus many are of the opinion that *the customs union model can be applied only in a limited way to integration among developing countries,* and only under certain conditions.

In the case of developing countries, "trade should not be liberalized, but rather promoted" (WIONCZEK 1966: 8). Since their internal development needs are the most important, and their economies are particularly vulnerable in world market competition, within the integration framework market mechanisms should be combined with a reasonable amount of protection. In some cases their interest is less in trade creation than in the creation of industry or in 'development creation'. The past decades have clearly shown that isolationist, autarchic policies have nowhere been successful, and a reasonable degree of openness can contribute far more to catching up in the world market. Customs union can be linked with a coordinated industrial development policy, and thus the members can together achieve rational specialization and develop competitive sectors capable of export. Taking into account the special characteristics of each country, it can also be decided what degree of protection they should maintain against each other and the outside world, and for how long.

5. THE THEORETICAL FRAMEWORKS OF THE COMMON MARKET

5.1. COMPARATIVE ADVANTAGES AND FACTORS OF PRODUCTION

At the beginning customs union theories did not deal directly with the question of the flow of factors of production. Common market models go further, and assume a free flow of production factors.

The question of the differing factor endowments and prices in individual countries soon attracted the attention of comparative analysis. The so-called HECKSCHER–OHLIN model included this topic area in the theory of comparative advantages. They set out from the assumption that different countries are characterized by different factor endowments depending on their level of development. As a result of this, the relative prices of factors differ. According to the HECKSCHER–OHLIN theory, it is capital that is plentiful in the developed countries, with the result that capital is relatively cheap there, and so it is in these countries' interest to export capital-intensive products. The converse is true of the less developed countries. There, labour is relatively plentiful and cheap, so in the international division of labour they specialize in producing and exporting labour-intensive goods. One important assumption of the HECKSCHER–OHLIN theory is that as a result of all this, purely through trade international equalization of factor prices takes place, even in the absence of an international flow of factors.

It has not been possible to verify these theses by means of calculations based on export structures. On the basis of an analysis of the export structure of the United States during the 1950s it turned out that the US actually had a comparative advantage in labour-intensive products, which became widely known in the literature as the 'LEONTIEFF paradox'.

With regard to assessment of the role of the factors of production (capital, labour, technology, entrepreneurship, etc.) our starting-point must be that here we are dealing with special commodities. The prices of these can by no means be deduced simply from their scarcity. Factor prices are performance-based (they are determined on the basis of their marginal productivity). Since they differ in quality, if countries are compared, then their prices necessarily differ, regardless of their scarcity.

According to the assumptions of classical theory, in the case of capital, comparative advantage and abundant supply are indicated in general by lower interest rates than those in other countries. A lower interest rate can increase producers' profit rate, which makes it possible for prices to be lower in the country in question, in otherwise similar conditions, and for comparative profit to be achieved. The chance of this is greater in the capital-intensive sectors, which thus tend to be concentrated in the developed countries.

By contrast, the less developed countries are really struggling with a shortage of capital, which in some cases is aggravated by a number of factors (wasteful consumption, insufficient willingness to save, etc.). At the same time labour sources are plentiful; in the labour market the ample supply keeps wages down. Social power relations have a similar effect, since the national elite often exercises its power in a dictatorial manner and restricts the freedom of action of democratic institutions (trade unions).

National capital expenditure and comparative differences in competitiveness depend on many factors, and among these relative plenty or scarcity represent just one factor. In determining the cost of capital, in addition to interest rates (the cost of debt) the debt/share ratio must be taken into account, and also tax burdens and concessions, the state of equilibrium of the budget, inflation and the various risk factors. In reality, therefore, interest rates are not adjusted directly to the relative scarcity of capital, and especially in recent decades, in the framework of active state intervention interest rates have in fact become one of the main instruments of economic policy.

In these circumstances interest rates by no means differ in accordance with levels of economic development. With the 'integration' of money markets, it has gradually become characteristic that interest rates are increasingly being determined internationally.

Interpretation of comparative advantages *with regard to labour* is an entirely different matter. Generally formulated, this occurs when in a given country it is possible to produce certain goods with lower wage costs. Unit wage costs, however, are determined by two factors: *the level of wages, and productivity*. Thus a generally lower level of wages is just one of the conditions or possibilities of comparative advantage.

In their dynamics, therefore, comparative wage-cost advantages in a country can through time develop in two different ways.

One possibility is that the growth of wages is held back and they rise more slowly than would be justified over a long period on the basis of increased productivity. An extreme case of this is the freezing or even reduction of wages. In the long-term, in response to such efforts various social and economic correction mechanisms go into operation. If wages are held down for long, especially in modern societies, this sooner or later provokes opposition on the part of trade unions and other political forces, and becomes unsustainable.

Though a relatively low wage level improves competitiveness for the producers, at the same time it reduces the chances of selling goods, and can become a source of serious market tensions and difficulties.[2] This

[2] Here we must touch separately on one of RICARDO's classical but ultimately mistaken theses relating to comparative advantages. According to RICARDO, one main possibility of increasing the general rate of profit is if in the manufacture of consumer goods (which contribute to the reproduction of labour) the increase in productivity is faster than average, which in comparison with other products pushes down the value of labour. Similarly it enables the rate of profit to be increased, if by exploiting comparative advantages the country through cheaper import reduces the exchange value of consumer goods (e.g. foodstuffs). As a result of the peculiar conditions in Britain in RICARDO's time (domestic prices for grain kept high by protectionism), undoubtedly it was not by chance that he concentrated his analysis on precisely this correlation and restricted it to this. Yet he came to the faulty conclusion that the rate of profit can be increased through exploitation of comparative advantages only if it results in the import of relatively cheaper consumer goods. On the basis of our earlier analyses it is clear that there is more to it than this. Comparative advantage, if the producer makes a comparative profit, always increases the profit rate, and RICARDO's assumption represents only one of the possible means for doing this. The macro profit rate is of course another matter.

may happen particularly when such comparative advantages are concentrated in the structurally disadvantaged sectors, that is, the products that are surplus to the domestic market cannot easily be sold on external markets. The picture may theoretically be modified somewhat by unemployment, but the downward inflexibility of wages proves that the mechanisms operate in this case, too. In the case of structural problems, what happens in the economy is simply that unemployment grows, or wages are depressed still further.

Similarly, it is a source of tensions if the relative level of wages rises, and as a result of pressure they increase faster than productivity. The country's products are thereby put at a wage-cost disadvantage. The economy generally 'defends itself' against this by means of inflation or recession, which can cumulatively harm competitiveness and upset the equilibrium of the economy.

On the other hand it is possible, and this is probably the more common case, that the level of productivity compared with that of other countries is raised faster than wage levels rise. This latter situation obviously involves less conflict, since in a given case wages can be raised in such a way that the comparative wage advantages due to the faster increase in productivity are maintained and can be exploited. In the last few decades most of the newly industrializing countries have taken this path. This was typical in the case of Japan, and its example is being followed by the other emerging developing countries of the Far East.

5.2. RELATIVE FACTOR PRICES AND COMPARATIVE ADVANTAGES ON GLOBAL MARKETS

Since in recent times, especially in global market circumstances, the potential static comparative advantages have become exhausted, it is possible to achieve comparative wage-cost advantages chiefly through a rapid increase in productivity. For this, what is needed most is rapid technical development and innovation, which is not really possible without adequate capital resources and research and development capacities. The economy of a given country can only dictate a pace of development, which over a relatively long period can guarantee it comparative wage advantage. Thus from the point of view of comparative wage advantages it was no accident that the countries that are rapidly catching up (Japan and South Korea) were in a more favourable position, but in a given field any relatively developed country may find itself in this situation. It is precisely because of their lack of development capacity that the countries lagging behind have the least chance of comparative wage advantages.

Structural and technical modernization is therefore the key to achieving comparative advantages. In a period that is characterized by rapid product innovation, structural disadvantages prevent the achievement of comparative wage-cost advantages, not to mention organizational or other infrastructural and marketing disadvantages. Thus the former socialist and developing countries did not get far with their lower wage levels, because these were 'taken away' by other disadvantages, or else they could not be exploited (or in some cases only with subventions) in products that were becoming structurally disadvantaged (becoming outdated).

From the above it logically follows that the assumption of the classical theorists, which concentrated on factor endowment while ignoring qualitative differences in factors of production, is now untenable. In achieving comparative wage advantages potentially it is precisely the countries with relatively abundant capital and a high level of technological development that are at an advantage, and there is even less guarantee today that comparative advantages achieved in labour can be coupled with a lower level of development. This is particularly true if we take into account the quality of labour (level of education and professional training). Historically the facts indicate that as a result of relatively high productivity over a long period it was in fact the United States that, in comparison with its competitors, was most capable of keeping down the unit wage costs of a broad range of products. So the 'LEONTIEFF paradox' was in reality entirely possible and logical, and by no means "paradoxical".

This is even more the situation at present. With regard to the factors of production, in today's world economy the chances of comparative advantages arising depend on the quality of these, and many situations can occur in which comparative advantage or disadvantage may arise in relation to all of a given country's factors of production. With relatively cheap capital there is the possibility of faster technical development and high-quality systems of education and training, on the basis of which, unlike in the case of a rapid increase in productivity, the level of wages can be kept down without any social or political conflict, and comparative advantage can be gained. On the basis of comparative profit the supply of capital and the possibility of development may improve, and the advantageous situation may become cumulative and long-lasting. This increases the possibility that internationally wages and the relative level of productivity will diverge enduringly and significantly, that is, in the developed countries, especially those modernizing rapidly, the conditions for securing comparative wage advantages are more favourable.

In the case of other countries development may lapse into a vicious circle. With a shortage of capital a country will probable lag behind technologically; it has less to spend on education and training, and this may lead to a slower increase in productivity. Thus despite a low or even declining level of wages it can find itself at a comparative disadvantage, especially if it is unable to utilize manpower adequately (as a result of poor organization, work morale or discipline). Good examples of this have been the former socialist countries and most of the developing countries, while in recent decades Japan and many other countries that are catching up have provided examples of the opposite kind of development.

In the last few decades the globalization of the world economy and the rearrangement of development rankings (with the newly industrializing countries breaking into the world market) have involved far-reaching consequences and structural changes. These have ultimately put the least developed countries at a serious comparative disadvantage precisely with regard to labour, because the new industrialized countries were able to use the most modern technology, in some cases more highly developed than that of their competitors, at the same time they have kept wages relatively low.

Special mention must be made of the interrelations between comparative wage advantages and relative labour endowments in today's world economy. The less developed countries undoubtedly tend to have ample sources and reserves of labour, which theoretically push wages down on the labour market because of the surplus supply. On the basis of the facts, however, the question justifiably arises, to what extent does the undoubtedly high unemployment in the less developed countries appear as genuinely effective supply on the labour market? In fact, unemployment in many developing countries is largely hidden, and does not increase, or only to a limited extent, the supply on the labour market.

In the developing countries, on the one hand the so-called informal sector, where millions barely subsist from day to day, is extremely large. On the other hand the surplus labour, except for unskilled types of work, in terms not only of its physical condition but its skills structure and industrial culture does not represent genuine supply capable of meeting real manpower requirements. In these circumstances despite the vast amount of hidden unemployment many less developed countries are characterized by a manpower shortage, and this applies particularly to the potentially competitive export sector. The problem of so-called structural unemployment appears in different dimensions in the CEE countries as well.

With regard to the connection between the supply of manpower and comparative wage advantages it must also be emphasized that, historically, even in classical capitalism the wage mechanism never operated smoothly. In other words, in spite of unemployment wages were always inflexible downwards ('sticky'), and wage demands were often difficult to suppress, even when there was surplus supply. In the developed countries today this is even more so, with the widespread system of welfare benefits.

5.3. COMPARATIVE ADVANTAGES AND INTERNATIONAL FACTOR FLOWS

For a long time the classical comparative analysis did not attach particular importance to international flows of factors. This later influenced integration theories as well. Of course, it contradicts the facts of the real world, and is not a permissible viewpoint. In what follows, therefore, extension of the theory in this direction is essential.

The most common motive and driving force in the case of capital export is *the possibility of excess profit.* Producers are motivated by the same interests and considerations as in seeking and exploiting comparative profit or savings in foreign trade. To put it simply, the individual producer transfers his capital or business activity abroad when there are no opportunities for comparative profit through foreign trade, or if these have been exhausted or are limited, and if in so doing he has prospects of greater extra profit. The businessman thus by exporting capital can somehow achieve a higher rate of profit than at home. Experience shows that capital export only takes place when this extra private profit is substantially higher than the profit rate attainable in the domestic economy.

In capital export, political, social, legal and other factors always play an important part. Naturally, minimal possibilities of normal production and business activity and non-excluding risk conditions are essential. Higher extra profit may also be justified by uncertain supplementary costs, and a higher level of commercial and political risk than at home.

Excess profit may arise in connection with capital export as profit deriving from operating-capital investment, as a difference in interest or exchange rates, as income from stock exchange or capital market speculation, or as income connected with various sorts of securities and bonds. These are many-layered, sometimes of considerable size, and short-term. Those active in the economy weigh up, on the basis of the given circumstances, which form of capital export to choose.

There can be many sources of excess profit that may be obtained by transferring capital and production abroad. Direct capital export is basically motivated by these. Through capital export, cheaper and more secure sources of foreign raw materials and energy can be obtained, and processing locally may enable substantial savings to be made. One important motive is always a lower level of local wages, which with the 'import' of relatively high productivity can be a source of comparative profit there. In connection with manpower, the motive may be a smaller 'welfare' wage-cost burden, the special quality of local labour (special skills or development capacities), or other subjective qualities of the manpower supply (discipline, work morale, etc.).

In recent times market acquisition and market security have increased in importance. Among developed countries the transfer of activities abroad may play a part in the acquisition of higher technology or cheaper sources of capital. The latter occurs when the foreign company can obtain cheaper capital on the local market because the interest rate is lower, conditions are better, or preferences are deliberately applied to lure in capital.

Recently, with the transnationalization of the company sphere, *the motives for transferring capital and business activities abroad have become more complex,* and it is not uncommon for capital to flow from less developed countries to more developed ones, for various reasons. (Here we are not talking about speculative capital flight.) This also proves that the HECKSCHER–OHLIN concept of development, factor supply and comparative advantages is highly questionable, in the light of reality.

In the world economy capital export on a substantial scale became characteristic from the end of the nineteenth century. The process was organically connected with the technological, economic and social changes that had taken place in the internal structure of capitalism, and with the readjustment of values in the international division of labour. One factor in capital export was the new period of colonization that began from the end of the 19th century, which certainly helped to establish the present structure of the global world economy.

In recent decades the international political, technological (computerized operations based on modern telecommunications) and legal conditions have been created in which these opportunities for excess profit can be exploited with great precision, flexibility and speed. An important factor in this has been the liberalization of international capital flows, which first for direct operating-capital investments, then in a widening sphere has opened up opportunities for free movement of capital. Another important factor is that the integrating international capital markets, based on modern technology, have enormously accelerated the circulation of capital and the return on resources, opening up the tremendous advantages of the international division of labour.

Integration of the capital markets is interpreted as consisting not just in deregulation and interconnectedness based on modern communications technology, but also the blurring of the various forms. This applies not only to operating capital (direct and portfolio investments), but also to overlapping with loan capital as well. In the globalizing world economy these opportunities are exploited in a flexible and complex manner. It often happens, for example, that from motives of optimization a transnational company finances its working capital needs by means of transactions involving securities or shares.

At the level of a specific company or bank the technical question of how to maximize total income may arise. Naturally the alternatives include trade based on comparative advantages, as one source of excess profit. Thus at the level of the individual company evaluation always seeks the most profitable possibility, and it will depend on the concrete conditions whether the businessman expands export capacity, lends his money, or invests abroad. With the above-mentioned globalization and integration of the capital markets these possibilities of choice have expanded to international dimensions.

Historically, in recent times the motives, directions and structure of capital export have undergone significant changes. Today in the globalizing world economy the functions of capital have acquired different values, and this has become an organic factor in the international division of labour.

I agree with András Inotai that one of the chief elements in the *'Copernican revolution'* observable from the 1980s onwards in the world economy has been the qualitative revaluation of the role of foreign direct investments, which has had far-reaching consequences in terms of its flow characteristics, its operating effect mechanisms and its importance for development strategy. With the increasing globalization of the world economy *the international capital markets are becoming more and more integrated,* and international capital movements are becoming organically interrelated with flows of goods, services and other factors of production (especially technologies, business information, etc.). This is closely connected with the requirements of the new technological revolution, the deregulation of the capital markets and the increasing, comprehensive internationalization of the various phases of the re-production process. As ANDRÁS INOTAI puts it, this change is manifested in the fact that "direct capital investments increasingly have comprehensive effects on modernization and competitiveness, is a carrier of the most up-to-date technology (or those capable of adapting to it), and of that portion of production that seeks sales channels in the world market. It is therefore an essential condition of national economies' adjustment to the world market, and their structural change, technological development and competitiveness" (INOTAI 1989: 327). Accelerated technical and scientific development has become the basic challenge for the national economy, involving qualitatively new structures and constituting a basic factor in catching up and keeping up in the world economy. Direct investment mediates this rapid technical development, and without its organic linkage with world economic processes is impossible. In the international division of labour new structures are coming into being, in which the re-production processes of the different countries form a continuous chain. This demands a new type of partner relationship in which direct capital relations are an indispensable element of cooperation. A country that is not capable of linking organically with this international production network, that cannot adjust its production structure to world economic trends, will be mercilessly left behind.

The crisis in the world economy at the beginning of the 1980s had complex effects on the international capital markets. The debt crisis and the general shortage of capital associated with it not only affected the money market in themselves, but also radiated to the demand for and supply of direct investments. Because of higher interest rates, only extremely profitable investments could be considered, and this from the outset caused the supply of direct investments to shrink. Thus long-term strategic and short-term cyclical factors alike lay behind the change in power relations among the direct capital-exporting and capital-importing countries. This means that in the future, though it is very likely that *the role of direct capital investments in modernization and world economic integra-*

tion will not just continue but will increase, nevertheless if there is general over-supply on the money markets, power relations will shift in favour of importers of direct investments. It would be a mistake, therefore, to assume that the existing power relations are given once and for all.

The great acceleration and expansion of international capital flows represent one of the general accompanying phenomena of the globalizing world economy, and this sphere has become one of the main areas where extra income is made. In the globalizing world economy the importance of these sources of growth in efficiency and revenue has increased. This is clearly shown by the fact that especially in the last few decades the international flow of capital has grown to gigantic proportions and is several times greater than the expansion of world trade.

The acceleration and expansion of capital flows has had fundamental consequences and has caused qualitative changes in the development of the world economy. Liquidity possibilities have been extended; together with the special consequences of the oil price explosions this created a dangerous debt trap which the majority of the countries of the world were unable to avoid.

At the same time, serious global problems of equilibrium arose, which partly explain today's crisis phenomena. The acceleration of capital flows and the increase in liquidity understandably raised the problem of inflationary tendencies, which in the special circumstances of the 1970s was able to emerge. Here it is a case of capital outflow that falls outside the jurisdiction of the national banks, and against it the effectiveness of anti-inflation economic policies is extremely questionable.

The development that took place in the 1980s, however, proves that the world is not entirely helpless in the face of international inflationary pressure. At the beginning of the 1980s one of the factors that proved decisive from the point of view of limiting the inflationary effects and regulating the capital market was the 'explosion' in interest rates. As a market mechanism this had corrective effects. It was also proved that national governments were only indirectly capable of influencing the international processes, especially when it was a case of a large country or if groups of countries acted collectively and in a coordinated way.

It also became clear that these coordinated actions took account mainly of the interests of those concerned, and were accompanied by serious consequences for 'outsiders'. From the beginning of the 1980s in the developed countries the inflationary processes were spectacularly brought under control, but since the causes were not eliminated, they were often simply 'passed on' to other countries. This was well demonstrated by the effects of American and German interest-rate policy.

The motives for the international flow of labour manifest themselves very differently. In the course of time they have changed greatly in the different regions, and the international flow of labour has become an important feature of the world economy in the past decades. It is a special characteristic of this sphere that in addition to economic considerations there are always many political, social and human factors (people seeking better living conditions, or fleeing from dictatorial political systems), and the process can often involve workers settling permanently in a given country (colonies of settlers are formed). The motives for the international flow of labour are complex; apart from higher wages and welfare provision, cultural and other human considerations (better educational opportunities, housing conditions, research facilities, etc.) may play a decisive part.

In the past decades there has been a substantial *international flow of other factors of production (technology, innovation, entrepreneurship, etc.)*. The problems of technology transfer and flow must be dealt with separately; the operation of many special laws can be observed in these.

It can in general be said, however, that the international movement of the other factors of production (technology, or entrepreneurship) is closely related to that of the two basic factors (capital and labour). In both the technical and the economic sense this is logical. Clearly, entrepreneurship or for example modern technology presupposes business activity, and for this, capital is needed. On the other hand, entrepreneurship and the flow of modern technology frequently involve international mobility on the part of individuals as well (as in the case of the brain drain). At the same time, in the world economy in recent years independent development of flows of some factors has been observable (expert advice to the developing and East European countries), and developed communications technologies are increasingly penetrating the barriers of geographical distance (company management from a transnational company headquarters).

5.4. THE THEORETICAL FOUNDATIONS OF THE COMMON MARKET

Theories of integration regard the common market as a real form of market integration, especially if it is accompanied by the creation of a 'single market'. Thus the free flow of goods and services is supplemented by liberalization of the movement of factors (capital and labour), completing the *'four freedoms'*. Even the Treaty of Rome went beyond the simple customs union and formulated the possibility of the free movement of capital, labour and enterprises among the member countries.

The classical customs union theories did not devote particular attention to the free international flow of production factors; indeed, they actually assumed the international immobility of the factors of production. Yet from the outset with the various efforts at integration it was clear that for maximum exploitation of the advantages to be gained from market integration, international liberalization of factor movements was necessary.

The fact that the classical customs union theories started out from the notion of the international immobility of the factors of production was due to a number of causes.

On the one hand, according to the HECKSCHER–OHLIN theory discussed earlier, there is no need for any international flow of production factors, because *factor prices are internationally levelled out through foreign trade.* Though in reality the growing volume of capital export contradicted this, the theses of the neoclassical economists greatly influenced customs union theories.

On the other hand, on the basis of the static and ideal system of assumptions of classical customs union theories the international movement of factors of production seemed unnecessary from the beginning. Explicitly or implicitly, they start out by assuming *general equality of levels of development*, full employment, balance of payments equilibrium and an equal distribution of trade advantages. To them, differences in development levels are merely structural, that is, they appear only in relation to certain products or sectors. With 'rival' economic structures the advantages of the customs union can thus be maximal for everyone. In the framework of the customs union increasing specialization carries out reallocation of output through foreign trade, and movement of factors takes place only between sectors. So there is no need for the international flow of factors of production.

Thirdly, in the framework of the customs union practical considerations also justified separate treatment of trade matters. *The creation of a customs union seemed simpler and more quickly attainable* than the liberalization of capital and labour flows. From many aspects trade liberalization was regarded as a precondition of the freeing of factor flows. Thus it seemed appropriate to preserve a certain order, and with some progress in the customs union the common market was put on the agenda.

The theoretical *starting assumptions* relating to the common market *were also based on the international levelling of factor costs and prices*. According to them, this is achieved through the international flow of factors. Capital and labour are transferred from low-productivity utilization to more profitable production, whereby the optimal international allocation of factors takes place. Capital flows to where labour is cheapest, while labour seeks the places where wages are highest.

The effects of factor flows on prosperity are mostly examined with the help of demand and supply models. We shall not go into the details of these, since the correlations are relatively simple, whereas certain assumptions of the modelling are highly debatable.

According to these assumptions, the reduction of barriers and freeing of factor flows may have positive effects on the prosperity of the countries concerned. If factor prices (wages and interest rates) differ between two countries (*A* and *B*) then the effect of liberalization is that they level out. Particularly in the case of wages this levelling will probably not be complete, since the physical and psychological costs of moving (migration) are considerable. According to the models it is assumed that foreign labour flows into the country (*A*) with high wages, and the supply of it on the labour market forces wages down. The opposite happens in country *B*, from which local labour flows out, and with the reduction of the labour supply market equilibrium is attained at a higher level of wages.

In country *A* the drop in wages means cost savings for producers. This is partly due to income redistribution to the detriment of local labour, which depends on the fall in wages and the shrinking of the labour supply. On the other hand, for producers employing the cheaper immigrant workers means pure profit; not only are the costlier local workers replaced, but with the increased demand for the new workers production is also expanded.

In the case of country *B* the local producers are the losers, since they have to pay higher wages; their losses are due both to the difference in wages and the reduction of output. The workers, however, gain from both the higher local wages and employment abroad.

The gains and losses are unequally distributed not only between the factors of production but also between the countries, which can give rise to many tensions (trade union action against the employment of cheap foreign labour). An argument in favour of liberalization, however, is that the 'world' as a whole gains because in country *A* the producers make net cost savings, while in country *B* the emigrant workers earn higher net wages. Obviously, the greater the difference in wage levels, the bigger the gains and losses.

A number of objections to these assumptions can be made. On the one hand the labour market is much less flexible, and it is very unlikely that wages would fall, despite the increased supply of labour. Experience suggests that this does not happen even when unemployment is high, and especially not if the surplus labour is foreign. The converse assumption, that with a fall in wages the labour supply would also shrink, is even less realistic.

The most serious objection and question concerns the validity of the assumption that wages become equalized internationally as a result of the flow of labour.

As we have seen, the national level of wages is determined by the general level of productivity. In these circumstances, naturally, the HECKSCHER–OHLIN assumption that national wages are levelled out through foreign trade is true only if it is accompanied by approximation of productivity levels. This tends to occur only under certain conditions, and contrary processes may emerge.

The tendency for price levels to become equalized among open economies can only result in the equalization of wage levels if productivity levels are also similar. Price equalization directly results in the levelling of unit wage costs (if we assume that other costs are equal), which means that with unequal productivity this simply rules out the equalization of wages. Thus *since with differences in productivity price equalization and wage equalization cannot be reconciled with each other, even with liberalization of factors the process is not possible.*

In fact, with the flow of factors in the long-term certain corrective mechanisms go into operation. With wage changes resulting from the flow of labour and with unchanged productivity, the countries concerned find themselves in a situation of comparative wage advantage or disadvantage. Though the inflow of foreign labour may bring wages down, this puts the producer at a comparative advantage, and with the expansion of his markets and sales he increases his output and his demand for labour. This drives wages up. The opposite happens when wages rise. The producer has a comparative wage disadvantage, and in a liberalized market he may be squeezed out of both his former export markets and the domestic markets. Deteriorating sales and cutbacks in production finally force the entrepreneur to reduce wages.

If we link in the flow of capital, clearly comparative wage advantages attract foreign capital, while wage disadvantages have a deterrent effect from the point of view of investment, and lead to capital outflow. Thus not even the comparative advantages deriving from better organization, management or enterprise can be maintained without limit.

It is another question to what extent free movement of factors contributes to the sort of resource allocation and development that leads in the long-term to actual equalization of productivity levels. In fact a country with lower wage levels (if in addition to other things the quality of labour is satisfactory) is more likely to attract advanced technology and capital, which raises productivity, and in the long-term brings equalization of wage levels.

Thus the classical common market models simply ignore differences in productivity (presumably they take productivity levels to be similar), and they attribute the equalization process exclusively to short-term labour market demand and supply effects.

The need for free movement of factors really arose directly and clearly in connection with *the dynamic customs union theories*. Optimal exploitation of large-scale production capacity, linkage of research and development, acceleration of technological development, and adaptation to changing conditions of competition necessarily imply the international flow of capital, labour and technical knowledge. With the development of the transnationalization process, in practice the order of flows altered, and that of capital became the top priority. At the level of macrointegration the free flow of capital was regarded as necessary in order to reduce regional and structural inequalities, and to deal with balance of payments equilibrium at Community level. By liberalizing labour flows it was hoped to reduce regional unemployment.

Thus the advantage of factor flows does not consist principally in the equalization of factor prices. The main point is that *as a result of free flows the possibility of structural allocation may improve, and with accelerated circulation the return on factors may be more favourable.* Thus structurally the fine-tuning of needs and factors becomes possible, and factor utilization will be more efficient. In the long-term this can contribute to the equalization of levels of development. It is mainly for this reason that the common market can be considered desirable and beneficial.

6. THE CUSTOMS UNION – THE COMMON MARKET – THE SINGLE INTERNAL MARKET

In connection with integration based on the classical customs union and common market, from the beginning many reservations and criticisms were expressed. Above all, it was far from being a case of the formation of 'internal market' relations free from any kind of restriction. The actual development of integration in practice confirmed this in many areas, and integration in many respects did not develop in accordance with expectations. As a result of the customs union trade between the members rapidly increased, but unrestricted flows of goods and factors of production were not achieved, and exploitation of the advantages became questionable.

With the customs union and the common market, unification of the member countries' markets *was for several reasons not fully achieved.*

1. With the customs union, only tariffs and quantitative restrictions were dismantled. In this way, within the region the main elements of normative, direct protectionism were eliminated, but the conditions of free trade were far from complete. Trade was impeded by *many direct non-tariff barriers,* among which the various kinds of technical, environmental and health regulations and administrative controls must be mentioned. In many areas efforts to make these uniform and to reduce them began, but in a far from comprehensive way.

2. In recent decades, with the increase in the regulatory activity of the state, the *so-called economic policy frontiers* have expanded significantly. Among these all the economic policy instruments, starting with direct subventions and tax concessions, must be mentioned (interest rates, exchange rates, taxes, etc.), which to a lesser or greater extent influence producers' cost conditions and therefore their competitiveness. In 1990 in manufacturing industry, state subventions as a percentage of value added amounted to 14.6% in Greece, 6% in Italy, 5.3% in Portugal, 3.5% in France, 2.5% in Germany and 2% in Great Britain (*The Economist,* August 8, 1992: 61).

From the start it was clear that these non-tariff barriers, or economic policy instruments could in a given case represent much more effective obstacles and trade-distorting factors than tariffs. It is not difficult to see that for a given producer a 10% devaluation of the national currency, or an equivalent-sized subsidy or tax concession can provide the same amount of support and market advantage as if a 10% tariff were to be imposed on the partner countries. It was not by chance that from the outset, as further development of the customs union, the idea of advancing towards economic union was formulated, which aimed at the stabilization of exchange rates, broad unification and harmonization of tax and monetary policies, and state regulation in many areas at Community level.

3. As a result of the customs union undoubtedly integration of the market for consumer goods was largely achieved. Yet *the principle of 'one market – one price' was not implemented* in accordance with expectations. In spite of the free movement of goods, *price differences remained considerable.* According to figures published by the sectoral trade association, in retail trade in electronic goods prices in Italy and Spain were 25–35% higher than in Germany or Holland, and in some cases (for certain TV sets) the price difference was over 100%. Companies explained the price discrepancies by referring to 'changing local competition conditions', taxes and national differences in distribution and other kinds of costs. At the same time, according to experts the differences in transport, distribution and servicing costs within the Community did not justify price differences greater than 5% (*Financial Times,* August 3, 1992). According to the European Carmakers' Association, exchange-rate fluctuations had a decisive effect on differences in car prices.

4. In the case of quite a few key industrial sectors *the main customers are traditionally the national governments*. Here, in addition to defence industry orders, we can list the energy and telecommunications sectors, pharmaceuticals and vehicle-manufacturing, in purchasing from which the national government's own companies are given priority. The 'state market' associated with the most modern technology amounts to 8–10% of national output. The limited competition in these sectors has contributed to European industry's relative technological lagging behind.

5. In recent times *services* have gained prominence in the economic structure. A considerable proportion of these are non-tradable, but at the same time they may be decisive in terms of the competitiveness of a given product or company. Services are heavily regulated, and national regulations and laws differ widely. From the point of view of international cooperation and penetration the regulation of the service sector is often discriminatory: foreign firms are at a disadvantage.

6. Among the factors of production it was mainly *the flow of 'direct investments'* that the common market formally guaranteed. In the framework of the common market, capital flows were assigned to four cate-

gories on the so-called A–B–C–D lists. From the beginning of the 1960s the capital movements that featured in lists A (direct investments, personal capital transfers, short- and medium-term commercial loans, life and loan insurance, and capital transfers relating to services) and B (sales and purchases of stock market securities) were liberalized 'unconditionally'. With regard to list C (unlisted securities, long-term commercial loans, medium- and long-term financial loans) liberalization was merely 'conditional'. In the case of list D (purchases of short-term securities, short-term financial loans and the opening of deposit accounts) the Community did not undertake any obligation to liberalize.

7. *In the flow of labour*, not only economic considerations but also political, social and cultural ones are important, and free movement has been hindered by many factors. Among the most decisive of these have been recognition of professional qualifications and degrees and the social conditions of employment abroad.

By the 1980s in these circumstances it was becoming increasingly clear that it was necessary to advance beyond the common market. This was indicated by the creation of the *program for the single internal market*. The single internal market is the most complete degree of market liberalization, and aims at total implementation of the principle of the four freedoms.

7. MEASURING THE EFFECTS OF INTEGRATION

The customs union theories provide a good basis for analysis of the advantages and costs of integration, and with the help of the 'classical' theories (trade creation and diversion or trade expansion and contraction) these can ultimately be expressed quantitatively in terms of the development of efficiency and prosperity. With the help of their relatively simple equations the 'classical' theories make it possible to measure costs and benefits accurately, and their great advantage is that they can be generalized to measure the effects of the reduction not just of tariffs but also of other trade barriers ('tariffication' of non-tariff barriers, or the trade-creating effects of the removal of exchange-rate risk).

Within the EU from the 1960s onwards many attempts were made to quantify the effects of the customs union (J. WAELBOECK, P. J. VERDOORN, F. J. M. MEYER zu SCHLOCHTERN, JAMES MEADE, BÉLA BALASSA, etc.). From their results, which are not comparable with each other and often directly contradictory, it nevertheless turns out in connection with the EC customs union that both the trade creation and the trade diversion effects did develop. It is another matter that these analyses, which are debatable in themselves, finally were unanimous in showing disappointingly minimal integration effects. On the basis of their calculations, T. SCITOVSKY and P. J. VERDOORN found that the gains deriving from the customs union came to just 0.05% of the member countries' GNP. Other calculations referring to the 1960s put it at no more than 0.5% of GDP. Yet it was in that period that the trade effects asserted themselves most dynamically.

In measuring the effects, one question is that of *the identification of trade flows*, and how to distinguish from the general trends the ones that really resulted from tariff reduction. It must immediately be pointed out that the analyses carried out so far (e.g. by SÁNDOR MESIEL for Hungary) indicated that there was little correlation between partnership agreement measures and the dynamics of trade flows.

The other question concerns *the calculation of cost savings.* There have been countless attempts at this. It really has to be examined product by product, therefore it would be very difficult to do aggregate calculations. H. G. JOHNSON and T. SCITOVSKY's estimate is theoretically acceptable, making allowance for the very great possibilities of error; they took as their starting-point *the percentage of tariff reductions.* Companies in the partner countries can gain cost advantages only in proportion to tariff reductions, and the same applies to trade diversion with regards to external producers in non-member countries. Clearly the cost savings on the trade creation associated with a 10% reduction in tariffs are likely to fall within the 0–10% band, since cheaper producers got in before the customs union, and higher-cost ones even after the formation of the union cannot enjoy its trade-creating effect. Thus the limits of the estimation of gains and losses are extremely wide.

In the case of the EC the very small gains can be explained by the fact that relatively low tariff barriers were reduced. In the case of Hungary and other candidate countries this may develop somewhat differently after accession, since higher tariffs will have to be reduced. In this respect from the producers' side the achieving of comparative advantages may have little effect. On the other hand the consumer may theoretically gain greater advantages. It is another question, how real will be the prevalence of price-reducing effects.

Later, to determine the balance of costs and benefits of integration, one of the most comprehensive effects-analyses in relation to the single

European market was carried out, which was summed up in the so-called CECCHINI report. The report examined the effects at both micro- and macrolevel and attempted to aggregate them. These relatively important and impressive analyses had an unexpectedly powerful effect, and played a large part in dispelling the 'Europessimism' of the early 1980s, which gave place to 'Europhoria', so that the program for the single market received general social and political support. Similarly wide-ranging analyses anticipated the effects of EMU and the introduction of the single currency. The Commission study (One Market, One Money) attempted to assess these from many angles.

The main directions of analysis and measurement of the advantages and drawbacks of the integration process are summed up below:

- trade effects (flows of goods and factors);
- effects on efficiency and prosperity (trade creation and diversion, trade expansion and contraction);
- competition effects;
- scale economy advantages;
- structural effects;
- growth effects;
- consumer effects;
- employment effects;
- regional effects;
- economic policy (e.g. budgetary) effects;
- measurement of social or sociological effects;
- identification of integration's winners and losers.

In connection with determining and accurately measuring the balance of costs and benefits, it is necessary to draw attention to some interrelations:

1. The advantages and disadvantages, the benefits and costs, cannot be statically analyzed in themselves. They are *policy-dependent*. Given effects can be examined in several scenarios depending on what political priorities and economic policy trends are implemented, and how effectively. The effects can be significantly influenced by good or bad economic policy. In a given case, therefore, it is not a question of considering whether on the basis of the static balance of advantages and disadvantages it is worth joining or not, but what conditions and methods may be applied to optimize the effects, reduce the costs and maximize the benefits, and what kind of policy can be followed to achieve the position that is most favourable to the interests of concerned.

2. It is essential to distinguish between *short- and long-term effects.* It is possible, indeed likely, that in the short-term the balance of stabilization or integration may be negative, but the long-term effects may amply compensate for this. The positive effects of modernization on competitiveness and prosperity can only be expected some time in the future, while many parameters of economic growth (a balance of trade deficit, heavy company reconstruction costs, etc.) may be negative in the short-term.

3. The development of the effects of integration depends largely on *cyclical conditions*. The integration process in the 1960s was positively influenced by the fact that it took place in favourable cyclical conditions. Later the long recession (between 1973 and 1983) caused serious disturbances in the integration processes, especially with regard to trade. At the same time, in the company sphere the constraints towards reconstruction generated by the crisis accelerated the integration process. From cooperation in production and company relations substantial cost savings were achieved. In its analysis of the cost-benefit balance of the 1992 internal market the CECCHINI report did not properly take into account the relatively severe recession that was just beginning in 1992. Particularly the macroeconomic analyses thus lost their relevance.

4. The advantages of integration may partly be *direct* ones, such as the increase in trade as a result of market opening, or the reduction in production costs through simplification of regulations. Other advantages may appear only *indirectly*. These include the advantages of efficiency and prosperity arising from bigger markets, exploitation of economies of scale, or more intense competition.

5. It would be a mistake to restrict the preparation of effects balances too much to budget transfers. Unfortunately, here too *we are tempted to use the budgetary approach.* Budget transfers and their balance represent only a very narrow segment of the advantages. It would be a fatal mistake if they were to unduly influence decisions in reality, on both sides. The biggest danger that threatens is from the EU, where many are inclined to condemn enlargement as 'too costly', while important advantages from the EU's point of view are not taken into account. But it may similarly motivate those seeking admission. As has already happened once or twice, particularly now it would be unfortunate if this question were to

be decided on the basis of budget balancing. From the EU's side, one of the most serious barriers and restraining factors hindering Eastward enlargement is considered to be the *expected burdens on the budget*, though for the period up to 2006 they will not exceed 0.15% of the EU's aggregate GDP.

6. The measurable advantages may be minimal or in a given case the effects may be negative, yet the effect of integration may still be positive. That is, in the absence of integration the negative consequences would have been even greater. It is possible, for example, that in the integration period the rate of economic growth may decline, as happened in the EC in the 1960s, but without the common market integration this slowing-down would probably have been much more significant. The annual average growth rate of the GDP of the six EC countries between 1950 and 1958 was 5.6%. Between 1958 and 1972 the rate fell back to 5.2%, in spite of dynamic integration. Many factors played a part in the process. From the point of view of integration the question arises, to what extent the dynamic effects of the customs union restrained this slowdown. This is why there is absolute justification for analyzing the *'non-integration' alternatives.*

7. In the case of *a small, open economy,* it is far from certain that the expected advantages *will materialize within the country*. The increased income resulting from tariff reductions can be shared between the exporting and importing firms. Who benefits is a question of power relations. Accession may cause domestic prices to fall in many areas. Whether this actually reaches the consumer or increases the price margin of the foreign supplier firms or wholesalers depends on many factors. With accession agricultural prices in Hungary will probably rise. This will partly have to be paid for by the consumer. On the other hand, how much of the surplus income from the price rise returns to the producer or remains in the country will depend on many factors. With the high rate of return on foreign investment the return may be such that in a short time several times the amount of capital invested leaves the country.

8. In connection with the measurement of integration *many methodological questions* can be raised; methods of measurement are often debatable. The difficulties begin with the accurate measurement of certain processes. On the other hand, often they concentrate on just certain effects, but because of the context the real effects cannot be distinguished. There have been many attempts, for example, to identify the trade flows prescribed by the customs union. Obviously the trade processes have been influenced by many other factors besides the formation of the customs union, but it is almost impossible to pick these out. It is even more difficult to estimate cost savings. Yet without these there is precious little we can say about the effects on the division of labour and on trade. The processes must be approached in their complexity, but this can make measurement extremely difficult.

REFERENCES

HAVELOCK, B. and Y. T. CLIVE (1969) Aspects of the Theory of Economic Integration. *Journal of Common Market Studies,* December.

INOTAI, A. (1989) *A működőtőke a világgazdaságban* (Operating capital in the world economy). KJK. Kossuth, Budapest.

M. S. WIONCZEK (ed.) (1966) Latin American Economic Integration (Experiences and Prospects). Praeger.

MEADE, J. E. (1956) *The Theory of the Customs Union*. North Holland Publishing Company.

MOLLE, W. (1994) *The Economics of European Integration (Theory, Practice, Policy).* Aldershot, Dartmouth.

MUNDELL, R. A. (1964) *Tariff Preferences and the Terms of Trade.* The Manchester School of Economic Studies, Vol. 32.

VINER, J. (1950) *The Customs Union Issue.* Carnegie Endowment for International Peace, New York.

B.

THE PROCESSES OF EUROPEAN INTEGRATION

I.

FROM THE CUSTOMS UNION TO THE SINGLE EUROPEAN MARKET

By

ÁKOS KENGYEL–TIBOR PALÁNKAI

1. THE PROGRAM OF THE SINGLE EUROPEAN MARKET

In practice, the program of the customs union and the common market was implemented by 1968. Up to the beginning of the 1970s these market frameworks enabled rapid integration. This applied particularly to trade flows, and also to labour mobility. Integration had a dynamizing effect on the economies of the member countries. From the end of the 1960s the idea of taking integration farther in the direction of economic and monetary union was considered, but the plan collapsed in the circumstances of the crisis that developed in the early 1970s. At the same time, the crisis drew attention to the inadequacy of the integration framework of the common market, since governments often tried to deal with their difficulties at the expense of their integration partners. It had become clear that the non-tariff (non-normative) instruments still untouched by trade liberalization could also be used against each other; state markets remained closed, and the common market measures taken so far had to only a limited extent affected the sphere of services. Thus, with the common market, success in creating real market integration and conditions of a real 'internal market' had been only partial. To ease the economic crisis it seemed especially vital to move forward. This was the purpose of the plan for the single European market.

The decision with regard to the plan to develop the so-called *single European market*[1] or European 'internal market' was taken in June 1985 at

[1] The name 'single market' (or Single European Market – SEM) is intended to express complete liberalization. In German the expression 'Binnenmarkt' ('internal market' in English) is used. In French, both 'marché intérieur' and 'marché unique' are applied.

the Milan summit meeting of EC heads of state and government. To create a completely integrated market, the *White Paper* presented by the Commission at the summit set out 300 concrete measures, with December 31, 1992 as the deadline for their implementation (European Commission, 1985). In accordance with the Commission's recommendations the Treaty of Rome was supplemented and amended, and the so-called Single European Act (SEA) came into force on July 1, 1987. One important legal and political result of the new legislation was that in order to make implementation of the single European market as quick and smooth as possible, they abandoned the formerly rigidly safeguarded principle of unanimity, and decision-making based on the majority principle was introduced.

In the interest of the single European market, the White Paper set the aim of *completely free movement of goods, services, capital and labour (citizens)*. These *'four freedoms'* were to ensure freedom of trade, free movement of labour, freedom to provide services and free choice of domicile, and free movement of money and capital. According to the White Paper, in order to create the single European market the various physical, technical and monetary (fiscal) barriers would have to be removed.

For the period 1985–1992 the EC laid down a detailed list of measures and timetable for their implementation (White Paper, Appendix, p. 135).

1.1. DISMANTLING THE PHYSICAL BARRIERS

Removal of physical barriers meant the abolition of national border controls. The White Paper basically envisaged the abolition of controls on the *movement of goods* at internal frontiers; later, with the coming into force of the Schengen Agreement, the framework for *free movement of persons* was established. After 1968, despite the removal of customs duties, control of the movement of goods at the Community's internal borders had to be retained for a number of reasons. In spite of the introduction of common external tariffs, the various countries applied different quantitative restrictions to external countries. Without examination of origin at the borders these would have been very easy to evade. Considerable differences between the various countries remained with regard to environmental, plant hygiene and veterinary regulations, as well as security norms. The preservation of border controls also fulfilled registration functions.

The single European market meant that after 1992 *quantitative restrictions* were applied *at Community level*, and with regard to external countries the various security, environmental and health regulations were standardized. New computerized methods of inspection and registration of the movement of goods were introduced, and responsibility for supplying data and checking the regulations passed to companies.

With the removal of border controls citizens could travel unrestrictedly within the Community without a passport; they were free to settle, study and work in any other member country. Citizens had equal rights to take advantage of certain social benefits in other countries (health services and education), and to enable this, attempts were made to harmonize social policies. From 1989 a common passport was introduced for travel outside the Community.

Controls on the movement of persons at internal borders were abolished with the coming into force of the *Schengen Agreement*. This was originally signed in 1985 by Germany, France and the Benelux countries. Its main aim was to eliminate controls at the Community's internal borders, to harmonize policies relating to visas, refugees and immigration, and to develop cooperation in policing. The treaty dealing with the implementation of the agreement was signed in 1990. In the early 1990s every EU country with the exception of Great Britain, Ireland and Denmark joined the agreement. It came into force in March 1995 with seven countries at first, but within a few years all the signatories were able to fulfil the obligations undertaken in the treaty and introduce the 'Schengen system'.

The Schengen countries standardized the regulations applied to citizens of non-Community countries (visa issuing practices, refugee laws, conditions of employment, etc.) and established the Schengen information system, which links every border crossing with a central computer database. With the Treaty of Amsterdam, which came into force on May 1, 1999, the Schengen regulations were incorporated into Community law, as a result of which after a 5-year transition period the EU is to form a common policy on immigration, refugee affairs and visas.

1.2. REMOVAL OF TECHNICAL BARRIERS

The abolition of technical barriers is designed to remove the major proportion of the remaining non-tariff trade barriers to cooperation, in order to achieve a real Community internal market. Among these, special attention is paid to the various national standards and regulations relating to products, the opening of the so-called 'state markets', and the deregulation of the services sphere.

With regard to the abolition of barriers, especially *standards and national regulations, three main methods* were recommended.

1. Compulsory *mutual recognition* of national standards and regulations, which means that "it is compulsory for all the countries of the Community to permit the entry and sale of all the goods legally produced and put on sale in all the other member countries". The 1978 decision of the European Court in the Cassis de Dijon case is cited as a precedent for 'mutual recognition'. What happened was that a German company, Rewe Zentral AG, wanted to import a French drink called Crème de Cassis into the FRG, but it turned out that because of its alcohol content it did not conform to the German regulations. The company applied to the European Court, which decided that the FRG had no right to prohibit the import of a product legally sold in France, unless this could be justified on health or consumer protection grounds, or by reference to unfair trading practices. On similar legal grounds the ban on sales of Community beers in the FRG was lifted; up till then this had been upheld by the regulations relating to 'the purity of the German national beer'. 'Mutual recognition' is considered one of the fundamental conceptual approaches in the development of the single European market, which enables many almost insoluble questions of technical and legal harmonization to be avoided, and facilitates the process of common legislation. Naturally the coexistence of as many as 15 different national standards or sets of regulations for a given product can cause great difficulties, but it is widely felt that the 'selection' or integration of these on the basis of the everyday interests of producers and consumers can be done automatically and quite easily. In consequence, 'selection' depends not on bureaucratic state regulations but on consumer preference. It must at once be said that this, the easiest of the three solutions, is the one that has been chosen for the great majority (about 80%) of products.

2. In certain areas with regard to standards and regulations *compulsory European harmonization and integration* are prescribed. The working out of standards at Community level has been in progress for a long time, but accelerated considerably with the creation of the single European market. In accordance with the so-called 'new approach', the characteristics of the uniform standards are formulated in the form of guidelines that define

the essential requirements. Precise technical specifications are worked out within the framework of the institutions responsible for matters concerning European standards. Standards have been integrated particularly in the areas of pharmaceuticals, engineering, chemicals, the electronics sectors producing high-technology goods, and telecommunications. Standardization is proceeding partly with a view to cost reduction (the advantages of economies of scale), and partly on the basis of consumer health protection and environmental considerations.[2]

3. *For the introduction of new standards and regulations, a compulsory Community notification procedure* is prescribed. Its aim is to prevent the creation of new technical and trade barriers in areas where standardization activity has remained within the national jurisdiction of the member countries.

After 1968 *freedom to take up employment* was allowed by the common market frameworks. This was possible without any great difficulty in the case of the simpler types of unskilled and skilled manual work, but with higher requirements in terms of professional qualifications and language skills increasingly great difficulties arose. In Western Europe – to a certain extent independently of common market measures – from the 1950s onwards enormous waves of foreign workers kept arriving. The main 'suppliers' of labour were the countries of the Mediterranean basin, while the recipients included non-EC countries like Sweden, Switzerland and Austria. Now it represented an advance, that over a broad area educational and professional qualifications and skills, including medical and certain engineering degrees, were *mutually recognized*. From then on, citizens could obtain professional qualifications in an educational institution (e.g. a university) in any other member country. Of course, liberalization did not solve the language problem. Clearly, without knowledge of the language no one can practise medicine in another country, or even find work as a commercial salesperson. For confidential positions, the possibility of excluding foreign citizens still remains.

In the framework of the 1992 measures determined steps were taken to *integrate the state procurement (public procurement) 'market'*. This represents

[2] According to the London management consultancy firm Ludwigsen Associates, for example, in 1987 the different national regulations and requirements relating to cars raised consumer prices in the Community by about 5.7%. The factors they list include such things as the differing national regulations concerning exhaust gases, and the strict requirements relating to flashing indicators on the sides and special wheel suspension in Italy, the reclining driver's seat and special rear lamps in the FRG, foglamps in Great Britain, and yellow headlight bulbs in France. It was no accident that the standardization proposals were received with unanimous enthusiasm by car manufacturers.

an enormous market, since state markets account for about 12% of the EU's GDP. According to estimates, in the EU member countries there are about 100,000 institutions with financial authority for procurement, and under the rules of the single market EU tenders have to be advertised. The number of such tenders advertised grew from 19,000 to 67,000 between 1988 and 1993.

Since 1977 – theoretically – for state purchases it has been compulsory in the Community to advertise tenders open to every company in the Community. Naturally the essence of this is that a national government or publicly financed institution cannot give priority – other conditions being equal – to a firm in its own country rather than one belonging to another member country. The fact is that, especially from the 1980s onwards, because of budgetary difficulties cheaper foreign suppliers were more frequently chosen, from motives of economy.

According to the new rules, tenders in this sphere are completely open as far as EU companies are concerned. They apply to all investment programs involving more than 5 million euros, and purchases worth more than 400 thousand euros (in the telecommunications sector the threshold is 600 thousand euros). According to estimates, annual savings by the countries of the Community as a result of these measures can amount to 20 billion euros (Cecchini 1988: 134). By opening the markets it was hoped to reduce state regulation and subventions. By 1990 state subsidies in the EU had fallen to 2% of GDP (*Financial Times,* March 7, 1994).

There has been dispute about the 'buy Europe' clause, which allows preference to be given to 'European tenders' as long as these do not cost more than 3% more than the best offer from a third country. Thus suppliers outside the EU will probably continue to be at a disadvantage in this sector of the market. Especially in telecommunications, aircraft manufacture and data processing, efforts are made to exclude foreign competition. According to American figures, overseas firms have secured only 2% of big public orders (*Foreign Policy,* No. 85, Winter 1991–92: 140).

In the EU it was the general opinion that the formerly protected nature of the state markets was to a large extent responsible for certain high technology sectors' lack of success in the world market. A typical example of this was the information technology and telecommunications industry. Because of differences in national standards, European companies manufactured, on average, three times as many types of the same product as their American rivals, and four times as many as the Japanese.

Liberalization of the market for services (transport, telecommunications, banking and insurance activities, etc.) required extremely complex and many-sided measures. When the program for the internal market was worked out, services accounted for almost 2/3 of the member countries' national product, while they produced less than 1/5 of export revenues, so it was clear that obstacles to the provision of services still existed among the member countries. In the field of services tariff-type barriers were less important; liberalization demanded mainly the abolition of restrictive legal prescriptions, and the harmonization of conditions and regulations (e.g. taxes).

Among services especial attention was devoted to *unification and integration of the money and capital markets*. In the framework of the common market, by the end of the 1960s capital flows connected with trade and direct investments had been liberalized. With regard to the plans for monetary integration, all financial and capital transactions (especially short-term and speculative ones) that might have a direct effect on exchange rates and monetary policy were excluded from the area of liberalization. In the interest of the single internal market, from March 1, 1987 the restrictions on the provision of commercial loans, the trading of unlisted securities and the sale of securities on other EC countries' stock exchanges were lifted. Within the framework of the program by 1990 all obstacles to the circulation of capital in the Community had been abolished; Spain and Ireland were granted a moratorium until 1992, and Portugal and Greece until 1995. As a result of complete deregulation, citizens can put their money in any other country's currency and banks, and can buy shares and raise loans there. On the other hand it is mainly in the commercial sphere that the insurance market has been opened up.

Acceptance of the principle of the single *licence* brought important changes, in the sense that once a bank or insurance company has obtained all the licences necessary for its operation, then without any further ado it can open branches in another member country and provide the services it is authorized to provide in its own country. This is the aspect of the single licence principle that makes it possible to settle freely in another member country. On the other hand the single licence makes it unnecessary to open branches, since freedom to provide services across borders is also guaranteed; that is, it is possible to provide services for a client in another member country without opening a branch there.

Liberalization had to be carried out in the markets for road and air transport and energy supply, as well as postal and telecommunications services. Since the deregulation of these sectors had serious legal and economic consequences, the opening of these markets to competition had to take place over a longer period. Deregulation of the road and air transport markets was implemented by the mid-1990s; in the other areas establishment of the legal conditions was generally completed by 1998. In most cases access to the network had to be provided; that is, the same conditions for use of the various networks had to be ensured for all service providers. These included equal conditions of the use of railway lines, access to the main telecommunications network, and the supply of electricity through the electrical power grid.

1.3. THE SINGLE MARKET AND TAX HARMONIZATION (REMOVAL OF FISCAL BARRIERS)

Financial (fiscal) barriers distort the conditions of competition mainly in the flow of goods and services. Obviously, different tax burdens or subventions can significantly alter the cost relations of the products concerned and have a decisive impact on their competitiveness. In the interest of the development of the internal market it was considered necessary to make fundamental changes particularly in the system of indirect taxation, above all by simplifying taxation, putting an end to all forms of double taxation, and equalizing tax burdens.

Turnover taxes chiefly affect the conditions of trade among the partners, while harmonization of corporate and capital gains taxes are important from the point of view of the free movement of capital, international company mergers and the single Community capital market.

As the first step in tax harmonization, *the changeover to a value-added tax (VAT)* took place in all the member countries by the end of the 1970s. VAT is a multi-level tax on value added, that is, turnover tax always has to be paid on that part of the value that in the production and distribution stages has been added to the total value of the product. The tax is paid by the retailer, and the level depends on how many hands the product has gone through before it is finished. The tax is always imposed only when the product changes owners. Ultimately the tax burden falls on the consumer.

The EC countries chose VAT principally because this type of turnover tax can best be reconciled with the effects of unrestricted, undistorted trade among the countries in a zone. As a non-cumulative tax, VAT is *'neutral' with regard to both the size of a company and the degree of specialization and cooperation*, and therefore from the point of view of its effect on the competitiveness of the various countries. The tax systems in which tax always had to be paid on the full production value in several steps led to significant tax accumulation in the areas of production and distribution, depending on the degree of specialization. This type of taxation favoured vertically integrated concerns, since within them it was possible to reduce the number of taxable end products. VAT, on the other hand, gave all products an equal chance in terms of tax burdens, regardless of whether they were produced by a small or a large firm.

VAT is considered *'an efficient regulator'*. That is, with VAT all the actors in the economy pay tax, and by changing the rate it is possible quickly to influence the whole economy. As a multi-level tax, VAT distributes the burdens more fairly among the different social groups, and by raising the rate just slightly the government can significantly increase its tax revenue. In the VAT framework, export can be effectively encouraged by means of the tax rebates given to exporters. The advantage of this system is that export can be subsidized in a way that does not conflict with the GATT/WTO rules. VAT can be an effective instrument with regard to outsiders, and can improve the balance of payments of the country concerned.

Even with a single rate of VAT, increased tax administration is involved, still it is seen as an advantage that it is one of the most efficient forms of taxation. Since payment of tax takes place with every sale, tax obligations can be clearly determined, and their fulfilment can be easily checked. With VAT tax fraud is more difficult. With it, taxing the non-producing sectors, especially services, can be made more uniform and comprehensible.

Thus in the first stage harmonization affected only the form of taxation, while considerable *differences* remained between the various countries in terms of *the number and levels of the rates applied*. This affected the price structure and the tax burdens on the various products, and was a source of differences in budget revenues. While apart from a 0% rate on exempted products Britain mainly used a flat rate of 15% and Denmark a rate of 22%, in France and Belgium the rate was 5–6%. In most countries the socially motivated concessionary rates were about 5–7%, but the maximum rates on certain products were set very high (38% in Italy, 36% in Greece, 33% in Spain and France, 25% in Belgium, and so on). According to the situation in 1992, the standard rate was 25% in Denmark and 21% in Ireland, but on the other hand only 14% in Germany and 13% in Spain.

In accordance with the recommendations of the White Paper it was intended that two rates of tax should be introduced. One was to be a preferential rate of 4–9%, while the other, the standard rate, was to be between 15% and 20%. In determining the bands, the experience gained in the US over several decades was taken into account: about 5 percentage points of difference could be allowed between the various states in turnover tax burdens on products, and they would still remain neutral from the point of view of trade.

In several respects the equalization of tax rates was a source of disputes. In certain cases *the price effects caused concern.* In Britain, for example, about 30% of goods were exempt (foodstuffs, children's clothes, books, etc.), that is, VAT was not payable on them. The recommended minimum rate of 4% would have caused price increases that could have resulted in social tensions. On the other hand, setting a uniform maximum rate would have caused considerable losses in terms of budget revenue in the countries with high rates. Moreover, the complete abolition of border controls between the countries resulted in 'redistribution' of tax revenues. In the absence of customs inspection the exemption of export between the countries (VAT rebate) was abolished, while in the importing countries it became impossible to separate internal and Community import inputs. The net exporting countries' budget revenues grew, while the opposite was the case in the net importing countries.

Finally, under the terms of the July 1992 agreement the EU decided to apply a uniform *minimum 'social' rate of 5% and a standard VAT rate of 15%,* with the exception of a few products, and to delay its introduction in certain cases. This meant that the 0–5% preferential rates remained on certain goods (in the case of the UK, retention of the zero rate for foodstuffs, heating fuels, transport and children's clothes was accepted). In practice a standard rate of 15–16% was introduced in every country except Denmark and Sweden, where the main rate was 25%.

There were similarly significant differences among the member countries with regard to *indirect taxes on consumption* (tobacco, alcoholic drinks, fuels, etc.) While in Italy, France the FRG, Spain and Portugal zero or practically negligible consumption taxes were levied on wine and beer, in Ireland the consumption tax on a litre of wine was 2.79 ECU and on a litre of beer 1.13 ECU, in Denmark 1.57 and 0.71 ECU, and in Britain 0.54 and 0.68 ECU respectively. Whereas in Italy, Ireland and Denmark petrol prices were high because of heavy consumption taxes, in Britain, Germany and Spain these taxes (and thus prices) were more moderate.

The plan for standardization of consumption taxes elicited especially fierce arguments. In the countries with low rates it would have caused certain barely perceptible price rises, while prices of alcoholic drinks would have dropped drastically in Ireland, Denmark and Great Britain. This would have had a painful effect on the budget, and conflicted with social and health considerations (restrictive taxation of drinks and tobacco). For the time being, minimum tax rates were introduced for these products.

2. SOME EFFECTS OF THE 1992 SINGLE EUROPEAN MARKET

In the framework of the single European market created in 1992, *a further qualitative step forward was taken in the direction of free trade and the development of a genuinely integrated market*:

– removal of the 'physical barriers' to trade and the flow of factors by the abolition of border formalities;

– reduction of structural and technical protectionism (linked with the quality or use value of the goods) through unification or mutual recognition of technical, security, health, environmental etc. regulations and standards;

– liberalization or harmonization of rules and regulations hindering trade in or the free flow of services;

– provision of the technical and social conditions for the free flow of labour (recognition of professional qualifications, social welfare entitlements, etc.);

– freedom of domicile and the establishment of certain Union citizenship rights (passport, voting rights, freedom of choice, etc.);

– complete freedom to carry on business activity in the partner countries;

– complete liberalization of capital flows (including 'speculative' capital);

– the further break-up of national market monopoly structures, mainly through the liberalization and Community regulation of state procurement (steps were taken earlier);

– further tax harmonization by standardization of VAT rates and indirect taxes (on energy, tobacco, alcohol – mainly by taxes on energy,

attempts are being made to reduce the differences in the tax burdens on an important factor of production).

At the same time, in many areas *the 'internal market' conditions,* like the national market ones, *reveal deficiencies*:

– in the period up to the introduction of the euro, because of the existence of the national currencies the market was not completely transparent; surplus costs and risks were associated with the use of the different currencies, but now this barrier has been removed;
– because of the differences between the national tax systems (corporation tax, profit and income taxes, etc.), despite the harmonization of turnover taxes relatively big differences between the countries still exist in public expenditure burdens;
– national wage-cost levels are no longer associated with different levels of productivity (artificial comparative wage advantages or wage disadvantages) because of differing tax and especially social security burdens;
– over a relatively wide area general competition-distorting and expenditure-distorting effects resulting from autonomous economic policies are noticeable; these may derive from national budget policies or from divergences in cyclical or structural policy in the widest sense;
– legal systems and legal regulations differ in the areas untouched by harmonization.

The plan for the single European market did not develop entirely in accordance with the originally determined timetable, but most of the measures were gradually adopted into the national legal systems and implemented. *Analysis of the effects* is not an easy task, since in the meantime the cyclical conditions have modified the conditions in several directions (the 1991–93 recession, the recovery in 1994–98, the international financial crisis of 1998–99, etc.). The measures connected with EMU have broadly affected the member countries' economies at every level, and many external factors have to be taken into account, which were not originally reckoned with. Nevertheless, some conclusions can certainly be drawn.

The single internal market established in 1992 *contributed greatly to the rapid transnationalization of company structures in Europe.* The measures carried out so far and the integration and opening-up that can be expected point in this direction. After 1990, as a result of the recession and the monetary crisis, the process slowed down, but at the end of 1993 it was still above the pre-1986 level. Up to the end of the 1980s it was concentrated mainly in industrial companies; in the 1990s consolidation took place chiefly in the service sector (banks, insurance companies, trading companies, etc.).

Large numbers of looser forms of company cooperation were developing. "On the assumption that many different national tastes in Europe will gradually blend, firms are also developing Eurobrands for 'Euro Consumers'. Luxury goods already fit the bill. But single marketeers hope also to tout such novelties as Euro-beers and Euro-wurst on Euro-satellite television. They run complex pan-European businesses, companies are hunting for multilingual European-minded managers" (*The Economist,* December 7, 1991). In the bigger deregulated market, intensified competition launched a new wave of restructuring. The increased emphasis on efficiency, adaptation, cost-cutting and competitiveness mainly affected sectors such as car manufacturing, electronics and the chemicals industry. On the basis of a survey by the Euro-Info Centre, which operates in the EU, it was particularly the companies that were prepared for the single European market that rapidly increased their sales in the partner countries, while reducing delivery times and costs. (European Commission 1994.) The gradual integration of the markets of Eastern Europe promises further opportunities; their structural adaptation may require new structures in the European division of labour.

The 1992 internal market *exercised a strong attraction on direct investment by external partners.* The chief investors were the EFTA countries, Japan and the United States. According to analysts, apart from the regulations of the 1992 single internal market this was also largely due to the fact that these countries were not included in the high technology programs (Esprit, etc.) and aggressive dumping procedures were used against them. According to BIS figures, the average volume of operating capital investment grew from $11.4 bn in the period 1975–1979 to $38.4 bn for 1985–89, and by 1990 had risen to $85.9 bn (Bank for International Settlements, 1991). In the 1990s there were some fluctuations, but capital inflow remained strong.

Despite fears of a 'fortress Europe', *with the single European market the EU became more open.* The 12 abolished 6,417 import restrictions of different kinds, and these were replaced by just a few Community quotas. Import documentation was made uniform, and the anti-dumping and anti-subvention procedures were simplified and speeded up. Countless analyses show that by becoming protectionist the single European market would have been disadvantageous to the EU as well.

The effects of the single European market *on macroeconomic performance* are difficult to judge. According to EU experts, 30% of the predicted effects had already been achieved by the time the program came into force. On the basis of the assumption that the single European market would materialize, as early as the second half of the 1980s there was an upswing in trade and investment, as a result of which relatively rapid growth (about 3.2% between 1986 and 1990) was achieved. According to calculations by the Commission in Brussels, the program increased the growth rate by about 0.4% annually after 1985.

The boom in the 1980s, at the same time, assisted the fulfilment of the program, particularly the implementation of unfavourable and unpopular measures and painful restructuring. Later, from the point of view of effects the main problem is seen to have been the fact that the actual establishment of the single European market in the early 1990s took place in crisis conditions, and therefore the real effects of the measures were distorted by the recession.

According to prior estimates, it was expected that as a result of the single market there would be an improvement in budgetary positions and payments balances, and that in the longer term about 1.8 million new jobs would be created. What happened was the opposite. From the end of the 1980s unemployment again rose to high levels, and was not brought down very much even during the upswing after 1994. Nevertheless, perhaps we can accept the view that without those measures the crisis could have been even more severe.

Trends in macroperformance were also significantly affected by the 1991 Maastricht decisions on monetary union. The Maastricht criteria strictly defined economic policy priorities and the use of economic instruments, which meant that the effects of the internal market created in 1992 could not evolve even in the long-term exactly in accordance with the original plans. "Even if the gains from completing the SEM are much less than the CECCHINI Report anticipates, the SEM has still proved to be enormously significant. For the plain fact is that the SEM was the centrepiece of the SEA; and the SEA is proving to be equally significant in the broadest sense. It is after all the SEA which helped to revitalize the Community: it has provided the springboard for the drive onwards the EMU and political union; it has helped to establish the Community as a major international economic actor; and it has exercised a magnetic effect on blocs such as EFTA and eastern Europe and key investors such as Japan" (SWANN 1993: 252–253).

While the general assumption is that fulfilment of the EMU convergence criteria restrained the rate of economic growth, the performance of the member countries improved with regard to inflation and their budgetary positions. The programs for the single market and monetary union had marked reciprocal effects on each other, and together determined the economic performance and integration processes of the 1990s.

3. THE STATE OF THE SINGLE MARKET AND FURTHER TASKS

2002 represents a turning-point in the further development of the single market, not only because implementation of measures aimed at completion of the internal market has been going on for a decade, but also because the euro has now become a reality and the negotiations on EU enlargement are nearing their conclusion. The latter development, however, means that considerable expansion of the internal market is due to take place soon.

Today 19 million firms can operate freely in the EU's internal market, and 377 million citizens have the possibility of living, working or studying in another member country. Within the past decade the most important barriers have been removed, but in many areas further measures still need to be taken. In order to achieve the aim set by the European Council in Lisbon – that Europe should become the world's most competitive and dynamic knowledge-based economy, capable of sustainable economic growth, the creation of more and better jobs, and stronger social cohesion – significant structural reforms are required. The frameworks for these can only be created by a successfully operating internal market (European Commission, 1999).

In the interest of the future successful functioning of the internal market, the EU will have to deal with some crucially important questions:

- promotion of the further integration of markets;
- improvement of the business environment;
- satisfaction of citizens' needs;
- preparation for enlargement.

3.1. FURTHER INTEGRATION OF MARKETS

In important sectors the single market still remains fragmented, though in these sectors increased market integration would result in significant benefits. Above all, further integration is needed in the network sectors and the financial sector, since they form the basis of a fully integrated internal market (European Commission, 2002: 9).

At the Barcelona session of the European Council the leaders of the member countries committed themselves to ensuring that in the area of *energy supply*, from 2004 not only large consumers but all non-household consumers will be able to choose freely the supplier from whom they obtain electricity and gas. It is very important that this commitment should now be embodied in concrete decisions. Market opening will become a reality only if the existing networks are developed and integration of the energy networks continues. In this connection, further development of the trans-European energy networks will play a particularly important part.

An integrated financial sector is undoubtedly an indispensable element in sustainable growth and the improvement of competitiveness. Such an integrated financial sector could bring surplus GDP growth of 0.5–0.7% annually (Zentrum für Europäische Wirtschaftsforschung, 2001). *Complete integration of the European securities markets and the financial services associated with them* could actually be achieved within a few years through implementation of the objectives defined in *the Lámfalussy report*.

Another area where progress is needed is the *public procurement market*. The proportion of publicly advertised procurement has gradually increased in recent years, but is still only about 15%. The proportion of contracts for the purchase of goods and services from other member countries is still below 2% (European Commission, 2002: 10). Above all, modernization of the legal frameworks is essential, because of the spread of new purchasing techniques and technologies (e.g. electronic purchasing).

In the area of the development of *uniform European standards*, serious problems exist. In some areas because of the fragmented nature of the market it has not taken place, even though the necessary Community legislation is in place. This is the situation with the guidelines laid down in the spirit of the new approach, in the case of the requirements set for products. It still takes on average 8 years for a new European standard to be developed. Moreover, in some key sectors such as construction industry products and engineering a real internal market has not developed: in the building industry the development of 150 harmonized standards has not yet been completed, and in engineering the number is 450 (European Commission, 2002: 11).

3.2. IMPROVEMENT OF THE BUSINESS ENVIRONMENT

Measures aimed at the creation of integrated markets will have the desired results only if an enterprise-friendly environment develops, which supports creative, dynamic businesses. To this end, progress is required in several areas.

Above all, improvement of the tax conditions within the EU deserves particular attention. The 'tax package' should help to eliminate obstacles caused by taxation, and end unfair tax competition. In the area of *corporation tax,* it is the definite opinion of the Commission that in the long-term, with regard to activities carried on within the Union, companies should be taxed on a consolidated corporation tax base. This is the only solution that will help to change the situation created by the present costly and inefficient practice. At present companies are taxed under 15 different tax regulation systems.

An important area of jurisdiction of the member states is that of regulation relating to *the establishment of enterprises.* Encouragement of entrepreneurial activity begins with making it simpler and cheaper to set up a new business. Many studies point out that in this area progress has been made in every member country, yet it is still not enough. Clear Union expectations should be developed, by determining concrete quantitative criteria. The Commission's present aim is to persuade the member countries to accept that establishment of a limited liability company should be possible within 18 working days and at a cost of not more than 213 euros, and that minimum primary capital should not exceed 3,000 euros (European Commission, 2002: 14).

An important regulatory question concerns the acceptance of *patent regulation at European level.* At present 86% of European companies regard the patent system as inadequate to protect their inventions and intellectual property rights. Obviously this hinders the innovation process, especially in rapidly developing sectors such as software innovation, the life sciences and biotechnology (European Commission, 2001). When the role of research and development activity is important, indeed decisive, in improving Europe's competitiveness, the creation of Community patent laws is absolutely essential.

3.3. SATISFYING CITIZENS' NEEDS

Market integration and improvement of the business environment are important aims in themselves, but they all contribute to the broader aim that the single market should bring palpable benefits for the citizens. When there is competition among retailers, they try to keep prices down, respond quickly to changing demand, and try to satisfy the consumer. Price differences between the various member countries have moderated in the past decade, but convergence has slowed recently. The explanation probably lies in the differing regulatory environment.

Experience has so far shown that in the areas where market opening has taken place, the citizens have benefited from lower prices and better-quality services. At the same time, wider possibilities of choice and more favourable prices have generally not jeopardized the consumers' safety or health. The free flow of goods and services has been accompanied by the approximation of *quality-assurance systems*. Measures to strengthen competition and increase consumer confidence should reinforce each other. The present level of informal cooperation among *consumer protection institutions* is inadequate.

To satisfy citizens' needs, further measures in the area of *environment protection and social policy* are required. The Commission has drawn up a plan for the introduction of a European health card, which would simplify the provision of treatment in another member country. To make it easier to work and take up residence in another country, modification and simplification of the current regulations relating to the coordination of the social security systems is another essential task.

3.4. PREPARATION FOR ENLARGEMENT

The conclusion of accession negotiations with the most thoroughly prepared countries is expected at the end of 2002. In the Country reports for 2001 the Commission envisaged the possibility that as many as 10 candidate countries might be admitted. Talks on the 5 chapters referring to the internal market have been completed with all 10 countries. The internal market is one of the clearly perceptible areas where it will immediately become clear whether a new member country is really ready, in practice as well as in theory, for integration.

The EU has several times called attention to the fact that the candidate countries' administrative infrastructure has to be adapted and strengthened so as to be able to apply the regulations relating to the internal market. The administrative capacity of the would-be members is rather weak in many areas. Further progress is necessary in the areas of *standardization, mutual recognition of degrees, public procurement and the problems of money-laundering*. The EU is providing assistance for the necessary changes, the main form of which is its *twinning programs*. In the twinning framework, experts from the corresponding institutions assess the existing situation in the candidate country and formulate concrete recommendations with regard to its functioning. The main aim is that the competent authorities' experts should cooperate with and understand one another, thus strengthening mutual confidence.

One important task is to ensure that every new member country *becomes a full, active member of the European institutions responsible for standards*. The conditions of membership of the CEN and CENELEC include adoption of at least 80% of the harmonized standards, acceptance of these organizations' policy on intellectual property rights, and the creation of a legal framework that defines standardization as a voluntary, non-governmental activity.

REFERENCES

Bank for International Settlements (1991) Annual Report. Basle.

CECCHINI, P. (1988) *Europe '92*. Nomos Verlag, Baden-Baden.

European Commission (1985) Completing the Internal Market. COM (85) 310 final.

European Commission (1994) Frontier-free Europe. *Monthly Newsletter*, April 1994.

European Commission (1999) Internal Market Strategy Communication. COM (1999) 624 final, 24 November 1999. Brussels.

European Commission (2001) Toward a Strategic Vision of Life Sciences and Biotechnology. Consultation Document. COM (2001) final. 4 September 2001.

European Commission (2002) 2002 Review of the Internal Market Strategy. COM (2002) 171 final. 11 April 2002. Brussels.

SWANN, N. D. (ed.) (1993) *The Single European Market and Beyond. A Study of the Wider Implications of the Single European Act*. Routledge, London

Zentrum für Europäische Wirtschaftsforschung (2001) Report on the benefits of a working retail market for financial services. Hamburg.

II.

ECONOMIC AND MONETARY UNION

1. THE BEGINNINGS OF MONETARY INTEGRATION IN EUROPE

1.1. FIRST EXPERIMENTS IN MONETARY INTEGRATION

In the first phase of EC integration monetary questions received only limited attention. Monetary conditions were regarded as important mainly from the point of view of exchange rate stability and the smooth functioning of the common market. Stable (if possible, fixed) exchange rates became an urgent priority from the second half of the 1960s, in connection with the uniform common prices accepted within the framework of the common agricultural policy.

In the interest of financial cooperation, the Monetary Commission was set up, but its functions were mainly limited to consultations. Monetary policy remained the responsibility of the national governments, and right up to the end of the 1960s the BRETTON WOODS exchange rate system operated by the IMF was considered an adequate framework for cooperation and stability.

As early as 1962 the Commission pledged itself to economic and monetary union, and the first plans were drawn up at the end of the 1960s (the BARRE plan in 1968, the WERNER plan in 1970). The main reason was the growing crisis in the BRETTON WOODS system, though the conviction was already gaining ground that the monetary sphere could not be omitted from market and complete economic integration.

Early in 1971, on the basis of the WERNER plan the *program for economic and monetary union* was launched, which was intended to be implemented by 1980. The plan was based on general theoretical assumptions about monetary union ("irreversible" currency convertibility, fixing of exchange rates, economic policy coordination and common monetary funds), and originally three stages were envisaged. The aim was the establishment of a common currency by the 1980 deadline.

In the Council of Ministers concrete agreements with regard to monetary union were reached in February 1971 only in connection with the first phase. The first phase ran from January 1, 1971 to December 31, 1973, and as the first step the band within which exchange rates were allowed to float in relation to one another was narrowed from the +/– 1% valid in the IMF to +/– 0.6%. In February 1970 a $2 bn short-term support fund was set up, and from 1971 a certain degree of economic policy coordination was agreed on.

From the EC point of view it was unfortunate that 1971 was the year of the spectacular collapse of the BRETTON WOODS-based international monetary system. In the years that followed, monetary cooperation was limited to crisis management, and monetary union no longer figured on the agenda.

As early as 1971 a number of decisions were taken in the interest of stabilizing the international monetary system. One of the most important was the so-called Smithsonian Agreement in December, which for the IMF countries broadened the floating exchange rate band from +/– 1% to +/– 4.5%. On the basis of this, in March 1972 the EC Council of Ministers again declared itself in favour of gradual stabilization of exchange rates, and narrowed from +/– 4.5% to +/– 2.25% the band within which exchange rates could float in relation to one another. Thus the "snake in the tunnel" came into being, which meant the narrower EC currency snake floated in the wider band in relation to the dollar. The March 1972 decisions were also approved by the countries seeking admission (Great Britain, Ireland and Denmark).

The 1973 oil crisis gave a further significant boost to the inflationary processes and to a large extent destabilized the member countries' balance of payments. Thus monetary union based on a system of fixed exchange rates became completely unrealistic in the given world economic circumstances.

With these negative external effects, the Community's internal political cohesion was not strong enough for the implementation of monetary union. The main reason was not the failure of the plans for political integration (a European Union), but rather the fact that the various governments had reacted to the crisis of the early 1970s with quite different economic policies. Ultimately only Germany, the Benelux countries, Switzerland and Austria had decided on strongly anti-inflationary policies, while the other countries (more or less irrespective of whether or not they were members of the EC) had sought a combination of monetary and budgetary policies for weathering the crisis. In economic policies and economic performance they diverged widely, owing largely to their differences in national policies but also in their social interest relations and structures.

At the beginning of the 1970s it appeared that the negative effects, which were present in varying degrees, would prove temporary. In any case, the various countries differed in their readiness to undertake the social costs of adaptation. Thus the conditions did not yet exist for effective macroeconomic policy coordination at community level.

1.2. THE EUROPEAN MONETARY SYSTEM – EMS

Monetary integration in the EC was resurrected in March 1979, with the creation of the so-called European Monetary System (EMS). Its chief declared aim was the creation of a "zone of monetary stability".

The central purpose of the EMS continued to be stabilization of the currency exchange rates of the member countries; in practice, it was intended that every member country should be included in the currency snake. The Exchange Rate Mechanism (ERM)[1] set out from so-called central parity, which was bilaterally established by the central banks for every currency.

The EMS was characterized by *bilateral setting and regulation of currency exchange rates*. On the one hand, floating bands for exchange rates in the framework of a so-called *parity grid* were established bilaterally for every currency. The band was set at +/– 2.25% for the so-called central currencies that had belonged to or joined the former currency snake. Within the framework of the system it permitted a maximum floating range between 2.25% and 4.5% depending on the situation of the various currencies, downwards compared with the strongest currency and upwards compared with the weakest one. For so-called external currencies (originally this referred to the Italian lira), the band was +/– 6%, similarly in

[1] Later, after the introduction of EMU it became known as "ERM 1".

relation to the strongest and the weakest currency. Thus the maximum floating range for the Italian lira was 9.75% (subtracting from 12% the maximum possible 2.25% between the strongest and the weakest currency).

In the event of floating the exchange rate out of the band, it was compulsory for the central banks concerned to intervene. Automatic intervention would take place in the currencies of the countries involved, and the degree of intervention was unlimited. In addition to market intervention, financial policy and other economic policy measures could be taken (interest rate changes).

An important new development in the EMS was the establishment of the European Currency Unit – ECU. Formally the ECU was identical with the European Unit of Account (EUA) used earlier (when it came into being, 1 ECU = $1.31). (Before 1971, one EUA = $1.) In fact it was a basket of currencies comprising the national currencies, weighted in accordance with the member countries' economic (and trading) power. In the ECU basket every currency was represented, even those that had remained outside exchange rate stabilization. The weightings were reviewed every five years. The fixing of the last basket before the EMU program began was carried out on September 21, 1989.[2] Parallel with the birth of the European Union, on November 1, 1993 the ECU basket was frozen in its September 1989 composition. The basket remained in effect until the ECU was replaced by the Union's single currency. In the private sphere it was often referred to as the ecu.

The other direction of exchange-rate stabilization was linked to the ECU. The ECU's daily exchange rate could also float in a band of +/– 2.25%, which was regarded as an exchange rate divergence indicator. From the point of view of exchange rate intervention the so-called divergence threshold was particularly important; this was reached already at 75% of the band. If a currency went over the "threshold", the government of the country in question was supposed to intervene in the currency market. In contrast to the compulsory intervention in the parity grid, here such action was conditional. The role of floating in relation to the ECU was therefore rather that of a warning system (a "rattlesnake").

[2] The percentage weights of the national currencies at that time in the ECU basket: DM – 30.53; FFr – 19.43; HFl – 9.54; BFr – 7.83; LIt – 9.92; DKr – 2.53; Ir£ – 1.12; UK£ – 12.06; Dr – 0.77; Pta – 5.18; Esc – 0.78.

Originally it was prescribed that within two years the European Monetary Fund should be established, and the ECU should be used unlimitedly as a reserve instrument for maintaining monetary stability. In the case of the EMS the plans for institutional reform were not implemented.

Within the EMS framework the member countries formed a 3-month collective reserve in the form of revolving swaps, amounting to a maximum of 20% of their gold and dollar reserves. Against the collective reserve the European Monetary Cooperation Fund (EMCF) issued ECUs, and these were used in transactions between the central banks. In addition to the former short- and medium-term loan possibilities, in the EC currencies so-called "very short-term credit facilities" (VSCF) were available in limited amounts to the various central banks through the EMCF in the interest of interventions. To promote greater economic convergence the economically weaker countries could receive subsidized credits through the European Investment Bank (EIB). Within the framework of the EMS in protecting exchange rates economic policy interventions and coordination took place, with which the EU went the farthest compared to every international financial institution.

Over the years, the international monetary functions of the ECU gradually expanded. Compared with earlier units of account it was more than simply an accounting unit; as a currency basket it was to become the basis of the EU's common currency. *It was not legal tender,* but despite this it became more and more widely used. With the liberalization of the capital markets after 1990 most of the member countries lifted the restrictions relating to currency markets which had prevented the ECU from becoming *a special parallel currency,* and had hindered the spread of its use in the internal market of the EU countries (e.g. Germany's currency rules were modified as early as June 1987, as a result of which German residents were allowed to open ECU accounts and receive ECU loans).

From the beginning the member countries used the ECU for accounting and lending among their central banks (as an *inter-state means of payment*). The common budget was drawn up in ECUs, and inward and outward payments were formally made in ECUs.

From the 1980s its use as a loan among commercial banks expanded, and it gradually developed into one of the elements of the European currency and bond market *(a real means of payment)*. The process accelerated particularly after the announcement of the plans for monetary union.

The ECU was used in transactions relating to exchange-rate stability (as an *intervention instrument*). Besides, the national gold and currency reserves were denominated in ECU, it constantly appeared and steadily accumulated in the accounts of the member countries' central banks (as a *special reserve instrument*). The ECU was most popular as a store of value, since as a currency basket it was ideal for eliminating currency risks.

From the mid-1980s commercial transactions were growingly carried out and accounts were kept in ECUs. Several transnational companies used the ECU in their internal accounting (transfer prices). In the private sphere the ECU was preferred as a means for investment and financing, and was less used for transactions. Mainly in Italy and France the ECU was used in export and import invoicing. Thus the ECU, to a limited extent, acted as a *means of exchange*, fulfilling the most basic functions of money.

From the outset the ECU was a *collective measuring instrument* for expressing the parity of national currencies and exchange-rate differences *(an exchange-rate indicator)*. In connection with commercial transactions world prices expressed in ECUs began to be used, enabling the ECU in a limited way to measure price movements. It was not used in the consumer market; consumer prices in ECUs did not exist. Union-level statistics were expressed in ECUs.

The ECU existed in bank accounts, but not in the form of cash or coins. In the private consumer sphere its use in credit card form was widespread. Gradually the ECU acquired the characteristics and status of an independent currency, but without being a legal tender.

From the point of view of the development of the EMS, the Nyborg–Basel Agreement of September 1987 was an important step towards reform; it introduced intra-marginal interventions, that is, central banks intervened before currencies reached their limits. The agreement expanded cooperation in the field of short-term interest rates, use of the ECU and the EMS short-term, automatically available credit facilities (VSCF). The member countries undertook an obligation to refrain from altering parity, which was successfully maintained for five years until September 1992.

After 1987 there was much talk of a "new EMS". This represented a transition between the "old EMS" (variable parities and capital restrictions) and monetary union. Parities were more or less fixed and capital movement was free, while monetary policies were formally decentralized. After functioning for five years, the "new EMS" collapsed in September 1992.

From the beginning, participation of all the member countries in the EMS was not achieved. For a long time Great Britain remained outside the exchange-rate stabilization system, and it joined only in October 1990 (with a 6% band). The British feared for the role of the pound as a reserve and petro-currency, and the liberal-minded British government was reluctant to commit itself to the necessary intervention obligations. From time to time the Conservative government tried to use entry to the ERM as a political card. In June 1989 Spain and in April 1992 Portugal joined the ERM (with a 6% floating band), while Italy went over to a narrower, 2.25% band in January 1990. Greece did not join the ERM.

As a result of the financial crisis in September 1992 Great Britain and Italy left the EMS for an indefinite period, while the currencies of Spain, Portugal and Ireland were devalued. From August 1993 the 2.25% *bands were widened to +/– 15%*, the narrower band remaining in force only between the German mark and the Dutch guilder. In the opinion of some, this in practice represented the collapse of the ERM; others emphasized the possibilities of more flexible adjustment (the "soft EMS"). After a few months of fluctuation, from the beginning of 1994 exchange rates stabilized more or less in the region of the narrower band. The international financial crises of 1997–98 did not really threaten the functioning of the EMS. After 1999, with the coming into force of the third phase of EMU, the EMS in its modified form was limited to the relation between the euro-zone and the countries that remained outside it.

1.3. THE EMS AND "EXTERNAL" MONETARISM

From the end of the 1970s *monetarist principles* predominated in the economic policy of more and more governments. This greatly influenced *the economic policy role of the European Monetary System.* Many came to believe that economic policies within the EMS could implement monetarist principles more decisively and effectively through exchange-rate stabilization than through regulation of the internal money supply. This applied particularly to the post-1987 "new EMS". In this spirit, NIGEL LAWSON, a former British Chancellor of the Exchequer, argued as follows: "It is, I think, nowadays widely recognised that the suppression of inflation requires firm monetary discipline. In theory, that discipline can be either internally based, through control of the domestic monetary aggregates, or externally, through control of the exchange rate. Historically, we have tended to follow the external route, whether via the gold standard, notably in the period up to the first world war, or via the dollar standard, during the period following the second world war. Today, when financial deregulation and the globalisation of financial markets have made the domestic monetary aggregates an especially unreliable guide, an external discipline, should there be one readily available, is clearly preferable" (*Financial Times*, October 8, 1990). This *form of monetary discipline linked to external (stable) exchange rates is called "external monetarism"*. It was generally believed that in the framework of monetary integration, particularly in countries where inflation is rising rapidly, the fixing of exchange rates can be a tougher and more efficient tool than national money targets.

In the second half of the 1980s, external monetarism became increasingly characteristic of the monetary policy of European governments. After 1987, through the fixing of central parities, *it was achieved by tying them to the low-inflation German mark*. The mark, as a leading currency, had an important disciplinary function. It was recognition of the possibilities latent in external monetarism that explained the October 1990 decision of the Thatcher government, otherwise opposed to closer monetary integration, to commit itself to joining the ERM. It had become clear that effective monetarist economic policy does not work in the traditional way.

The switch to the international version of monetarist doctrine corresponded to microlevel business interests as well. "One reason for the shift, widely held in the business community, was the view that exchange rate stability against the country's most important trading partners was a good in itself. Another was that it would be better to tie the UK to the pragmatic monetarism of the Bundesbank than to attempt to stabilise the British economy directly" (*Financial Times*, October 4, 1991).

Opponents of exchange-rate fixing call to mind the negative experiences of the 1930s. In the literature on the history of economics the "Great Depression" of 1929–33 is attributed to the fixing of rates to gold or a strong currency, and to the rigidity of exchange rates. In 1925 the dollar–pound sterling exchange rate was fixed on a similar basis, resulting in the mining crisis, a wave of strikes and a colossal rate of unemployment. When the pound was devalued in 1931, and interest rates were reduced, years of prosperity followed. This did not take place in the so-called "gold bloc" countries (Belgium, France, Holland, Switzerland and Poland), with the result that the recession lasted longer and recovery was delayed until 1935–36, when currency devaluation could not be avoided in those countries either.

Many warn about the experience of the British government's "stop-go" policy after the Second World War (cyclical restraint of economic growth in the interest of balance of payments and exchange-rate stability), which because of insistence on an unrealistically high exchange rate for the pound significantly hampered development of the British economy in comparison with its competitors. After 1990 this argument again gained strength, since it was clear that exchange-rate stability had to be paid for with high interest rates and recession. Indeed, the case of Great Britain proves that in the countries that left the ERM in September 1992 recovery began in 1993, while every country that clung to the narrow-band ERM produced negative growth. The same could be observed in the case of Italy and Spain; in the latter, between September 1992 and the end of 1993 the three devaluations of the peseta clearly contributed to an improvement in competitiveness and the recovery.

According to others, the parallels drawn with the 1930s are false, because at that time cooperation between the world economy actors was missing, and the degree of integration was significantly lower. In that period not even minimal collaboration and coordination among the central banks was achieved. Today the situation is different. As ALBERTO GIOVANNINI argued: "The single currency designed at Maastricht is superior to the interwar gold standard and to the BRETTON WOODS regime for a simple reason: it removes monetary policy from the attempts of national governments to exploit it for temporary advantage at the expense of their neighbours" (*The Economist,* July 11, 1992: 6). The events of September 1992 seemed to contradict this.

All in all, the experiences of the 1980s undoubtedly showed that it was no longer possible to achieve better economic performance with more flexible exchange rates. Inflationary effects were not accompanied by higher growth or improved performance in terms of employment. The example of the ERM countries indeed proved that the sacrifices of adaptation after a certain time reaped their reward, and from the end of the 1980s, with low inflation, these countries were capable of more rapid growth.

Thus the EMS assisted governments' anti-inflation policies, and had a disciplinary effect on inflationary wage demands. Fears that the huge amount of money put into circulation to protect exchange rates had inflationary effects cannot really be justified. It obliged governments to exercise greater discipline in their monetary and budget policy. The EMS had a beneficial effect on "expectations" (about exchange rates, inflation and interest rates), which had a stabilizing effect with regard to speculation. The disturbing effects of the recession at the beginning of the 1990s and the September 1992 currency crisis only *strengthened the arguments in favour of monetary integration.*

It can be interpreted as a positive effect of the EMS that "there is more than circumstantial evidence to indicate that participation in the exchange rate mechanism served, at least for a large part of the period under consideration, as an important additional instrument in the fight against inflation; and this seems to be particularly true of France, Italy and Ireland. Participation in the ERM acted as an external constraint on domestic monetary policies, while the exchange rate has also been used, as an instrument of disinflation" (TSOUKALIS 1993: 195). These countries "tied their hands to the DM anchor", and this proved beneficial for them (GIAVAZZI and PAGANO 1988).

From the end of the 1970s the EMS satisfied real needs and fulfilled important functions. It was in every country's interest to curb extreme fluctuations in exchange rates and stabilize the currency markets. Every country regarded the EMS as a means of stabilizing the prospects for investment and profit and accelerating economic growth. Adaptation to the changed conditions in the world economy meant giving priority to structural and technological modernization of the community economy, and every member country recognized the importance in this of a stable monetary integration background. The EMS undoubtedly *did contribute to monetary stability*. It proved to be a relatively flexible construction, with which even very serious crises were successfully weathered, since by adjusting the central parities it was possible to prevent the collapse of the parity grid.

The EMS strengthened the "cooperative" behaviour among governments in economic policy. In the absence of coordination, governments can easily engage in competitive devaluation or upward revaluation, which can cause relatively greater production losses in the course of their anti-inflationary efforts, or boosting production may lead to higher inflation, than if they were to cooperate. "The EMS has the merit of limiting, or removing, such inefficiencies resulting from non-cooperative use of national policy instruments" (THYGESEN 1989: 9).

2. ECONOMIC AND MONETARY UNION – EMU IN EU

2.1. THE THEORETICAL BASES OF ECONOMIC AND MONETARY UNION

From the 1990s with the launching of *Economic and Monetary Union* the European integration process *entered a qualitatively new phase.* Customs union, the common market and single market represented liberalization ("negative integration"), that is, the complete opening of markets to one another. Even customs union and the single market required certain common policies (chiefly competition and commercial policies), but these mainly served to ensure the normal functioning of the market. Economic union meant qualitatively more, since the establishment of new institutions and economic policies was required ("positive integration"), and the reallocation of former functions to union level. *Economic union* goes beyond the common or single market and implements comprehensive integration over a wide range of economic policies.

The post-war literature on integration did not clearly define economic union. The concept was always understood to include the common market, which BÉLA BALASSA supplemented with certain "economic policy harmonization" for the sake of "elimination of discrimination" (BALASSA 1962).

In the wider sense, economic union involves three main stages of economic policy integration:

– *Unification and harmonization of economic policies,* a typical example of which is represented by value-added tax (VAT). Unification of economic policies means that identical economic policy forms, mechanisms and solutions are applied, but the participating countries retain their autonomy in economic policy.

– *Economic policy harmonization* can be defined as concerted action in selecting economic policy aims and the means for implementing them. Prior to EMU this included certain, but weak conjuncture policy coordinations, and exchange rate interventions, in the framework of EMU. With economic policy coordination, national sovereignty and autonomy are to a certain extent restricted.

– The "highest level" of economic policy integration is represented by community-level unification of national economic policies (community, "common" or union policies). The first areas of *common policies* were the common competition policy, common commercial policy and common agricultural policy. Later, from the 1980s the single market was regarded as the basis of economic union, and economic union meant the necessary policies and institutions for the smooth operation of the single market (PELKMANS 1997: 296).

European integration theory links economic union to monetary integration, a central element of which is *the introduction or creation* of a *"common"* or *single currency*. Economic union thereby extends to monetary union. The common currency leads to the raising of monetary policy to community level. The functions of the union are thus mainly economic; as J. PELKMANS states, they are directed towards the achievement of "efficiency" and "stabilization" (PELKMANS 1997: 296). In the EU many elements of economic union had already been created (for example, the common agricultural policy), but EMU meant the full completion of these.

Even the very first forms of market integration (customs union, common market, single market) had multi-directional monetary implications. In the customs union from the beginning maintenance of equilibrium in the balance of payments and "exchange-rate stability" (if need be, fixing) were regarded as important conditions, since in principle there was a possibility that after the removal of customs tariffs, their role could be replaced by exchange-rate manipulations. In the framework of the common market the liberalization of capital flows indicated the necessity of eliminating exchange-rate interventions, but in most of the member countries certain restrictions on (mainly speculative) capital movements were permitted, to protect the balance of payments. With the single market, the need to guarantee the stability of exchange rates was more pressing, since in conditions of complete capital liberalization this was no longer easy to achieve. There is extensive literature dealing with the idea that monetary integration follows logically from the single market, but the two were not necessarily linked on the basis merely of exchange-rate stabilization. Ultimately it was the common or single currency that represented the final "fixing" of exchange rates.

Fundamental strategic and political considerations were always bound up with the plans for monetary union. Monetary union and particularly a common or single currency were obviously inconceivable without a wide range of institutional and regulatory reforms, and ultimately without *political integration*. The common currency may be a means of achieving the aim of political union. In giving up their national currency, the participating countries lose one of the main symbols and attributes of national independence.

The question of whether political union necessarily follows from EMU is widely debated. It is an indisputable fact that from the outset, the plans for economic and monetary union were closely linked with aspirations to political union in the EU. "Money was also a means to an end, and the end was the political union. This function of monetary union was widely recognized and aptly summarized by the French: 'la voie royal vers l'union politique'" (TSOUKALIS 1991: 160). The Germans and others saw an urgent need for monetary union to counterbalance the excessive weight and dominance of Germany within the European Union. As HELMUT SCHMIDT, the former German Chancellor put it: "Unless the D-Mark is replaced by a single European currency, the German currency will one day be 'overwhelmingly strong'. This would eventually make the Germans the 'masters' of the European Community – a position which would rebound on Germany by making it vulnerable to 'coalitions' of European states formed to curb its strength" (*Financial Times,* September 9, 1993).

From the first, the implementation of monetary union was envisaged on the basis of *the following main principles:*

– Full convertibility of the member countries' currencies, as a logical concomitant of the freeing of capital flows.

– "Complete and irreversible fixing" of exchange rates relative to each other, on the basis of which a common or single currency could be created.

– Creation of monetary reserve funds for balance of payments stabilization.

– Coordination of monetary and economic policies and, where necessary, community economic policy action and the establishment of (monetary policy) mechanisms.

Unlimited convertibility and strictly and irrevocably fixed exchange rates were considered necessary partly in order to eliminate all market restrictions. Apart from their stabilizing role, it was much more important that they were seen as the road leading to a common currency within the union. For if currencies are fully convertible and their exchange rates are fixed, then all the currencies become equal in value (at a certain rate). After this, the creation of a common currency, whether alongside or in place of the national currencies, is seen as merely a technical question.

As a result of the development of economic and monetary union *fundamental changes take place in the operating mechanisms of the economy.* With a common or single currency *all possibility of changes in nominal exchange rates disappears*, whereby *national macroeconomic policy loses an important, autonomous means of adaptation*. With complete liberalization of capital flows, governments cannot make use of capital restriction measures either. Determination of interest rates becomes the responsibility of the European Central Bank.

The exchange rate is a special type of price mechanism that serves to bring the different national economies into equilibrium, and to equalize price levels. This may operate as a market automatism (equilibrium exchange rate), but in recent decades it has been actively used by governments as an instrument, since they could use devaluation to compensate for a decline in competitiveness. Exchange-rate corrections, therefore, could be used directly to counterbalance comparative cost disadvantages. With devaluation profitability improved, and the producer was able to stay in the market. But with devaluation ultimately real incomes decreased, though gradually and less painfully. Obviously, if exchange rates are "irreversibly" fixed, and exchange rate mechanisms disappear, then problems of equilibrium arise in a modified form, and handling them requires new forms and methods.

With the elimination of the possibility of exchange rate corrections, the most important element of the changes is that maintenance of competitiveness finally becomes directly dependent on the *flexibility of prices and wages*. This leads to fundamental changes in the operating mechanisms of the macroeconomy, and macrolevel economic policies are confronted with new requirements.

At the same time, the literature promoting EMU stressed already from the beginning, that the assumed effect of exchange-rate changes had so far been somewhat doubtful.

The limited effectiveness of the exchange-rate correction mechanisms was pointed out in critiques of neoclassical equilibrium theories. KEYNES and his followers agreed that devaluation policy does not solve problems of equilibrium, and does not bring lasting results from the point of view of competitiveness. Devaluation can only temporarily improve competitiveness, and the economy may get into a harmful spiral of devaluation and inflation, which in the long-term adversely affects the country's position in the world economy. If a country devalues, "it not only makes its exports cheaper, but it makes its imports more expensive. Its costs rise. If wage bargainers react by pushing up pay settlements, it may not be long before the rise in the level of domestic costs and prices has eroded the initial gain from the devaluation. Devaluation makes a country cheaper for a time, but it also pushes up inflation. It is thus more like postponing an adjustment than actually making it" (EMERSON and HUHNE 1991: 13). Devaluation can genuinely improve competitiveness only if the increase in real wages is less than the increase in producer prices and productivity.

In the last few years the liberalization of capital flows, and the spectacular expansion and globalization of the money markets, have made financial markets and exchange rates extremely vulnerable. Every day about 880 billion dollars change hands on the currency markets. According to some estimates, in autumn 1992 about 200–300 billion dollars were held in high-yield, at that time weak currencies, which enormously increased the vulnerability of the European money markets. From the point of view of the development of exchange rates, the role of capital flows becomes particularly important, and the resulting movements by no means coincide with commercial interests. "In practice, 95% of currency trades are done by investors and speculators, not by people with goods and services to sell. Floating exchange rates often overshoot for years at a time" (*The Economist*, August 7, 1993: 78). *So exchange rate adjustments as an economic policy instrument for regulating trade were relegated to the background, while their financial policy role grew more prominent.*

With the growing *mutual dependence* of economies, exchange rates as a means of economic adaptation and adjustment *have lost their effectiveness in the short-term, as well.* On the basis of the high degree of integration of economies, through import inputs devaluation today can more quickly and with some products sooner and more thoroughly destroy profitability than more favourable export prices can actually be achieved on the market. The experience of the past few years shows that increasingly in highly interwoven economies devaluation has lost its ability to improve competitiveness even in the short-term. "In open economies, the competitiveness gain acquired by a devaluation is likely to be small since imported inputs and final goods will rise in price immediately. If, in addition, real wages are sticky downwards, discrete realignments would destabilise the price level even more" (PELKMANS 1997: 290).

Thus the exchange-rate mechanism ousted by EMU does not represent an irreparable loss. "The main potential cost of EMU is that represented by the loss of monetary and exchange rate policy as an instrument of economic adjustment at the national level. This loss should not be exaggerated since exchange rate changes by the Community in relation to the rest of the world will remain possible, whereas within the EMS the nominal exchange rate instrument is already largely abandoned, and EMU will reduce the incidence of country shocks. Relative real labour costs will still be able to change; budgetary policies at national and Community levels will also absorb shocks and aid adjustment, and the external current account constraint will disappear" (One Market, One Money. *European Economy*, 1990: 11).

2.2. THE MAASTRICHT DECISIONS ABOUT EMU

The Delors plan for monetary union was published in April 1989. The plan follows logically from the program for a single European market. Complete liberalization of the capital markets threatened the effectiveness of national monetary policies, and the only possible way of "escape forwards" was the creation of a single currency. "The economic advantages of 1992 are certainly not fully achievable without a single currency, especially in the field of financial market integration. In addition the EMS in its present stage of development may not be compatible with complete capital market liberalization as required by 1992" (One Market, One Money. *European Economy*, 1990: 17–18). According to PADOA–SCHIOPPA, the single market tries to undertake an impossible task, that of reconciling the four priorities of economic policy, namely free trade, completely free movement of capital, fixed exchange rates and "national autonomy in following monetary policy". "These four elements form what I call an 'inconsistent quartet': economic theory and historical experience have reapetedly shown that these four elements cannot coexist, and that at least one has to give way" (PADOA-SCHIOPPA 1989: 373). Thus in the interest of the normal functioning of the single market, monetary integration, or EU-level centralization of monetary policy, is required. This is achieved with EMU. Monetary union is supported by the complete integration of national markets, and by efforts to promote political union.

According to the DELORS plan, monetary union was to be implemented in the 1990s in three stages. This timetable was approved at the December 1991 Maastricht summit meeting.

The plan formulated the required measures on the basis of the traditional conditions of monetary integration, which were to be fulfilled by the end of the second phase:

– complete and irreversible convertibility of national currencies;
– complete liberalization of capital transfers, in addition to complete integration of financial and money markets;
– the narrowing of the bands for floating exchange rates and finally the irreversible fixing of currency parities;
– coordination of economic policies.

Of these conditions, the first two were implemented by the time of the Maastricht decisions, in the framework of the program of the single European market, while the "irreversible fixing" of parities was to take place at the beginning of the third stage of the EMU.

The launching of the *first phase* took place in July 1990. By January 1, 1994, capital flows were liberalized in every country in the Community, and between member states and third countries, and exchange-rate controls were abolished. According to the plan, every member country was supposed to join the exchange-rate mechanism. Certain "convergences" in economic performance were expected, and steps were taken towards making the central banks independent.

As a condition of entry to the monetary union *stringent (membership) convergence criteria* were set for participants:

– Price stability measured by the consumer price index. The annual inflation rates of member countries must not diverge by more than 1.5% from the average of the three best-performing countries.
– Stable monetary positions. The budgetary deficits have to be kept under 3% of GDP and the national debt under 60% of GDP.
– Convergence of interest rates. Long-term nominal interest rates should not diverge from the average of the three best-performing countries by more than 2%.
– Stable national currencies. No devaluation against the national currency of any other member country allowed within two years.

The given monetary union construction expressed the firm intention of the decision-makers to implement EMU and especially the single currency with a low and controllable level of inflation. The plan cannot be regarded as breaking with the economic policy of the 1980s; on the contrary, it caused monetarist considerations more decidedly to prevail. "The future currency of Europe will be stable. The Treaty of the European Union considers price stability as main aim of monetary policy" (European Union. European Commission. 1993, November. 1993: 4). The single currency, for Germany in particular, was acceptable only if it was not more inflationary than the German national currency had recently been. This in general coincided with the interests of all the other member countries.

So it was no accident that the Maastricht convergence criteria laid emphasis on monetary and fiscal stability. In fact, among macroperformance factors only inflation was singled out, while the others were only apparently target criteria, and amounted to the definition of the use of economic policy instruments. The monetary conditions were thereby comprehensively tightened up, thus severely restricting the traditional field of play of economic policy. With interest rate convergence, the range of instruments available for exchange-rate stabilization was reduced, and it was not possible simply to replace monetary policy with budgetary instruments either. Since devaluation was automatically ruled out, the traditional means for improving the balance of trade and payments were lacking. Moreover, it was not possible to operate by restricting or increasing the national debt.

The 3% budget deficit and 60% national debt reflected the developed central countries' indices at the beginning of the 1990s. On the other hand, they comply with FISCHER's "golden rule" for community financing, that is, while current expenditure must be covered from taxes, debt can be increased for capital expenditure. In the EU countries budget investment expenditures are about 3% of GDP. If we take the indices for GDP and inflation, then the 3% budgetary limit is in harmony with the 60% national debt criterion.

The strict prescription of the monetary criteria was an attempt to reduce the member countries' room for manoeuvre in economic policy, in order theoretically to improve performance in the sphere of the real economy. It was assumed that approximation in the performance of the different countries would enforce greater discipline in economic policy and could be a source of powerful constraints towards adaptation.

An important item in the Maastricht protocol was the principle of "irreversibility", which was aimed at preventing any country from being able to veto the introduction of the single currency.

The *second stage* began on January 1, 1994. The European Monetary Institute was set up, headed by ALEXANDRE LAMFALUSSY, who was appointed for a three-year term. The Institute strengthened monetary cooperation among the central banks, supervised the operation of the EMS, promoted financial policy coordination among the member countries in the interest of price stability, and supported use of the ECU. As the December 1993 summit communiqué declared: the EMI has to play an important role in coordination of monetary policies of the member states, and in supervision of EMS (European Council. Presidency Conclusions. SN 373/93, December 10 and 11, 1993: 22). The EMI was seen as the forerunner of the Union's common central bank.

At its December 1995 meeting the Council of Europe decided on the name of the single currency and the timetable for its introduction. The Union's new single currency was named the *"euro"*. On the basis of the March 1998 Convergence Reports of the Commission and the EMI, the Council at its May 2, 1998 session defined the group of member countries to take part in the third stage. Basically, advancement to the third stage *was judged on the basis of fulfilment of the convergence criteria*. Of the 15 member countries, 11 were included in the first round, while the other four (Denmark, Greece, Great Britain and Sweden) remained outside for various reasons.

When the Maastricht agreement was accepted, Great Britain and Denmark had already indicated that they attached conditions to their participation in EMU, even though they met the convergence criteria. The two countries expressed reservations mainly with regard to political unification. Great Britain made its advancement to the third stage and participation in it, when the time came, dependent on a separate decision by Parliament and the cabinet. The Danes reserved to themselves the right to decide through a referendum whether to accept the single currency and take part in the third stage. The British at first did not even sign the Social Charter, which allows the member countries to decide by a simple majority on questions relating to employment and social affairs. Later the British Labour government gave its assent. They did not accept the formula of a "union with federal aims" originally proposed, but in the interest of economic policy approximation and coordination they supported the principle of "ever closer union".

Sweden did not take part in the exchange-rate mechanism and the Swedish krone was allowed to float in relation to the EMS currencies. Sweden did not adjust the status of its central bank to conform to EMU norms. It would have met the convergence criteria, but the Commission was unable to recommend its joining the euro-zone. Sweden did not commit itself to taking part in the third phase of EMU. On a political basis Swedish public opinion and its political parties were too deeply divided on the issue.

Only Greece remained outside the third phase on account of its unsatisfactory economic performance. The Greek government and public opinion wanted to join EMU and did what they could to achieve it. From January 1, 2001, when they had fulfilled the requirements, membership of the euro-zone was opened to them.

The *third phase* of EMU began on January 1, 1999. As a first step, the exchange rates[3] between the currencies of the 11 euro-zone member countries and the euro were irrevocably fixed. The euro became a real currency, while the official ECU basket simultaneously ceased to exist. ECUs were "converted" to euros at par (1:1). The participating countries now record their new national debt in euros. The central banks follow a uniform monetary policy, and all conduct external currency transactions in euros. The national currencies remained as legal tender, and use of the euro was optional. Supermarkets, department stores and other retail units displayed their prices in both the national currency and euros, and credit cards, bank cards and cheques in euros were accepted. Tills were automatically converted to cope with euros. Banks and credit card companies allowed euro accounts to be opened. Consumers were able to make mortgage, rent and public utility payments in euros.

Firms, by mutual agreement, were able to keep their accounts and transact business in euros. Stock exchanges and money markets began to deal in euros.

Until January 1, 2002, the euro functioned only in accounts. Then euro banknotes and coins were put into circulation, and with slight differences between countries, for roughly two months euros were used parallel with the national currencies. Then the latter were withdrawn from circulation. From February 2002 in the 12 euro-zone countries *the euro became the only legal tender and means of payment.*

The euro's becoming real money was one of the most important events in European integration. "The euro-zone is more than just the sum of its constituents. It is an economy in its own right, with its own economic statistics and distinct economic characteristics. Individual members of the euro-zone no longer exist as relevant macroeconomic units" (*Financial Times*, February 26, 1999. The Pink Book. Quarterly Review. European Economy 2).

[3] The conversion rates to 1 euro fixed on January 1, 1999 were as follows: 40.3399 Belgian francs (100); 5.94573 Finnish marks (1); 6.55957 French francs (1); 2.20371 Dutch guilders (1); 0.787564 Irish punt (1); 40.3399 Luxembourg francs; 1.95583 German marks (1); 1936.27 Italian lire (1000); 13.7603 Austrian schillings (1); 200.482 Portuguese escudos (100); 166.386 Spanish pesetas (100).

For those who remain outside, *participation in ERM–2* is available. Joining in ERM is not compulsary but voluntary, but the requirement of two years' exchange-rate stability can be fulfilled only by countries that take part. The main aim of ERM–2 as well is the maintenance of exchange-rate stability.

ERM–2, similarly to ERM–1, is based on central exchange rates, but these define a given country's currency in euros. The difference is not only that the euro has replaced the ECU, but also that in contrast to the parity grid characteristic of ERM–1, in ERM–2 the euro is the official "anchor currency", that is, every other currency is pegged only to the euro. So, compared with the multilateral parity grid, it conforms to the "hub-and-spokes" model. ERM–2 is not a strictly tied exchange-rate system; the central exchange rate can be adjusted, in a concerted manner and at an appropriate time. In the interest of maintaining the exchange-rate system, any participant and the European Central Bank can initiate adjustment. To make flexible adaptation possible, a wide (15%) floating band is permitted.

In ERM–2 *intervention in defence of the exchange rate is mandatory, automatic and unrestricted*. For successful intervention, the ECB and the member countries' national banks make use of both monetary and fiscal instruments. Reciprocal cooperation agreements can be concluded between the ECB and member states outside the system, in the framework of which the floating band can be narrowed, or intervention can be carried out within the floating band. The ECB and the member countries can suspend intervention and financing if it is likely to jeopardize the maintenance of price stability.

This construction was created for the member countries unable to fulfil the convergence criteria. For non-members, and therefore for the candidate countries of Central and Eastern Europe, the possibility of participation will be open after admission. For Hungary, participation can be considered only after full membership is achieved.

With the introduction of the euro, the openness of the zone to external trade underwent a fundamental change. With the single currency, trade between the members became "internal trade"; only the exchange of goods with non-member countries could be regarded as foreign trade. Since earlier the majority of the member countries counted as small or medium-sized economies, their total export of goods amounted to about 35% of their GDP, which meant that they were characterized by a relatively high degree of openness to external trade. Now with the introduction of the euro, the proportion of export fell to just 14% of GDP. In size and quality this is hardly more than the similar indices for Japan (10%) and the US (8.5%).

The replacement of the national currencies with the common currency was in itself a question of *political commitment, will and decision. Its objective economic basis* was the economic relations among the participating countries, the *intensity* of the division of labour, as a result of which the benefits of the changeover may come to outweigh the costs. After several attempts at EMU these foundations had been established by the 1990s, since about 2/3 of trade are conducted among the members, and cross-border cooperation in production, company contacts and financial and capital transactions are intensive.

The European business sphere (and not just the transnational one) is in favour of EMU, and the population as well (as workers or tourists) expect many benefits from it. This commitment is indicated by the great intensity of preparation on the part of banks and the company sphere in the past few years, and the sacrifices they have made in terms of expenditure. Measures in the single internal market have strengthened the pressure towards integration. It is thanks to the massive economic interests involved that EMU is successfully being implemented.

2.3. THE PERFORMANCE OF THE EURO AND THE EURO-ZONE ECONOMIES

It is difficult to pass judgment on the trends in macroperformance since the launch of the euro in 1999, and to distinguish which are short-term effects of recession, and to what extent we can speak about long-term structural processes. It is not entirely clear, either, how far expectations have been fulfilled, either the anxieties or the hopes of positive effects. Evaluation is made difficult particularly by the fact that in economic performance in recent years in many respects contradictory tendencies have developed. After 2000 unfavourable external developments powerfully affected the performance of the euro-zone in a negative way. While the 1998 financial crisis did not especially affect the EU countries' economies, the recession that developed in the world economy from the end of 2000 was increasingly felt. It was particularly unfortunate that growth in Germany, the Union's leading economy, after a brief upswing in 2000 (3% growth in GDP), fell back sharply (to 0.5–0.7% in 2001–2002). The strengthening of inflationary trends was largely attributable to steeply increasing oil prices.

In recent times, with fluctuations of varying intensity in both directions, *the euro exchange rate has been relatively unstable*. Over the first two years the euro generally weakened, and continued to fall. Compared with its initial rate of $1.17 its devaluation culminated on October 26, 2000 at 82.3 cents, which represented a drop in value of about 30% compared with its January 1, 1999 level. From the end of 2000 the euro exchange rate began to rise again, and in July 2002, after bigger and smaller fluctuations it again reached 1:1 parity with the dollar. The strengthening of the euro was a reflection not so much of improvement in the health of the zone's economy, but rather of the weakening of the US economy. Despite its steep fall, the euro did not sink nearly as low as the "record depth" in 1985 (when the ECU was worth 69 cents). The *euro's ups and downs* have been *more moderate* compared with both the historical movements of the ECU and the fluctuations of other currencies.

According to Bank of England calculations, in contrast, the "synthetic euro's" trade-weighted nominal exchange rate, weighted retrospectively with all the component currencies, in October 2000 was just as low as in May 1985 when the dollar exchange rate was at its peak (*Financial Times*, September 17, 2000).

Similar contradictions can be seen in the macroeconomic performance of the euro-zone countries in the period following the launch of EMU:

Table 1. Macroperformance of the (11) euro-zone countries 1998–2002

Year	Growth rate (% of real GDP)	Inflation, %	Unemployment, %	Budget deficit (% of GDP)
1998	3.0	1.1	11.1	2.3
1999	2.0	1.8	10.0	1.7
2000	3.4	2.4	8.9	0.4
2001	1.5	2.7	8.3	1.3
2002*	1.2	1.4	8.6	1.2

* 2002 – prognosis.
Sources: Eurostat and OECD Statistics.

From the beginning, the economic policy of the member countries *gave priority to the curbing of inflation*. When the third stage of EMU began, the European Central Bank set *a ceiling of 2% for the inflation*, which meant that the Union aimed at a level of inflation lower than the 3% level defined in the international literature as "desirable inflation". There was debate about whether or not *such a strict interpretation of price stability* would have deflationary effects on the economy. The setting of a rigorous inflation ceiling was not accidental, because a decisive condition of support on the part of Germany for EMU was that the new single currency should not be weaker or more inflationary than the German mark.

In the preceding years *most of the member countries had already succeeded in fulfilling the low inflation requirement*. In 1995–97 the average level of inflation in the EU countries was around 2.5–3% (in the case of "EU North", 2.2%), and in the euro-zone countries by 1998 inflation had fallen to just 1.1%. Performance in terms of inflation deteriorated somewhat in 1999 compared to 1998 (to 1.8%), but was still kept below the 2% level set by the ECB. Several countries showed very satisfactory performance. Among the euro-zone countries, in Austria, France and Germany inflation was just 0.6%, while prices in only a few countries (Holland, Portugal and Spain) rose a few tenths of a percentage point above the ECB's 2% ceiling. The picture is particularly satisfactory, if we examine the level of "core inflation". In 1999 this price index, which excludes prices of energy and foodstuffs (defined as core inflation) amounted to just 1.1–1.3%.

Apart from central bank policy, *certain favourable structural processes* played a part in the relatively benign trend of inflation. Deregulation and liberalization within the single market had a beneficial effect on prices. Particularly the liberalization of the telecommunications and electrical energy market stimulated keen price competition, which pushed prices down. In those years a drop in oil prices contributed to low inflation.

From the beginning of 2000 these favourable price trends were interrupted, and the economy of the zone had to face increasing inflationary pressure. Forecasts for 2000 had projected an inflation level of about 1.8%, but it became increasingly clear that it could not be kept below the 2% ceiling. In the euro-zone inflation rose from 1.8% in 1998 to 2.4% in 2000, which although it was not a significant rise, was still above the ECB target. In addition, the spread among the different countries increased. In 2000 price rises remained below 2% only in France and Austria (1.9%), while in several countries they were above 3%: in Ireland, 5.3%, in Spain 3.5% and in Finland and Belgium, 3%. Core inflation in the zone remained at 1.3–1.5%, but the new developments forced even the ECB to do some hard thinking.

A number of factors in the strengthening of inflationary pressure, despite this rigorous monetary policy, must be mentioned.

– A continuing highly inflationary factor was the depreciation and undervaluation of the euro. According to a study by a US investment bank, Goldman Sachs, the euro was too much undervalued, by about 30% on a trade-weighted basis compared to the dollar, and by more than 40% compared to the Japanese yen. Many economists reckon that the "correct value" of the euro is about $1.10 (*The Economist,* September 16, 2000: 91). According to CHRISTIAN NOYER, a vice-president of the ECB, the euro was "dangerously undervalued". Thus inflationary effects steadily grew.

– Energy (oil) prices rose sharply from the middle of 1999, pushing up the inflation rate. The higher oil prices were increasingly "built into" product prices. According to a Commerz Bank estimate, compared to core inflation oil prices raised the inflation rate by about 0.5%, while increased prices of imports due to devaluation raised it by a further 0.5%.

– From the point of view of production costs it was not only energy prices that caused problems. According to the Economist Intelligence Unit, in 2000 the prices of industrial raw materials rose by 15%, which particularly affected the input costs of products that required such materials.

– According to the ECB, in certain periods, the increase in demand that accompanied accelerated growth also put strong pressure on prices.

– A special question that arises is that of "catching-up" by countries with lower price levels, as a result of increased competition, and the convergence of costs. In the low-price-level countries this caused inflation to accelerate, pushing prices up towards the average. This price convergence is regarded as normal by the experts. According to the ECB as well it is acceptable if differences in inflation rates are not increasing, but temporary, and reflect the less developed countries' "catching-up". Others point out that similar price differences can be seen between the south and west of the US, and between its north-eastern and mid-western states.

In recession conditions the inflationary process continued to strengthen in 2001, and a turning-point was reached only in 2002, when the inflation rate was once again brought below the Central Bank's ceiling. Moderation of oil prices, and the gradual upward valuation of the euro, played a positive role in this. From the second half of 2002, the instability of oil prices created renewed inflationary pressures.

In the EU low inflation has in the past ten years been accompanied by a high level of *unemployment* (around 10%), and a moderate rate of economic growth (around 2.5%). At the same time, EU analyses highlight the fact that the formerly presumed close correlation between slowing inflation and unemployment (the PHILLIPS curve) has become highly debatable. The tendencies observable from the end of the 1990s confirm this. Between 1998 and 2001, unemployment fell by almost 3% from 11.1% to 8.3%, while at the same time the inflationary process also showed improvement. It is true that as a result of the recession, unemployment has risen slightly in 2002, but a breakthrough does seem to be beginning in this respect, even if it is questionable. Since 1997, in the euro-zone countries 5 million new jobs have been created, and unemployment has begun to decrease. At the same time, at above 8% in 2002 it is still too close to the magic 10% threshold. We can also say that several countries have had to pay for low inflation with high unemployment, and the Union has so far not been able to match the remarkable achievement of the US economy at the end of the 1990s (rapid growth, with zero inflation and full employment).

There is general agreement that the problem is not connected with the recession, and that a "breakthrough" can be expected only as *a result of structural reforms.* This is also indicated by the fact that in the countries where reforms have begun (Great Britain, Ireland and Holland), spectacular success in reducing unemployment has been achieved. In all three countries at the beginning of 1990s unemployment was still above 10%. In 2000 in Holland unemployment fell to a level of 2.6%, which can be regarded as virtually full employment, while in Ireland it dropped from its 1990 level of 14.5% to just 4.3%.

The other positive result of the rigorous monetary policy has been *a spectacular improvement in budgetary positions*. After the beginning of the 1970s, in practice balanced budgets could not be maintained, and in the long-term deficits ran at 4–6% (of GDP). In harmony with the Maastricht convergence criteria, a condition for joining the monetary union was that budget deficits had to be kept below the level of 3% of GDP. In the course of the 1990s the member countries made strenuous efforts to achieve this, and by the end of the 1990s they had succeeded in "over-fulfilling" the targets set. The zone's aggregate budget deficit in 1999 was around 1.7% of GDP, and falling. In 9 of the euro-zone countries in 2000 a budget surplus was recorded. In 2000 the overall budget deficit for the euro-zone was 0.4%, while in the EU as a whole a surplus of 0.5% was achieved, in which substantial revenues from privatization played a part. Budget consolidation had a beneficial effect on the inflationary processes. As a result of the recession, budget positions deteriorated in the member countries, and in many countries the surplus recorded in 2000 was followed by a deficit. A typical example of this was Germany, where the 2000 budget surplus of 1.5% turned to a 2% deficit for 2001. It has become clear that despite its commitment France will not be able to return to a balanced budget by 2004, while Portugal has overshot the 3% ceiling as well (with a deficit of around 4% in 2001), which has raised the possibility of application of the Stability Pact sanctions.

1999, the first year of the introduction of the euro, saw a slowing down of growth. We can also say that the preparation for the euro, the restraints applied in order to meet the convergence requirements, led to *a mild sort of mini-recession in 1999*. Economic growth fell from its 1998 level of 3% to 2% for 1999, even though the international financial crisis was more or less over. Especially poor performance in terms of growth was achieved by Italy (1.2%) and Germany (1.4%), but from 1998 to 1999 in economic growth only Spain among the euro-zone countries (up from 3.5% to 3.7%) and Sweden, ouside the zone (up from 2.9% to 3.5%), managed a slight acceleration.

From 2000 growth trends again showed improvement. And this was not by chance, because after a certain time the weakness of the euro was bound to make its beneficial effect increasingly felt. That is, against the inflationary tendencies, economic growth in the Union began to move in a positive direction in 2000. For the whole of 2000 on an annual basis 3.4% growth was achieved for both the EU and the euro-zone.

Undoubtedly in this process a large part was played by the advantageous possibilities provided for leading European companies by the devaluing euro. The effect of this was felt more and more. In 1999, for example, Airbus secured 55% of the market for passenger aircraft, and in terms of orders beat Boeing into second place. The successes of German carmakers on the US market can also be attributed to the euro's low exchange rate. In 2000 Mercedes sales in the US grew by 18%, and Volkswagen sales by 20%. According to data issued by the Japan Automobile Importers' Association in 2000 from Europe parallel import grew by 40% in the sector compared with the previous year (www.ft.com/globaleconomy). The successes of Alcatel, and of the whole French economy in 2000, were largely due to the weakness of the euro. According to the European Commission, wage costs for the whole euro-zone had not been so low since 1986. Domestic consumption also perked up in many countries.

From the end of 2000, signs of a slowdown appeared in the European economy (and especially in the German economy once more). Thereafter, the recession of 2001–2002 in the world economy brought a sharp deceleration (to 1.2–1.5% growth) in the expansion of the European economies. The economic performance of Germany and Italy was again particularly poor, but from the end of 2000 the pace of economic growth declined in every member country.

It must be emphasized that apart from short-term cyclical changes, *significant long-term changes in growth trends* can be expected only if structural reforms are consistently pursued. It is a question for the future, whether in the coming decades the long-term "ranking" in terms of annual growth that characterized the previous period (US 3.5%, EU 2.5%, Japan 1.5%) can be altered. This process has begun in the last few years, largely as a result of the single internal market. It was no accident that the international financial crisis of recent years left Europe largely untouched, since it erupted in circumstances, and anyway only in certain localized areas of the world economy, when the stability of the real economic sphere was able to counterbalance it. Clearly, for a "big crisis", the simultaneous collapse of both spheres would have been needed. This was not the case, and it applied not only to the US but to a certain extent to Europe as well, for the above reasons. The introduction of the euro also had a beneficial effect on developments in business life.

The strict monetary stability criteria may continue to confront economic policy with complex and difficult tasks. Though Maastricht restricted specifically only inflation, because of the rigorously defined monetary policy criteria there were from the outset fears that convergence would be attainable only at the expense of the other macroeconomic performance indices. Thus while inflation-curbing performance and monetary equilibrium are improving, this may mean a slowdown in economic growth and a drop in real incomes or a rise in unemployment, especially in certain member countries. This much can be said, that thanks to the introduction of the euro on January 1, 1999 and its comprehensive consequences (and to some extent its antecedents), in the European Union *new development trends* seem to be unfolding since the end of the 1990s. Despite contradictory economic performances, it appears that the strict monetary policy introduced earlier is bearing fruit.

2.4. STRUCTURAL PROBLEMS AND THE NEED FOR REFORMS IN THE EU

In assessing the performance of the EU economies it is repeatedly said that the deficiencies in performance and the economic difficulties are attributable to structural factors. Though there is no obstacle to the integration process, still structural weaknesses express "deficiencies" in integration maturity. According to experts, stabilization of the euro and the economies of the zone, and consolidation of long-term growth trends, can be achieved only by consistently *pursuing structural reforms*. So structural reforms can enable fine-tuning of integration maturity.

It must be emphasized that the EU is one of the most highly developed areas of the global world economy, with modern economic structures and technologies, and its products and companies can hold their own in world market competition. Germany, the world's third strongest industrial power and its second largest exporter, has innovative, highly productive and competitive companies. In the past decade it has managed to integrate East Germany, with its population of 17 million and outdated structure, while still remaining one of the world's most highly developed states. This is not to deny that many consider Germany at present the "sick economy" of Europe, and a typical example of the fact that this can scarcely be changed without radical structural reforms. On the basis of productivity, development, entrepreneurial qualities, the knowledge-based nature of the economy, and competitiveness, the same can be said of France, Great Britain, Italy and indeed increasingly even of Spain. In respect of productivity, the "gap" between the EU and the US economy has narrowed.

In the last few decades the *economic structure* of the EU countries has undergone enormous changes, and the direction and nature of these merit the label "post-industrial society". In accordance with globally developing tendencies, the European economies have become increasingly *services-oriented*. The proportion of the services sector at the turn of the millennium in the member countries' average in terms of value added was more than 2/3, and similar proportions have developed in respect of the number of people employed. As a percentage of GDP, the proportion of services was highest (70–72%) in Denmark, Belgium, Britain, France and Holland, but the relatively low level in Greece and Italy was still 66–68%. At the same time, in the EU in respect of value added the share of manufacturing industry fell to 1/3, and that of agriculture to less than 3%. At the turn of the third millennium, it can be said that *economic structures have grown more similar*, both within the Union and in relation to global competitors. Thus the "structural problems" are basically *relative*.

The chief indications of Europe's structural problems are considered to be its *moderate economic growth and relatively high unemployment*. With relatively slow growth (2–2.5%) in the last 20 years unemployment has stabilized at a level of about 10%, and it is only in the last few years that a modest improvement has been achieved. In contrast, in the US with low inflation, growth has continued steadily above 3%, and in recent years unemployment has dropped to 4%, a level regarded in America as full employment; in 1999 almost 75% of the potential working population was in employment. In that year in Europe the number of those employed was less than 60% of the potential workforce. The result was that although in the productivity of labour Europe closely approximated to the US, in per capita GDP it remained almost 1/3 lower. In 1998, taking the US as 100, in the euro-zone output per hour of work was 94%, but output per worker was 82%.

From the 1990s a new development was the increasingly keen competition and world market challenge from *the newly industrialized countries*. These have a low level of wages and social expenditure, while with their technology and productivity they are competitive and pursue aggressive marketing policies. Competition from the 'emerging countries' represents a challenge particularly for the European welfare states.

The structural weaknesses of the EU economies have several dimensions:

1. The structural problems are partly *of a technical or technological nature*. Bridging the so-called "technology gap" was from the beginning one of the basic considerations in European integration. In the past 40 years Europe has shown contradictory performance in catching up. In the case of many high-tech sectors and products there is no question of its lagging behind; indeed, Western Europe leads the US and Japan. Especially in certain products or product groups Western Europe has the advantage. These sectors include the nuclear power industry, aircraft construction, pharmaceuticals, the manufacture of telecom equipment and among the so-called traditional sectors food-processing, the car industry and many branches of engineering.

Yet it was in technical development that the main symptoms of the so-called "European disease" appeared. Europe lagged behind particularly in the development, production and sale on the world market of some high-tech products that represented technical progress (computers, semiconductors, robots, etc.). Western Europe's consumer electronics industry was one of the spectacular losers in the rapid technical revolution. In the most important products of the high-tech sectors, from the mid-1970s in Western Europe a considerable trade deficit and import-dependence developed. In world trade, with regard to modern industries Western Europe lost ground.

The events of recent years have continued to provide a contradictory picture. According to a study by Goldman Sachs, the EU is indeed at a disadvantage compared to the US in terms of computers and communications technologies, but the euro-zone's "new economy is capable of narrowing the gap with the US". In 1995 knowledge-based branches of industry accounted for 48.4% of the added value of the business sector in the EU, while in the US the figure was 55.3%. Investments into the knowledge-based sectors amounted to 8% of GDP in the EU, and around 8.4% in the US. In 1997 expenditure on information and communications technology came to 5.9% of GDP in the EU and 7.8% in the US (Eurozone Economy. February 25, 2000: 5, *Financial Times*). According to data for 1998 from the European Information Technology Observatory, the proportion of informatics hardware in 1996 was 2.26%, while the corresponding figure in Japan was 2.51% and in the US 4.08%.

According to German Bundesbank estimates, if investment in Germany in computer technology equipment is calculated on the basis of American prices, then since 1991 instead of the official figure of annual 6% growth the real increase was 28%. This looks rather better in comparison to the US (*The Economist,* September 2, 2000). Particularly if we look behind the averages, there is no justification for speaking of a "gap" between the US and the developed European countries. Technological catching-up in many fields is far more necessary within Europe than in the relation between the two continents. This particularly will apply after Eastern enlargement.

Against the possibility of 'technological gap', it is an important argument that among the developed countries, in the present highly internationalized world economy, *it is impossible to maintain for long any technological advantage.* On the basis of the close and wide-ranging cooperation in research, production and sales, a relatively rapid and unrestricted flow of technologies is characteristic, and it is no longer possible today for one or two companies to exercise a monopoly. Technical and product innovation advantages are largely temporary, and although they can result in big profits, it is not possible to prevent others from gaining access to the results. The flow of technology today takes place basically within the framework of transnational companies, and it has become intensive through increased internationalization. Among analysts there is general agreement that the loss of its world market position by West European industry is attributable not really to technological backwardness but to other factors such as its *slower innovation or its lagging behind in modern company organization and management.*

2. *Europe is lagging behind in its modernization of some service sectors.* This is especially noticeable in comparison with the US. While the productivity and competitiveness of manufacturing companies are satisfactory, and actors in this area, because of global competition, simply cannot afford to lag behind significantly, in some service sectors this is not the situation. It is a matter of the problem of 'tradable' and 'non-tradable' products, where in the case of the latter the constraining forces of global competition are largely indirect, weaker or absent. Among such 'swollen and over-regulated' branches we can list telecommunications, air transportation, and the banking sphere. Europe's disadvantage in these areas is due to the high proportion of state ownership, over-regulation and the relatively closed nature of internal markets. This harms Europe's competitiveness. As a result of 'internal market' measures and privatization, improvement in these areas can be expected only at the beginning of the 2000s.

3. The root of the structural problems is *the relatively undeveloped nature of the factors (capital and labour) markets*. Analysts call attention above all to *the liquidity of the capital markets and the relative scarcity of risk capital*. In the Anglo–Saxon countries the openness of the capital markets, the ease of access to the capital markets, ensures the conditions for expansion of these economies, because through this, as Professor EDMUND PHELPS of Columbia University states, the entrepreneurs could start "new economy" ventures as the corresponding institutions are available (*Financial Times*, August 9, 2000). By contrast, in Europe entrepreneurs are squeezed bureaucratically by the big trade unions and the interfering state, and the capitalization of their economies is considerably lower. While in 1988 the share of the stock markets in GDP in the US, Canada and Australia was about 50% (and in the UK, almost 80%), the figure in Germany, France and Italy was only 20–25%. In 1995 in the US and Canada the proportion of the workforce with higher education qualifications was 1/3, by contrast in France and Germany it was 20–23%, and in Italy only about 8%.

Unfavourable infrastructural conditions (a shortage of low-rent accommodation, the undeveloped nature of the property market, and the absence of favourable transport facilities) contribute largely to *the poorly-developed state of the labour market*. In the US there is virtually no regional unemployment, because the labour force reacts relatively flexibly and rapidly to regional changes in the economic conditions. This in Europe places particular emphasis on the need for skills training and re-training, and for the improvement of the infrastructural conditions.

4. A significant proportion of structural problems derive from *institutional and regulatory deficiencies*. Among the structural problems, critics mention inflexible regulation of the capital and labour markets, high prices of factors, especially high wage costs, and delay in long-overdue reform of the public service sectors (health, education and state administration). One of the main factors in weak economic performance is the excessive level of state redistribution, especially over-expenditure by the welfare state (delay in reform of pensions and social welfare) and in connection with this, excessive taxation and over-regulation of the economy.

4.1. While in the US the total *burden of taxes* amounts to just 31% of GDP, the average in the euro-zone is about 43%. Considering the relatively wide dispersion, reduction of this 'disadvantage' is imaginable only in the long-term. High taxes restrain investment and employment and are unfavourable in general from the point of view of economic growth.

4.2. The inflexibility of European factor markets is regarded more or less as a commonplace. Legal rigidity and over-regulation, the highly organized nature of the European labour force, centralized wage agreements and complicated labour law conditions all play a part in this.

The inflexibility of factor market regulation is apparent in areas such as the definition of working hours, wage guarantees, and the rigorous and complicated legal and financial conditions of dismissal. According to a UNICE study, it takes a bankrupt company in the EU eight times longer to clear creditors' claims and start again than in the US. According to European entrepreneurs, the laws protecting workers against dismissal are 14 times stricter than in the US (*The Economist*, July 22, 2000: 31). According to the OECD, the burdens of administrative, regulatory and competition law are more than two and a half times greater in Italy, France and Belgium than in the UK. In the case of Germany and Sweden, they are twice as great. In France in 2000 the 35-hour working week was introduced. As the OECD report warns France, this will reduce unemployment only if it does not push up wage costs.

4.3. One of the main weak points in Europe's competitiveness is *the high level of wage costs,* which result in significant wage-cost disadvantages compared with other developed regions and particularly the ambitious newly-industrializing countries. Wages in Europe are burdened with significant social contributions, and there are big differences within Europe in this regard. The total tax burden on wage costs in the US amounts to just 23.8%, while in the euro-zone on average in 1999 it was 39.8%. This proportion is the highest in Belgium, at 44.8%, but it is over 40% in Germany, Finland, Austria and France, as well.

In 1999 Germany's manufacturing industry wage costs per hour came to $28, 40% of which went on *social security contributions and social taxes.* The same wage costs in Japan amounted to $22, and in the US, $19. Social burdens amounted to only 1/3 of US wage costs. The wage cost level was $18 in France, and in Britain $17. Social burdens amounted to almost 50% of French wage costs. In Great Britain this proportion was just 1/4 (Swedish Employers' Confederation). In the Union on average 30% of earnings go on tax and contributions, but the proportion in Belgium is 42%, and it is close to 40% in Denmark and Germany.

In many countries *excessive wage rises* are regarded as one of the main causes of unemployment. Excessive wage demands destroy jobs, and the increasing taxes on wages to finance unemployment raise the cost of labour even further. This prompts firms to replace workers with machines, and to transfer production abroad.

4.4. On the basis of the new pressures to adapt, once again arguments have intensified in connection with *reform of the European welfare state.* High unemployment has been accompanied by continuing high social expenditure, which even in the 1980s proved impossible to curb. Social expenditure in Germany grew from 26.7% of GDP in 1970 to 32.4% in 1980 and to 33.1% for 1992. The 'most dynamic' growth was observable in the area of unemployment benefit. In GDP terms social transfers in the EU were 50% higher than in the US, and 78% higher than in Japan.

The main area of structural problems is the crisis in public service areas such as pensions and the health service. OECD figures show that in the coming decades Europe will face a serious pensions crisis, and comprehensive reforms, in the light of demographic trends, cannot be further postponed. According to calculations, by 2030 in the 5 biggest EU countries (the UK, Germany, France, Italy and Spain) the number of people aged over 65 will amount to 25% of the total population, compared with just 9% in 1950.

The rise in the average age and early retirement, together with the generous pension systems, lay increasingly unbearable burdens on budgets, and seriously add to the wage costs of those in employment. It is calculated that if reforms are not carried out, pension costs between 2000 and 2040 as a percentage of GDP will grow in Germany from 11.5% to 18.5%, in Italy from 12.6% to 21.4%, and in Spain from 9.8% to 16.8%, while as a result of reform based on private pension funds the proportion in Great Britain may rise from 4.5% to just 5%.

Thus in the global world economy not just companies but national economies and also, we can say, social and economic structures are in competition with one another. Europe's global companies, despite certain deficiencies, are leading participants in this worldwide competition, and their *competitiveness problems* in the light of the above figures are related mainly to their *costs* (especially wage costs). Europe's weakness, therefore, derives largely from its *social and economic structure,* and its place in the global competition of the coming decades will to a great extent be determined by how far it is capable of carrying out the necessary structural reforms. It must be emphasized that *the welfare state, the great achievement of European civilization, must not be dismantled, but reformed.*

2.5. STRUCTURAL REFORMS AND THE EURO

Structural changes and reforms are multi-factor processes, and in recent times they have taken place at several levels, in several directions. The fundamental restructuring and modernizing processes in the past few decades in Europe, as elsewhere, have been chiefly influenced by *the decisions and measures taken by large (transnational) corporations and national governments.* In addition, a major role has been played by national economic policies and integration mechanisms. Efforts have been made in the EC/EU to promote structural changes in two directions: on the one hand, with the help of *integrative market mechanisms* (e.g. the single internal market); on the other hand, by the use of various sorts of *economic policy instruments,* from sectoral policies (industry policy, agricultural policy, energy policy, etc.) to functional economic policy (a common budget, monetary union, etc.).

In the new structural policy strategies of the past decade, market mechanisms and forces have continued to have a prominent role. The 1992 plan for the *single internal market* aimed at rapid development of the 'technologically advanced sectors', as a means of accelerating economic growth. This policy is based on the concept that companies are the developers and carriers of the most modern technology, and the market frameworks provided for them are of decisive importance. Structural processes and changes fundamentally affect their decisions and activities, and within the framework of their intensive cooperation these companies transmit them internationally.

From the beginning of the 1990s, the formation of the single internal market removed further obstacles to integration, and set free market forces that increased pressure towards further structural adaptation.

An important new phenomenon in recent times has been the start of transformation at company level; entrepreneurs have tried to sidestep the rigid legal rules and the consequences of costly state regulation *by concluding direct agreements with their employees.* In Germany, for example, in the past 10 years trade union membership has fallen to 1/3, and only 1/4 of German workers can be regarded as organized. Dividing lines between employers and employees are becoming increasingly blurred. In just the last 3 years, share ownership by households in western Germany rose from 10% to 21%. According to some figures, in Germany there are more shareowners than trade union members. In more and more companies, employers conclude direct agreements with employees on wages, hours of work, working conditions and the level of services, simply ignoring rigid state laws or trade union rules (e.g. on opening hours, flexitime, part-time employment, etc.). This is characteristic particularly of so-called 'dotcom' companies. We can observe similar tendencies in France and the other EU member states.

The March 2000 summit meeting is officially recorded as *a turning-point* in the history of the EU. The Union committed itself not only to modernization, structural transformation and reform, and the improvement of global competitiveness, but also to the preservation of social justice and social stability. The Lisbon Council meeting where the 'e-Europe' program was approved has often been referred to in the press as the 'dotcom summit'. The Council supported measures to be taken in the interest of the 'New Economy' and accepted the program whereby Europe by 2010 was "to become the most competitive and dynamic knowledge-based economy in the world, capable of sustainable economic growth with more and better jobs and greater social cohesion" (Presidency Conclusions, Lisbon, European Council, 23 and 24 March, 2000).

Analysts unanimously acknowledge that the EU has committed itself to radical structural reforms, and the defined aims and tasks are relevant.

If they are implemented, the Union's efficiency and competitiveness will really improve significantly. Of course, the decisions have to be actually carried out.

It appears that the introduction of the single currency has initiated further important changes in the economy of the Union, and these can be expected to have far-reaching internal and external consequences in the longer term. EMU seems to be confirming the expectations that it would *speed up the process of structural adaptation* both in the business sphere and in government policy.

The introduction of the euro has had palpable effects in transforming business life. The number of mergers has grown, especially in the financial sphere, and in more than one case has taken aggressive forms (hostile takeovers). "The battle for European capitalism has begun in earnest. In the three months since the single currency was launched, the sleepy world of continental European corporate finance has burst into frenetic activity. The speed with which companies have adopted previously foreign techniques, notably the hostile takeover, has been astonishing" (*Financial Times,* April 16, 1999). The euro is greatly increasing competition among European companies.

The effect of the euro on capital markets has been to speed up their transformation. "Europe's capital market is being transformed even more radically, thanks to the euro. The integration of European financial markets and the elimination of currency risk and restrictions on cross-border investment by pension funds within the euro area has created a deeper, more liquid capital market. This has intensified the pressure on firms to be more responsive to shareholders and to seek to raise rates of return" (*The Economist,* September 16, 2000).

Recently, positive changes have begun in the area of the labour markets as well. Workers have been prepared to show moderation in their wage demands, part-time employment and casual work are becoming more widespread, and labour market flexibility is increasing. The growth of real wages is lagging behind productivity growth, which with improving budgets governments can counterbalance by reducing social security contributions. The reduction of social security contributions should encourage companies to increase employment.

According to some, part-time employment and the spread of casual work in Europe will probably play a greater part in improving the level of employment than the British method of moderating wages and taxes. According to ECB data, casual employment in the EU involves 15% of the labour force, while part-time employment involves almost 17%. In the period between 1995 and 1999 more than half of net job creation was due to this. The example of Holland must be mentioned in particular; there, 40% of all those in employment, and 70% of women, work part-time. Perhaps it is no accident that in Holland unemployment is below 3% that is, they have virtually returned to full employment.

Despite all the difficulties and weaknesses, *structural transformation has achieved the 'critical mass' when its effects can now be felt.* "So far Europe's recovery has been largely cyclical, thanks to a cheap euro and strong global demand. But there are also good grounds to hope that the rate of growth it can sustain in the medium-term could soon increase, too. One reason is that many governments have indeed been making their labour markets more flexible. As the old rules have been loosened, firms have hired more workers, often on short-term contracts or as part-timers, with less strict job protection and lower social security contributions. As a result, after a long period of stagnation, employment has grown slightly faster in the euro area than in the United States over the past two years. A revolution has also been sweeping Europe's boardrooms, with a wave of mergers and hostile takeovers, as global competition forces managers to lift their rates of return. This promises to boost future productivity growth" (*The Economist*, September 2, 2000: 17).

Recognition of the need for structural changes and reforms, and growing commitment at every level to carrying them out, are not in themselves enough. Many uncertainty factors must be reckoned with. Structural modernization depends on the private sector, and as long as it is a question of the direct competitiveness of companies, this is not a problem. At the same time, implementation of large-scale infrastructural programs has never gone according to prior expectations, but there is hope that 'e-Europe' will not meet a similar fate. The individual national governments, although despite similar political platforms they differ significantly in their philosophies and public support (French, German and British socialist or social democratic governments), will probably carry out the reforms (planned tax reforms and modernization of social welfare systems) in a consistent manner. If not, it will be difficult to improve Europe's performance.

3. THE ECONOMICS OF MONETARY INTEGRATION

3.1. THE COSTS AND BENEFITS OF MONETARY INTEGRATION

Multiple advantages are expected from EMU, which are very important from the point of view of support for and implementation of the plan for monetary union. At the same time, the costs of monetary union, as we have seen, appear mainly in reduction of the scope of national economic policies, which can adversely affect some sectors and economic actors. The changeover to the common or single currency in itself involves considerable technical, but non-recurring, costs (withdrawal of national currencies, adaptation of computers and tills, etc.) Presumably the inflationary effects of the switch to the new single currency (rounding–up of prices) will also be one-off effects.

Monetary union brings many *micro- and macroeconomic advantages,* though the costs must not be ignored. The effects on the main actors in economic life (companies, workers, households, the money markets and the state) are examined in three traditional dimensions of economic policy: microeconomic efficiency (optimal allocation of resources, cost savings, etc.), macroeconomic stability (inflation, production, growth and employment), and the distribution of the effects among countries and regions.

The main microeconomic benefits and costs:

– The elimination of exchange-rate uncertainty and risk in internal relations are beneficial from the point of view of the business environment and investment development. This contributes to the expansion of trade i.e. it has 'trade-creating' effects, and as capital sources become cheaper and more mobile, makes investment and development more advantageous. The exchange-rate risks are costly, and the floating rates can be considered as taxes on trade.

– The possibility of exchange-rate changes makes relations uncertain from the point of view of the consumer, and obtaining of investment goods. Because of this, more expensive but more dependable domestic suppliers are often preferred. This may hinder closer cooperation in production (e.g. of components), and uncertainty concerning exchange rates makes accurate calculation of costs more difficult. According to some large European companies (e.g. Ford and Bosch), expectations relating to exchange-rate movements have always played an important part in the choice and allocation of plants and production bases. So monetary integration could be *an important integrative factor in the sphere of the real economy.*

– Prices for goods and services expressed in the single currency improve 'price transparency', which is beneficial from the point of view of allocation of resources and consumer evaluation, makes business decisions and calculations easier and increases trade and competition. Information costs and price discrimination are reduced. As a result of all this, price approximation can be expected.

– Increased money market security enables the general risk premiums charged by banks and stockmarkets (and thereby *interest rates*) to be lowered, with the result that more can be spent on investment and growth. More stable, lower interest rates are particularly beneficial to the interest-sensitive sectors (e.g. property markets, the construction industry and consumer services).

– With integration of the bond and capital markets liquidity improves, and on the bigger money markets *cheaper long-term loan opportunities* open up. This could improve the development possibilities and competitiveness particularly of the capital-intensive sectors.

– As a result of the introduction of the single currency, *transaction and conversion* costs connected with currency conversion drop significantly (the latter more or less disappear in trade between member states). This benefits companies, private individuals and tourists alike. Banks thereby lose an important source of income, but in the expanded money market there is a greater chance of compensating for such losses.

In the EU, as a result of the introduction of the single currency, the considerable reduction in conversion costs in connection with currency conversion amounts to about 1/2% of the Union's GDP (13–19 bn euro annually). According to Commission estimates, every year about 200 million cross-border transfers take place, each amounting to less than 2,500 euro. According to the EU's Consumer Protection bureau, the charges on individual transfers range between 7 and 40 euro, which is on average 20 times the amount charged on transfers within a country. What deters many small enterprises from engaging in cross-border trade in either the export or the import field is the fact that the bank charges on cash transfers simply eliminate profit. Sending a bank cheque from France takes five days, and costs 12% of the amount. In trade within the EU transaction costs take away 15% of profits. Transaction costs in the case of open, small countries with weak currencies amount to 1% of GDP. By comparison, the CECCHINI report estimated the savings to be gained from the abolition of border formalities, in the interest of free movement of goods, at 1/4% of GDP.

The macroeconomic benefits and costs of monetary integration:

– The plan for EMU should contribute to *price stability and the approximation of inflation rates*, an important condition of which is the independence of the central bank and the reduction of inflationary expectations by the determination of a clearly fixed program of monetary integration.

– One of the most important benefits of participation in monetary union is the *significant reduction of the costs of disinflationary policy*. At the same time, because of disinflationary policies, much of the income from seigniorage is lost. This mainly affects countries which formerly had high inflation. With participation in EMU, on the one hand the efficiency of the tax system improves, while on the other hand because of the nominal convergence of interest rates the costs of financing the state budget are reduced. As a result of falling interest rates, *financing the national debt* becomes cheaper, which is a greater saving than governments could have made, had they retained the possibility of printing money.

– Monetary union is expected to *improve macroeconomic performance*. Budgetary savings and dynamic efficiency benefits will result in greater economic growth, which should improve employment opportunities. Pressures towards technical and structural modernization will be felt in the bigger, more integrated market, and this will give rise to many benefits. As a result of monetary integration the global competitiveness of the Union should increase. With price stability and higher incomes, overall prosperity will grow.

– The basis for the success of monetary union is budgetary stability, and it is also one of its benefits. At the same time, the price of rigorous monetary and budgetary policy in countries struggling with structural weaknesses may be higher unemployment and slower growth. In normal circumstances the costs will appear mainly in the short-term; on the basis of its long-term effects of transforming structures and improving efficiency, the Union balance will very probably prove positive.

– *Reduction of national autonomy and competence in economic policy* is seen as one of the greatest 'prices' of monetary integration. Monetary union goes with integration of monetary policy. Thus, exchange rate and interest rate policy is removed from the national sphere and becomes unified.

These instruments cannot be independently used to protect or help the national economy or individual sectors or regions within it. There is some anxiety about how, with uniform interest rates, the more backward countries will be able to achieve the long-term growth 'surplus' needed if they are to catch up in the foreseeable future. This is a realistic consideration in relation to EMU participation by the CEE countries. At the same time, the pressures towards adaptation arising from monetary union may compensate for it. Economic policy has other means at its disposal, including budgetary policy, which can offer considerable room for manoeuvre.

Regional and community effects:

– With the introduction of the single currency there is a significant reduction in *the official central bank international reserves*, while considerable gains should result from the role of the single currency as an international money and as a reserve. As a result of EMU, the Union's *presence and influence in international financial forums* will grow.

– As a result of EMU, the dependence of the countries of the Union on *exchange-rate movements* will decrease. A considerable proportion of former foreign trade will become internal trade, and in this internal market prices and price movements will approximate more closely. The more integrated Union will have better positions from the point of view of the development of trade conditions, both at company level and with regard to securing more favourable commercial contracts. This will benefit particularly the smaller countries (e.g. Hungary, in the future).

– Monetary integration could have significant *income-redistribution effects*. The rigorous stabilization constraints will affect the various social strata in differing ways, and this applies to unemployment as well. Monetary union is expected to increase *regional differences* in particular. These effects will be felt to a varying extent in different countries; the whole territory of some less developed countries may be defined as a backward region. This will demand regional support ('cohesion') mechanisms.

In contrast to the 1992 single internal market (see the CECCHINI report), comprehensive summaries quantifying the net effects of EMU have not been prepared. With regard to the main priorities of economic policies, chiefly efficiency, stability and equilibrium, the overall effects and the EMU aggregate balance seem positive. As the Commission's report states in summing up: "The EMU, similarly to 1992, is a positive-sum game" (One Market, One Money, 1990: 9). All in all, according to the Commission, gains deriving from EMU could amount to 0.5% of GDP.

3.2. ECONOMIC AND MONETARY UNION – INTEGRATION MATURITY

It is an important new development in economic union, or 'positive integration', that member countries and others interested must fulfil complicated conditions, and thus participation by even the most highly developed countries cannot be automatic. With economic union, the question of *integration maturity and preparedness for integration* arises directly and unavoidably.

On the question how mature and well-prepared a country or group of countries is for economic and monetary union in market-economy and structural terms, guidance is provided by monetary economics, and within it, especially theoretical analyses of the so-called "optimum currency area", which developed out of the debates in the 1960s about fixed versus flexible exchange rates. On the basis of the various approaches, we can interpret the optimum currency area as follows:

– Flexible and properly functioning factor markets; that is, in addition to mobility of capital and labour, factor prices are capable of adjusting to external price movements.

– The region achieves such a degree of internal homogeneity that it is not threatened by external "asymmetric shocks".

– To deal with economic difficulties, there is the possibility of appropriate budget transfers.

Theoretical approaches to the optimum currency area express *the most important* (market economy, structural, financing) *factors in integration maturity*. Monetary integration does not assume identical levels of development, but structural convergence contributes to the avoidance of asymmetric shocks. The officially accepted *membership criteria* in the EU are narrower than this; in practice they were limited merely to *achievement of monetary and fiscal convergence* (the Maastricht criteria). The concrete definition of the *membership criteria* extends to *institutional questions, as well (the independence of the central bank).*

3.3. MARKET ECONOMY REQUIREMENTS FOR MONETARY INTEGRATION

According to R. A. MUNDELL, father of the theory, the most important attribute of the optimum currency area is the free and unlimited movement of factors, *flexibility in the factor markets*, which ensures that adjustment of prices and wages among the participants concerned takes place without large, serious losses or shocks (MUNDELL 1961: 657–664). *The flexibility of factor markets is the extension* to economic and monetary union *of the market economy criterion of integration maturity*, defining it *in all its complexity*.

The opinions of analysts of EMU are divided concerning the extent to which the EU can be considered an 'optimum' currency area. One of the key questions is how far it fulfils the requirement of *free movement of factors and market flexibility*.

The fact that the 'optimum currency area' requirement is not fulfilled "means that economic integration inside the EC has not yet reached the level

– where capital and especially labour mobility could act as near substitute for changes in the exchange rate;

– or that wage and price movements in different countries correspond to changes in productivity rates so as to make exchange rate realignments redundant;

– or even that the EC economy is sufficiently homogeneous so that different countries and regions are not frequently subject to asymmetric external shocks" (TSOUKALIS 1991: 194).

From the point of view of factor mobility it was an important development that from 1990 the member countries *abolished all restrictions on capital flows*. Earlier these restrictions had protected each country against speculative attacks, and cut off national interest rates from international market fluctuations. Their abolition showed that internal interest rates were becoming more closely linked to those of the euro-market.

The liberalizing measures introduced in the framework of the 1992 single European market program did not by any means cause the EU money and capital market to become integrated. The experiences of earlier years in the EMS showed that even with the fixing of currency parities and complete liberalization of capital, certain differences between interest rates could remain (for instance, the difference was about 4 percentage points between Italy and Germany). With the transition to the third stage of EMU interest rates became uniform, thereby causing capital market conditions to approximate even more. The euro capital market took off, and intensive cooperation and concentration began among the banks. From the aspect of capital flows there seem to be no serious obstacles to implementing EMU, though complete integration of the capital market may take several years.

The most important factor in the common monetary policy is interest rates which are applied uniformly throughout the euro region. At the same time it is a fact that there are still significant differences between the member countries of the Union in their monetary structures, so that monetary measures reach the real economies in different ways, through different channels and transmissions. As a result, a given increase in the interest rate affects the various national economies differently depending on the recession situation and also on the form in which the monetary 'message' is conveyed, and on its intensity.

One key question of *the effectiveness of the common monetary policy* is in what way and how quickly national economies react to monetary measures. Raising this question brings us in fact to the problem of *monetary transmission*, namely, in a given economy, how is the official interest rate translated into market interest rates? What makes monetary transmission especially important is that the common monetary policy is of the "one size fits all" type, so every economy has to maintain its equilibrium within the same monetary framework, while they differ in the *structure and level of development of their money markets*, which determine the effectiveness of the 'transmission' of the 'message'.

Differences also exist with regard to *the time needed for monetary transmission*. On the basis of the earlier period Union members can be divided into two groups. One is the group of those where the economy reacts only after a relatively long lapse of time to monetary measures (e.g. restrictions) but then there is a strong response from the real sphere – production drops significantly. The other group consists of those where transmission is rapid; in their case production adjusts with minimum delay to reduced demand.

The efficiency of monetary transmission is dependent on many factors:

– What differences can be shown between the member countries *in the (relative) weight of credit and non-credit type financing*? The data call attention to the enormous difference that exists among some EU member countries in terms of loans and other ways of raising capital (e.g. share issues). Loan financing is a decisive source for German and Spanish firms, while Finnish and Dutch companies rely mainly on non-credit financing possibilities. It is a special characteristic of the EU and EMU that in general non-bank loan financing is of little importance everywhere. This is due to the peripheral role of share issues. In contrast to the US, in Europe companies make little use of this possible means of financing.

– Differences in the efficiency of monetary transmission can also be due to the fact that despite similarities in the global weight of bank loan financing, in one country non-banks chiefly make use of *short-term financing possibilities, while elsewhere long-term ones are preferred.* Obviously the greater the weight of short-term bank loan financing in an economy, the more rapid and efficient its monetary transmission.

– *The monopolistic character of the banking sector* and the lack of intensity of competition represent an important factor. Among other things this indicates the trend of banks' profitability, which is mainly expressed by their net income from interest. The dispersion of this index not only shows the varying abilities of banks to generate income, but calls attention to the limited nature of competition within the banking sector. In the course of the 1990s convergence of interest margins was definitely observable among the EU member countries.

– *The financing role of stock exchanges and its level* increased steadily in the EU member countries throughout the 1990s, but despite this they still play a much smaller part in financing than in countries overseas. The value of securities registered on stock exchanges in the EU is 32% of GDP, compared with 68% in the US and 65% in Japan.

– The effectiveness of monetary measures may be influenced by *the net financial position of the non-banking sector*. Are companies and households in the position of debtors or creditors in relation to the banking sector? If the non-bank sector is a net debtor, then society and a wide swathe of the economy reacts to any monetary measure, since the burden of existing debt – debt-servicing and interest payment obligations – may rise proportionately.

– *The personal savings structure* varies from one country to another. In some countries the greater proportion of personal savings are held in cash and in bank deposits; elsewhere significant investments in long-term (or annuity) securities dominate. As regards the effect of monetary policy measures on personal consumption expenditure, we must mention the growing money market role of pension funds and life insurance companies. An ever-increasing proportion of personal savings is absorbed by the special non-banking institutions; they offer income owners a form of investment where yields are only indirectly affected by the central bank interest rate.

– From the point of view of transmission, finally, *the openness of economies* deserves attention. Where the economy really is open, that is, even after the formation of the Union the relative weight of the 'external economy' and 'foreign trade' is considerable, more efficient monetary transmission can be hoped for. The less the importance of external relations, that is, the exchange of goods and capital with economies outside the EMU, then the less efficient monetary transmission will be.

Those who think that the EU is not an optimum currency area justify their opinion by pointing out *the inflexibility of labour markets and the limited mobility of labour.* According to a study by the Brookings Institute, in the US there is virtually no regional unemployment, because the labour force reacts relatively flexibly and rapidly to regional changes in economic conditions. According to estimates, in the US out of every 100 employed 65 leave the state in question, 5 leave the labour market, and just 30 stay (*Financial Times,* June 18, 1992). In the EU the reverse is the case. If as a result of the single European market regional specialization develops similar to that in the US, then in the absence of mobility considerable regional differences in levels of employment could arise.

According to traditional economic theories, then, the EU is not an 'optimum currency area' mainly because labour is insufficiently mobile. In most countries the level of trade union organization of the workforce is high, as a result of which wage rises also react inflexibly to changes in the situation. It is no accident that compared with its partners the EU suffers from higher unemployment and more frequent social conflict.

In Europe, owing to the unfavourable housing policy and situation the mobility of unskilled labour even within a given country is very poor. The problems of some backward regions of Europe (southern Italy and the north of England) have remained unsolved for decades, or even centuries.

The EU labour market is characterized by many tensions (regional inequalities, the deteriorating age composition of the labour force). In spite of high unemployment there is a shortage of highly-qualified 'white-collar workers', especially engineers, technicians and researchers. This market tendency may increase in the future, as with the growth of the intelligence content of products and services the earnings of managers, engineers and multi-skilled workers rise. This raises wages, but naturally in the long-term it can be assumed that they will be covered by increased productivity.

The above contradictions, though with certain differences, arose in a concentrated way in the past decades in the development of a number of countries. The 1980s showed that the European trade unions preferred higher unemployment to any reduction in real wages. Higher wage claims were traditionally linked with promises of higher productivity, and any short-term time slippage could be satisfactorily bridged by adjusting the exchange rate, without any loss of competitiveness. Similarly it was possible to correct the linkage between wage rises and inflation. The trade unions generally insisted that prices should first be lowered, and only after that could any reduction in wage demands be expected. In this respect the ERM offered a certain scope for exchange-rate adjustments. With the advent of the single currency, this possibility ceased to exist.

From the point of view of wage and labour market flexibility, a distinction must be made between sectors according to the extent to which they are exposed to the effect of market (foreign trade) competition. BALASSA and SAMUELSON drew attention to this (BALASSA 1964, SAMUELSON 1964). The situation is different in the sectors that are involved in world trade with so-called 'tradables' – mainly manufactured goods – and in those that sell chiefly on the domestic market ('non-tradable' products – mainly services). According to the so-called *BALASSA–SAMUELSON effect,* owing to competitive pressures in the 'traded goods sector' productivity will grow faster than in the non-tradable sectors. The strong productivity growth in traded goods will probably lead to high wage increases, but without affecting output prices. If these wage increases spill over to sectors producing non-traded goods, as a result of their lower productivity growth their output prices are likely to rise. Depending on the role and proportions of these sectors, the wage-price mechanisms may work in a distorted way, and may lead to lower or higher inflation.

The *BALASSA–SAMUELSON effect particularly applies to the catching-up countries* (CEE candidates), where the relatively faster growth in productivity and wages, then the spilling over to non-tradables, may produce a higher inflation rate compared to other EMU members. This, however, is normal and can be accepted, as it means *price convergence* between the lower and higher price level countries. The effects of *non-tradable sectors* should be analyzed for *the developed countries also*. From 1/4 to 1/3 of the labour force is employed in the area of such services. These will probably not be affected by the disciplinary power of EMU and it will take time for wage differentials to adjust to the new conditions. The experience of the past has shown that in the services sphere inflation rates were higher, amounting to almost twice the level of price increases for material goods. The mid-1992 price index for material goods was 2% in the US and France and 3% in Great Britain, while in Italy it was almost 5%. The same indices for services in these countries were 4.6% and 10% respectively. The burden of reducing inflation continues disproportionately to affect producers of manufactured goods.

Naturally, with monetary union *price differences do not disappear*. Differences in wage levels due to productivity differences remain, but particularly in such spheres as house and commercial property prices, or energy prices, big differences can appear. Despite the integration based on the single currency, price differences between, for instance, the provinces of Canada are not smaller than those between the EU countries.

Monetary union should set up strong market barriers against inflation and wage demands that outstrip productivity, which is one of the most important arguments in its favour. With the common currency, faster wage growth erodes profits and competitiveness, and has to be paid for in higher unemployment. As the Commission report evaluating EMU emphasizes, the regional labour costs should remain in harmony with productivity differences, because otherwise the unemployment increases (One Market, One Money, 1990: 38).

By the 1980s the example of France, Denmark and Ireland had shown that where industry and trade unions were incapable of flexible adjustment, bringing down inflation involved lost production and higher than average unemployment.

Certain measures in the Social Charter can assist more rational mobility of labour (e.g. transferability of pensions), while others (like the minimum age limit for employment) may hinder it.

A developed capital market (loan conditions, property market, etc.) is also *indispensable from the point of view of ensuring a flexible labour market. Improvement of the infrastructural conditions* is particularly important (the housing situation, transport, telecommunications, skills training). Measures within the single internal market (recognition of degrees and other professional qualifications) could contribute to greater mobility of labour.

The dangers of monetary union arise with greater complexity if structural weaknesses underlie competitiveness problems. In the long-term monetary restrictions may hinder technical and structural modernization, and generate tensions in the system. This, with the single currency, may *take the form of an increase in regional differences.*

With monetary union, therefore, differences in competitiveness as balance-of-payments problems formally disappear, but *they remain as causes of decline in the given regions*. Regional differences have never become apparent at state level because the EU member countries show a relatively high degree of homogeneity among themselves. Their regional problems even now are greater than those in the US. In the absence of appropriate regional policies, these could worsen in the future. Thus instead of exchange-rate policies, regional policies are set to gain prominence. The need to deal with regional inequalities increases the importance of structural policies and budgetary transfers.

3.4. 'ASYMMETRIC SHOCKS' – CONVERGENCE – FINANCIABILITY – COHESION

Economies can suffer various kinds of unexpected external or internal effects (negative or positive) or shocks, as a result of which the performance of the given economy may suddenly and drastically change. On the basis of their causes, such shocks may be

– structural in origin (crisis in 'sensitive' sectors; oil crisis, debt crisis, etc.);
– conjunctural character (slump, unemployment, bad harvest, etc.); or
– results of unforeseen events (natural disasters, conflicts, wars, etc.).

These 'shocks' differ more or less from one country to another (they are 'asymmetrical') in their nature, location, consequences and timing. The basis of these so-called 'asymmetric shocks' consists in differences between countries:

– in the structure of their economy and of production;
– in their potential for growth;
– in their external and internal market positions;

– in the forms of regulation of the economy and the markets;
– in their institutional structure; or even
– in the forms and traditions of social behaviour.

On the basis of all these, the literature distinguishes between:

– 'country-specific',
– 'sector-specific' and
– 'region-specific' shocks.

EMU is based on the transmission of monetary policy to union level. If the 'shocks' affecting countries are 'asymmetric', this runs counter to unification of monetary policy, since different countries would need measures differing in nature and direction. *So the effectiveness of the common monetary policy assumes the elimination of the asymmetries of such shocks*. The *danger of asymmetric shocks* indicates that the given group of countries *does not fulfil the structural criteria of integration maturity for EMU.*

There is general agreement that monetary union is less exposed to the troublesome effects of asymmetric shocks, the more closely integrated are the units within the union (national economies and regions), the more diversified the production structures that have developed, and, with the convergence of economic and commercial structures, the higher the level of intra-sectoral trade. *P. Kenen stresses the need for a high degree of diversification of economies*, as a condition of the optimum currency area (Kenen 1969). On the basis of the highly stratified nature of economic structures there is a greater chance that the effects of disturbances and external shocks will be more moderate. It could be particularly beneficial if there are considerable intra-sectoral trade flows and a significant proportion of these are balanced. One important index can be the relatively low weight of so-called 'sensitive sectors' in the trade structure.

Thus ultimately it is a question of the *coordination of economies, the synchronization of economic cycles*. Strengthening integration obviously helps in the transmission of the various kinds of shocks among the regions of the union, that is, it increases the speed of diffusion of shocks. This, however, proportionately reduces the development of shock effects. According to R. McKinnon, from the point of view of the optimum currency area *the degree of openness of the economies* affected varies so much that it must be taken into account (McKinnon 1963). Open economies are more sensitive to external shocks, but the diffusion of these is also faster.

The total amount of foreign direct investment from partner countries (through both outflows and inflows) has risen sharply in the Community countries in the past few decades. The total of foreign direct investment amounts to almost 1/5 of GDP, and the counterbalancing effect of these relations in tempering asymmetric shocks are undeniable. If a capital-exporting country is affected by an asymmetric shock, the loss of income resulting from the negative changes is well compensated for by profits made on investments in the unaffected partner countries. Approached from another angle, the strengthening of direct capital relations results in the spreading of shocks, so that they tend to develop into general negative processes affecting all the member countries. The spreading of shocks, however, moderates the losses suffered by any one economy. This clearly makes the task of the common monetary policy easier, since every member of the system *needs similar monetary measures.*

The question arises, how EMU affects the participants' economic structure, and to what extent it modifies cycle synchronicity. Researchers support two types of hypothesis. According to one concept, the operation of EMU in itself results in closer trade relations between the members, so their economic structure becomes increasingly similar, and with increased cycle synchronicity the likelihood of asymmetric shock effects is reduced. This conclusion seems particularly justified when shocks occur in demand and when the weight of intra-sectoral trade is considerable (EICHENGREEN, BAYOUMI, GIAVAZZI, DE GRAUWE, DECRESSIN, FRANKEL and ROSE 1998). In connection with internal homogeneity, in the wider sense this simply means the approximation of levels of development and economic structures, and their close interconnectedness, despite the differentiation resulting from specialization.

In the opinion of PAUL KRUGMAN, a higher level of integration is not necessarily accompanied by reduction of sensitivity to assymmetric shocks (KRUGMAN 1993). In fact, as integration deepens it is not the case that production structures become more similar, but that more intense regional specialization takes place, since it is through territorial concentration of production that the benefits of economies of scale can be exploited, but this increases specialization of production and trade. The vulnerability of some regions to the dangers of specific shocks is thereby definitely heightened. While in earlier times regional specialization was firmly restrained by international trade barriers and substantial transportation costs, with the creation of the single internal market and through technological changes the former obstacles to specialization are being removed.

Many dispute KRUGMAN's theses. Experts emphasize the efforts at product differentiation. Since competition is not perfect, in international trade – and internal trade within the Union – a significant volume of turnover of similar-type goods takes place. In respect of manufactured goods, perfect replaceability never exists. As a result, a certain amount of parallelism remains, in spite of integration and trade liberalization. Despite the advance of territorial specialization, within the sphere of integration a significant proportion of trade takes place within sectors, so Union members are increasingly likely to face symmetric shocks in the future.

According to the Commission's arguments in favour of monetary union, EMU should in fact reduce the occurrence of country-specific shocks and make them easier to handle, while the risks deriving from exchange-rate instability and uncoordinated monetary policy will disappear. "While the possible occurrence of country-specific shocks cannot be eliminated, they are likely to become less probable for three reasons. First, integration as a result of 1992 and EMU leads to changes in industrial structures in the direction of deeper 'intra-industry' trade and investment relations, which means that most countries become involved in both exporting and importing the products of many industries. Old-style comparative advantage, in which countries specialize their production in distinct commodities, become less important. As a result sector-specific shocks become to a lesser degree country-specific in their impact. Secondly, a credible monetary union will affect the behaviour of wage-bargainers. They will be more careful about risking becoming uncompetitive, given that devaluation will not be an option. Thirdly, EMU will eliminate an important category of country-specific shocks which originate in exchange-rate movements themselves and imperfectly coordinated monetary policy" (One Market, One Money, 1990: 24).

For avoiding 'shocks', 'perfect functioning' of markets is often mentioned. In fact, the most important (most effective) shock-absorbing mechanisms are ensured by free markets and their perfectly flexible functioning. It is not by chance that the single internal market in the EU represents the basis of monetary union, and was defined as virtually a starting condition ('first phase'). With regard to commodity and financial markets this criterion is in practice being fulfilled. The situation is different as regards the labour market.

From the point of view of the smooth functioning of monetary union, the most critical question is to what extent coordination of the participating economies, the alignment of the functioning of these economies, is assured. It is not a condition of Union membership that the member countries should all be at the same level of development. The acceptable degree of deviation in development levels is determined by the Union's convergence capacity, that is, the extent to which it is able to initiate mechanisms and policies that narrow the performance gap between member countries. If the Union really does function successfully, then in the medium-term *convergence in the real economy (and with it, in society)* will follow.

The weaker regions can hope to catch up only if they set out on a path of more dynamic growth than the leading economies. At the same time, optimum functioning of the Union should not mean a zero-sum game; stronger growth in the 'catching-up' countries should not be achieved at the expense of weaker performance by the stronger economies. From the Union's point of view it is very important how far national economies can be expected to achieve parallel development, if possible a positive change in levels of performance, or whether fundamentally different shock reactions in the various economies will have to be faced.

From the point of view of 'internal homogeneity' it is easy to see that in the Community in the last two decades the integration process has surged ahead, and thus the cycle asynchronicity among the member countries has significantly decreased. Intra-sectoral trade in industrial goods has grown enormously. The strongest development can be observed in connection with the late entrants, the relatively less developed countries (Portugal, Spain, Ireland and Finland).

Experience suggests the probability that in response to exchange-rate adjustments, wages and prices will fall more slowly and react more inflexibly, with the likely result that production will fall and unemployment will rise. Governments' room for manoeuvre will thus be reduced, and in order to provide assistance, debatable *budgetary transfers* may become necessary. With regard to the optimum currency area, many (e.g. *G. D. A. MacDaugall and P. R. Allen) emphasize the need for a high degree of budgetary integration,* to ensure the effectiveness of intra-Union transfers and maintenance of stability (MacDaugall 1983).

In relation to EMU, then, *so-called financeability criteria* directly come up. Since most of the EU member countries are barely capable of fulfilling the structural criteria, in the interest of supporting the less developed member countries and strengthening their social cohesion, it became clear that compensatory budget transfers were needed. With these, regional environmental and structural programs are financed in member countries where per capita GDP is less than 90% of the average for the community. In accordance with these decisions the *cohesion fund* was set up, and the structural funds were substantially increased. Expansion of the funds was urged particularly by the less developed countries and regions (Germany's new Länder are also entitled to assistance). These transfers are important conditions of *social support for monetary integration.*

4. EMU AND ECONOMIC POLICY COORDINATION – INSTITUTIONAL CRITERIA

Economic and monetary union implements integration in the economic policy sphere. It represents unification of economic policies (certain tax harmonization), their coordination (budgetary policies) and the development of common policies (monetary policy). From the point of view of monetary integration, *common monetary policy* is especially important (interest rate and exchange rate policy), and this is closely connected with *coordination of certain economic policy areas*. With EMU, the system of economic policy institutions and its new operational structure is developing, which in the EU has many special features compared with other 'federal systems'. While in terms of monetary policy new Union responsibilities and competences are emerging, in the peculiar structure of its institutional system the 'intergovernmental character' remains predominant (fiscal policy). The problems of the functioning of EMU will obviously to a great extent determine the direction of future institutional reforms.

From the point of view of *Union monetary policy*, a special part is played by the European Central Bank (ECB). The Maastricht protocol made provision for the establishment of an *independent European Central Bank*, and of the European System of Central Banks (ESCB). The ESCB consists of the ECB and the national central banks. The main task of the ECB is to safeguard 'the maintenance of price stability', which the Bank defined as 'keeping inflation to between 0 and 2%', and monetary policies must be subordinated to this. The ECB, like the Bundesbank, was endowed with independence. It is the responsibility of the ESCB to define and execute the community's monetary policy, carry out foreign currency transactions, handle the member countries' official currency reserves and ensure the 'smooth functioning of the monetary system'. The ECB and ESCB began their operation on January 1, 1999.

From the beginning there was agreement that for monetary integration *a central bank was needed that was independent and had the necessary jurisdiction.* Independence means that the bank cannot be given instructions by national governments and EU institutions. National monetary policy, in fact, is often subordinated to short-term government and electoral interests, and governments have bought votes with policies that, in the longer term, have had inflationary effects. "A growing pile of research shows that the more independent a country's central bank, the lower its inflation rate will be over the medium- and long-term. Allow governments much say over the setting of interest rates, and they will use that power to produce booms just before elections, followed by inflationary busts once the votes have been counted" (*The Economist,* April 20, 1991). "It is difficult to avoid the conclusion that there is a strong link between central bank independence and price stability. Germany and Switzerland have the two most independent central banks, and enjoy the lowest inflation rates" (EMERSON and HUHNE 1991: 68).

The recommendations expressed the conviction of experts and decision-makers that there really is a close connection between the central bank's independence and low inflation, although there was some disagreement on this point. The bank has to possess all the attributes of national central banks in order to fulfil its function. The single currency must have a guaranteed role as legal tender, that is, no one can refuse to accept it. In the financing of national debt and deficits three important golden rules must be kept:

– no possibility of financing deficits by printing money;
– no possibility of financing deficits from privileged sources, only from the money markets;
– no possibility of rescue action (bail-outs) to help governments in trouble.

With regard to the Central Bank, from the beginning there have been arguments about the transparency of its activities and its reporting obligation; in fact, about the interpretation of 'independence'. The president of the Bank does indeed report regularly to the European Parliament, but the latter does not have the right to review or change the Bank's status and policy. By contrast, the Chairman of the American Federal Reserve Bank not only reports to Congress, but the latter has wide-ranging powers to change the Bank's status and viewpoint.

EMU raises *monetary policy to Union level,* while *budgetary policies,* apart from the conditions defined in the Stability and Growth Pact, basically *remain within the competence of national governments.* "The EMU block will be almost unique among the world's currency unions in having no central fiscal authority with a substantial role in taxing and spending" (CRAWFORD 1996: 299).

The main forum for economic policy coordination is ECOFIN (the European Council of Economic and Finance Ministers). Decision-making is still the responsibility of ECOFIN, although the finance ministers of the 11 euro-zone countries can hold unofficial consultations outside the so-called Euro-11 framework. Any attempts by the Euro-11 to take decisions have so far met with rejection. In the second half of 2000 one innovation under the French chairmanship was that the Euro-11 were named 'the Euro Group', and it was proposed that the finance ministers should be given the right to set the ceiling for inflation. This idea, which would greatly reduce the independence of the Central Bank, was most decisively rejected by Germany.

– every year the Council defines comprehensive economic policy guidelines, the budget and exchange rate stability;

– it decides whether any country in the euro-zone has too big a deficit, and if so, makes recommendations for putting an end to that situation in the country concerned;

– since the euro was introduced in 1999, it has the right to impose punitive measures on any countries belonging to the euro-zone which have too big a deficit; this is based on so-called 'multilateral surveillance', introduced by the Council in 1990 and later confirmed by the Maastricht Treaty.

Within the framework of the Amsterdam Treaty in 1997 the member countries approved the *Stability and Growth Pact,* according to which the member states committed themselves to a stability program planned to last for several years. The member states must continue to prevent deficits in excess of 3% of GDP, but in the medium-term they aim to achieve 'balanced budgets'. If a given country does not fulfil the budgetary indices, it receives a warning from the Council. In the event of non-fulfilment, at the end of a special procedure the member state can be required to make a deposit of 0.2% of its GDP in a non-interest-bearing Community account. If the member state is unable to put its budget in order within two years, this deposit is converted into a non-returnable fine. The penalty is not automatic, but can be imposed with the approval of a majority of the euro-zone members. If the country is hit by a recession, it can be exempted from 'punishment'.

Exchange-rate policy decisions remain the responsibility of the Council of Ministers. On the other hand, international currency market interventions are the task of the ECB.

Apart from determination of budgetary equilibrium, in budgetary policy national governments have kept their independence. Although the single market would require tax harmonization, this would tie national governments' hands with regard to the flexible application of budgetary policy. At the same time, meeting the convergence criteria requires the possibility of flexible manoeuvering on the part of member states. The budget is an important means of handling asymmetric shocks, and this too is an argument in favour of flexibility. As far as harmonization is concerned, in the last few decades it has become clear that this is a politically highly sensitive area, since the 'sovereign right' to tax is a fundamental element of national (financial) sovereignty.

Many are also anxious about whether supervision of national governments' budgetary policy is appropriate from the point of view of achieving anti-inflation aims. In cases of over-spending by national governments it was a limiting factor that the burden of interest on their debts grew, and they risked having to devalue their currency. As the danger of currency devaluation grew, the money market would demand even higher interest, and so the barrier rose even higher.

With the coming of the single currency, the danger of devaluation was removed, and in theory governments could with less risk increase their debt, while raising interest rates not only for themselves but for the whole community. With the elimination of currency risk, therefore, an important force for discipline as far as national governments are concerned has disappeared.

In the opinion of others, the disciplinary power of the market has not disappeared, only it makes itself felt in different ways. Since devaluation is not possible, the money market can be expected to exercise even stricter selectivity with regard to national governments, and restrain them from irrational behaviour. "Financial markets are perfectly capable of discriminating among governments, as among private borrowers, on the basis of creditworthiness. In Europe, EMU will sharpen this credit-risk discrimination by shifting the markets' attention from inflation, current-account imbalances and other warnings of currency changes to the narrower question of budget deficits and the accumulation of public-sector debt. As a result, the arithmetic of public finance will come into much clearer focus. Governments, no longer able to print their own money, will be judged just like companies – which is as it should be" (*The Economist,* December 15, 1990: 61). So with the integration of the money markets, market evaluation of national budgetary policies is becoming more refined. There may be stronger political pressure for more effective budgetary policy, which could contribute to improvement of the efficiency of public services or stricter enforcement of fiscal discipline.

Keen competition may develop between national governments for more favourable loan conditions, and may compensate for the loss of the disciplinary effect of exchange-rate risk. The relevance of these interrelations is confirmed by the experience of federal states (e.g. in the US and Canada). With integration of markets, governments could find themselves competing with consumers and producers to keep taxes low, which will help to enforce budgetary discipline.

For the enforcement of budgetary discipline it is of course necessary that the monetary position of national budgets should be transparent, and the governments should not be able to count on any sort of community rescue action (the no-bail-out rule). The central bank should not be able to print money to finance governments' budget deficits. Rigorous community competition policy is important, to prevent national governments rushing to assist their companies with export subsidies. These possibilities are strictly ruled out by EMU.

Others are of the opinion that in the future, integration of budgetary policy is unavoidable, and that later, in order to deal with asymmetric shocks and promote stabilization, so-called *fiscal federalism* will be indispensable. One important characteristic of fiscal federalism is that *cohesion transfers are largely automatically carried out* by the budgets of the various federal states, in such a way that by means of progressive income tax and social benefits, income is redistributed from richer regions and social strata to poorer ones. *From the fiscal point of view it is a weakness of EMU* that in the EU budget such automatic mechanisms do not exist. On the other hand, community transfers from the various 'cohesion and structural funds' *do not come close to the amount that is likely to be needed and is typical in federal states.* In contrast to the structural funds' 0.46% share of GDP, such 'cohesion transfers' in other federations amount to 3–4% of GDP. This could be a source of tension from the point of view of enlargement, as well.

Most of the special literature on EMU still takes the view that the structure taking shape in the EU could function satisfactorily in the long-term, and there is no absolute need to develop 'fiscal federalism'. National budgets are capable of handling any tensions and adaptation constraints arising from EMU. As JACQUES PELKMANS says: "The conclusion is that the EU is not less a suitable currency area merely because it does not have, or plan to have, a centralised fiscal stabilisation policy. Decentralisation may do. Extreme forms of decentralisation can only be a stable solution in the absence of labour (and voter) mobility across borders. Thus, the strong EU preference to retain national fiscal stabilisers, interacts favourably with the strong preference to seek jobs in the national economy, in turn also permitting some degree of diverging social policies and regulation. In conclusion, it would seem that such an EMU, without much redistribution and no stabilisation at central level, is possible and may well be stable" (PELKMANS 1997: 293).

There are some who think the single currency in itself demands political integration. Behind a strong currency a fundamental requirement is a strong state. The euro at Union level lacks that, and it is uncertain to what extent the strong, independent Central Bank can replace it. Thus in connection with monetary and political integration there are many question marks, and only the future can provide the answers.

4.1. FIRST EXPERIENCES OF COORDINATION OF MONETARY POLICY AND ECONOMIC POLICY

The success and effectiveness of monetary policy can best be measured by inflation performance. True, the ECB itself was unable to keep below the strict 2% inflation ceiling it had set, but euro-zone inflation has remained below 3%, that is, *basically the price-stability requirement has been fulfilled.* This applies especially to core inflation; that is, actual inflation was raised by factors that fall outside the sphere of monetary policy (oil prices, a financial crisis). So it was not without justification that the ECB argued that despite hectic exchange-rate fluctuations, the euro can be regarded as one of the world's strongest currencies.

In monetary policy the Central Bank can make use of *interest-rate adjustment and currency market intervention as instruments*. In spite of the arguments to the contrary, the Bank has used these instruments in a restrained and well-considered way. In recent times it has made use of *interest-rate* adjustment on a number of occasions, and it can be said that this has contributed to its success in maintaining the chief directions of monetary policy. In contrast to the Fed's practice of frequent interest-rate adjustments, it has preferred to follow a strategy of less frequent but more concentrated changes.

– In April 1999 it reduced the standard interest rate from 3% to 2.5%.
– In November 1999 it restored it to the 3% level.
– In February 2000 it raised the rate by 0.25%.
– In March 2000 there was a furhter rise of 0.25%.
– In April 2000 there was another rise of 0.25%.
– In June 2000 it was raised by 0.5%.
– In September 2000 there was a further rise of 0.25%, whereby the standard rate reached 4.5%.
– In October 2000 by further 0.25% increase interest rate peaked with 4.75%.
– In May 2001 standard interest rate was reduced to 4.5%.
– In August 2001 further reduction was made to 4.25%.
– In September 2001 by 0.5% reduction the standard rate was set at 3.75%.
– In November 2001 by further 0.5% reduction the rate was decreased to 3.25%.

In the circumstances of the slump in growth in 1999, at the beginning of the year the Bank yielded to the pressure to lower the interest rate. Slow growth in the economies of Germany and Italy was the main cause of the slump. *The increase in inflationary pressure* based on the further crumbling of the euro exchange rate from the end of 1999 forced the Bank to intervene more frequently and decisively. Accelerating inflation caused growing anxiety and dissatisfaction in business circles, though there was agreement that it would not be advisable to slow down growth too much. This applied particularly from the second half of 2000, as the recession in the world economy made itself felt in the European economy. From 2001 the Bank made virtually no use of the possibility of interest rate adjustment, or only in a very limited way. The high level of inflation did not allow the reduction that was desirable in view of the recession, but precisely because of the latter it also ruled out any further increase. This is in sharp contrast to the Fed's policy, which at the beginning of 2002 took the interest rate down to the historically low level of

1.50%. True, thanks to the recession, inflation in America which stood at 3.4% in 2000, despite this fell below 2% by 2002.

In a new move, in accordance with the decisions it took on August 31, 2000, the ECB also undertook *currency market intervention,* which up to then it had been reluctant to do. Experts justified their reservations about intervention in the currency market in defence of the euro mainly by saying that they felt it would be ineffective. Considering the volume of daily turnover on the currency markets these days, central banks do not have sufficient reserves to be able to take effective and convincing action against speculation by selling or buying a given currency. This was well demonstrated by the events of the 1992 currency crisis.

In mid-September the Bank carried out currency market transactions to the value of about € 2.5 bn. For this, interest income from bank reserves was used. Officially, the Bank did not describe the transactions as 'intervention'. The markets, however, interpreted it as the Bank's first admission that it was prepared to intervene in the international currency markets in defence of the euro by selling its foreign currency reserves.

The *first officially declared and coordinated currency market* intervention took place on September 22, 2001, and involved the cooperation of the American, Japanese, British and Canadian central banks. These G–7 banks bought euros to an estimated value of $3–5 bn, as a result of which the exchange rate of the single European currency immediately rose from 85 cents to 90 cents. Though according to experts the rich countries 'acted courageously', this step cannot be regarded as a commitment by the partner countries to defend the euro. Such intervention "works best if it is aimed at squeezing out a speculative bubble, if it signals a change in underlying policies, if it is strongly supported by all parties, and if they are prepared to intervene repeatedly and in large amounts. None of these conditions pertain in the case of the euro" (*The Economist,* September 30, 2000: 23). This was made very clear by the fact that the American Treasury Secretary, LARRY SUMMERS, felt it necessary to announce immediately that there was question of giving up the 'strong dollar' policy. It was no accident that the euro exchange rate soon fell back again.

At the beginning of November the ECB once again intervened, this time unilaterally. Now that it had become clear that the weakness of the euro was increasingly threatening price stability, the monetary policy priorities entirely justified intervention. At the same time expert opinion remained unchanged: the effectiveness of interventions was still highly questionable, and tended to damage rather than strengthen the Bank's credibility. With the stabilization of the euro, in the period that followed currency market intervention no longer figured on the agenda.

The recession in the member countries was accompanied by *deteriorating budget positions,* on the basis of which the Stability and Growth Pact gained in importance. By 2002 in Germany and Italy the budget deficit came close to the 3% ceiling, while in Portugal it even went through it. With this being an election year, in Germany the issuing of warnings in itself created tension.

The experience of the initial period draws attention to *the dangers of a 'one-size-fits-all' monetary policy*. This arises especially in connection with the policy of uniform interest rates, in relation to differing growth rates and rates of inflation. From the point of view of growth, the countries of the euro-zone can be divided into 3 groups. One is the group of countries with dynamic economies achieving annual growth of about 3–4% (in 1999 Portugal and Spain achieved 3.6% growth, Finland about 5%, and the 'Celtic tiger', Ireland, 7%), which was well above the average 2% level of growth for the whole zone in 1999. The second group consists of the slightly above average countries, Belgium, Holland, France and Austria, with growth rates of 2.2–2.5%. Finally, the third group consists of Germany and Italy, with growth probably around 1.8%, that is, more or less stagnating economies. This means that with identical interest rates the difference between the two extreme values for the rate of economic growth is a factor of 4.

The uniform interest rate policy clearly does not correspond to the interests of divergent economies. While the April 1999 reduction in the interest rate was necessary from the point of view of the stagnating German and Italian economies, in the Irish economy it increased the danger of overheating. The inflationary aspects are especially problematic.

In Germany with 0.1% inflation the 2.5% nominal interest rate is equivalent to a real interest rate of 2.4%. In Portugal with 2.7% inflation this results in virtually negative real interest rates, which are not needed for growth, but result in further boosting inflation. In Ireland particularly the turbulence in the property market caused tensions where they were already confronted with 'bubble-economy' phenomena. In 1999 property prices in Ireland rose by 20% in one year. Similar problems were experienced in Spain. Low interest rates led to an explosion in borrowing and spending; the demand for credit in the private sector grew by 30% for the year.

According to some, problems were caused by the fact that the new European Central Bank did not always rise to the occasion, and neither in its basic principles nor in its operation has it yet found its proper place. As MARGIT RÁCZ states, "the euro's 'free fall' on the international currency markets in those first 6 months was partly due to the fact that the 'monetary authority' created to protect the new currency had not yet really taken characteristic form" (*Üzleti Hét*, June 28, 1999). Opinions concerning the Brussels Commission are no better. "The Brussels officials do not command sufficient respect, and the Stability and Growth Pact does not inspire too much confidence either, though it might be expected to enforce objective and automatic compliance with the fiscal and monetary convergence criteria" (ANDOR, *Figyelő*, May 18–24, 2000: 24). When at the beginning of September 2000 in contrast to the Commission and the ECB the German Chancellor SCHRÖDER announced that the weakness of the euro was decidedly favourable, the markets immediately reacted in a negative manner.

With the raising of monetary policy to Union level, for the individual countries *the role of other economic policy spheres gains in importance.* As a simple comparison, opposite Union monetary policy stand national fiscal policies. The scope of fiscal policy is limited by the fact that it is subordinated to monetary priorities. The Stability Pact is designed to ensure this. Therefore other areas, such as *income policy or structural policies* could and should be given *a more prominent role.* For the time being this does not seem to be working, at least not to the extent that it did in Germany, where the Bundesbank could count on the well-established cooperation between the trade unions and entrepreneurs' organizations. This is lacking at present, so the ECB cannot count on it.

In *wages policy* there are very big differences among the various countries. On the other hand, union coordination is largely absent among those that exercise influence on wage negotiations. In Germany and Austria well-organized regional wage-negotiation mechanisms operate; Ireland has a national incomes policy, while the Dutch labour market has to a large extent been deregulated. In France and Italy wage increases are in the hands of the government, while in Holland and Spain there are no restrictions on above-average wage increases. In Italy the system of national collective agreements causes trouble; these guarantee minimum wages for workers in the various economic sectors. This 'concertazione', collective negotiations involving the government, trade unions and employers, which has been one of the chief characteristics of economic policy, will be difficult to maintain in the new circumstances. Problems are caused by the fact that whereas the Bundesbank was able to indicate what it considered 'excessive' wage demands, politically the ECB is not in a position to do so. It can, however, send signals through its interest rate policy.

According to many people, the market is capable of regulating these processes. Companies, with growing European and global competition, are becoming extremely sensitive to increases in wage costs. In spite of the different wage policies and bargaining practice of individual countries, regulation of wage increases tends more and more to take place at company level. Above-average wage rises can be afforded only by companies that can compensate for them by raising productivity.

With the introduction of the euro the single financial market is taking shape, supported by monetary policy instruments. There are increasing complaints that this in itself is insufficient. Ultimately *unified bank and money market supervision* will be needed.

It is no accident that to promote *reform of the capital markets*, the Union's finance ministers, at the instigation of the French finance minister LAURENT FABIUS, have set up a 7-member committee (a 'Council of Wise Men') headed by SÁNDOR LÁMFALUSSY. The committee examined the present regulations concerning the functioning of the stock market, and made recommendations in favour of cross-border stock exchange associations and technical innovations, and also regulatory convergence and the facilitating of day-to-day cooperation. This may contribute to the creation of a single capital market in the coming years, and a single market for financial services.

4.2. THE EURO AND INTERNATIONAL MONETARY COORDINATION

The foreign trade regulatory system in relation to the euro has been particularly widely criticized. Monetary policy largely concentrates on internal monetary stability and does not emphasize the external exchange rate of the euro; competences relating to this are also uncertain. In exchange-rate policy responsibility is shared between the ECB and the finance ministers, and in this way governments' political interests are able to play a part. Since the weak euro suits the finance ministers, the Central Bank is obliged to accept this, despite the risks of inflation. The ECB's occasional currency-market interventions cannot be expected to change the picture significantly.

Many people expected that with the euro better-regulated conditions would emerge in international monetary affairs, and that the state of 'benign neglect' would cease. This was how the post-war behaviour of the US was described, which 'benignly' just ignored the role of the dollar as a key currency, and the world economic consequences of this, always subordinating monetary policy to the country's domestic interests. Now many hoped that cooperation among the world's three leading currencies would become technically easier and more feasible, and at least in their own thoroughly-understood interests they would in some way coordinate their exchange-rate policies. As the main concern of ECB is price stability, and the exchange rate is much less important, the policy of "benign neglect" remains the property of euro, as well.

The various sides have so far rejected any kind of exchange-rate policy cooperation. Particularly the US Treasury and Federal Reserve have shown a negative attitude, whether it be a question of mobilization of reserves in defence of exchange rates, or the designation of 'target zones' limiting exchange-rate movements. Against money market interventions it is often said that the daily volume of international currency trading is such that the world's central banks simply do not have sufficient resources to be able to exercise any real influence on the markets. Perhaps the Japanese would be more cooperative, but so far the occasion has not arisen. Yet many think it would be advisable, since excessive fluctuations in exchange rates, whether upwards or downwards, are harmful to everyone's interest. The Nobel Prize-winner ROBERT MUNDELL, and FRED BERGSTEN, director of the Institute for International Economics in Washington, have both urged the G–7 to undertake intervention and exchange-rate policy coordination.

In plans and discussions relating to monetary cooperation or integration the question of a 'parallel currency' has often arisen. In the literature a parallel means of payment is mentioned when the proportion of a given foreign currency in internal circulation is more than 10% of the amount of money in circulation. The parallel currency becomes official if the laws allow entrepreneurs and consumers a free choice of means of payment, and the external currency is accepted as legal tender. This means that a company can pay not just wages but official dues as well (taxes, social security contributions, etc.) in foreign currency (e.g. in euros). This requirement may arise particularly in sectors covered by transnational companies or built on intensive integration relations.

In Europe the parallel currency question arose in relation to EMU partly

– *as one of the possibilities of development of the common currency,* and partly
– *as a consequence of the introduction of the common currency.*

"The basic idea of the parallel currency approach is that a European currency which is made attractive enough will readily be used by economic agents, and in so doing drive the national currencies out of the market. At the end of the road we will have monetary union. One of the main intellectual attractions of this approach to monetary unification is that the movement and the speed toward EMU will be determined by the free choice of European citizens, and not by decisions taken by politicians and bureaucrats. In addition, the competition provided by this parallel currency will force the national monetary authorities to behave better. As a result, this strategy will have the interesting side-effect of reducing inflation" (DE GRAUWE 1994: 169–170). It must be noted that this idea is consonant with HAYEK's theory that in money creation competition reduces inflation.

When in 1969–71 the plan for monetary union was worked out, concrete notions about the creation and introduction of the common currency had not yet been formed. It was considered equally possible that the common currency, the name of which had not even been decided at that time, could be used alongside the national currencies (as a 'parallel currency') or introduced in place of them.

The first concrete plan relating to the common currency appeared in 1972; it was produced by JOHN WILLIAMSON and GIOVANNI MAGNIFICO, who recommended calling the new currency unit the 'Europa', and would have tied it to the national currencies. They designed the new unit to be less inflationary, which would make its use attractive to the various actors in the economy. Later the proposal was taken over by an international group of economists, and they published their ideas in the November 1, 1975 issues of *The Economist* under the title "All Saints' Day Manifesto". According to their plan, the 'Europa' would be issued in the framework of the European Monetary Agreement, and would go into circulation in every member country. Its value would be tied to the strong national currencies, whereby it was hoped to ensure the permanence of its purchasing power. This would have meant its value steadily rising against the weaker currencies, which, in view of the population's dislike of inflation, would have caused its use to become more and more widespread. In connection with the plan, apart from technical objections chiefly political reservations were expressed, and outside narrow professional circles it did not arouse much interest.

When later the plan for economic and monetary union gradually had to be abandoned, the question disappeared from the agenda. An important element of the *European Monetary* System established after 1979 was *the creation of the European Currency Unit (ECU).* In practice the ECU, especially as it increasingly took over some of the functions of money, operated as a special 'parallel currency'. The ECU, however, did not prove attractive enough, either in its money functions or in its soundness, to match up fully to the above assumptions with regard to the 'parallel currency'. Since its exchange rate was expressed as a basket consisting of all the members' currencies, obviously compared to the strongest currency it was inflationary. It was used only within a narrow circle, in whatever function of money (means of exchange, reserve or exchange-rate measure).

The DELORS plan and its program of economic and monetary union ruled out from the start the 'parallel currency' possibility. By so doing it was intended to express and emphasize the determination that the new currency should be *a single currency*. There were other ideas and suggestions (e.g. JOHN MAJOR's proposal of the 'hard ECU'), according to which the ECU would always be pegged to the strongest currency, and would never be devalued against any national currency, but these were rejected by the member countries. Governments were not ready to declare the ECU legal tender (e.g. for paying tax). Yet without this, the population could hardly be expected to switch over en masse to the ECU in preference to their national currency.

On the basis of the DELORS plan, according to the original proposals the single currency would at a given moment (e.g. on January 1 one year) replace all the national currencies, that is, 'parallel' use was ruled out. Later it became clear that a 'big bang' method like this was in practice not technically feasible. Coins and banknotes could not be replaced from one hour to the next, and the situation was the same with the adaptation of computers and tills (or, for example, filling-stations). So it was decided that the euro should function for 3 years in the form of a parallel money, while the introduction of euro coins and banknotes would take place over about 2 months. Since exchange rates were fixed, only formally could there be any question of "parallelism".

A different question concerns the emergence of the euro as *a parallel currency in the monetary systems of countries outside the Union*. We can adduce many examples of the development of a 'parallel currency' in the world economy. Alongside national currencies the dollar is most widely used as a second currency (in a dual currency system) in various countries of the world. Today there are about 30 countries where use of the dollar is officially recognized, and in practice the dollar has become the national currency. This phenomenon is often called 'dollarization'. On the analogy of this, 'euroization' is frequently mentioned.

Several possibilities exist for establishment of a parallel currency, or 'dollarization':

– One is the introduction of a *currency board,* which means that the exchange rate of the national currency is pegged to some strong foreign currency, and money can be issued only up to the value of the international currency reserves. This can be considered a very tough stabilization policy, reducing the scope of monetary policy, and in fact of all economic policy, to a minimum. "In its strictest definition, a currency board is an arrangement in which one country pegs to another currency at a fixed level and the issue of domestic currency is fully backed by the foreign currency. One could even say that a currency board is a form of unilateral and reversible monetary union. In a currency board regime, a country gives up sovereignty in monetary matters" (GIORDANO and PERSAUD 1998: 154). With regard to the currency board, they consider the latter argument as more important. It can be added that the currency board is seen as an institution that "would be purely passive, with no monetary policy role of its own, nor any commitment to, or clear definition of, the monetary or institutional development" (PADOA-SCHIOPPA 1994: 157). In recent years such a currency board has been created among others in Estonia, Bosnia and Bulgaria, pegged to the German mark, and in Hong Kong and Argentina, pegged to the dollar.

– The spread of *the use of some kind of foreign currency as a means of payment alongside the official national currency*. This can take place illegally (e.g. before 1990 with the dollar in Poland, or the German mark in Yugoslavia), or governments acknowledge it and in law it does not count as a punishable offence (the dollar in certain Latin American countries). In these cases the reason for the use of the foreign currency is the weakness of the local currency, and lack or diminution of confidence in it. The phenomenon is generally closely linked with hyperinflation, as was the case in Poland at the end of the 1980s, or in Yugoslavia and many Latin American countries. "This process is usually called 'dollarization'. It rarely starts before inflation exceeds 100 per cent per annum. When inflation reached several hundred percent per annum (and even went above 1,000%) in Argentina and Israel in the late 1980s many domestic transactions were carried out in dollars. A similar process occurred in Yugoslavia where the DM was used instead. In all these cases the use of the foreign currency for domestic transactions stopped when the domestic currency was stabilized" (GROS and THYGESSEN 1992: 169).

– Simple replacement of a weak national currency by a strong foreign currency. The use of the latter is done in such a way that the given country does not enter into monetary union with the country of issue of the foreign currency. Such proposals have been on the agenda in countries like Peru and Argentina.

Experiences of dollarization have so far been contradictory, and not very helpful with regard to the future. As GUILLERMO CALVO, who teaches at the University of Maryland in the US, noted, the experiences of dollarization are so limited that at present any evaluation would be very misleading (*IMF Survey*, Volume 29, No. 10, May 22, 2000: 164). And opinions are divided about whether, particularly for 'emerging economies', floating or fixed rates should be considered. From the point of view of curbing inflation, undoubtedly the latter seem advisable. This would favour a form of dollarization or euroization that supports the fixing of the exchange rate.

Thus it has to be examined as a real supposition, now that the introduction of the single currency is irrevocably taking place in the EU member countries (at least in the euro-zone), to what extent the use of it is spreading in the other member countries and especially in the candidate countries which have weaker currencies. It can be expected that despite the rigorous EMU entry requirements the possibility cannot be ruled out that the single currency, simply on the basis of the selection mechanisms of the market, will become dominant in some external countries, as well. More than a dozen countries (Monaco, Liechtenstein and the franc-zone African countries) are more or less automatically switching over to the euro, or pegging their national currency directly to the euro.

Forecasts predict parallel use of the euro in countries outside the euro-zone particularly after 2002, when its introduction in cash form has taken place. It is the general opinion that even in developed external countries as well (e.g. Great Britain, or Switzerland) the euro will be used in internal transactions too and may circulate parallel with the national currency. At the same time, Toyota Motor and Unilever announced initiatives encouraging their British suppliers to invoice in euros. According to data released by the Association of Payment Clearing Services, in Great Britain already in March 2000 euro bank accounts were held by 55,000 businesses and 20,000 private individuals. There are signs that these numbers are rapidly growing, and the "euro-creep" is a realistic assumption for the future.

It is especially vital to deal with the possibility of 'euroization' in the so-called *'pre-accession' countries* that will still be in transition and have not reached the stage of joining EMU. In some cases proposals for these countries' 'euroization' have already been made (e.g. in Estonia and Croatia), which means that they may change over to the euro even before joining the EU. And it is also necessary to consider the question even in the case of countries (like parts of the former Yugoslavia or Ukrain) that are not seeking to join the EU for the time being, or in the future.

The spread of use of the euro as *a parallel currency* in the candidate countries is regarded by many as very likely. "When Hungarian companies transact their foreign business in euros, in many cases it is in their interest to make domestic money transfers in the same currency. It would be advisable especially in Hungarian companies' longer-term agreements if preference were given to the relatively stable euro in money transfers. The importance of the euro is clear, in view of the large number of Western countries that have set up headquarters in Hungary, for whose products payment in euros ought to be made possible. To an increasing extent this is already happening. The euro, therefore, over time will be not just a foreign currency but a means of payment parallel with the forint" (LŐWE 1999: 2).

There are several reasons why the euro is likely to become a parallel currency. "In trade with the Union, increased use of the euro can be expected for two reasons. On the one hand, the euro is already the dominant transaction currency in intra-Union trade, in the case of medium-sized and larger companies. Since these firms generally invoice in euros, it is in their interest to transact their business with Hungarian companies in the same currency. On the other hand, the value of the common European currency is basically more stable than that of the forint, therefore the euro – particularly for long-term contracts – is a more suitable contractual means of payment." (Ibid.) The costs and risks involved need to be carefully analyzed, and a suitable strategy is necessary.

Many unforeseeable tensions may arise in relations between the strong euro of the 'core' countries and the national currencies that will remain outside for the time being. One strategic question in connection with the 'parallel currency' is examination of *the crowding-out effect*. The more stable and freely convertible single currency may on the basis of market mechanisms and judgment of value simply crowd out weaker and less valuable national currencies from the market and from circulation. Such 'crowding-out effects' could involve *significant costs*. The point is that in relation to the parallel currency national governments could be forced to adopt costly and socially painful measures (budgetary restrictions, wage freezing, etc.), the consequences of which (heavy debt burdens, or recession) would be difficult to counterbalance. So weaker countries would have no choice but continuous defence of the national currency through tough stabilization measures, or else simple acknowledgement in the given country of the vicious circle of devaluation and inflation. In the less developed CEE countries it cannot be ruled out that the crowding-out effect of the stronger currency on the weaker ones will really make itself strongly felt. After all, there have already been numerous examples of this in countries with dual currencies (e.g. in Latin America and the Balkans).

The implications of possible 'euroization', therefore, should be carefully analyzed. In the case of a parallel currency, the following problems should be considered:

– the cost of interventions to stabilize exchange rates;
– the necessary monetary policies to offset the pressure of increased inflation expectations;
– the uncertainty of control over the amount of money in circulation and its inflation effects.

In relation to the parallel currency, a 'contrary crowding-out effect' may be observed on the part of the weak currency. This is none other than the operation of 'GRESHAM's law', when *it is actually the weaker currency that crowds out the stronger*. With regard to this, PAUL DE GRAUWE refers to the 'shopkeeper effect' (DE GRAUWE 1994: 174–175). According to this, with a parallel currency it is in fact in the customer's, or taxpayer's, interest to carry out his purchases and transactions in the weaker currency because thus he makes a profit. If he converts the strong currency he holds into the weaker one, he will gain in proportion to the devaluation.

Therefore he offers the stronger currency and asks for the weaker, and uses the weaker in his transactions. Clearly the shopkeeper's only defence against this is automatically to raise prices in proportion to and parallel with devaluation. So the parallel currency would automatically stimulate the inflationary process and set it spiralling in the economy. There is some justification for the supposition that in such circumstances the cost of stabilization policy in sacrifices on the part of society and the economy would be greater than that of equally drastic economic policy measures taken in the interest of immediate accession. At the same time, as the experience of recent years has shown, from the point of view of speculative pressure even just a commitment to joining the euro-zone can have a stabilizing effect.

Officially, the EU is against any 'euroization'. According to an ECOFIN report, "It should be made clear that any unilateral adoption of the single currency by means of 'euroization' would run counter to the underlying economic reasoning of economic and monetary union (EMU in the treaty). Euroisation would not be a way to circumvent the stages foreseen by the treaty for the adoption of the euro" (*Financial Times*, November 8, 2000).

Many argue in favour of *quickly joining the EMU*, precisely because of the *crowding-out effects*. The question can be formulated in this way: will the stabilization costs arising in connection with the parallel currency (exchange-rate stabilization interventions, monetary policies to counterbalance the pressure of increased inflation expectations, uncertain control of the amount of money in circulation and the inflationary effects of this) not be greater than the burdens involved in the forced stabilization expected on the basis of the convergence criteria? If the answer is yes, and the general conditions can be fulfilled, then there is no sense in postponing entry. If a candidate country satisfies the structural and convergence criteria for membership of the EMU, it is in its interest to become part of the euro-zone as soon as possible.

5. EMU AND THE CEE CANDIDATES

Although the *Europe Agreements* signed with 10 CEE countries referred to promoting the convertibility of the currencies of CEE partners, they did not *contain any monetary provisions*. The CEE countries were already associated with an EU that had a single market and was constructing EMU, but the monetary relations or 'cooperation' had to be built outside these agreements. The rapidly growing and restructuring cooperation under the Europe Agreements had broad monetary implications, but the agreements dealt basically with unilateral steps and measures on the part of the CEE countries. It was clear from the beginning that successful implementation and full exploitation of the possibilities of association, convertibility and relative stability of the currencies of the CEE partners should be secured as soon as possible.

First steps to *convertibility* were made immediately after the democratic changes, and in some countries (Hungary and Poland) well prior to them. The notion of convertibility was on the agenda both in expert discussions and in political declarations, particularly in the reforming countries, after the 1970s. In Hungary, the proposal of 'forint convertibility' was raised from time to time after 1968. It was an important development when Hungary joined the IMF and the World Bank in 1982. Real steps toward convertibility of the national currency were made only after 1988. For the Visegrád countries, *convertibility was achieved* for current account transactions and foreign direct investments *by 1996*. (The same stage was completed in Western Europe by 1958.)

Although Hungary, like other planned economies in the region, applied dual exchange rates (trade and tourist rates) in its external transactions, as a reforming country (like Poland also) it used *the (trade) exchange rate as an 'active' economic policy tool* after 1973. This meant, first, anti-inflationary revaluations, and later, devaluations for import (energy) savings and to improve export competitiveness. The overvalued tourist rates served as a form of taxation of foreign tourists, because of the subsidized food and services in all these countries. Unified exchange rates were introduced in Hungary in October 1981 and in Poland in 1982.

Since 1989–90, *the exchange-rate policies of CEEs* have been an important part of their monetary policies, but the countries have followed different priorities. In some countries and in some periods monetary stability and anti-inflationary considerations were given priority; in others, competitiveness was the primary concern. Although all these countries turned to unified exchange rates after 1990–91, the CEEs pursued *diverging exchange-rate policies* in the following years, some favouring fixing (e.g. the Czech Republic), some the crawling peg (Poland after 1991 and Hungary after 1995)[4] and others relatively free floating (the Czech Republic since 1997, and Poland since 1998).

After the unification of its exchange rates, between 1981 and 1991 the rate of the forint was fixed to a currency basket which largely reflected the currency structure of Hungarian foreign trade. The structure of the basket changed during the 1990s, and from January 1, 1999 the forint was linked to a basket comprising 70% euro and 30% dollar.[5] From the point of view of our gradual approach to the euro-zone, it was an important step that the exchange rate of the Hungarian *forint was linked (pegged) fully to the euro from January 1, 2000.*

Full pegging to the euro means that Hungarian monetary policy "will be more strongly related to the monetary processes of the euro-zone and the monetary policy of the European Central Bank. As a result of closer relations, the monetary and real-economy shocks of the euro-zone will be more strongly transferred to the forint than in the previous years" (*Világgazdaság,* October 19, 1999). By that step, the monetary policy of the Central Bank became more transparent, inasmuch as the effects of changes in cross rates were eliminated. The exchange-rate risks were reduced substantially.

The fixing of the forint to the euro was no doubt a step in the right direction, but owing to the subsequent strong devaluation of the euro, in

[4] Monthly rates of devaluation of HUF:

March 12	1995	1.9%
July 01	1995	1.3%
January 01	1996	1.2%
April 01	1997	1.1%
August 15	1997	1.0%
January 01	1998	0.9%
June 15	1998	0.8%
October 01	1998	0.7%
January 01	1999	0.6%
July 01	1999	0.5%
October 01	1999	0.4%
January 01	2000	0.3%
April 01	2001	0.2%

The crawling peg was abolished on October 1, 2001.

[5]

December 9, 1991:	USD 50% – ECU 50%
August 2, 1993:	USD 50% – DM 50%
May 16, 1994:	USD 30% – ECU 70%
January 1, 1997:	USD 30% – DM 70%
January 1, 1999:	USD 30% – Euro 70%
January 1, 2000:	Euro 100%

the short run it caused some difficulties, particularly in terms of the anti-inflationary policy aims of the Hungarian government.

The Hungarian National Bank introduced *several new measures* in its monetary policy *during 2001,* which clearly were aimed at preparing the country for its approaching entry to the European Union.

In the pegging, the *monthly devaluations were abolished* from October 1, which ended the crawling peg policy pursued since 1995.

From May 4, *the band of free floating of the forint was widened* from the earlier +/– 2.25% to the +/– 15% applied by the ERM countries.[6] According to the Board of the National Bank, the main aim in widening the band was 'sustainable reduction of inflation', which was halted by several factors. Inflation got stuck around the 10% level and the government could not achieve its target of reducing inflation in 2000 and 2001, first as a result of increases in energy prices, and later owing to the rapid rise in prices of food and some services. It was realised that more monetary rigour was needed.

In the enlarged band in 2001 the forint was revalued by about 10–12%, which contributed to the moderating of inflation in a perceptible way. Although inflation decreased from 9.8% in 2000 only to about 9.2% on an annual basis, in monthly terms it fell from the 10.8% peak in July to about 7.2% by the end of the year 2001. According to experts, although the anti-inflationary effects were moderate in 2001, for 2002 a 1.8–2% reduction in inflation can be achieved (*Üzleti 7,* May 14, 2001). The fears of increased volatility of the forint proved to be unfounded; the Hungarian currency's fluctuation was about 15% (€240–270) in the 6 months following the enlargement of the band. As some experts point out, by sensitively reacting to international financial turbulence (in Turkey, Argentina, Poland and after September 11), "the exchange rate of the Hungarian forint has been globalized" (*Népszava,* November 20). From time to time, this may have negative effects in terms both of the fight against inflation and of competitiveness.

From June 15, 2001, the remaining restrictions on external transfers were abolished: capital transactions were fully liberalized. *After 70 years, the Hungarian forint became fully convertible again.*

[6] Intervention bands for HUF:

from	July 1,1992	+/– 0.3%
	December 22, 1994	+/– 2.25%
	May 4, 2001	+/– 15%

The liberalization measures meant:

– abolition of compulsory home transfers of revenue earned abroad;
– freedom for Hungarian companies or individuals to open bank accounts abroad;
– free transfer and holding of foreign currencies by Hungarian and foreign citizens;
– unlimited possibilities for Hungarians abroad of acquiring partial or full ownershp of foreign property;
– free and unlimited holding and cross-border export–import of foreign currencies;
– access of foreigners to the securities and forward markets, etc.

As a logical step, 'currency (exchange-rate) stability' as a primary *monetary policy objective* was replaced by *inflation targeting,* as in Poland and the Czech Republic after these countries floated their currencies. The National Bank and the Central Statistical Office of Hungary agreed on a uniform calculation of core inflation, which will be also used in deciding on the necessary monetary policy measures. The interest rate is considered a major tool of monetary policy. The objectives are ambitious: according to the National Bank, consumer price rises should be brought down from about 10% to 5.5% in 18 months, by the end of 2002, and then by 1–1.5% in each of the following years.

Compared to countries involved in previous enlargements, the CEE candidates will enter not simply a common market but a Union which is already at the stage of EMU. From the first moment, they will have to 'coexist' with the single currency, and therefore the full EU membership of CEE candidate countries assumes EMU participation. This corresponds to the membership requirements set by the Copenhagen criteria, namely they should have the "ability to take on the obligations of membership, including adherence to the aims of political, economic and monetary union", and they have no possibility of opting out. The CEE candidates, however, are not expected immediately to join EMU upon gaining membership, but only after a certain transition period. *After accession, they will first join the EMS and the exchange-rate mechanism (ERM–2),* and *entering EMU* can realistically be done only some years later.

As CSABA LÁSZLÓ, the Hungarian Finance Minister stated, Hungary could join the euro-zone even as early as 2007, however "not by forcing, but by naturally growing into it" (*Népszabadság*, July 24, 2002). Earlier, for several reasons some assumed that the transition period between joining the EU and entering EMU might last for many years, probably more than a decade. We do not exclude that possibility, but the transition should not be too long and for Hungary and some other countries it could be realised around 2007, as is officially planned. Some other candidates entertain similar expectations. In the light of the recession and related difficulties, the target date for joining EMU might be postponed, but probably not long.

According to GYÖRGY SZAPÁRY, vice-president of the Hungarian National Bank, the anxieties of the ECB and some experts that early joining of the euro-zone by Hungary and others would endanger the price stability of the zone, are unfounded. "The economies of new EU members are too small to exert perceptible negative influences, and before entry there is enough time to achieve real convergence" (*Frankfurter Allgemeine Zeitung–Magyar Hírlap*, May 28, 2001).

One can realistically assume that the CEE candidates, including Hungary, will be able to join ERM–2 upon their entry into the EU, and the conditions seem to be assured by that time. The Hungarian National Bank is prepared in terms of both staff and structure for the tasks in connection with exchange-rate interventions. It would be an important condition on the part of the EU to open and provide the monetary funds necessary for exchange-rate interventions.

Participation in ERM–2 would require a closer relation between inflation and the stability of the exchange rate in terms of economic policies. This would assume the consolidation of the Hungarian economy to such an extent that its participation in the ERM does not threaten 'sustainable economic growth' or its export competitiveness (the restriction of devaluation), and the difference to the EU inflation rate is not more than 2–3%. This aim can be achieved if consistent stabilization policy is maintained in the future.

From the point of view of stabilization policies, *the budgetary constraints of 'deepening' and 'enlargement'* are one of the most serious problems, in fact, for both sides. Although the euro-zone member countries have managed to bring down their budget deficits in recent years, the 2001 recession seems to have led to some deterioration. The budgetary implications for CEE candidates of adjustment and preparation for membership are enormous, particularly in terms of infrastructure, the environment and structural modernization. According to calculations, after closing the chapter on the environment, Hungary needs investments of several hundred billion euros in environment improvement in order to meet EU standards. The transfers envisaged by Agenda 2000 are relatively modest in the light of these needs, and the national budgets of the candidates can cope only partly with these problems. Since 1991, Hungary has not managed to bring down its budget deficit below 3%, and contrary to previous expectations, this aim will have to be postponed for a few more years. The estimated budget deficit of Hungary in 2002 was 3.3% of GDP, and in the following years the country hoped to meet the Maastricht criteria. But in reality the deficit in 2002 was around 5% (effects of the recession and the election year), and realistically it could be brought down below 3% only by 2005–2006. The other candidates, in this respect, performed better, and all met the Maastricht ceiling by the end of the 1990s. Owing to postponed structural reforms and the 2001 recession, the budgets of many countries deteriorated (the Czech Republic, Poland, Slovakia and Romania) and deficits increased well above the magic figure of 3%. Of course, the financing of adjustments could be done mostly on a commercial basis, but this depends on several economic and political factors. The budgetary implications are probably the most complicated dilemmas of economic policy on both sides.

Joining EMU involves *different stages,* which candidates have to go through:

1. Integration into the Single European Market (the first stage of EMU). If we copy the timetable of the EU members, a precondition of EMU is complete implementation of the four freedoms: the liberalization of the movement of goods (this involves integration into the CAP), services, capital and labour. Integration into EMU postulates full market integration in all fields.

In accordance with the White Book of June 1995, implementation of the internal market program has already started in all the candidate countries. The complex tasks of law harmonization, institution-building, application of EU standards, reform of public services and policies will take a long time, but they should mostly be completed by 2004. WERNER RIECKE, a vice-president of the Hungarian National Bank, stresses that from the point of view of EMU preparation the most important thing is that "the Hungarian economy should be able to hold its own in the European single market" (*Magyar Nemzet,* January 15, 1999).

The real question marks arise about transition periods, which seem to be unavoidable in certain important fields. Originally both sides agreed that with too long a transition period the single market could be undermined, and for that reason both sides strive to minimize derogations. The compromise involving a 5–7-year transition period with regard to free movement of labour (with the same delay in acquisition of arable land in the CEE candidate countries by foreigners) created a new situation. Of course, one can argue that really it is only the free movement of capital that counts from the point of view of the smooth functioning of EMU, and that will be fulfilled. Although labour mobility is considered important by the theories of the optimum currency area in terms of avoiding aggravation of regional differences, from the point of view of the CEE countries' joining the euro-zone these limitations are not serious problems. The question of arable land is also a marginal issue. The question remains, could the transition period prior to full single market integration be overlooked, or does it automatically imply the same transition period prior to joining EMU? Could *the fulfilment of the convergence criteria* (the second stage of EMU) be enough for joining EMU, or is it irrelevant without integration into the single market? To put it differently, some countries may well fulfil the Maastricht convergence criteria, but still remain unprepared for EMU.

2. The meeting of the convergence criteria is important as a way of stabilizing the economies of the candidate countries. Recently, candidates started a 'pre-convergence program', which becomes obligatory upon full membership. According to the Joint Assessment of the Economic Policy Priorities of the Republic of Hungary, the convergence of the Hungarian economy is to be consolidated by 2006–2007, including the requirement of exchange-rate stability. The chance of stabilization still supports the idea of early EMU joining, while such a commitment may contribute to the process of that stabilization. As CSABA LÁSZLÓ, the Hungarian Finance Minister, stated, "the commitment to early joining of the euro-zone is one of the most important factors which make the program of disinflation credible in the eyes of market agents" (*HVG*, July 27, 2002: 19).

Some feel that the CEE candidate countries, being far below the level of development of the present EU members, should probably face stricter conditions, because their meeting of "the Maastricht criteria in themselves would not secure the stability of the European currency" (A study by the German HypoVereinsbank published by Eubusiness. *Világgazdaság*, May 3, 2001). It is suggested that CEE countries should spend more than two years in ERM–2 prior to EMU entry, and keep their exchange rate within a 2.25% band (unlike, for example, Greece, which enjoyed the 15% band).

Of course, we cannot exclude the possibility of a prolongation of the stabilization process if liberalization puts too great a burden on the economy, especially if this effect is strengthened by external factors, such as unfavourable development of the European or international economic situation. The 2001 recession justified those reservations. It is not clear how full membership will affect national budgets. Even if the transfer of 4% of GDP from the EU budget were realised, the net effect on the national budget could be negative (payment of about 1.27% of GDP into the Community budget, burdens of co-financing, indirect budgetary requirements, while budget transfers to CEE countries do not improve the budget balances). If that is the case, this stage might become longer, especially if on entering EMU the CEE countries are called more strictly to account for their fulfilment of the convergence criteria than the present members.

3. *Joining of EMU by CEE candidates, and replacement of their national currencies with the euro* (the third stage of EMU): The member countries gave themselves 3 years for the accomplishment of this task. CEE candidates do not have to stick to the same schedule and pace, but they may have to face some difficulties. The preparation of the micro- (especially the commercial banks) and the macrospheres may be done continuously and it is possible that the transition can be completed in less than three years.

If we consider the above circumstances, in the case of the CEE countries integration into the internal market, meeting the convergence criteria and the changeover from national currencies to the euro could and should be achieved parallel. The separation of these stages in time will not be necessary, though it was with the original members.

Fulfilment of the structural and institutional requirements (how they fulfil the demands concerning the 'optimum currency area') has to be examined also in the case of CEE candidate countries. The fulfilment of the convergence criteria set up in Maastricht is only the second thing to observe. We have to emphasize that *fulfilment of the structural and convergence criteria is not only a precondition of integration but also the only way in which the advantages of integration outweigh its costs*. This is the only way in which integration serves their interests.

How are the CEE candidates meeting the requirements of the 'optimum currency zone'?

– *The mobility of 'factors':* Theoretically, liberalization of the movement of capital and labour is one of the important preconditions. Owing to its relatively low internal mobility it is hard to tell how mobile the CEE workforce could become under international conditions. (In this latter dimension, we do not have to take the underdeveloped real-estate market into consideration, but we have to pay attention to certain other factors – the lack of knowledge of languages, the hardships of fitting into a different society; but the huge differences in terms of wages may have a strong motivational effect.) The relations between the factors mentioned above require further research in terms of both the sectoral and the regional mobility of the labour force. While the regional mobility of the Hungarian labour force even inside the country has proved to be modest, the situation is different on a sectoral basis. There has been a substantial shift from industry and agriculture to services in the last ten years. International mobility is another question. It is widely estimated that the Polish labour force would probably be the most mobile among those of the Visegrád countries. But the fears expressed by the derogations in terms of labour mobility seem exaggerated, particularly in the long run, and for the whole Union. Not only the EU but most of the candidate countries also are demographically deficit regions, and they need immigrants to fill the gaps in the labour market. This is the case with Hungary, only estimates differ as to how much foreign labour we shall need in the near future. As a result of enlargement, the threat of a 'flood' of foreign labour is relevant only in certain regions (commuting in the border regions of Germany or Austria), and only in certain sectors (construction, tourism).

The movement of capital has been and will be liberalized by the candidates upon their entry to the EU.

– *The flexibility of 'factor prices':* The years of transition proved that wages are much more flexible in the CEE countries that wish to join than had been assumed. What is more, they are more flexible than in the majority of the EU countries. The great decreases in real wages in the CEE region, accompanied by intra-sectoral mobility, took place without any serious social turbulence. Real wages dropped in Hungary by nearly 14% between 1993 and 1996, and showed positive growth only in 1994 (election year). As is proved by the demonstrations against the closing down of certain factories in Belgium, France and Germany, the social and political limits of wage-flexibility are stricter in the EU countries than in CEE. However, the tolerance of CEE (and Hungarian) society may change in the future. The labour market regulations of CEE countries introduced after 1990 were generally more liberal than those existing in the EU members, and the recent Hungarian labour laws secure rather satisfactory market flexibility.

– The *possibility of 'asymmetric shocks'* (sectoral or regional): For structural reasons, this possibility is relatively greater in the candidate countries than in the member countries. Owing to the export-dependence of these countries, this results in a high degree of sensitivity towards international business cycles. At the same time, the proportion of 'sensitive products' in Hungarian export, which was about 58% in 1989, has dramatically decreased to below 15%, and the increasing share of intra-sectoral trade may reduce these countries' vulnerability to external shocks. In this respect, the trends of recent years have been encouraging.

– *Budget transfers:* These could be the most important constraints of enlargement. It should be examined how the 'costs' of these and of competitive devaluations relate to each other on both sides.

The structural reforms that are essential for successful integration into the unified market (law harmonization, modification of economic planning structures and institutional reforms) will take a long time and all the fields of the integration process will be affected by them. A lot of EU documents call the countries to account for the sluggishness of 'radical structural reforms' (the Country Reports). When planning the integration process, it is absolutely essential not only to work out the schedule of EMU-related harmonization but also to calculate its effect on the balance of the budget, as well.

As far as the institutional conditions are concerned, in Hungary the 1991 law created an independent national bank, and the recently-proposed amendments mostly correspond to EU requirements. The HNB has well-trained staff. As was stated before the European Integration Committee of the Hungarian Parliament, the Hungarian commercial bank sector was fully prepared for receiving the euro from January 1, 2002. The same can be said about most of the other candidates.

To sum up, the effects of EMU on the CEE candidates will be complex. Some of them are quantifiable and some not, and they can be influenced for good or ill by proper policies. The candidates will enjoy the same benefits and face the same losses as the present member countries.

For CEE candidates EMU will mean getting into a monetary zone the safety of which would hardly be achievable for them if left to their own devices. For countries where the currency was for decades completely valueless (owing to its non-convertibility) and then, in the years of transformation, went through rapid devaluations (which slowed down somewhat as a result of stabilization), joining the EMU is a *benefit of unique significance.*

A Europay International survey conducted by SBS International about the reception of the euro in 12 European countries indicated that among the countries outside the euro-zone, Hungary showed the greatest interest in the euro (*Világgazdaság,* April 30, 1999). About one-third of Hungarians (30%) favour the euro because it brings economic stability, while another third (31%) like it because it means convenience and savings. 94% of those questioned in Germany, and 91% in France, knew of the possibility of paying in euros with bank cards. While 82% of citizens of the euro-zone countries were aware of that possibility, the proportion was only 59% in the non-euro-zone countries, but 77% in Hungary.

– *The promise of a stable single currency* had great influence on public opinion in the member countries. It happened to be fairly negative in Germany, since the citizens did not want to lose their strong national currency. The case is opposite in the candidate countries. The socio-psychological potential of this fact is an important factor as far as the relation of public opinion to European integration is concerned.

The introduction and taking over of the single currency would mean savings which in many respects, if quantified, would be substantial. According to calculations by the Hungarian National Bank, for economic actors the gains due to *savings in conversion costs and transaction expenses* would be around 0.1–0.2% of GDP on an annual basis (Hungarian National Bank, 2001). The higher degree of monetary stability will make it possible for the banks and stock markets to *reduce their general risk premiums,* even if as a function of national financial positions they may remain divergent. This would mean that for example Hungarian companies and institutions could substantially reduce their present 3–4% risk premiums. One of the most important gains will be *a reduction in the costs of anti-inflation policies.* With decreased rates of interest, *it will be easier to manage the state budget (and the national debt).* This may be crucial from the point of view of Hungary, with its high level of debt and debt service (in 1999, interest payment on debt took nearly 6% of GDP). The gains for Hungary from lower real interest rates may bring about a 0.4% 'growth surplus' in GDP in the coming 25 years (ibid.).

The single currency may *contribute to the expansion of trade* (it may have a significant trade-creating effect, according to some analysts), and it may improve the competitiveness of given sectors and the potential of national economies. The increased trade as a result of participation in the euro-zone may generate about 0.1–0.3% annual growth in GDP (ibid.). Exchange risk will be excluded to some extent, which may create *a better commercial environment* from the point of view of both the development of trade and investment decision-making. The benefits would be mutual.

Joining the EMU is likely to *make the country even more attractive from the point of view of foreign investment*. The EMU may become an important factor in real integration. Analyses show that exchange-rate expectations play an important role in determining where the leading companies choose to invest their capital. This might be the 'most important impact' of enlargement for all sides. (Views of RICHARD BALDWIN, JOSEPH FRANCOIS and RICHARD PORTES.) At the same time, recently with the establishment of the euro-zone we have experienced certain investment diversion effects from CEE to euro-zone countries. (Investment by Toyota was diverted from Hungary or Poland to France, among other places, on the grounds of euro-zone considerations.)

The euro may take over the role of the dollar on the energy (oil) markets, since Russia, the Mediterranean and the Arab oil countries may later on prefer the euro to the dollar. In this respect, EMU could mean for CEE candidates that they would buy oil for their own currency. Probably after a seemingly longish period of weakening following the introduction of the euro, in the longer term the dominance of the dollar will be replaced by a bipolar or tripolar international monetary system.

The BALASSA–SAMUELSON effects are often cited as risks of early EMU joining. These are realistic assumptions, as in recent years in Hungary inflationary expectations in the non-tradable sectors were more than double those of the other sectors. Above-average inflation may mean low or negative real interest rates, which may have an accelerating effect on inflationary processes, and may frustrate efforts at disinflation. On the other hand, low or negative interest rates may greatly help in the maintenance of higher growth rates and the convergence process, which is important from the point of view of closing development gaps. Higher inflation may make CEE goods overvalued in terms of euro exchange rates, which may worsen competitiveness and may have a negative effect on growth in these highly export-dependent countries. On the other hand, overvaluation may support disinflation, and promote increasing productivity and efficiency. To sum up, it is clear that early euro-zone joining raises several risks, but these risks can be avoided and the conflicting processes can be reconciled by careful selection of economic policies and by proper policy mixes.

A concrete and comprehensive cost-benefit analysis would require more precise data and knowledge of conditions in order to enable quantitative estimates to be made regarding the factors mentioned above. This would be very important and should be done later if it is possible. But it is clear even without such estimates that if these countries meet the basic criteria (structural and convergence as well), *the net balance of integration into the EMU of the CEE countries (including Hungary) is favourable and positive for both sides*. According to the Hungarian National Bank, the aggregate effects of joining the euro-zone may mean about 0.3–1% annual growth surplus in the coming 25 years (Hungarian National Bank, 2001). The introduction of the euro will contribute to a 'stronger Europe', which is also a basic CEE interest.

REFERENCES

ANDOR, L. (2000) Örömtelen valuta (Joyless Currency). *Figyelő*, May 18–24.

ARTIS, M. (1994) *European Monetary Union*, The Economics of the European Union. Eds M. ARTIS and N. LEE. Oxford University Press, Oxford.

BALASSA, B. (1962) *The Theory of Economic Integration*. London.

BALASSA, B. (1964) "The Purchasing Power Parity Doctrine: A Reappraisal". *Journal of Political Economy*, 72.

BERTHOLD, N. (1993) Fiskális föderalizmus Európában mint a sikeres gazdasági és valutáris unió előfeltétele? (Fiscal federalism as condition of successful EMU?) *Közgazdasági Szemle*, No. 6.

CRAWFORD, M. (1996) *One Money for Europe? The Economics and Politics of EMU*. Macmillan Press Ltd., London.

DE GRAUWE, P. (1994) *The Economics of Monetary Integration*. Oxford University Press, Oxford.

EICHENGREEN, B., BAYOUMI, T., GIAVAZZI, F., DE GRAUWE, P., DECRESSIN, J., FRANKEL, J. A. and ROSE, A. K. (1998) The Endogeneity of the Optimum Currency Area Criteria. *The Economic Journal*, Vol. 108.

EMERSON, M. and HUHNE, C. (1991) *The ECU Report*. Pan Books, London.

FELDSTEIN, M. (1992) The Case against EMU. *The Economist*, June 13.

GIAVAZZI, F. and PAGANO, M. (1988) The advantage of tying one's hand: EMS discipline and central bank credibility. *European Economic Review*, No. 32.

GIORDANO, F. and PERSAUD, S. (1998) *The Political Economy of Monetary Union. Towards the Euro*. Routledge, London.

GIOVANNINI, A. and SPAVENTA, L. (1991) *Fiscal Rules in the EMU: a No-entry Close*. Centre for Economic Policy Research. Paper No. 516.

GROS, D. and THYGESSEN, N. (1992) *European Monetary Integration*. Longman, London.

Hungarian National Bank (2001) *A forint útja az euróhoz* (The Forint's Road to the Euro). November.

KENEN, P. B. (1969) Theory of Optimal Currency Areas: Electic View. In R. MUNDELL and A. SWOBODA (eds) *Monetary Problems of International Economy*. University of Chicago Press, Chicago.

KRUGMAN, P. (1993) *Lessons from Massachusetts for EMU*. Adjustment and Growth in the European Monetary Union. Cambridge University Press, Cambridge.

LŐWE, J. (1999) *Az euró jelentősége a magyar gazdaság számára* (The Importance of the Euro for the Hungarian Economy). *Valóság*, No. 10.

MACDAUGALL, G. D. A. (1983): *The 'Discussion Paper' Report of the Study Group on Economic and Monetary Union in 1980.* Annex II. The Commission, Brussels, 1975; and P. R. ALLEN: Cyclical imbalance in a monetary union. *Journal of Common Market Studies*, Vol. 21.

MCKINNON, R. (1963) Optimum currency areas. *American Economic Review*, 1963, Vol. 53.

MONTANI, G. (1993) Crisis of the EMS: What is to be done? *The Federalist Debate*, 1993, VI. No. 3.

MUNDELL, R. A. (1961) A theory of optimum currency areas. *American Economic Review*, 1961, Vol. 53.

One Market, One Money. An evaluation of the potential benefits and costs of forming an economic and monetary union. Commission of the European Communities. *European Economy*, No. 44, October 1990.

PADOA-SCHIOPPA, T. (1989) *The EMS: long-term view*. EMS. CEPR.

PADOA-SCHIOPPA, T. (1994) *The Road to Monetary Union in Europe*. Clarendon Press, Oxford.

PELKMANS, J. (1997) European Integration (Methods and economic analysis). Longman, Open University of the Netherlands, Heerlen.

SAMUELSON, P. A. (1964) Theoretical Notes on Trade Problems. *Review of Economics and Statistics*, Vol. 46.

SCHUL, J. J. (2000) No Stable Euro Without Europe. *The Federalist Debate*, Year XIII, Number 2, July.

THYGESEN, N. in GIAVAZZI, F., MICOSSI, S. and MILLER, M. (eds) (1989) *The European Monetary System*. CEPR. Cambridge University Press, Cambridge.

TOBIN, J. A proposal for International Monetary Reform. *Eastern Economic Journal*, Vol. 4.

TSOUKALIS, L. (1991) *The New European Economy*. Oxford University Press, Oxford.

III.

THE BUDGET OF THE EUROPEAN UNION

1. THE CHARACTERISTICS OF THE EU BUDGET

The EU budget differs from those of nation states and other international organizations. This applies to the financing and the structure of budgets and also their functions and macroeconomic effects.

National budgets (both at federal and local state levels) generally rely on income from taxes or tax-like revenues (e.g. customs duties, fees) and these vary in size but tend to amount to 40–50% of a given country's GDP. Taxes are paid directly by citizens and legal persons, and we can define these as *the national budgets have their 'own resources'.*

Through their expenditure, national budgets traditionally fulfil four major *functions*:

– financing of state projects or developments (infrastructure, armaments, etc.);
– purchase and provision of public goods and public services (health, education, public security);
– regulation of the economy;
– income redistribution (cohesion, i.e. redistribution of income from the rich to the poor).

The budget, therefore, is *one of the important tools of economic policy (regulation),* and it fulfils all these functions on the side of income (the cyclical and social effects of tax concessions) and also of expenditure (e.g. state investments – growth stimulation and income redistribution – social policy, etc.). National budgets are cohesive in nature. Redistribution of income from the rich to the poor takes place virtually automatically, on the one hand by means of progressive taxation (or a higher rate of purchase tax on luxury goods), and on the other hand by means of social expenditure benefiting the needier strata of society. These mechanisms are called 'automatic stabilizers'.

In drawing up budgets theoretically the aim is to achieve equilibrium, but in practice this rarely happens. In most countries budget deficits are characteristic, which governments can cover by printing money or by taking up loans. A budget deficit has inflationary effects (non-covered printing of money) and increases the national debt. There may be some point in a budget surplus if it is used to reduce the national debt, or to build up needed reserves. On the basis of its broad economic effects the budget balance can be used as an economic policy 'tool'. Increased expenditure (a deficit) can be an instrument for creating demand (Keynesian economic policy).

The budgets of *international organizations* (e.g. NATO or the UN) are basically derived from member states' contributions, generally defined as a certain percentage of each country's national income. So the financing of international organizations is based on transfers of a 'membership fee' from states; such organizations do not possess their 'own resources' in the strict sense. Such budgets are used mainly for the maintenance and operation of the given institution (e.g. upkeep of premises, employees' salaries) and they do not fulfil regulatory functions similar to those of national budgets. At the same time, for example in the case of the IMF or the World Bank it is possible to a limited extent to speak of such functions. The World Bank's resources can finance important development programs, and by supporting poorer countries they carry out global redistribution of income. By supporting the balance of payments, the IMF helps to stabilize economic policy.

The EC/EU budget shows many peculiarities and occupies an intermediate place between the budgets of national states and those of international organizations. It shows these special characteristics:

- in the financing of budget incomes;
- in the size of the budget and the requirement of equilibrium;
- in the functions fulfilled by the budget;
- in the principles relating to programs financed from the budget.

1.1. PRINCIPLES AND CHARACTERISTICS OF BUDGET FINANCING

The Community budget was established in special historical conditions which left their stamp on its structure and means of financing. To avoid unproductive and obstructive arguments, the principle of 'own sources of income' was built into the budget of the Coal and Steel Community, since there was a danger that if the member countries made the budget dependent on any year's contributions, then this could always be used to enforce concrete short-term national interests, and in a given case could paralyze the operation of the organization.

In the case of the Montanunion, its 'own resources' meant *a direct tax, calculated as a percentage (maximum 1%) of steel and coal production,* which had to be paid directly into the budget of the organization.

In the case of the EU they consist of:

1. *Customs duties:* all revenues related to import from non-member countries, based on Common External Tariffs.
2. *Agricultural duties and sugar levies:* which are imposed on agricultural products coming from outside the EU. Sugar levies are paid by producers to cover market support and storage.
3. *A proportion of national VAT:* a rate of standardized VAT is applied to an identical range of goods and services for all member states, the base of which is subject to a ceiling (originally 55%; since 1995, 50% of the GDP of a given country).
4. *GNP-based contributions – 'the GNP factor';* which means setting the same proportion of GNP as the contribution for all member states. The resource, which was introduced in 1988, supplements the revenues from other sources up to a given ceiling expressed in GNP terms.

For collection and tax administration the member states are entitled to a certain amount of reimbursement.

It was originally intended that financing based on 'own resources' should be introduced on July 1, 1967, but agreement was reached only in April 1970. Since customs and agricultural duties by the early 1970s no longer covered expenditure, a third resource was added to these, namely a proportion of national value added tax: in fact, 1% of national VAT income, calculated on an identical basis for all the member countries. For various technical reasons (e.g. the working out of comparative VAT bases for trade in goods and services) the VAT element was not fully incorporated until 1980. Since revenues still did not keep pace with expenditure, the VAT ceiling had to be raised in 1984 to 1.4%, but after 1995 it was gradually reduced again to 1%. The VAT base was limited to 50% of GDP, instead of the former 55%.

From 1988 a so-called *fourth resource,* based on GNP, was introduced (the proportion was then about 10%). The new tax was calculated on the basis of the difference between GNP and the VAT base, and the 'own resources ceiling', taking account of all four sources, was set at 1.20% of current GNP; that is, the fourth resource supplemented the other three within this limit. (After 1992 the GNP ceiling was gradually raised to 1.27%.) Thus the growth of income was directly linked to economic growth, more or less applying the principle of ability to pay.

Table 1. Income structure of the common budget (as %)

Year	Customs duties	Agricultural duties	VAT	Fourth resource
1971	25.4	31.2	43.4*	–
1980	36.8	12.5	41.7	–
1987	25.0	8.6	66.4	–
1996	15.5	2.7	48.9	32.9
2000**	13.0	2.3	38.1	42.3

* Other items apart from VAT income are included.
** Under income a 'miscellaneous' item amounting to 4.3% appears, consisting of interest on arrears, fines and the previous year's surplus.

Source: Statistical Annex. European Economy, June–July 1993; Commission, The Community Budget: The Facts in Figures, 2000.

The exact definition of 'own resources' has remained vague and controversial since the beginning. As the Rome Treaty states, "the financial contributions of Member States could be replaced by the Community's own resources, in particular by revenues accruing from the common customs tariff" (Article 201). The first two items are often referred to as "traditional own resources" (TOR), while VAT and particularly the GNP-related component of transfers do not completely correspond to the notion. The tariff revenues were related to "common policies" (common external tariffs and common agricultural policies), and even VAT was considered as pre-eminently an EC tax, particularly as it is a tax paid by all the Union citizens.

The application of the principle of own resources, even in the case of the traditional ones, was limited by the fact that, unlike national states, the EU has no tax-raising and managing authority, but its revenues are collected by the member states. "It is argued that the TOR is the only true own resource of the EU and that its importance is diminishing. Moreover, member states collect these duties and tend to regard them as national contributions" (JONES 2001: 201).

After the introduction of the GNP factor, this was even more the case. In fact, the principle of 'own resources' was further weakened, and the contributions took on the character of membership fees. The financial autonomy of the Union remained limited and the question of contributions was further politicized. "The implications of this lack of financial autonomy are judged to be threefold; first, it has made the EU increasingly dependent on intergovernmental transfers, leading to budgetary conflicts, and has encouraged member states to seek to maximize national benefits from the budget; secondly, the EU financing issues have become entangled with domestic politics, so that citizens lack knowledge of the EU-wide priorities at stake; thirdly, it has obscured democratic accountability, because of the lack of a direct relationship between citizens and taxes paid to the budget" (JONES 2001: 201).

The member states cannot withhold these revenues, but they should be automatically transferred. *Automatic financing* is an important principle of the operation of the EC/EU budget.

Later, the notion of 'own resources' was specified by the Commission, which stated that they are regarded as "tax revenue allocated once and for all to the Community to finance its budget and accruing to it automatically without the need for any subsequent decision by the national authorities" (European Commission, 1989). This implies that any type of tax may be defined as a source of financing of the EU budget. The Commission definition repeatedly implies the automatic character.

EC/EU budget expenditure also shows a number of special features, and has undergone considerable changes through time.

Between 1970 and 2000 EC/EU budget expenditures rose from ECU 3.4 bn to €8.94 bn, or from about ECU 20 per capita to more than €238. In recent years they amounted to 1.10–1.20% of Community GDP (in 1970 they came to 0.74%, but in 2000 1.11%), which indicates that they are still marginal compared with the 40–50% proportions of national budget expenditures in GDP terms (in 1999 the EU average was 47%). EU budget expenditures represent about 2.5% of the total public expenditure of the member countries.

Table 2. The main items of EU common budget expenditure (in millions of ECUs)

Items	1970	1985	2000
Common agricultural policy	3 108	20 546	40 994
Structural transactions	95	3 745	31 802
Structural funds	95	3 038	29 002
Cohesion fund	–	–	2 800
Internal policies	–	–	5 675
R&D	63	707	3 600
External transactions	2	–	3 611
Assistance for CEE*	–	–	1 696
Administrative expenses	115	1 333	4 704
Reserves	–	2 600**	906
Total	3 385	29 374	89 387

* Assistance given to the Central and East European countries and the successor countries of the former Soviet Union. In 2000, pre-accession aid.
** "Other expenditures".

Sources: Commission; HM Treasury, European Community Finances.

The greater proportion (about 80%) of common budget expenditure consists of agricultural subsidies and the so-called 'structural funds'. In the common budget the following structural funds are available for structural transactions:

- the European Regional Development Fund;
- the European Social Fund;
- the Agricultural Budget Orientation Fund; and
- the Fisheries Guidance Instrument.

The so-called *Cohesion Fund* is also available for structural transactions.

The expenditures are divided into *compulsory* and *non-compulsory* items. The compulsory expenditures are those "necessarily resulting from the Treaty" and they are mainly related to common agricultural policies and expenditure on third countries. The non-compulsory expenditures cover principally the structural funds. The compulsory items represent certain types of automatic financing on the expenditure side.

The power of decision-making in relation to the budget is shared between the Council and the European Parliament. In the case of the compulsory items, however, the final decision is in the hands of the Council. The EP may propose modifications, but the Council can reject them.

In accordance with the Treaty of Rome, *the Community is obliged to balance its income and expenditure,* and thus there is *no possibility of financing a deficit* by borrowing, as national states do. It is possible to roll over a minimal deficit (by deferring obligatory payments), but in the case of a larger deficit the only solution would be modification of the budget. Surpluses are carried over to the following year. "Balancing the budget" means that the revenues must equal the *payment appropriations,* which are the amounts available to be spent during the year, to meet the commitments of the current and the preceding year. On the other hand, the *commitment appropriations* are defined as the total costs of legal obligations related to activities during the current financial year and which lead to payments in the current and future financial years.

Apart from this, through loan transactions *resource transfers* are carried out by the European Investment Bank (EIB), the European Investment Fund (EIF) and the European Development Fund (EDF – for the support of developing countries) and a number of other programs.

The budget is prepared for a calendar year. In order to increase the predictability of the budget, since 1988 the expenditures have been projected for several years as "financial perspectives". The first financial perspectives were worked out for 1988–1992, but after that they were extended to 6 years. The currently valid Financial Perspectives are planned for 2000–2006, and they are called Agenda 2000. The revenues and expenditures have been calculated in ECUs since 1979, and in euros since 1999.

In the system of budgetary control the *Court of Auditors* (CoA) plays an important role. It is responsible for verifying the legality and regularity of Community revenue and expenditure. The court provides an annual statement of assurance on the reliability of the EU accounts and the legality and reliability of transactions. The Commission has its own internal system of financial supervision, including an anti-fraud office, named OLAF (Office de la Lutte Antifraude).

1.2. THE ECONOMIC POLICY FUNCTIONS OF THE EU BUDGET

In the Montanunion and the early years of the EC, it was mainly administrative and organizational tasks that were financed from the common budget. From the 1960s, with the common agricultural policy the EC/EU budget gradually acquired real developmental, regulatory and redistributive functions. This differentiates it notably from other international organizations. In this spirit the MacDougall Report published in April 1977 decisively formulated the basic principles to be followed in the Community budget (MacDougall Report, 1977). According to the report, *the Community budget must also fulfil the main stabilization, allocation and redistribution functions of macroeconomic policy.* It must ensure the promotion of price stability, expansion of economic activities, employment and the efficient use of resources.

Of course the possibility of exercising these functions is basically determined by the size of the budget, its internal structure, the financing principles and not least by political will, the extent to which the member countries are prepared to increase the financial autonomy of the budget. Since for a time the last-mentioned was lacking, real expansion of the functions progressed only slowly and inconsistently. Opinions are sharply divided concerning the economic policy role of the EC/EU budget, and this situation is likely to persist with regard to the future, too.

Understandably, the EC/EU budget, compared with national budgets, in many respects exercises its economic policy functions in a special way.

1. Though in a limited way, the EU budget does *fulfill allocation and development functions*. The common agricultural policy, through price support, has carried out substantial transfers of resources to agriculture, and its role in modernizing European agriculture is undeniable. Significant investment in agriculture has taken place, output and productivity have increased, and as a result of improved competitiveness European agriculture has largely overcome its comparative disadvantage compared with its overseas competitors. Modernization of agriculture has also been directly supported from the Orientation Fund, though the amounts have not been significant. With the Structural and Cohesion Funds financing of development was extended to other sectors as well. The EU funds play a part in the development of infrastructure throughout Europe and in the support of scientific research. Compared with the allocation effects of market integration the possibilities of the budget are limited, but in certain spheres and countries (e.g. the cohesion countries) the effects of these resources can be felt. With the e-Europe program the EU's role in development has been extended and has acquired qualitatively new dimensions.

2. With regard to the provision of public goods and services (public administration, public security, education and health), national budgets

have retained their exclusive role, and in this respect no significant changes can be expected in the near future. National governments treat these spheres as strategic and political questions, and there are only limited possibilities of rationalization at Community level. Despite this, the EU budget does in fact *purchase certain public goods and services on a small scale*. Here we can mention the Social Fund expenditures on retraining, the educational exchange programs at various levels, and research projects financed from framework programs. Another question is that free movement of people in itself raises many problems that would make it rational to develop EU-level forms of financing (of health and social services).

3. As far as the *regulation functions* of the EU budget are concerned, it is probably one of the most controversial issues. Many feel that even after about thirty years of reforms of the budget, no real economic policy functions of the budget have developed. "It is interesting to ask whether the EC budget can be made to perform proper fiscal policy functions, i.e. can it be used to reduce income disparities between the member nations? Can it perform stabilizing functions? Even with the new and increased own resources, the budget will not do much in this respect" (EL-AGRA 1990: 299). From this point of view, the sheer size and character of the budget are important limiting factors. The macroeconomic stabilization role is particularly questioned. "An important difference is that national budgets are functional budgets, whereas that of the EU is an accounting type of budget. The budget itself is concerned mainly to raise revenues to balance its financial expenditure; it is not engaged in macroeconomic Keynesian stabilization policies of running budgetary deficits to stimulate demand in order to reduce persistently high levels of unemployment" (HARROP 2000: 243). As it is more explicitly formulated, "the EC budget is not a device for fiscal fine-tuning" (PENKETH 1992: 51).

On the other hand, none can deny that through common agricultural policies the budget has had far-reaching impacts on agricultural production and incomes, and in general on the welfare of the whole of society. These impacts have been substantial enough not only in the agricultural sector but, by means of their interconnections, throughout the whole economy. With the dynamic increase of structural funds these roles have been extended.

Some feel that despite its marginal macroeconomic stabilization and regulation role, the EU budget "is significant for the following reasons:

– many important EU policy areas are influenced by the budget;
– tangible gains and losses from membership can be identified, although the extent of these may be challenged;
– the net contributions from the EU have a significant impact on the economies of small countries" (BARNES and BARNES 1995: 146).

Similarly, we can speak about the relatively *strong redistribution function* of the budget, right from the beginning. In the framework of the CAP, significant income transfers were made in favour of agriculture, and they had broad impacts on income relations and the social positions of related groups. It is another question that the CAP had contradictory effects on income distribution both in terms of intra-country relations and concerning social groups, and it was by no means satisfactorily 'cohesive'. The Cohesion and Structural Funds try to correct these distortions, and they implement more consistently the principle of cohesion. "Thus, the redistributive function of the EU budget is already a reality; certainly limited, when compared with the size of the inter-regional distribution of resources inside member countries and federal systems outside the EU, but no longer negligible. Net flows for at least three out of four cohesion countries now have a significant macroeconomic effect, and the gradual shift of emphasis from the CAP to the Structural Funds, which also means a shift from consumption to investment, makes these inflows even more beneficial in the long run" (TSOUKALIS 1997: 219).

1.3. PRINCIPLES OF PROGRAM FINANCING

Programs financed from the Community budget have to *fulfil numerous special criteria and principles.*

The first principle is *externality*, that is, the assumption that in connection with a proportion of the activities, partner countries are involved in the costs and the benefits, which may require appropriate inspection and compensation.

Indivisibility means that certain activities, for reasons of economies of scale and functional considerations, cannot be distributed among the member countries, and therefore should be financed at Community level.

According to the *cohesion principle*, every citizen of the Community must be guaranteed services, welfare and a minimum level of development (From Single Market to European Union. Commission of the European Communities, April 1992: 15). The Single European Document officially established the principle of "economic and social cohesion and solidarity among the member countries".

In accordance with the *principle of subsidiarity*, functions must be delegated to the lowest possible level (e.g. local authorities), if there is no advantage to be gained from exercising them at a higher level (e.g. through Community institutions).

According to the *principle of co-financing* or *partner financing*, a determinate part of the cost of programs supported by the EU must be borne by the beneficiaries.

2. THE MAIN DIRECTIONS OF REFORM OF THE COMMON BUDGET

The budget financing construction set up in the beginning proved inadequate for two reasons. On the one hand, incomes grew more slowly than national output (regressivity); on the other hand, the budget was unable to provide the desired cohesion, that is, the reallocation of income from the rich to the poor developed rather inconsistently.

The regressivity of incomes was partly a result of the gradual reduction of customs duties and agricultural duties, but this phenomenon characterized VAT income as well. The relative decrease in budget revenues (mainly customs duties) resulted from:

- a gradual shift in trade turnover towards internal partners;
- the EC/EU's numerous free trade and partnership agreements;
- GATT liberalization (reduction of common external customs duties);
- the decrease in agricultural duties due to similar factors, but mainly to the fact that agriculture was becoming increasingly self-sufficient;
- a similar effect resulted from the shrinkage of VAT-bases within national income, as with economic development the emphasis shifted from consumption to savings and non-VAT services.

The other problem with the Community budget was connected with the *weakness of cohesion*. Not only did the common budget not automatically redistribute income from the rich to the poor, but because of its internal structure and automatisms in many respects it actually did the opposite. In spite of reforms, *the net contributions of some countries are not proportional* to their level of development. The internal disproportions of the common budget have so far not been successfully removed.

The cohesion distortions in the transfers between countries are indicated by the fact that until very recently several of the most highly developed countries were among the net beneficiaries, and in some cases received relatively more significant support (in terms of transfers per capita) than the poorer countries. This is clearly shown in terms of budget transfers by the net positions of the various countries, both in the order of contributions and in the scale of benefits.

Table 3. Net contributions to the EU budget

Country	Net contribution						Per capita GDP compared to EU average (%)
	1986			1995			
	Million ECUs	ECUs per capita	Rank order	Million ECUs	ECUs per capita	Rank order	
Germany	3 742	613	2	13 431	1 646	1	106.7
UK	1 438	253	4	4 720	807	6	98.2
Holland	–217	–149	8	2 005	1 297	2	100.4
France	561	101	5	1 727	296	9	107.2
Sweden	–	–	–	937	1 055	5	95.3
Austria	–	–	–	905	1 129	3	109.3
Italy	195	34	6	614	107	10	101.7
Belgium	284	287	3	311	306	8	110.4
Finland	–	–	–	165	323	7	92.5
L'bourg	59	1 603	1	45	1 106	4	128.2
Denmark	–421	–822	10	–306	–586	11	112.0
Ireland	–123	–3 744	12	–1 887	–527	15	85.3
Portugal	–219	–221	9	–2 381	–242	13	67.9
Greece	–1 273	–1 278	11	–3 489	–333	14	60.0
Spain	–95	–25	7	–7 218	–184	12	76.1

Source: Court of Auditors Report: European Commission.

It is noticeable from these figures that even in the mid-1980s Holland and Denmark, which count among the most highly developed members, were net beneficiaries of the budget, while among the less developed only Ireland and Greece received bigger transfers. Spain and Portugal received relatively moderate-sized transfers, and without the corrective mechanisms they would have been net payers. In contrast, in both absolute and relative terms Germany, Great Britain and France were substantial net contributors. It was only relatively recently that highly-developed Denmark became a net payer.

The question of Great Britain's contribution was hotly debated for years after it joined. As the world's biggest importer of foodstuffs, it would have been a substantial net financier for countries with a much higher per capita income than Britain's. The British government refused to accept this, and in March 1975 the Community agreed that Britain should receive a *rebate* on its excess gross budget contribution. In 1984, in connection with the raising of the VAT ceiling this was fixed by means of determinate mechanisms (2/3 of the net surplus contribution was repaid), thus for the first time applying the 'ability to pay' principle. The British rebate agreement was periodically renewed.

Disproportions arose on both the contributions and the benefits side, and these can be traced to a number of causes:

1. In the given consumption structure customs duties and agricultural levies burden more heavily lower-income, less-developed countries, because more highly processed goods, on which more duty has to be paid, feature more dominantly in their import than in that of more developed countries. The situation can be even worse if they are also in the position of net agricultural importers.

2. VAT revenues depend on propensity to consume, and by their nature they are more of a burden on the poorer strata, and thus on the less developed countries.

3. It is a source of distortions in contributions that in some countries (mainly the Netherlands and Belgium) customs revenues are significantly higher owing to their ports, which serve as gateways for the entry of foreign goods into the whole Union market. This is often called 'the Rotterdam effect'. Rotterdam and Antwerp are major entry ports for large regions of the northern part of the EU (especially Germany). While the customs revenues are collected by these two countries, the burdens are borne by consumers elsewhere in the Union.

4. On the expenditure side, distortions have mainly been connected with the agricultural subsidies, the principal beneficiaries of which have been the agricultural producing and net exporting countries, while net importers (especially Great Britain) find themselves in the position of contributors. Such a position has no direct relation to the level of development, and in some cases it has actually been the most highly developed countries (Denmark and Holland) that have been the net beneficiaries of this mechanism.

5. The cohesion functions of the CAP are even more problematic if we look at its domestic redistributive effects in individual countries. "Within countries, the CAP has a positive redistributive impact because on average it is transferring income from richer, urbanized and industrialized regions towards poorer regions where agriculture accounts for a relatively large share of regional production. In contrast, the overall impact of the CAP on social cohesion (interpersonal income disparities) appears to be negative. Higher food prices have a regressive effect on consumers, because lower-income households spend a higher share of their budget on food. On the other hand, a policy which operates on the basis of guaranteed prices favours mostly the better-off farmers, the amount of subsidy being a function of the total size of production" (TSOUKALIS 1997: 214).

In the course of time the structure of the budget has followed the development of current interest relations. In the 1960s agricultural policy and financing were a means of compensating for the presumed market advantages enjoyed by Germany, with its more competitive industry, compared with France and (to a lesser extent) Italy, as agricultural exporters. Since in the budget agricultural subsidies predominated, the net beneficiaries were necessarily the countries producing and exporting agricultural products. Later the relations between contributors and beneficiaries changed, and especially with enlargements a new situation arose. Budget reforms, particularly in the interest of cohesion, laid emphasis increasingly on the structural funds, which chiefly benefited the less developed countries and regions.

Reform of the common budget has been implemented in several waves, in an attempt to correct the above-mentioned distortions. After the introduction and refinement of the VAT resource, by the end of the 1980s the Community was in a situation in which radical reform of the budget had become unavoidable. In 1987 the EC once again faced a financing crisis, and decisions could no longer be postponed. It was clear that a solution to income regressivity had to be found, and the principle of cohesion, in view of the new, poorer Mediterranean countries, must be more effectively applied. The proportion of customs and agricultural duties in income fell from about 50% in 1980 to less than 34% in 1987, while the proportion of VAT contributions rose from 42% to 66%. This was no longer enough to cover expenditure. In 1987, to balance the budget, 1.9% of VAT revenues would have been needed.

The most important measure in the 1988 reform was the introduction of the so-called *'Fourth Resource'*, which at least *brought contributions into line with GNP growth,* thus eliminating the regression. The most important effect of the reform was that at least in terms of revenues in general it tried to apply *the principle of ability to pay,* even if with the given structure of expenditures it was still far from the *just return principle,* according to which countries would get back from the budget roughly what they put in.

In addition, the reform altered *the nature of budget financing and the structure of expenditure.* The reform stipulated a reduction in expenditure on agriculture, and on the other hand greater expansion of the structural funds. In the budget the principle of economic and social cohesion was adhered to more decisively, with the aim of reducing regional differences and assisting the weaker economies in facing the increasing competition in the single internal market. In accordance with this, the so-called DELORS (I) package of 1988 doubled the amounts prescribed for the structural funds for the period 1988–92.

Table 4. The structure of expenditures of the EU budget (as %)

Year	CAP	Structural operations	Internal policies	External policies	Administration	Reserves*	Pre-accession aid
1970	92	5	–	–	3	–	–
1980	69	16	2	3	5	5	–
1985	70	14	3	4	5	4	–
1990	58	24	5	3	5	5	–
1995	50	31	6	5	5	3	–
2000	46	36	6	4	5	1	2

* Miscellaneous before 1995.

Sources: European Economy, and Bulletin of the European Union. General Budget of the European Community, General Budget of the European Union, Court of Auditors.

A significant increase in the structural funds took place between 1975 and 1980 (from ECU 392m. to ECU 2,765m.), which meant that the proportion of these rose from 6.3% to 16%. In the following ten-year periods they almost doubled in volume, but their proportion of the budget grew only moderately (by 1985 to 19.6%, and by 1990 to 20.2%). After 1988 the situation changed significantly; by 1994 the proportion of the structural funds had risen to 30.5%, and by 2000 it was over 36% of expenditure. By increasing the structural funds *the 1988 reform strengthened the redistributive functions and cohesive effect of the budget.*

The above aims were directly served by the so-called *Cohesion Fund,* which on the basis of the Maastricht Treaty was set up in 1994 to support countries with GDP below 90% of the EU average (Greece, Ireland, Portugal and Spain). The Cohesion Fund assists development of the transport and communications infrastructure, and helps in fulfilling Union environmental requirements. Transfers from the fund are dependent on fulfilment of the convergence program. In the case of "a very big budget deficit" the Commission was authorized to suspend payment.

Thus in the Community budget the structural funds represent the traditional redistributive function, which channels resources from the rich to the poor. 70% of the structural funds go to the less developed regions, where 27% of the Union's population lives.

In connection with the budget the member countries continue to be divided by heated arguments. The net payers, especially Germany, are struggling to secure a fairer 'distribution of the burdens', while the less developed countries insist on the transfers and positions they have so far enjoyed. Serious debates are going on concerning reform of Community policies, especially agricultural policy and the reduction of the financing burdens connected with it. The net payers would like to freeze expenditure at least, while in relation to EMU and enlargement the arguments are in favour of further expansion of the budget.

Many warn that *the disputes* about the budgetary burdens and their distribution between the net payers and the beneficiaries are *misleading*. "Budgetary transfers should not be confused with the costs and benefits of membership in the Community. Community policies have many and varied economic effects, and the budgetary accounts provide only a partial and distorted view. In general, net budgetary transfers do not, by definition, take account of costs and benefits outside the budget and therefore they cannot become a basis for measuring the costs and benefits of economic integration" (Hitiris 1998: 101–102).

1. The main economic effects of integration are related to market opening for goods, services and factors of production, and they are due to exploitation of scale economies, intensified competition and technological development. In this respect, the gains (and also the losses) directly accrue to enterprise sectors, while for the whole society the benefits are enjoyed only indirectly. The bulk of the tax burden, however, is borne directly by consumers, that is, by all citizens. These different dimensions of gains and losses are often obscured, and usually politics is unable to bridge them. "Gains and losses through the budget are much more easily identifiable by politicians and by the public at large than, say, the trade effects of the customs union and the CAP, which are, however, more important in economic terms" (TSOUKALIS 1997: 210).

2. It should be borne in mind that Community expenditures serve the interests of all the member states, even if the links are often indirect and vague. Road construction in a Central European country creates improved trade opportunities for all the member countries, and in general the same applies to its economic and political stability. In most cases there are direct complementarities between Community and national budgets, and EU budget expenditures mean direct savings in national budgets.

3. The gains and losses of the CAP are particularly obscure, and are by no means clearly expressed by balances of budget transfers. Price interventions favour producers, and make them more competitive with their external market rivals. At the same time, they increase food prices for the whole Union, which in some cases means that the burden of subventions is doubled for individual citizens, first as taxpayers and then as consumers. The subsidies mostly go to rich farmers, and inequities are recreated.

4. The net balance of budget transfers does not fully or accurately indicate who reap the benefits and who bear the burdens of the various programs. Great part of cohesion transfers goes back to the donor countries, which are usually in better position to gain public tenders and procurements. According to Commission figures, for every 10 ECUs received by Portugal, 4 ECUs return directly to the donor countries. For the construction of the Athens metro, which at ECU 2.4 bn counted as the biggest EU structural assistance program, 50% was non-refundable EU support, 40% had been lent by the European Investment Bank, and the Greek government had to cover the remaining 10%. But the import content was over 75%, so Greece provided mainly manpower.

5. The 'Rotterdam effect' should also be mentioned in this context, insomuch as the customs revenues are collected in the country of entry, while the burdens are borne somewhere else, in other member countries.

In spite of sharp disputes, further reforms of the budget are unavoidable. "Two events may cause significant changes in budgetary strategy. The first would be caused by real progress being made towards EMU. The Edinburgh Agreement was not an adequate response to the challenges of the monetary union. If there is to be EMU, the size of the Structural Funds will need to be looked at again. Similarly, the issue of expansion of the EU was not properly addressed, largely because this was still a hypothetical issue at Edinburgh. Both these developments will require a new strategy towards the distributional aspects of the budget" (BARNES and BARNES 1995: 161).

The reform and particularly any substantial expansion of the budget raise the question of the introduction of new sources of financing, if possible by strengthening the principle of 'own resources'. In this respect, several proposals have been made:

1. Introduction of a *European corporation tax,* which would correspond to the Single European Market program. It is opposed, however, on various grounds. Countries' interests differ greatly and there are several technical problems, which would require broad harmonization. There are differences in definition of corporate income, and in some member countries corporate and personal income are not clearly separated. It may be an unstable resource, as business profits fluctuate widely.

2. An energy or eco tax, which may limit the polluting use of energy. The idea of a carbon tax on fuel in order to limit CO_2 emission was raised by the Commission as long ago as 1978, but it was opposed by most of the member states and interest groups. As it was coolly received by the main industrial partners (the US and Japan in particular), it was clear that unilateral introduction would hurt the competitiveness of European goods.

3. European excise duties on alcohol or tobacco. Although it would generate substantial revenues, would be relatively easy to collect and would promote health, it would create inequities as consumption rates vary greatly between member states, and probably it would be anti-cohesive.

4. Several individual, unofficial *proposals* have been made *on taxing* mobile telephones or air tickets, or speculative capital transfers (a sort of Tobin tax). As member states are not prepared to give financial autonomy to the Union budget, these proposals have so far been neglected.

3. THE COMMON BUDGET AND EMU

It was recognized even at the time of the WERNER plan that the regional distorting effects of monetary union must be counterbalanced by appropriate Community level policies and resource transfers. The regional inequalities within the Community were increased by the oil price shocks and by the enlargements. Monetary union failed, but by 1975 the Regional Development Fund had been set up.

In Maastricht, though strategic decisions were taken with regard to monetary union, budget decisions were postponed. When the 1988–92 budget agreements (DELORS II) expired, a new 'package' was needed. Agreement was made difficult by the fact that bigger budget transfers were allocated to the less developed members as the price of their support for the Maastricht plans. Spain in particular insisted on an increase in net transfers to the less developed countries in return for backing for the Maastricht decisions. The countries of the southern European region were afraid that with the approximation of real wages, resources would tend to flow to the more developed regions, and the new members in northern Europe might be the beneficiaries of investments. The less developed members favour a system of Community transfers similar to the German financial equalization (Finanzausgleich) system, which automatically allocates resources to the poorer Länder.

Decisions on increasing the budget on the basis of the DELORS (II) budget 'package' were taken at the Edinburgh summit in December 1992. The more highly developed countries, especially Germany and Great Britain, the main net contributors to the budget, opposed the budget increase (to 1.37% of GDP, according to the original proposal). In their view there was no need to raise the current limit of 1.20%, because in the next 5 years, as a result of economic growth, incomes would automatically increase and according to British calculations would cover 3/5 of the increased requirements. The British recommended the reduction of agricultural expenditure, and it was clear that the EFTA countries then joining would be net contributors. There was also strong opposition to financing the research and development programs urged by DELORS to strengthen "the competitiveness of industry", on the grounds that any possibility of support for "lame duck" industries must be excluded. The Maastricht Treaty also included a statement on the necessity of the Trans-european Networks, involving construction and development of road, rail and energy systems and telephone networks.

At the Edinburgh summit the ceiling for Community budget expenditure was set at 1.27% of GDP. In the decisions great emphasis was laid on increasing the structural funds, which were supplemented as a fourth resource by the Fisheries Guidance Instrument. In the six years between 1994 and 1999 more than ECU 140 bn was allocated to the structural funds, and by the end of the decade they accounted for more than 1/3 of the common budget expenditure.

In May 1994 the Council approved the Cohesion Fund specification of ECU 15.15 bn for the period between 1993 and 1999. In 1993 on the basis of the transitional agreement ECU 1.56 bn was allocated to the four least developed countries, and after this was approved, financing of long-term programs became possible.

At the December 1995 European Council meeting in Madrid the Commission was asked to draw up the Union's budget plan for 2000–2006, taking prospective enlargements into account. On July 16, 1997 the EU Commission presented the plan (Financial Perspectives), entitled Agenda 2000, to the European Parliament. This document outlines the development of the Union, taking into consideration the necessary internal reforms, the prospects of enlargement, improvement in macroeconomic performance (reduction of the high level of unemployment while keeping inflation low), and enhancement of competitiveness in global markets. At its December 1997 meeting in Amsterdam the European Council accepted Agenda 2000 as matter for discussion, and after more than a year of argument, on March 26, 1999 at its Berlin summit a compromise decision was reached. Agenda 2000 sketched out the planned development of the Union budget *for the period between 2000 and 2006,* with the reform of the relevant policies. What was very important, it also assumed as a working hypothesis that *enlargement of the Union by 5+1 countries could be implemented from 2002.* There would be gradually increasing budget transfers to the countries joining and waiting to join.

The Union's budget income *ceiling* is held *at 1.27% of GDP* until 2006, so any increase in income and expenditure can only come from economic growth. Average economic growth for the period up to 2006 was estimated at 2.5% annually.

According to Agenda 2000, the Structural and Cohesion Funds should amount to 1/3 of the budget, that is, 0.46% of the member countries' GDP. For these 6 years, for financing structural policies a sum of €213 bn is at the disposal of the 15 member countries, of which €195 bn goes into the Structural Funds and €18 bn to the Cohesion Fund. The annual maximum structural support any member country can receive is the equivalent of 4% of its GDP.

In the future 3 main objectives are to be financed from the structural funds. The first objective involves support of backward regions where per capita GDP is less than 75% of the Union average, or which belong to the categories of the so-called most distant regions (e.g. France's overseas territories), or areas with exceptionally low population density. In the framework of the second objective, support is given to regions struggling with economic and social transformation, and difficulties arising from structural changes. The third objective directs resources to the modernization of the system of education, training and employment and the relevant policies. Roughly €24 bn has been set aside for this. Five per cent of the resources allocated to the structural funds is used to finance three Community initiatives: INTERREG (cross-border cooperations), EQUAL (elimination of labour market inequalities and discrimination) and LEADER (rural development).

In accordance with a decision of the council of economic and finance ministers (ECOFIN), in the next budget period Community expenditure on agriculture must not exceed an annual limit of €40.5 bn The agriculture ministers demanded €7 bn more than this, but their proposed package was rejected by the Council. The Council requested that the Commission prepare a detailed report by 2002 on agricultural expenditure and possible savings. Appealing to the principle of financial solidarity, they did not accept a proposal for co-financing of agricultural subsidies by the members.

In harmony with the theoretical assumptions relating to the optimum currency area, the cohesion transfers are an attempt *to reduce the rigidity of the factor markets and to facilitate factor mobility*, and therefore the emphasis is placed on *infrastructure developments*. Thus Community cohesion transfers cannot be automatic income compensation, but must indirectly finance infrastructure or environmental programs. It has become recognized that among these, in addition to transport and communications, special attention must be paid to raising the standard of public education and professional training.

The budget decisions relating to monetary union have been the subject of much criticism. A number of studies show that the planned Community budget transfers are not likely to compensate for the effects of EMU of increasing regional disparities, and that the Community transfers from the various 'cohesion and structural funds' *fall far short of the amount likely to be needed and typical of federal states*. The structural funds amount to less than 0.5% of Community GNP, whereas in the federal budget of the US and Australia the corresponding transfers amount to between 3% and 5% of GDP. The same conclusion was reached by a study by the US National Bureau of Economic Research, according to which the level of internal integration of the European economy is lower than that of the US economy, and the funds planned in the EU whereby these tensions could be resolved do not match the federal budget transfers. In these circumstances, in EMU for the peripheral countries of Europe low inflation will "not come cheap" (SALA-I-MARTIN and SACHS 1991). The German currency union is a warning that the price may be higher unemployment in weaker economies, while increasing financial transfers become unavoidable.

The enlarged structural funds and the sums deriving from the new 'cohesion' fund are intended to alleviate the difficulties of the less developed countries. If the developed countries themselves fulfil rigorous conditions and are faced with disturbances, it is not certain that sufficient resources will be produced (partly because of the automatisms of the common budget).

The equalizing role of structural subsidies is also criticized. In a certain respect subsidies have a negative structural policy effect, since resources are directed to the poorest regions, while the relatively more developed regions of the given country (Madrid, Valencia, Catalonia, etc.) are left out of consideration. With transfers the balance of payments improves, but the effects on the balance of trade and the national budget may be negative. Concrete deliveries improve the export chances of the donor countries, while the compulsory national contributions force governments to carry out surplus expenditure. In the long-term this may improve the economic structure of the given country, but in the short-term it may have contradictory effects on fulfilment of the convergence criteria.

4. FISCAL FEDERALISM

Many argue that with the establishment of a properly working economic and monetary union, the future integration of budgetary policies is unavoidable, and in order to deal with asymmetric shocks and to secure stability, progress towards fiscal federalism is a necessary development. "Existing monetary unions, such as the USA, Canada and Australia, rely heavily on interstate fiscal transfers to compensate for the absence of state monetary and exchange rate policies in response to region-specific inequalities and disturbances. The European Union is not yet a fully-fledged federation. But as it progresses towards EMU, what is urgently required is a larger central budget which in combination with national fiscal policy will enable the member states to deal with national macro-economic and regional problems which otherwise might have negative spillover effects on the stability of the Union. It will also empower the Union to pursue its external economic objectives, such as to assist potential members of the Union in Central and Eastern Europe to adapt to the requirements of membership and to aid the development of associate countries. Therefore, the European Union would need a substantially larger budget. Whether it will be called federal or not makes no difference" (HITIRIS 1998: 114–115).

The EC/EU budget can be regarded as only an "embryo centre of a federal system" (referred to by EL-AGRA 1990: 290) and so far only slow and contradictory steps have been taken towards any type of federal budget. In fact, one can rightly ask whether we can speak about any such progress, inasmuch as federal union is not yet an objective declared and accepted by the member states. The issues of a federal budget were raised by the MACDOUGALL Report as long ago as 1977, but owing to the far-reaching political implications, these recommendations lapsed into oblivion.

The MACDOUGALL Report envisaged three stages of federal budget integration:

- pre-federal integration with Community public expenditures, amounting to 2–2.5% of Community GDP;
- federation with small public sectors, with expenditures of 5–7% of GDP;
- union with large Community expenditures, reaching 20–25% of aggregate GDP.

By the early 2000s, the European Union, transferring little more than 1% of its total GDP among the members countries, is only about half-way even to a "pre-federal budget", and the disputes about the budget reforms suggest no spectacular breakthrough in the foreseeable future.

The case for fiscal federalism can be supported by many arguments, but at the same time the main points can also be used against it.

1. Already, in the present state of integration, particularly as a result of the single market and monetary union, increasing the Community transfers is more and more necessary, and this calls for strengthening the role of the Union's budget. "Among this set of arguments for a larger EU central budget is the need to compensate, first, for the regional impact of the single market and EMU, and, second, for the constraints which tax harmonization imposes on the members' ability to raise tax revenue" (HITIRIS 1998: 110). The budget, therefore, should evolve along the lines of fiscal federalism in the future.

2. In the EU, compared to the US labour mobility is lower, labour markets are imperfect and wages are more rigid. Under these circumstances, short-term shocks may lead to large regional income disparities and unemployment. In the US, under more favourable conditions, the inter-regional transfers are relatively substantial (according to some studies, about 30–40% of short-term shocks are offset by automatic transfers), therefore the lack or inadequacy of these transfers in the EU threatens it with serious social consequences and tensions (SALA-I-MARTIN and SACHS 1991).

3. Factor market integration may also call for budgetary centralization. Differing regulations and budgetary conditions may interfere with optimal allocation of factors and cause inefficiencies. Harmonization of regulation is needed and unilateral incentives for dislocation of factors should be avoided. To put it simply, higher unemployment benefits or more favourable social provisions may attract movement of labour, leading to further market distortions. Budgetary harmonization or centralization is the only proper way to solve these problems.

The bulk of the EMU literature, however, is of the opinion that the structures emerging at present in the EU can be operational and viable even in the longer run, and there is no urgent need for progress toward fiscal federalism in the foreseeable future.

1. All the tensions and constraints generated by the operation of EMU can be dealt with effectively by the national budgets. As JACQUES PELKMANS stresses: "The conclusion is that the EU is not less a suitable currency area merely because it does not have, or plan to have, a centralised fiscal stabilisation policy. Decentralisation may do. Extreme forms of decentralisation can only be a stable solution in the absence of labour (and voter) mobility across borders. Thus, the strong EU preference to retain national fiscal stabilisers interacts favourably with the strong preference to seek jobs in the national economy, in turn also permitting some degree of diverging social policies and regulation. In conclusion, it would seem that such an EMU, without much redistribution and no stabilisation at central level, is possible and may well be stable" (PELKMANS 1997: 293).

2. According to others, if disturbances of equilibrium are due to structural causes, then these must be handled by means of appropriate policies. "To the question whether in the EC a central fiscal policy is absolutely necessary in the event of the establishment of a European currency union, clearly the answer is no. If the causes of macroeconomic equilibrium disturbances are to be found in the imperfect national economic and political markets, then there is not much point in reacting to shocks with centralized process regulation. The appropriate therapy for such causes would rather be an effective policy of order, that is, correction of the operational frameworks of the economic system, which would help to reduce vulnerability to the causes of shocks, and the extent and seriousness of the shocks themselves" (BERTHOLD 1993: 480).

3. There are marked differences among the EU countries not only in terms of per capita incomes and consumption structures, but also in historical, political, cultural and geographical respects (it extends from the far north to the Mediterranean). These factors run counter to fiscal harmonization, and enforced centralization would do more harm than good. The provision of basic public services should remain on the national level, and budgetary regulation should reflect local interests and preferences.

4. Fiscal federalism is characterized by automatic cohesion transfers. From the fiscal point of view, one of the greatest weaknesses of EMU is that in the EU budget such automatic transfers and stabilizers simply do not exist. As the chances of any essential transfer of income taxes and provision of public services to federal level are minimal, such mechanisms will not develop in the foreseeable future.

5. Premature and hurried budget centralization may further increase the 'democratic deficit' and weaken democratic accountability and control. "The essence of this argument is that the EU should develop its constitution and institutions along democratic principles before contemplating any substantial increase in the size and functions of its budget" (HITIRIS 1998: 113–114). The European Parliament should acquire real responsibility for and control over any federal type of budget.

There is no doubt that the establishment of monetary union has created a new situation from the point of view of the importance and possible role of the EU budget, but any development towards fiscal federalism will be primarily a function of the future progress of political integration.

REFERENCES

BARNES, I. and BARNES, P. M. (1995) *The Enlarged European Union*. Longman, London.

BERTHOLD, N. (1993): Fiskális föderalizmus Európában mint a sikeres gazdasági és valutáris unió előfeltétele? (Fiscal federalism in Europe as a condition of successful economic and monetary union?) *Közgazdasági Szemle*, No. 6.

EC Commission (1989) *Community Public Finance – The European Budget after the 1988 reform*. Part 3, Chapter 13. Office for Official Publications of the European Communities, Luxembourg.

EICHENGREEN, B. (1991 *Shocking Aspects of European Monetary Unification*. University of California.

EL-AGRA, A. M. (1990) The General Budget. In: A. M. EL-AGRA, ed. *Economics of the European Community*. Philip Allan, London.

EMERSON, M. and HUHNE, C. (1991) *The ECU Report*. London: Pan Books.

HARROP, J. (2000) *The Political Economy of Integration in the European Union*. Edward Elgar, Cheltenham.

HITIRIS, T. (1998) *European Union Economics*. Prentice Hall Europe, London.

JONES, R. A. (2001) *Politics and Economics of the European Union*. Edward Elgar, Cheltenham.

MACDOUGALL Report (1977) *Report of the Study Group on the Role of Public Finance in European Integration*. Commission of the European Communities. Vol. II. Brussels.

PELKMANS, J. (1997) *European Integration (Methods and economic analysis)*. Longman, Heerlen, Open University of the Netherlands.

PENKETH, K. (1992) The Budget of the European Community. In: F. MCDONALD and S. DEAREN, eds. European Economic Integration. Longman, London.

SALA-I-MARTIN–J. SACHS (1991) *Fiscal Federalism and Optimum Currency Areas: Evidence for Europe* from The US National Bureau of Economic Research. Working paper No. 3855.

TSOUKALIS, L. (1997) *The New European Economy Revisited*. Oxford University Press, Oxford.

IV.

STRUCTURAL POLICY ROLES AND DIRECTIONS

By

ÁKOS KENGYEL–TIBOR PALÁNKAI

The EU members belong to the *developed industrial countries*, with a modern industrial structure, highly-developed money markets and banking and service sectors, a modern continent-wide infrastructure network, a concentrated transnational company sector, and developed state regulation and welfare systems. In recent years the EU countries' *economic structure has become increasingly 'post-industrial' in character* as the European economies are becoming *service-oriented*: the service sector now has a weight of more than 2/3 of GDP.

According to official EU statistics, in 2000 the average per capita GDP of the Fifteen (purchasing power parity) was €20,613 (European Commission – EUROSTAT 2000: 11). In respect of GDP per capita only the figure for Luxembourg was markedly (94%) higher than the EU average; a group of countries (Denmark, Ireland, Holland, Belgium and Austria) were 10–20% higher in their level of development, while the per capita GDP of the least developed, Greece and Portugal, was about 70% of the EU average, and that of Spain 80% of the average. The figures for the other countries were around the Union average. This means that *there are not really substantial differences in levels of development among the majority of the EU member countries.* With the Mediterranean enlargements in the 1980s relatively significant differences did appear, but in the past decade these countries have been rapidly catching up.

The process of European integration was characterized from the beginning by considerations of structural modernization. It was always its fundamental aim to improve the competitiveness of the European economy and to bridge the 'technology gap' between it and the US, and later Japan (POSNER 1992), and to improve the world market positions of European companies. In different periods the roles of EU structural policy underwent significant modification. Despite efforts at adaptation and modernization *the 'gaps' kept reappearing, and the continent's structural crisis seemed to be an acute problem.* At the same time from the 1990s Japan's spectacular technological advance ran out of steam, its economy lapsed into recession, its stock exchange became depressed, and its share of high-technology markets stopped growing.

Until the beginning of the 1970s the EC/EU was characterized by a *passive structural policy,* and the Union did not at first undertake a decisive structural policy role. In the first phase of the integration process, it was expected that the liberalization of trade and the competition developing within the common market would bring about the necessary structural changes. The Treaty of Rome laid the main emphasis on competition policy, which was understandable at that time, when industrial output was growing rapidly. In those circumstances it was important to concentrate on ensuring the conditions of fair market competition.

The EU's passive structural policy meant that at first it was not considered necessary to provide extra support for particular branches or activities; *basically it was left to market forces to carry out modernization of the economic structure.* In this period only a few bilateral and trilateral intergovernmental cooperative agreements were concluded in strategic areas like aircraft manufacture and space research.

In a few branches an active role was undertaken at the beginning of the integration process. Among them were the iron and steel industry and supervision of coal mining, within the framework of the European Coal and Steel Community. This was motivated by the need to deal with post-war difficulties, to increase output and eliminate shortages. In the 1950s the main purpose of interventions was to maximize prices, in contrast to the situation two decades later, when in circumstances of over-production the chief concern was to fix a minimum price level. The other area to which special attention was paid was the atomic energy, as the energy source of the future. Cooperation in the field of atomic energy research was the fundamental aim formulated in the establishment of Euratom. In the area of Union structural policy intervention the development of regulation of the agricultural sector became the most striking feature. Because of the many special circumstances that typified the sector, agricultural policy became one of the first EU areas to be regulated, and in the greatest detail.

Significant changes took place in structural policy in the period after 1973: *a prolonged structural crisis resulted from the oil-price explosion and the deep recession.* The traditional branches underwent a serious crisis; this marked the end of the period when the iron and steel industry, shipbuilding, heavy industry and textiles were the main motors of the economy. The EU member countries faced serious challenges: the crisis in the key sectors of the economy had somehow to be dealt with. The solutions tended to be hasty ones, reflecting a short-term view. The governments of the member countries laid the emphasis on support for the branches hit by the crisis. After 1973 they also devoted more attention to energy policy.

At EU level the structural policy that evolved approved national subsidies, *gave priority to support for the traditional sectors, and financed losses;* adopting OECD terminology, we can call this *negative structural policy.* Instead of supporting the improvement of competitiveness, changes in the economic structure and technological renewal, negative structural policy preserves the existing faulty structure. This policy, which the EU followed until the 1980s, largely contributed to the relative decline in competitiveness of the European economy, and its loss of ground in world markets. The EU was tardy and slow in joining the new technological revolution.

At national level, re-evaluation of the theoretical and strategic bases of economic policies started at the beginning of the 1970s. *Monetarism was even then gradually gaining ground in practice in the economic policies of several countries. Radical practical steps, however, were taking place only about 10 years later. The most important ones involved a shift away from policies of subsidies and protectionism, and drastic changes in the structure of national budgets.* Accelerated structural change and technological development created a new situation from the point of view of European integration as well. It was clear that in the interest of adaptation new integration strategies were needed.

From the beginning of the 1980s, in the framework of national structural policy state intervention began to turn its attention to structural transformation, technological renewal and support for research and development. It had become clear that significant reduction of the capacity of the traditional branches was needed, together with development of sectors in this area carrying out smaller-scale but more efficient production. This change of viewpoint altered the direction of structural policy at EU level also.

The positive structural policies that evolved at EU level *were characterized by emphasis on support for technical development, the promotion of structural change, and development of sectors capable of surviving in market competition and satisfying the new demands*. In 1984 the first Union budgetary program for research and technical development was launched. To further improve the conditions of competition among economic actors and promote structural modernization of markets, in 1985 the program for a single internal market was approved, and its implementation was completed by the end of 1992. The change of approach in structural policy was reflected in the new form of support for the traditional sectors: in these support was now concentrated on improving efficiency and on development of smaller, more specialized production capacity creating greater added value.

In implementing the single internal market special attention was paid to the information and communications technologies, as the motors of development. From the 1990s a number of documents of strategic importance were drawn up, relating to *the information society, the knowledge-based economy and support for the development in Europe of the electronic economy (the e-Europe)*, and the creation of the necessary conditions at Union level. This strategic approach is particularly important in view of the present pace of development of the informatics revolution, when competitiveness in the world economy is based on knowledge, innovative ability, access to information and linkage with the various networks.

1. INDUSTRIAL POLICY

Industrial policy at Union level is characterized by dualism. *The policy of improving the general conditions for economic development appears in the form of comprehensive measures relating to full implementation of the single market, while the narrower approach aimed at dealing with the situation of the branches in crisis and applying new technologies appears in the form of sectoral programs.* Considering that the EU does not possess the necessary means and resources to carry out a completely independent policy, the main task of Union-level industrial policy consists in defining common objectives and ensuring that the activities of the member states do not conflict with one another. This demands the formulation of common targets and strategies.

1.1. THE DEVELOPMENT AND AIMS OF INDUSTRIAL POLICY

The origin of the role of Community-level industrial policy can be linked to the establishment of the European Coal and Steel Community (ECSC) in 1951. In the framework of the ECSC, coal mining and the iron and steel industry in the then 6 member countries were placed under the direction of the High Authority. In the Rome Treaty which established the European Economic Community the need to establish an industrial policy was not formulated; only the development of certain sectoral policies was highlighted (e.g. agricultural policy and transport policy).

To deal with the structural crisis that developed in the 1970s various kinds of measures were taken in the member countries, and it became clear that some sort of action at EC level was also needed to cope with the crisis.

Naturally, the gradual implementation of the common market had its effect on Community industry, especially the consumer goods (domestic electrical appliances, car manufacturing), but at the same time it had less effect on the high technology sectors (information technology and telecommunications), where generally big national companies dominated the market. In the latter area change came only with the implementation of the single market. Long years passed before any member country realised that Community-level industrial policy was needed to deal with common structural and sectoral problems.

With the coming into force of the Maastricht Treaty, improvement of the competitiveness of industry became one of the Union's expressed objectives: strengthening of the competitiveness of Community industry was included in Article 3 of the Treaty. *Article 130 (now 157) of the Treaty on European Union specified that the Community and the member countries must ensure development of the necessary conditions for the competitiveness of industry in the Community.* To this end – in harmony with the system of open and competing markets – their activities were to be directed at the following:

– acceleration of adaptation to structural changes in industry;

– strengthening a favourable environment for the establishment and development of enterprises;

– creation of a favourable environment for development of cooperation between enterprises;

– promotion of better exploitation of the industrial potential of innovation and R&D policies.

The member countries, together with the Commission hold joint consultations and coordinate their activities to the extent necessary. The Commission can carry out any initiative that is useful for assisting such coordination. In connection with activities aimed at improving the competitiveness of Community industry, it is emphasized in Article 157 that the aims formulated cannot serve as a basis for introducing any measure that would result in distortion of competition.

This article created the legal basis for Community-level action. The Community's industrial policy is based on three main principles:

– consistent harmonization of all common policies affecting industrial activity, with special emphasis on environment protection;
– improvement of access to markets outside the Union, introduction of measures to combat unfair business practice, and promotion of international cooperation in industry;
– positive adaptation to industrial changes through a well-thought-out approach.

Besides implementation of the program directed at complete realization of the single market, improvement of international competitiveness became the key issue of EU industrial policy. *The most comprehensive approach to industrial policy in the EU was contained in the White Book entitled "Growth, Competitiveness, Employment – the Challenges and the Ways Forward into the 21st Century"*, which was published in December 1993 (European Commission 1993). The White Book pointed out that in the previous two decades:

– the rate of growth of the European economy had slowed from 4% annually to 2.5%;
– unemployment had steadily increased;
– the proportion of investment had dropped by 5 percentage points;
– the Union's competitive position relative to the US and Japan had deteriorated in the areas of employment, its share of export markets, R&D and innovation, and the introduction of new products.

The White Book stresses the key importance of assisting the adaptation of companies to the new competition situation based on globalization and mutual dependence. In view of all the factors, EU industrial policy must be directed at improving competitiveness:

- the Union must develop the strengths of Community industry;
- active policies promoting industrial cooperation are required;
- a harmonized approach for creating strategic alliances must be worked out;
- measures must be taken to ensure market competition.

Although European industry has much to gain from the single market, the EU still faces new challenges. *The globalization of economies and markets,* which is increasing the intensity of international competition, favours not only the exploitation of possibilities of economies of scale but also specialization in well-defined market segments. The actors in the European economy must pay more attention to the development of factors that improve productivity: technological development, investment in the field of research and development, full use of capacity, the training and the cost of labour, and company management skills.

In addition to the challenges arising from the globalization of markets and competition, European industry must prepare to meet the challenges of the *new industrial revolution* resulting from developments in information and communications technology. The present development processes are increasingly blurring the traditional boundaries between electronics, information technology, telecommunications and the audiovisual sector. This revolution could have spinoff effects on the structure of production and the development of methods. Competitiveness is increasingly dependent on innovative ability, which offers the possibility of developing new products and services.

1.2. SECTORAL POLICIES

To prevent sectoral measures taken by individual national governments from jeopardizing common interests, and to promote structural change in European industry, there is a need to develop sectoral policies formulated at EU level. The Union's policy has developed in the sectors that are most important internationally, where intervention is necessary because the markets (steelmaking, shipbuilding, textiles) are saturated, or because support at European level is required (the aircraft industry, informatics, telecommunications).

1.2.1. THE STEEL INDUSTRY

The Union-level policy directed at transforming the steel industry was its first and most comprehensive industrial policy intervention. The steel industry was one of the two strategic sectors at which the treaty that created the ECSC was aimed. This sector provides good examples of all the problems of industrial policy operated at Union level, since traditionally this sector operates with significant state involvement, and is a sector where the EU has exceptional authority, and where serious crises occur. This is the branch where substantial intervention is needed, in the form of coordination and provision of financial subsidies for restructuring, and even the restriction of competition.

Despite the modernization that was carried out in the period of rapid economic growth up to 1973, production costs in the steel industry compared with its competitors outside Europe remained high; its disadvantages were due to failure to develop sufficiently large-scale plants. The protectionist environment characteristic of this sector of industry did not promote the necessary changes. Even in the 1960s the EC's share of world steel production had begun to decline; the European steel industry remained basically within national frameworks, and only a handful of companies carried out production in more than one country. As a result of the first oil price explosion and the subsequent recession, demand for steel products fell by 14%. As a consequence fierce competition developed: producers wanted to retain their market share, and this pushed steel prices down by 35-45%. The European Commission proposed the introduction of voluntary restraints on production. In response to the new wave of recession, in 1980 compulsory production quotas were introduced, and 'recommended prices' were applied.

The main aim of the measures formulated by the EC was to reduce the capacity of the steel industry within an organized framework, so as to improve the sector's efficiency and profitability. There can be no doubt that if the transformation of the sector had been left to international market forces, the process would have been very painful. The Treaty of Paris provided the legal basis for Community intervention; it gave the ECSC High Authority (later the Commission) wide-ranging powers to prevent the formation of cartels, to promote research and development and to support re-training. Subject to the approval of the Council, the Commission had the right to declare a state of 'imminent emergency' and introduce minimum prices. If such a situation arose, it could also announce a state of 'manifest emergency', in which the application of production quotas became mandatory. Until the mid-1970s there was no occasion to make use of these provisions. In October 1980 on the basis of Article 56 of the Treaty of Paris the existence of a state of manifest emergency was declared. This was called the DAVIGNON *plan*, after the relevant member of the Commission, and it *introduced mandatory production and delivery quotas.*

By the end of 1985 the EC steel industry had got over the worst of the crisis. In future all forms of state subsidy were banned, with the exception of support for plant closures prompted by environmental considerations or loss-making. At the time of the manifest emergency output fell by 19% and the number of those employed by 40% (BARNES and BARNES 1995: 234–236). The social costs of restructuring were very high, but at least the state that was absolutely necessary for the normal, efficient operation of the sector was reached. The effects of the introduction of production quotas were generally judged to have been beneficial.

As the European economy once again began to decline at the beginning of the 1990s, the steel industry faced a new crisis: steel prices fell by 30% between 1991 and 1993. At the end of 1993 the Commission confirmed that an emergency had again arisen in the sector. In the interest of better use of capacity, the EC decided to reduce its 185-million-ton raw steel capacity by 20–25 million tons. In spite of further subsidies, it did not succeed in carrying out a substantial reduction of capacity: even among state-owned companies only half the reduction in capacity was carried out, and the private sector showed no real willingness to cooperate until the state sector committed itself to the necessary cutbacks. The state sector was in fact a hostage to domestic interests: the location of steel works meant there were very limited possibilities of workers finding new jobs, since the plants already operated in areas of high unemployment. The EU's contribution to bearing the social costs of closures was inadequate. Support for re-training proved insufficient to compensate for the jobs lost in areas suffering from high unemployment.

At the same time it must be noted that the structure of the European steel industry has altered significantly in the last few decades. The traditional picture of the steel industry as a branch employing large numbers of workers is no longer realistic: the number employed in this sector has fallen by 70% in the past 25 years. *As a result of the various structural changes and the privatization of formerly state-owned companies, production has been rationalized and substantial technological investments have been carried out.* The competitiveness of the sector has improved, partly owing to strategic cross-border alliances. At the end of the 1990s 5 groups accounted for 60% of steel output, compared with 23% at the beginning of the decade (European Commission 1999).

The European steel industry has proved successful thanks to the close links forged with users – companies operating in the sectors manufacturing investment goods (e.g. the construction industry, engineering) and the branches producing consumer goods (car manufacture, domestic appliances) *in the field of innovation directed at developing new products* (e.g. flexibility, resistance to corrosion, weight). As a result of the introduction of new technologies, rationalization focussing on efficiency, and reduction of the size of the workforce, operating costs have fallen considerably. In consequence, productivity of the EU steel industry is among the highest compared with its competitors in the Triad.

The Union's steelmakers face competition principally from companies in countries with comparative cost advantages, where labour, energy prices and the level of taxation are more favourable, or there are less strict regulations concerning state subsidies and environment protection. The future situation of the sector will be seriously affected by the intention, expressed by the majority of the OECD countries at the Uruguay Round of GATT negotiations, to abolish customs duties on steel products by 2004.

1.2.2. SHIPBUILDING

Shipbuilding – which, like the steel industry, has become a crisis sector – had already lost its importance in the world economy from the beginning of the 1960s. In 1960 the EC still accounted for half of the world's shipbuilding, but by 1975 it represented only 22%. The oil crisis and the recession that followed cut back orders drastically and an enormous amount of surplus capacity developed in the sector. In a policy statement in 1978 the Council emphasized that *there was a need for the survival of a healthy, competitive shipbuilding industry,* which was of strategic importance not just on account of its own economic and social weight, but also because it provided a basis for *development of the Community's overseas trade.*

At the same time in the absence of the appropriate concrete authority the Commission was unable or unwilling to play a serious part in restructuring the sector. The only means available to Union sectoral policy relating to shipbuilding was coordination of national subsidies. To date, 7 guidelines relating to support for shipbuilding have been approved.

In 1989, under the aegis of the OECD multilateral talks aimed at regulating the international framework of shipbuilding got under way, involving countries accounting for more than 70% of the world output of the sector (the EU, Japan, South Korea, Norway and the US). As a result of their agreement, all obstacles limiting the conditions of normal competition had to be eliminated from January 1998. Consequently the EU issued a Council decree on subsidies for shipbuilding and ship repairing. The Commission's *main aim was to harmonize the national forms of subvention relating to shipbuilding* and to make them transparent, while permitting budget support by the member countries to help develop the sector.

1.2.3. THE TEXTILE AND CLOTHING INDUSTRY

From the end of the 1960s the textile and clothing industry faced increasingly serious difficulties. The problem was partly the slow growth of domestic demand and partly competition from imports from developing countries. In this sector Europe had lost its cost competitiveness compared to countries where wages were relatively low. In addition, in many cases Union producers had to contend with unfair business practices, while high tariff barriers and non-tariff obstacles made market access difficult for their products.

In the EC through the European Social Fund support was successfully provided for the re-training of workers who had lost their jobs in the textile and clothing industry. At the same time this was only a piecemeal solution, and by no means a substitute for development of a comprehensive Union-level sectoral policy. Such a policy *began to take shape at the beginning of the 1990s,* and it had two aspects, an internal aspect and an external one. Within the Union the Commission supervises national subventions and tries to prevent effects that transfer employment difficulties and structural problems from one member country to another. Many sectoral subsidies have been banned, or permitted only in a different form.

The external aspect of textile industry policy is directed at ensuring adequate room for manoeuvre in foreign trade for the Union's industry, without hindering the developing countries' efforts at development of the sector or giving rise to conflict. At international level the signing of the 'Multifibre Agreement' (MFA) approved within the framework of the GATT Uruguay Round made possible the gradual liberalization of world trade in textiles and clothing industry products. In view of this the EU concentrates on opening external markets and stimulating export, and takes stern action against dumping, subsidies and fraudulent origin- and brand-labelling.

The current situation and future development of the EU's textile and clothing industry are characterized by the following processes (European Commission Enterprise DG 2001):

– *Globalization and liberalization.* The sector is exposed to increasing competition from (mainly Asian) countries with low labour costs, but at the same time, despite the huge labour-cost differences, the European textile industry has remained competitive thanks to its higher level of productivity, and on the basis of competitive strengths such as its innovative ability, high quality, creativity and fashion design.

– *Continual structural transformation and modernization.* The sector is quick to introduce new technologies, as regards not only informatics and communications technologies but also new manufacturing techniques. The EU textile industry plays a leading role in development of new products.

– *The operation of many small and medium-sized companies.* The average company is family-owned and employs 20 people. Subcontracting is very widespread; it accounts for between 10 and 60 per cent in some member countries and particularly in certain regions plays an important part in the maintenance of employment and provision of income.

– *Outsourcing and outward processing.* Many companies transfer low-value-added, labour-intensive activities outside the EU, chiefly to candidate and Mediterranean countries. Thanks to the geographical proximity of these countries, Union companies are able to supervise the outsourced production processes and react rapidly to changing market demand.

1.2.4. AIRCRAFT MANUFACTURE

The aircraft manufacturing has for several decades been among the sectors of industry that promote economic growth, and its technological development has spinoff effects on other branches of industry. Aircraft manufacture is a strategic sector. More and more attention is being devoted to this sector, since it could play an important role through the international division of labour in replacing branches of industry relocating to developing countries.

In the course of the 1970s cooperation within the EC went furthest in the field of aircraft construction, though not at Community level but in a bilateral form (the Concorde and Airbus projects). At the same time, these bilateral and multilateral forms of cooperation often functioned alongside contrary national policies; there was no unified Union strategy or joint financing. Both the Concorde and the Airbus programs scored technically remarkable successes, and Airbus represented an immediate breakthrough in the commercial field as well. The 'Airbus' consortium offered serious competition in the field of civil aviation to the previously unchallenged leading role of the US.

In the field of aircraft manufacture Union policy is based on legislation of a non-compulsory nature: harmonized projects are formulated and consultation takes place among the member countries. The competitiveness of the sector depends above all on research and development activity. In recognition of this, since 1989 the EU has *provided co-financing for research in the aircraft industry.* The chief aims of the research are to develop design and manufacturing technologies of a high technical standard, to decrease energy consumption, to reduce noise and pollution emission, and to increase operating safety.

1.2.5. INFORMATION TECHNOLOGY SECTORS

Development of information and communications technologies plays a crucial role in improving the competitiveness of European companies. *Economic development is increasingly based on the use of information and knowledge, access to which is made possible by the enormous development that has taken place in the field of information and communications technology.* The digitalization of information in every form (text, picture and sound) has fundamentally transformed many areas of operation of the economy and society. Working methods have changed, and so has the organizational structure of companies, the emphasis as regards the content of education, and modes of interpersonal communication. Information technologies are gradually acquiring great importance in the operation of every producing and service sector, and already in the social services too (health, education, transport, entertainment and culture) their significance is steadily increasing.

Access to information, to the networks ('information highways') that convey it, and to services that facilitate the use of data (databases) is of fundamental importance. The EU Commission has defined four major priorities in connection with the promotion of the continuous spread of the information society:

– improvement of the business environment through *complete liberalization of telecommunications* and coordination among the relevant regulatory authorities;
– investment in the future through support for *research and training* related to the information society;
– giving people priority by guaranteeing *access to a wide variety of services;*
– responding to global challenges by *linking up networks,* ensuring the interoperability of services and protecting intellectual property rights and personal rights.

On the basis of the Commission's proposals the Council worked out a number of programs to encourage creating of the information society. For example, a program planned to last for several years was designed to develop the presence of 'European digital content' on global networks and to support the promotion of linguistic variety. The main aim of this program is to create a favourable environment for business initiatives that can exploit in the field of commerce Europe's creativity, its cultural variety and its technological strengths.

The approval of the guideline published in January 2000 relating to the guaranteeing of acceptance of electronic signatures was the first step in creating a European regulatory framework for e-commerce. Six months later the *guideline on electronic commerce* was also approved; it harmonizes the chief legal aspects, including indication of the headquarters of providers of services, the validity of electronic contracts, the transparency of the contract-concluding process, the responsibilities of Internet service providers, the possibility of online exchange of information, and the role of national governments.

After the Council of Europe meeting in Lisbon in March 2000, the Commission approved the *'e-Europe' implementation program and the action plan relating to it,* which dealt with the removal of the main obstacles to use of the Internet and the creation of the essential conditions for development of the 'new economy'. The chief aim of the action plan was the creation of cheaper, faster and more secure use of the Internet, support for acquisition of the appropriate skills, and encouragement of widespread use of the Internet [COM (2000) 330, 24 May 2000]. The strategic aim was to enable the EU to catch up on its global competitors in competitiveness by 2010.

1.2.6. TELECOMMUNICATIONS

The digital technologies developed by the information technologies enable integrated transmission of voice, text and pictures through a single communications system. These highly developed communications technologies and services create crucially important links between the various sectors of industry, the service sector and the market, and between peripheral areas and economic centres.

The EU's common policy in the field of telecommunications was developed in the 1990s, and focuses on four main groups of issues:

– the creation of a single market for telecommunications equipment, with the help of standardization;

– liberalization of the market for telecoms services;

– promotion of the technological development of the sector through Union support for research;

– promotion of the balanced development of the EU regions through construction of the Transeuropean telecommunications networks.

The creation of a single European market for telecoms equipment was the purpose of the Council decision dealing with the *standardization* needed in the field of information technology and telecommunications. Standardization makes possible the creation of a European telecoms market and the exploitation of the possibilities of a large market, plays an important part in preventing the distortion of competition, and also ensures the smooth exchange of information.

Creation of a single market for telecom equipment made it necessary to *open the telecom markets,* which traditionally operated as state monopolies. The chief means for liberalizing telecom services was the provision of free access to networks. The guideline approved in 1990, dealing with the creation of an internal market for telecom services, laid down the twin principles of open and efficient access to and use of telecom networks *through introduction of the Open Network Provision (ONP).* On the basis of the ONP it is prohibited to limit access to telecom networks and telecom services.

Research in the field of highly developed communications technologies and services, as the basis of *technological development* of telecommunications, is *supported within the framework of EU research and development programs.* The main aim of the research program to promote the development of user-friendly information society is to support the application of excellent technical solutions and the widest possible use of them, including the development of broadband networks, which play an important part in the fast transmission of data.

Particular attention is paid to *the development of the Transeuropean telecommmunications networks,* based essentially on coherent linkage of the national networks. *Telematics* have a central role in the development of the Transeuropean networks. Numerous action plans and directives have been issued with reference to the creation and operation of a telematics network that will allow electronic data exchange between government offices, especially in fields that are necessary for the operation of the internal market and the application of joint policies. Telematics applications assist, for example, the linkage of university and research institute networks, the development of connections between library services, co-operation among local authorities in the field of tele-working and tele-services, and the use of telematics devices in the area of road traffic.

2. THE COMMON AGRICULTURAL POLICY

The Common Agricultural Policy (CAP) was one of the first policies developed in the European Union, and one of those regulated in the greatest detail. For many reasons, right at the beginning of the integration process the member countries taking part considered it important to establish a common policy to regulate and provide support for the agricultural sector. In the past decades this policy has undergone several changes, but it has retained a strongly protectionist character: a high level of subventions and an internal market protected by high customs tariffs and other means.

2.1. THE REASONS FOR THE DEVELOPMENT OF THE COMMON AGRICULTURAL POLICY

The situation and development of agriculture at the beginning of the integration process was from many points of view a question of special importance in Western Europe. At that time about 25% of those in employment worked in the agricultural sector, and in addition their income level was very low (around 40% of the national economy average). *This low income did not provide workers with an adequate standard of living and was insufficient from points of view of the investment needed* to raise the technological level of agriculture and improve productivity. The low level of incomes, together with the outdated structure, was in itself main justification for support of agriculture.

Another argument in favour of the development of a subventions policy was the fact that the member countries of the Union, as far as agricultural output was concerned, *were at a comparative disadvantage with regard to producers in other parts of the world* – especially the US, Canada, Australia and New Zealand. Thanks to their climate and soil endowments and more favourable distribution and use of arable land, these countries could produce much more cheaply.

For the EC countries, right from the beginning of the integration process the *provision of security of supply* of foods, that is, achieving *the minimum import-dependence,* was an important consideration. To this end, however, their low level of self-sufficiency had to be improved, since at the end of the 1950s they were self-supporting with regard to only about 40% of the main types of produce. Being self-supporting from their own resources meant that the less efficient, less economical Union producers had to be *protected against external competitors.*

Apart from support of agriculture, *political considerations* also played a part. Because of the size of the agricultural population, those who earned their living in agriculture represented a significant base for all political parties, and thus every government sought to gain favour with agricultural voters.

There were also *social considerations.* If there were no agricultural subsidies, then it would not be possible to live decently by farming, it would not be worth to carry on agricultural activities, unemployment would grow, and a significant proportion of the rural population would migrate to the cities. In these circumstances the cities' infrastructure would have to be developed; transport, housing, schools and hospitals would have to be provided. The costs of all these would be far in excess of the sums allocated as agricultural subsidies.

It must be added that this consideration is still valid today, embodied in the *comprehensive rural development program.* The aim of rural development continues to be the preservation of the level of population, but now not only by supporting agricultural activities but by enabling a living from other activities as well.

Taking all this into consideration, in drawing up the Treaty of Rome the member countries declared that support for agriculture was important, and that a common agricultural policy must be developed for this purpose. A common agricultural policy was necessary also because a *common market* for agricultural produce had been created, which would not have functioned properly without agricultural subsidies. If the national subsidies had been allowed to remain, then competition in national subsidies would have developed in the common market: a bigger market share would have been gained by whoever got a bigger subsidy from his national government. Thus *the common market for agriculture* could be implemented *only within the framework of a common subventions policy.*

2.2. THE REGULATION AND OPERATION OF THE COMMON AGRICULTURAL POLICY

Article 33 (formerly 39) of the Treaty of Rome formulated the aims to be pursued by the joint agricultural policy, which were:

– *to increase agricultural productivity* by stepping up technological progress, by expanding agricultural output and by optimal use of manpower;
– *to ensure a decent standard of living* for those working in agriculture by increasing incomes;
– *stabilization of markets;*
– to guarantee *security of supply;*
– to ensure *supply to consumers at reasonable prices.*

The working out of the policy began with the coming into force of the Rome Treaty. In the course of the development of the CAP 3 main principles were declared to be important:

1. *The development of a common market* (the principle of market unification): free trade, common prices, competition rules and prescriptions;
2. *Community preference*: protection against external competitors, preference given to EU producers;
3. *Financial solidarity:* joint financing regardless of which products or countries were involved in subsidies.

The CAP went into operation in 1962. To finance it, the European Agricultural Guidance and Guarantee Fund (EAGGF) was set up. The components of the operating mechanisms of the policy are:

- application of guaranteed prices;
- state intervention;
- export subsidies;
- protection against import competition.

Guaranteed wholesale prices are central to the policy; these are determined annually for the main types of products. In setting guaranteed prices production costs are taken into account, and also the need to ensure the desired level of income, and the level of revenue needed for saving and investment. When the policy was established, *the guaranteed prices were about 30–40% higher than world market prices. In the last few decades this big difference has gradually been reduced, and at present it is about 10%.*

When significantly divergent wholesale prices develop on the market, then the EU *through state purchasing agencies intervenes* in the processes. Characteristically this is done in the form of intervention buyings; that is, when prices are lower than the guaranteed prices, then demand is created by the intervention buyings and this pushes prices up to the desired level. If the guaranteed prices are higher than world market prices, *export has to be supported*: the low export price obtainable on external markets is supplemented to the level of the guaranteed price.

To protect its own producers the EC introduced de facto extremely *high customs tariffs against cheaper import,* and also imposed quantitative restrictions. Import levies were applied, which prevented imports from entering the market at prices lower than internal prices. The variable import levies were imposed on the current import price, so that it always supplemented the import price to the internal prices. After several decades of international protest against it, import levies were finally abolished in June 1995.

As a result of the agricultural policy that had been developed, thanks to high prices and guaranteed state intervention buyings, agricultural output grew rapidly from the 1960s onwards. One of the chief political aims, the attainment of a state of self-sufficiency, was achieved by the second half of the 1970s. Thanks to the system of subventions everyone produced as much as they could, for there were no market restrictions on production: if the market did not accept the high prices, then state stepped in by intervention. The consequence of all this was that *over-production was general*. In the second half of the decade 20–25% surpluses accumulated.

In these circumstances *financing of CAP became unsustainable*. As much as 2/3 of the EU common budget was now being allocated to the agricultural policy. For consumers too, consumer prices far higher than world market prices were becoming more and more intolerable; the whole of society was having to pay to maintain them, while the proportion of the population engaged in agriculture had decreased drastically in the past decades, to around 3–4%. The protectionist nature of the policy and the high level of its export subsidies distorted the whole of world agricultural trade, causing conflicts with countries where agriculture was genuinely efficient. The EU's main competitors protested in every international forum against the protectionist and discriminatory character of the Union's agricultural policy.

As a result of the CAP agricultural *productivity has improved, and significant technological modernization has taken place;* the quality of agricultural produce is higher, and average yields have risen. The agricultural 'infrastructure' has been developed: that is, the storage capacity, means of transport and cold-storage essential to efficient agriculture. Intensive farming, however, caused serious environmental damages.

Thus on the whole the internal situation that had developed by the second half of the 1980s (over-production and financing difficulties), together with external pressure made comprehensive reform of the CAP unavoidable. Several attempts at reform were made, the most important so far being the package of measures approved in 1992 and known as the *MacSharry reform* (European Commission 1992).

The main reform measures were as follows:

– separation of prices and incomes policies (producers' income level should not be supported through high prices, but instead, direct payments should be provided, conditional on fulfilment of certain requirements);

– reduction of guaranteed prices, to approximate to world market prices;

– production quotas (supports only up to a certain quantity);

– laying out of land from agricultural use;

– re-training programs (aimed at withdrawing labour from agriculture);

– early retirement (support for retirement at 55, if the farmer gives up production);
– support for young farmers (wide-ranging support for farmers under 35, loan arrangements).

Simultaneously with the internal reform measures, external obligations were undertaken in the GATT Uruguay Round. This round of negotiations dealing with the liberalization of international trade included on its agenda for the first time liberalization of agricultural trade. Not by chance, the Uruguay Round (1986–1993) was the longest in the history of the GATT, because the agricultural questions – mainly owing to the EU's opposition – proved extremely difficult to settle. Finally it was agreed that in agriculture the only legally permissible means of protection in trade policy was the customs tariff. Every other form of protective device must be abolished, or "tariffed", but subsequently their gradual elimination should be started.

The following international obligations came into force from the summer of 1995:

– application of customs duties, abolition of import levies;
– reduction of internal subsidies by 20% within 6 years;
– reduction of export subsidies and customs tariffs by 36% within 6 years.

On the basis of the document entitled Agenda 2000, drawn up by the Commission, at its March 1999 meeting in Berlin the Council of Europe approved further reform measures. Agenda 2000 urged the continuation of the reform process that had been begun, through further reduction of internal prices, an increase in the proportion of direct support for producers, with greater emphasis on food safety and quality, increased extensiveness of production, and more attention given to environmental considerations. The measures were still very cautious, and did not basically alter the existing system of agricultural subsidies and concessions. No one dared to undertake radical reform (European Commission 2002b).

The real importance of Agenda 2000 lay in its outlining of *rural development, as the 'second pillar' of the common agricultural policy*. The EU recognized that the future of the agricultural sector would largely depend on the balanced development of rural areas. In addition to market policy measures to improve the competitiveness of European agriculture, attention must be paid to comprehensive development of rural areas, which account for 80 per cent of the territory of the Union. The main aim of rural development policy is to create consistent, long-term frameworks that will guarantee the development of rural areas and their ability to preserve and create jobs.

One of the main basic principles of rural development policy is recognition of the *multifunctionality of agriculture,* which means that not only the food-producing role of the agricultural sector must be supported, but also many other, chiefly service activities. The other main feature of rural development is a *multisectoral, integrated approach,* promoting diversification of activities and the creation of new job opportunities. Another important aspect is the preservation of the 'rural heritage'.

All in all it can be stated that as a result of internal and external pressure the Union's agricultural market is less closed off from the world agricultural market, less isolated, thanks to the reform measures that have been carried out. Internal prices are closer to world market prices, and customs tariffs and export subsidies have been reduced, but they are still very high. At the same time, almost half of the Union's common budget is still devoted to financing the common agricultural policy: in the period from 2000 to 2006 €40.5 bn is available for expenditure on agriculture. Precisely as a result of the development and modernization carried out within the framework of the CAP the competitiveness of agriculture in the EU countries has significantly improved, and in fact, the existing level of development no longer justifies preservation of the present system of agricultural subsidies and protection.

3. RESEARCH AND DEVELOPMENT POLICY

In the course of the last few decades the European Union has gone through a considerable economic and social transformation, and the traditional structure of industry has undergone serious changes. The crisis phenomena and process of decline observable in the traditional sectors of European industry can only be counterbalanced by the strengthening of the new high-technology sectors. These *new branches and technologies,* which characterize the post-industrial society, the so-called information society, *are of decisive importance from the point of view of the competitiveness of the European economy, job creation, the future standard of living and the sustainability of economic growth.* Scientific research and technical development provide the basis for sustainable economic and social development and the competitiveness of the EU in the world economy.

The research carried out in the EU member countries was originally at a disadvantage in the international comparison, because the various countries pursued divergent research and development policies, and thus resources were often frittered away. It was clear that it was indispensable to develop R&D policy at Union level, with the chief aim of coordinating national policies and defining and supporting research programs that represented European interests.

3.1. THE NECESSITY FOR A COMMON R&D POLICY

In terms of the main index most frequently used to demonstrate the technological gap, the *proportion of R&D expenditure in relation to GDP,* in recent decades Europe has increasingly lost its earlier advantage. In the index for the whole of the EU, Europe lags behind its two main competitors in the world economy, Japan and the US. In 2000 Japan devoted 3.04% of its GDP to research and development; in the US the corresponding figure was 2.64%, while that for the EU was only 1.9% (EUROSTAT 2001).

At the same time significant differences exist between the EU member countries: R&D expenditure is highest in Sweden and Finland (3.8% and 3.19%); next come Germany and France, with indices of 2.44% and 2.19% respectively. In terms of the volume of expenditure, the latter two countries carried out 35% and 20% of the research done in the EU in 2000. At the other end of the scale stand the southern countries: the ratio of R&D expenditure to GDP in Greece was 0.51%, in Portugal 0.76%, and in Spain 0.89%.

The challenges facing the European economy – and therefore the main aims of scientific and technical research – change from time to time, yet certain generally valid considerations can be formulated, which justify the promotion of activities connected with research, the conscious definition of the directions of the research supported, and the development of cooperation among institutions in the various member countries.

The *chief aim of state intervention is to encourage research and development activities on a larger scale and to promote innovation,* through which the economy can improve its performance and international competitiveness. Support for basic research that offers possibilities of a wide range of applications is obviously a desirable area. Intervention makes it possible to prevent *duplication of research* and to *coordinate efforts*. Support in the field of research linked to the market may be justified, if the existing disadvantage of the given sector in international competition has to be reduced.

The development of new technology is often regarded as the task of the private sector, which may be true in cases when the market brings the desired results, in other words, the cost of research activity is quickly recouped. *The closer research activity is to the market, the more willing the private sector is to take responsibility for it.* This is understandable from the point of view that the only research worth making sacrifices for is the kind that promises commercial returns.

In most cases this does not happen: *research involves too great risks and requires serious capital expenditure,* which companies are usually hesitant to undertake. That is, if there were no deliberate state intervention, the market on its own would 'underperform'. In our experience, companies generally do not willingly undertake basic research. Instead they pursue a strategy of exploiting others' efforts and building on their results to enter the market.

One of the basic aims of intervention is *to promote cooperation between business and the research institutes.* The greatest advantage of this support strategy is that it creates a regular connection between the parties involved. There are several arguments in favour of large-scale cooperation:

– *reduction of costs,* through savings due to the advantages of economies of scale, among other things, and the exploitation of accumulated experience;

– *the possibility of cross-border application of technological results,* which also means there is no need for duplication of the high costs of R&D;

– *risk-sharing,* especially with large-scale projects where there is a risk of failure;

– *elimination of the problems of technical standards,* since standardization of the new invention no longer takes place at national level;

– *greater market power,* which means that the results of the cooperation will not be wasted because of the small size of the market or insignificant presence on the market.

At the same time it must be emphasized that in connection with R&D policy supporting cooperation several kinds of problem may arise:

– because costs and risks are shared, there is no sense of ownership, that is, a project to be carried out within a cooperation framework receives less attention than one of its own initiated within the institution;

– cooperation involves very serious costs at the beginning of the development of the program, on account of the necessary journeys and development of the appropriate communications channels;

– development and implementation of joint projects is a very time-consuming task.

In view of all these it must be considered whether the positive effects to be expected from cooperation outweigh the negative consequences. These considerations, apart from being generally sound and explaining the state's involvement, are particularly worth taking into account in connection with the successful development of the process of European integration. In the case of the EU there is even more justification for providing a common framework for the research and development activities carried out in the Union, since this is a question that fundamentally determines competitiveness.

The R&D policy followed at EU level cannot regard it as its task to eliminate national intervention, because in any case it does not have sufficient resources to be able to provide support for every sector. The main task of Union-level policy aimed at the development of new technologies is to eliminate national policies that compete and conflict with each other and to formulate strategy evolved within the European framework.

3.2. THE DEVELOPMENT AND REGULATION OF R&D POLICY

The need for a common policy on R&D only gradually became obvious. The basic agreements did not give the EU institutions any kind of authority to support or even merely coordinate the research carried out in the member countries. In the field of the responses to be made to the spread of the new technologies, at the beginning of the integration process promotion of research and development activity was formulated only within the framework of Euratom, in the area of the peaceful uses of nuclear energy.

In 1967 the council of science ministers met for the first time. In six fields – transport, oceanography, iron-smelting, environment protection, information technology and telecommunications – the council decided that studies should be prepared, examining the need for action to promote technological development. *In 1971 they set up the COST group (European Cooperation in the field of Scientific and Technical research),* the task of which was to facilitate such cooperation (BARNES and BARNES 1995: 252). Alongside the already designated fields COST included research in medicine, food technology, meteorology and agriculture. All the OECD countries of Western Europe took part in COST, which created a useful framework in the area of applied research for developing pan-European cooperation, but it distanced itself increasingly from the EU and led to the concluding of individual cooperation agreements.

The energy crisis that exploded in 1973 gave new impetus to the development of Union policy on R&D. In 1974 it was agreed that the Union should take part in the encouragement of scientific and technological development, and the Commission was given the task of coordinating national science policies. Though these were important decisions, a real breakthrough came only in 1979, when under the leadership of DAVIGNON, the official responsible for industry policy, with the participation of the 12 biggest European electronics firms the European Information Technology Industry Round Table came into being. These companies, in collaboration with the EU Commission, worked out the ESPRIT program (the European Strategic Programme for Research and Development in Information Technology) (SANDHOLZ 1992).

ESPRIT came into being to support development in fundamentally important fields such as microelectronics, software technology, information-processing, office information systems and computer-controlled manufacturing processes. Thus ESPRIT was the EU's first program supporting cooperation in R&D, its chief purpose being to eliminate the separation of R&D efforts within the Union. The program was launched in 1982, and from 1984 it was included among the Union's R&D framework programs.

ESPRIT became the model for all subsequent programs of support for high technology. It encouraged cooperation among the various institutions on the basis of the following characteristics:

– the participants must come from more than one member country;

– at most, half of the research costs would be borne by the EU budget;

– the project aims must be clearly defined, and the time allowed for implementing them was limited;

– this support was by way of being supplementary to national efforts.

By the mid-1980s a definite conviction had grown in the EU that the competitiveness of the European economy could be significantly improved by expanding R&D cooperation at Union level and making it more effective.

In 1985 virtually every country in Western Europe shared in the launch of the so-called EUREKA (European Research Coordination Agency) program. EUREKA was the broader European 'answer' to the US 'Star Wars' program (the Strategic Defense Initiative, or SDI, 1981), and its main aim was to promote improvement of the competitiveness of the European economy by organizing market-oriented development projects.

It was in this period that it was decided that the EU must formulate *a comprehensive strategy aimed at development of the new technologies, in the form of R&D framework programs*. In the Single European Document it was stated for the first time that the main aim of R&D policy at European level was to strengthen the scientific and technological basis of European industry, to increase its international competitiveness, and to promote economic and social development.

The present Article 163 of the basic agreement states that it is the Union's task to encourage high-level research and technical development activities on the part of companies, research centres and universities, and to support the cooperation developing among them. The aim of support is to enable companies to exploit to the full the advantages offered by the internal market, and this exploitation must be assisted by opening the member countries' procurement markets, by establishing common standards, and by removing the legal and fiscal obstacles to cooperation.

In order to implement the specified aims, the EU, supplementing the member countries' activities, carries out the following:

– *implementation of research, technical development and demonstration programs;* cooperation with companies, research centres and universities, and promotion of cooperation among them;
– *fostering cooperation* in the field of Community R&D *with third countries* and international organizations;
– *dissemination of the results of* Community *research and development;*
– assisting *the mobility and training of researchers*.

To harmonize R&D activities, *framework programs covering several years* were initiated; the first of these actually preceded the approval of the Single European Document, and applied to the four years from 1984 to

1987. Since 1987 5-year framework programs have been prepared, overlapping in time with a view to the more advantageous functioning of the projects currently running. Program 6 refers to the period between 2002 and 2006.

Expenditure on the R&D framework programs has gradually increased over time. Support grew from ECU 3.75 bn for 1984–1987, to ECU 5.4 bn for 1987–1991, to ECU 5.7 bn for 1990–1994, to ECU 13.2 bn for 1994–1998 and to €14.9 bn for 1998–2002. For the period 2002–2006 €17.5 bn has been allocated, which represents 4% of the EU budget and 6% of the research carried out in the Union (European Commission DG for Research 2002).

Support is provided within the framework of various programs, including the following:

– ESPRIT in the electronics and IT industry;

– RACE (Research in Advanced Communications technology for Europe) in the telecommunications sector;

– BRITE (Basic Research in Industrial Technologies for Europe) in the field of development of manufacturing technologies;

– BAP (the Biotechnology Action Programme) in the field of biotechnology research;

– EURAM (European Research in Advanced Materials) in the area of production of new materials.

In addition to the framework programs as forms of indirect support for research, it is important to mention the direct role undertaken by the EU. Under the terms of Article 171, the EU can set up joint companies and any other kind of structure necessary for implementation of shared research and development programs. Thus *the EU can take part in the promotion of R&D activity not only indirectly but by itself establishing research institutes.* These research institutes *operate within the framework of the Joint Research Centre (JRC).* The JRC, as the Union's independent chief directorate, operates as the Union's scientific, technological and reference centre. The JRC's biggest institutes are to be found in Ispra in Italy, but specialized institutes also operate in Geel (Belgium), Petten (Holland), Karlsruhe (Germany) and Seville (Spain).

3.3. THE NEW R&D FRAMEWORK PROGRAM AND THE EUROPEAN RESEARCH AREA

R&D framework program 6 for the period 2002–2006 has as its main aim support for the development of the *European Research Area (ERA).* The plan for the establishment of the ERA is based on the Commission report published in January 2000 (Commission, 18 January 2000). The purpose of the ERA is closer coordination of European research and innovation policies, consistent introduction of regional, national and European research programs, efficient use of research capacity, support for greater mobility of European researchers, and more successful exploitation of the links between science and society. Through the ERA an open research area should develop, characterized by free movement of researchers and better use of scientific results. One new aspect is the fact that the framework program also supports social science research; its priorities include the knowledge-based society, and governance and the citizen.

At the March 2000 session of the Council of Europe in Lisbon, the Union's leaders declared R&D and innovation policy to be a question of strategic importance for the future of the EU. They announced that research activities carried on at national and Union levels must be better integrated and coordinated, to make them as efficient and innovative as possible, and to ensure that Europe offered attractive prospects for its best intellects. The heads of state and government considered the establishment of the ERA to be crucially important for increasing Europe's competitiveness (European Commission, 2001). At the Lisbon summit they formulated the intention that *within the next decade (by 2010) the EU should become the world's most competitive and dynamic knowledge-based economy,* capable of sustainable economic growth while creating more and better jobs and achieving greater social cohesion.

The current framework program introduced new methods: one of these is support for the development of *networks of excellence,* which encourage long-lasting integration of the research capacity of the network partners; another is support for *integrated projects,* involving research projects of a suitable size with clearly defined scientific and technological aims. In the framework of the integrated projects, in contrast to the networks of excellence, support is given for the achievement of precisely defined results that lead to the introduction of new products, processes or services in the short- or medium-term.

4. COMMUNITY ENERGY POLICY

Because of the special economic and political importance of energy supply, in the industrially developed countries the energy sector was one of the first areas of early state intervention. The organization of energy production and supply involves many tasks that affect the whole of society. Generally an electricity grid or gas pipeline system can rationally be constructed only on a nationwide scale, not to mention the importance of linkage with international networks. General social problems have arisen for the state with regard to energy management and environment protection, which in the course of development have increasingly become global problems. In addition, individual countries have always tried to exercise control over foreign trade in energy products.

Historically, the energy policies to be developed have always been subordinated to *three* basic priorities:

– *provision of cheap energy,* as far as possible, in suitable quantities in terms both of production and of consumption. Relatively cheap energy is a condition of the general development of the economy, rapid and balanced economic growth, public supply and an acceptable standard of living. Cheap energy is of decisive importance from the point of view of competitiveness with other countries;

– the importance of stability of sources and particularly *security of supply*. This permits the smooth operation and development of the economy, consumer supply and the possibility of free choice, and also safeguards military and security interests;

– *harmonization of energy policy and environment considerations.* Energy provision is one of the most environment-polluting sectors of the economy; use of the various energy sources involves different kinds of environmental risks. Among the hydrocarbons coal is regarded as the most polluting; at the same time hydroelectric and especially nuclear power plants – though directly 'cleaner' – are associated with greater risks of environmental damage.

4.1. THE ENERGY SITUATION OF THE MEMBER COUNTRIES

From the 1950s, parallel with rapid economic growth, energy consumption also grew rapidly in the developed countries. In the period before 1973 gross energy consumption in the EC countries too outstripped the general rate of economic growth. The member countries reached a level of energy consumption similar to that of the developed countries. Meanwhile significant changes in the structure of energy consumption were taking place. In line with world trends, in respect of use as the primary fuels, in the energy balance coal gave place to hydrocarbons. In 1950 in the Union's fuel balance coal still accounted for 2/3 of the total, while oil represented barely 10%. By the beginning of the 1970s the proportion of oil had risen to over 60%, and natural gas accounted for almost 12%. The proportion of coal had fallen to 23%.

These structural changes were accompanied by greatly increased dependence on energy import. Coal had been largely an internal source of energy, though production was unevenly distributed. Three-quarters of coal production took place in West Germany, though France and Belgium also mined significant amounts of coal. At the same time, import from non-members was not a disadvantage; indeed, the problem was that through cheap import some countries gained comparative advantages.

With the dominance of oil and natural gas the situation changed. The EC did not possess major sources of oil, and only Holland had large reserves of natural gas (58% of the output of the Six in 1972). Thus the EU was obliged to import large quantities of hydrocarbons. In 1960 in the Six domestic production provided 70% of primary energy. By 1973 this proportion had fallen to 37% (later, in the Nine also it was less than 40%).

Thus even from the mid-1960s oil was by far the most important source of energy in the EC member countries: dependence on oil reached its highest level in 1973, when it covered 67% of energy consumption. Because of this heavy dependence on import, the oil price explosion and the energy crisis caused severe shocks and enforced a gradual reduction of dependence on oil. As a result of this process, by the end of the 1980s the role of oil had shrunk to 45%. At the same time, more than 70% of the oil used in the Union still has to be imported. Thus the EU's fuel balance has changed considerably in the last few decades. At the turn of the millennium, in the Union's energy consumption structure oil accounted for 41%, gas 22%, solid heating materials 16%, nuclear power 15% and renewable energy sources 6%.

Table 1. The EU fuel balance
(in oil equivalent, as %)

Year	Types of energy				
	Oil	Natural gas	Coal	Nuclear	Renewable energy
1950	14	–	83	3*	–
1960	31	2	63	4*	
1973	61	12	23	4	–
1985	46	18	23	12	1
1992	44	19	22	13	2
2000	41	22	16	15	6

* Electricity.

Source: European Commission DG Energy and Transport: EU energy and transport in figures. Pocket book. Brussels, 2001.

The geographical endowments of the EU severely restrict the Union members' room for manoeuvre in the energy sector: *the EU is at present obliged to import half of its energy requirements and according to estimates this proportion will rise to 70% by 2030.* EU import dependence today is 72% in the case of oil, 45% in the case of gas, and 47% in the case of solid heating fuels (coal, lignite). Within 20–30 years import dependence could be 90% for oil, 70% for gas and 100% for coal (European Commission, 2002a).

Even if the EU were capable of reducing energy intensity, it appears that the annual 1–2% increase in energy consumption is unavoidable. *Households and the service sector are chiefly responsible for increasing energy consumption, in the form of electricity and also for transport and heating. The energy requirements of industry have stabilized, but the transportation sector has undeniably become the main determinant of demand for energy.* The transport sector is also the main consumer of oil, and is 98% dependent on oil. At present 2/3 of oil consumption is devoted to satisfying the needs of the transport sector.

The EU is a key player in the world energy market: it accounts for 14–15% of world energy consumption, and is the biggest importer of oil and gas. The Union's main sources of oil are the Middle East and the OPEC countries: half of its import comes from 8 OPEC countries. To reduce the high degree of concentration it is considered advisable to strengthen relations with Russia and the countries in the area of the Caspian Sea. In the case of natural gas import, Russia and the CIS countries account for 40%, Norway about 30%, and Algeria 25%: so there is a high degree of dependence on individual suppliers.

For the EU, therefore, unexploited possibilities exist only in the area of renewable energy sources. North Sea *oil reserves are also limited;* according to calculations they are sufficient for only another 25 years, and in addition the extraction costs are already significantly higher (2 to 7 times higher, depending on the location) than costs in the Middle East. In the case of natural gas the situation is similar. From the mid-1970s the Union's supply of natural gas developed favourably: on the basis of the Dutch and North Sea gas fields the EU was at first 80% self-sufficient, but owing to the limited nature of these sources and increasing consumption its self-sufficiency has gradually been eroded.

Costs are high in coal-mining too; there would be stocks, but extraction is unprofitable because costs are 3–4 times the level of world market prices. In addition, coal pollutes more and has lower calorific value than hydrocarbons; and also it is more difficult to transport and store. Its main advantage is its low and relatively stable world market price. Only in Great Britain is there any realistic chance of maintaining competitive coal-mining.

Nuclear energy contributes positively to the security of EU energy supply. Thanks to its negligible emission of carbon dioxide it is a beneficial energy source from the point of view of climate change as well. It is used exclusively to produce electricity, and at present 1/3 of the Union's electricity needs are supplied from this source. Despite this, *the future of the nuclear energy sector is uncertain*. In some member countries decisions to gradually close down nuclear reactors have already been taken, and they are being replaced by traditional power stations, partly based on renewable energy sources. No member country except Finland is planning to build new nuclear power plants.

The so-called *alternative energy sources* (solar, wind, water, geothermal energy, bioenergy, etc.) have not gained a significant share of EU energy production. In the 1990s the proportion of these in the energy balance remained below 3%, and since 2000 is still not more than 5–8%. The EU aims to reach 12% in this area by 2010.

4.2. THE MAIN DIRECTIONS OF COMMUNITY ENERGY POLICY

The need to deal with questions relating to the energy sector first arose within the framework of the ECSC, in the field of coal mining and trade, then in the case of EURATOM in the area of nuclear energy research.

When the EEC was formed, no decision was taken on the development of a common energy policy; it was the oil price explosion that drew attention to the need to establish cooperation in energy policy within the framework of the Union. On the basis of authorization contained in primary legislation, as has been the case with many other sectoral policies, we cannot speak of a common energy policy even now. Despite this, the Union's energy policy did develop in secondary legislation, the basis of which is the series of authorizations relating to the internal market and the regulation of competition.

Security of supply gained in importance in the course of the first decade and a half of the integration process, with rapid economic growth and the changeover to an oil-based economy. For the majority of countries oil was an imported resource, and import dependence led to economic and security vulnerability. *The oil price explosion and energy crisis of the 1970s made security of supply a critical energy policy issue.* After 1973 the EC countries were in a difficult situation, as a result of which more decisive steps were taken towards formulating a common energy policy. Because of their high degree of import dependence, the member countries' balance of trade and inflationary processes in particular were unfavourably affected by the oil price explosion and the energy crisis. In these circumstances the member countries' system of energy policy aims and instruments, which was developing within the framework of international and bilateral cooperation, was extended, and national governments undertook more active and decisive intervention in the energy sphere.

As a result of the first oil crisis national energy programs to reduce oil-dependence were drawn up. On the other hand, multilateral cooperation came into being under the aegis of the OECD: in 1974 the *International Energy Agency (IEA)* was set up. Within the framework of the IEA an agreement was concluded on the maintenance of strategic reserves to ensure security of supply, and on the handling of supply. At EC level, too, the need to develop common strategies was becoming clear: the Community energy policy now taking shape manifested itself mainly in the form of recommendations made to the member states. The Community-level energy policy strategies formulated (for example, the 'New energy policy strategy' in 1974, and the 'Energy program of the European Communities' in 1979) played an increasingly important role in the handling of energy questions. From the 1970s, in response to the new situation the role of the various international institutions (the IEA, the World Bank, summit meetings of the industrially developed countries) expanded, and on occasions these became forums for collective international action.

The EC's first important document dealing comprehensively with energy policy issues was the *'New energy policy strategy'* approved in December 1974, in which the Commission *recommended* to the member countries *that they increase production and improve exploitation of domestic resources*. The program recommended a significant increase in investment in the nuclear energy sector. Under the terms of the recommendation, nuclear capacity was to be increased to 160 gigawatts by 1985, so that the proportion of nuclear power in electricity generation would rise from 7% to 45%. However, it soon became clear that the nuclear power station programs could not be implemented, and construction came up against significant economic and political obstacles. The programs were reviewed in 1979, and the prescriptions were reduced to 127 GW by 1990.

By the 1980s among the member countries only France was pursuing an active nuclear power plant program, while Holland and Italy had stopped launching new programs. Implementation in Great Britain and West Germany of the plans worked out in the early 1970s was also abandoned. In spite of rising oil prices, nuclear power did not become cheaper; on the contrary, the investment costs considerably increased. Later, as oil prices fell, this was even more the case. Mainly because of environmental objections (especially after Chernobyl), *significant political and social opposition to the nuclear programs developed.* Implementation of the plans *to stabilize coal production* (and even increase it) did not take place either. Coal output declined slightly faster than consumption, so net import into the EC increased. 80% of the coal extracted was traditionally used in the producing countries, thus mutual supply among the member countries was always minimal. In any case, the importing countries, particularly France and Italy, tried to obtain most of their import from cheaper external sources. North Sea *oil production* began in 1976. By the beginning of the 1980s annual British oil production was more than 120 million tons, making the country a net exporter of oil. At the same time, North Sea oil was of only limited importance to the EC, since it was capable of covering only about 20% of total consumption. In addition, extraction of North Sea oil was a costly undertaking.

In energy policy priority was given to *reducing consumption and improving energy-saving*. In its various energy policy programs the EC mainly limited itself to formulating collective recommendations. In accordance with the decision reached at the June 1980 summit in Venice, as a result of energy-saving a ratio of 1:0.6 was to be attained in the rates of economic growth and annual energy consumption. This was in fact achieved. Between 1973 and 1985, while GDP grew at an annual rate of 2.3%, the annual increase in energy consumption was less than 1% (1:0.4). In the period between 1986 and 1990 this tendency was somewhat modified by lower oil prices, and the annual rate of increase in energy consumption rose to 1.9%. With annual GDP growth of 3.1%, however, this was still close to the 1:0.6 ratio.

In May 1992 the Commission recommended the introduction of a Community-level energy tax to combat global warming. According to the plan, from 1993 in oil parity terms a tax of 3 dollars a barrel would have been imposed, rising it gradually to 10 dollars by 2000. This would have increased the price of petrol by 6%, and that of diesel oil by 11%, whereby it was hoped to hold CO_2 emissions down at the 1990 level. Since they wanted to avoid the negative effects on competitiveness, introduction of the tax was made dependent on whether the US and Japan took similar action. These partners rejected the recommendation, which was also severely criticized by the oil-exporting countries.

Energy policy has always laid special emphasis on *trade in energy products*. From the end of the 1970s the EC made great efforts to *freeze or reduce its import of oil*. Up to the mid-1980s these aims were fulfilled. Compared with 1973, by 1983 the member countries' oil import had been reduced by 47%. At the same time, their over-fulfilment of import reduction was largely due to moderate economic growth and the introduction of internal resources (North Sea oil), production of which accelerated from the second half of the 1970s onwards, reaching the level of about 150 million tons annually by the 1980s, which covered roughly a quarter of consumption. After 1983, however, oil import began to increase again.

One important direction of improvement of security of supply was *diversification of import sources*. Earlier, the Union's energy import (especially of oil) was characterized by concentration on a few sources of supply. In 1973, 97% of petroleum import to Western Europe came from the Middle East and Africa, and within this about three-quarters of deliveries came from just five Arab countries (Libya, Saudi Arabia, Iraq, Kuwait and Algeria). Diversification of import sources accelerated particularly after the events in Iran in 1979. Attempts were made to ensure that no single supplier country had more than a 10% share of import.

An important means of increasing the security of supply was the agreed creation of *emergency reserves*. Attempts at such agreements among the consumer countries were made in a number of institutions and forums. As early as December 1968 the Council of Ministers issued a directive that the member countries should create emergency reserves of crude oil and oil products sufficient for at least 65 days' consumption. This directive was modified in December 1972, and from then the minimum emergency reserves had to be raised to the equivalent of 90 days' consumption. Later this directive was strengthened several times, and the IEA also committed itself to creating 90 days' emergency oil stocks. Subsequent recommendations urged the introduction of 120-day emergency oil reserves.

The chief tasks of the EU's present energy policy were most comprehensively formulated in the Green Paper (For a European Union Energy Policy) approved in 1995, and in the White Paper that followed this (An Energy Policy for the European Union), in these terms (Commission, 26. 06. 2002):

– energy supply must be secure and efficient;
– in price-setting the costs of environment protection must be taken into account;
– the member countries must work together;
– the necessary standardization must be carried out jointly;
– uniform taxes on the products affected must be introduced;
– the internal market should be free, but easily supervised;
– investment must be encouraged, and network development should increasingly be financed from private resources.

The events of the past three decades and the development of the main directions of Community energy policy demonstrate that in the framework of energy policy strategies, *an acceptable compromise in energy supply between cheapness, security and environment protection has been sought*. After the price explosions – apart from brief shocks – it became clear that considerations of economy and competitiveness were still not being subordinated to security considerations, and different means of implementing the policy of security of supply were sought. In several countries exaggerated security interests and pressure from certain lobbies (e.g. coal-mining) led to decisions to develop unprofitable domestic resources, but generally these have not been implemented. The undeveloped nature of EU energy policy strategy is often criticized, but undoubtedly it has so far played a positive role, from the point of view of security of supply, rational development of the energy structure, and also environment protection, in the development of the member countries' energy consumption.

REFERENCES

BARNES, I. and P. M. BARNES (1995) *The Enlarged European Union.* Longman, London.

Communication from the Commission. Towards a European Research Area. Brussels, 18 January 2000.

European Commission (1992) *Agriculture in Europe: Development, Constraints and Perspectives.* Brussels.

European Commission (1993) *Growth, Competitiveness, Employment – the Challenges and the Ways Forward into the 21st Century.* COM (93) 700 final.

European Commission (1999) *The state of the competitiveness of the steel industry in the EU.* COM (99) 453.

European Commission (2001) *Research and technological development activities of the European Union.* 2001 Annual Report, 12. 12. 2001, COM (2001) 756 final. Brussels.

European Commission (2002a) *Energy: let us overcome our dependence.* Office for Official Publications of the European Communities. Luxembourg.

European Commission (2002b) *Mid-Term Review of the Common Agricultural Policy.* COM (2002) 394 final, 10. 07. 2002. Brussels.

European Commission DG for Research (2002) *New Framework Program Launched.* A Fact Sheet. Brussels.

European Commission Enterprise DG (2001) *Textile and clothing industry in the EU: A survey.* Enterprise Paper No. 2, 2001. Brussels.

POSNER, M. V. (1992) *International Trade and Technical Change.* Oxford Economic Papers, Oxford.

SANDHOLTZ, W. (1992) ESPRIT and the politics of international collective action. *Journal of Common Market Studies,* March 1992.

V.

THE EU'S REGIONAL POLICY

By

ÁKOS KENGYEL

One of the major endeavours as well as one of the consequences of the European integration process is to reduce the differences in development between individual countries and regions and to support the less developed areas in catching up with the others. This process requires joint action to strengthen the predominance of free market forces, as well as the establishment of a support system for the regional policy managed at EU level. *If the EU did not undertake as one of its main goals the reduction of differences in income levels and in standards of living, this would jeopardize the future of the integration as a whole,* since, in the long run, people living in various regions of the union would find it unacceptable to live in significantly different conditions.

Achieving a position of complete levelling out cannot, of course, be a realistic goal, partly because of the dissimilar historical and geographical circumstances, social expectations and economic resources. Completely equalizing the differences in the standard of living among the individual regions is not only impossible but would not be desirable either, as it would eliminate the basic motivating forces that influence economic activity. On the other hand, however, it is necessary to continuously stimulate regional development and protect the standards of living attained and accepted.

"Cohesion" is a strategic goal within the EU, serving to reduce social and regional differences. The EU's social policy and regional policy are the two areas where measures are taken to facilitate cohesion. The latter focuses on increasing the competitiveness of the less developed regions, while the former considers it as its main function to strengthen and harmonize employees' rights.

The most important factors that support cohesion are the improvement of the conditions of employment and the strengthening of the economic potential of the more backward regions. The crucial element in accelerating the process of catching up in these regions is to improve the conditions of economic development, since these regions are in a disadvantageous position in every respect. It should be noted that *the measures promoting cohesion are not meant to replace the EU policies driven by free market principles, but are applied parallel and in harmony with them:* the cohesion measures are a concession to interventionism, but within the general framework of the market.

1. THE NECESSITY OF AN ACTIVE REGIONAL POLICY

Theories of regional economics have produced serious arguments in support of the idea of concentrating advanced economic activities in different regions. These include taking advantage of economies of scale, exploiting the so-called agglomeration benefits, the division of labour, favourable labour market characteristics, the "external profitability" arising from the accumulation of knowledge and the existence of the leading role in innovation. The spread of activities in manufacturing industry can also be supported with a number of arguments: the geographical rearrangement of the distribution of the labour force and the development of transport and telecommunications networks in the peripheral regions, preventing saturation and congestion in the central regions.

There are numerous arguments to back an active regional policy as opposed to the view that spontaneous market adaptation has sufficient impact:

– the major consideration is *the necessity to handle the structural weaknesses* resulting from the inflexibilities of the market, the conditions of access to the market and the structure of production;

– the problem of *utilizing the factors of production:* the reallocation of resources may be slower than would be socially acceptable. Though the classical theory of international trade postulates the free flow of factors of production, which ensures complete utilization, even ADAM SMITH remarked that the factor hardest to mobilize is Man. In times of recession the employment situation is difficult everywhere, and as a result the potential advantages of areas with abundant manpower disappear. The low mobility of labour prevents the levelling out of inequalities within an economic union;

– *the need to handle the distortions arising from the allocation of resources.* Capital has a tendency to move toward the more developed regions: here private investors can expect a faster return and can save the major part of the costs of infrastructure development. This tendency of the developed to become even more developed, while the less developed, in the optimal case, remains at the level already achieved, ensures significant gains for private investors on the one hand, and involves social costs on the other. From the above it follows that if private investors' decisions are not influenced by government policies, then considerable social costs may be incurred;

– in the supported region *state subsidies,* and consequently public expenditure, *can be reduced* in the long-term. The incentives provided by the state and the support of economic activity can accelerate the development of the given region, unemployment may be reduced, social costs may decrease and tax revenues may increase;

– though regional policy targets a particular region, *the positive influence of the benefits can be felt not only in the targeted region* but in other regions as well. Integration will deepen and the factors of production will be better utilized;

– besides the economic arguments underlining improvement of efficiency, certain political aspects are no less important. *Solidarity* and tolerance are crucial in every social community. In the course of creating the union, regional inequalities must also be reduced, which requires *reduction of the growing and intolerable differences* in welfare between regions at different levels of development.

The most important argument supporting the need for an EU-level regional policy is that to spread the welfare gains resulting from economic integration requires active tools, since, with market forces working freely, the benefits arising from integration cannot necessarily be felt in every region, but on the contrary, development may become even more concentrated in the central regions of the EU.

Among the factors determining regional inequalities, differences in infrastructure and human resources largely contribute to the competitiveness of individual regions. The historically low level of infrastructural investment has undoubtedly hindered the improvement of productivity and employment levels in the least developed member states of the EU.

The infrastructural background, the quality of human resources, the levels attained in research and development activities, and, as a consequence of all the above, the region's ability to attract working capital, are all factors determining competitiveness, which clearly reflect the development level and prospects of a region. The EU's regional policy has to improve these conditions that influence competitiveness in such a way that the given region becomes more attractive to investors, the spirit of enterprise is stimulated, and, as a result, economic growth takes off.

The system of objectives in regional development depends on the country's economic policy, the general approach to regional policy, and the nature of the existing regional processes. *One of the characteristic properties of this system of objectives is that it comprises long-term ideas, since the processes of regional development are very slow to alter.* One of these long-term goals can be, for example, the reduction of regional inequalities of development, more efficient utilization of national resources, the lowering of unemployment rates or easing of demographic pressure on over-populated city centres. The individual elements of this system of objectives may certainly emerge differently in terms of time and place and in different combinations, depending on the characteristics of the different types of regions.

To implement the tasks of regional development, to properly adjust to regional conditions and to select the tools for development it is necessary to establish a vertically and horizontally structured system of institutions. As a consequence of ever-increasing state intervention and the growing number and complexity of the tasks, *the system of institutions of regional development has become rather diverse in the last half-century. In all the European countries the development of regions and settlements has become the duty of one sub-national level or another.*

Within the European Union the economic and cultural role of the regions is growing, and as a result, with their increasing economic weight, they are able to exert an ever-growing influence on the social and political conditions of their own countries. The general tendency that can be observed is that regional policy is most successful where the regional level, beyond having the right to determine its own developmental priorities (the principle of subsidiarity), also possesses significant decentralized functions in public administration. Thus it is able to make the local machinery of public administration serve more effectively and inexpensively the development projects adapted to the endogenous conditions and needs.

2. REGIONAL DEVELOPMENT DIFFERENCES IN THE EU ECONOMY

The economic inequalities within the union are sufficiently demonstrated by the distribution of GDP in purchasing power standard terms. Beyond measuring a country's economic output, GDP can also be used to compare incomes. The most suitable method is comparison of GDP in terms of the purchasing power parities, so we have used this in the comparisons that follow. This index provides a picture of the changes in the relative position of the individual countries and of the relative development of the member-states' economic performance compared with the EU15 average.

Table 1. GDP per capita in purchasing power standard terms, 1960–2002 (percent – EU15 =100)

Country	1960	1965	1970	1975	1980	1985	1990	1995	2000	2002
B	99	100	102	107	109	106	105	112	111	112
DK	116	118	113	108	106	113	104	111	120	119
D	123	120	117	113	117	118	116	110	104	104
E	57	67	71	78	71	70	74	78	81	82
F	106	108	111	112	112	111	110	104	99	97
GR	43	50	57	63	64	62	58	66	69	71
IRL	61	59	60	63	64	65	72	93	119	127
I	88	89	96	95	102	103	103	103	102	102
L	169	146	152	137	128	132	144	171	194	201
NL	113	109	110	110	106	103	101	109	117	117
A	95	93	96	102	106	106	106	110	110	109
P	40	44	50	53	55	53	59	71	74	74
FIN	88	89	92	97	97	101	102	97	103	104
S	123	126	122	121	112	114	107	102	102	102
UK	123	114	104	101	97	100	100	96	104	104
EU15	100	100	100	100	100	100	100	100	100	100

Source: European Commission: European Economy No 65, 1998.; EUROSTAT: GDP per capita in Purchasing Power Standard (PPS), General Statistics, 15/10/2001.; European Commission: European Economy No 72, 2001.

The data show that the development level of the current member countries compared with the EU average ranges between 71% in Greece and 201% in Luxembourg. On the basis of the two extreme values, it can be determined that the existing developmental difference between the EU member countries is 2.8-fold. If we disregard Luxembourg, considering its small size, the three countries with the highest GDP that follow are Ireland, Denmark and Holland. Their GDP figures range between 117 and 127. From these data it can be established that *the difference in development between the most and the least developed countries of the union is 1.7-fold.*

On regional level the differences are much more significant: compared with Ipeiros in Greece, with a figure of 42% of the EU average and thus the lowest level of development, Inner London has a figure of 243%. Consequently, the developmental difference between the two is sixfold. *The difference between the 10% of the regions with the highest per capita GDP and the 10% with the lowest per capita GDP is 2.6-fold.* The GDP per capita figure in the highest 10% is on average 60% more than the EU average, while the lowest 10% are 40% below that level. Looking at the developmental difference between the highest and the lowest 25%, we are faced with 137% of the EU average compared with 68% of the EU average: the difference is twofold. At the end of the 1990s, of the 208 NUTS2 regions 47 did not reach the developmental level of 75% of the EU average, and in these regions 19% of the EU's population lived (European Commission 2001).

The regional development differences are also significant within the individual member countries: in most member countries the difference between the most and the least developed region is more than twofold. For example, in Belgium Brussels shows a value of 169% of the EU average, while Hainaut shows 79%, in Spain Madrid shows 110% while Extremadura shows 50%, in Italy the figure for Lombardy is 135% while for Calabria it is 61%, and in Austria Vienna shows 163%, while Burgenland has a figure of 69%. There are some member states where the developmental difference is still higher: in the case of Germany and Britain it is threefold.

An important development in EU integration is that over the past few decades a process of *levelling out among the less developed member countries has been taking place,* as can be seen in the three countries currently the least developed, and in Ireland, though at a pace varying from country to country. Several factors have played a part in the approximation of development levels, which, combined, have resulted in economic growth faster than the EU average. *This rapid growth had several causes: an investment boom, increasing openness to the world economy and the structural adaptation of the national economies.* The performance of the four countries has at times shown similarities, but by the late 1990s their courses of development showed remarkable differences, and significant disparities have emerged between them in their rate of catching up.

In 1960 the four countries had a low level of GDP per capita in purchasing power parities: Portugal had 40%, Greece 43%, Spain 57% and Ireland 61% to the average of the EU. By 2002 Portugal had achieved 74%, Greece 71%, Spain 82% and Ireland 127%. It can be seen that *in the four decades there has been considerable approximation between the performance of the peripheral member countries and the union's average development level.* Regional policy support is, of course, only part of the explanation for this process, and several other factors have also contributed to this successful catching up. At the same time, as a result of the strengthening of the regional policy, in the 1990s subsidies from the EU played a decisive role in the convergence of economic performance.

In the process of convergence between the development levels various periods can be distinguished. The period of the fastest catching up in the countries of the southern periphery preceded their EU membership, so in this period subsidies from the EU played no role. *For Greece and Portugal the most dynamic period in terms of the convergence of development levels was the period up to 1973:* Greece approached the level of 60% and Portugal achieved more than 50% of the EU average. Convergence was interrupted by the oil price explosion and the subsequent world economic crisis.

During the 1980s the two countries' paths of development diverged. While Greece was only able to stabilize its position, since the mid-1980s Portugal has seen a fast convergence period and its GDP per capita grew from 53% in 1985 to 74% of the EU15 average in 2000. Greece's position worsened during the 1980s: from 64% in 1980 it fell back to 58% of the EU15 average in 1990. Only in the 1990s did the country's performance begin to slowly catch up with the Union average, which has resulted in roughly a 10% improvement in its position in nearly a decade: by the year 2000 its GDP per capita increased to 69% of the EU average.

Spain also achieved rapid convergence in the period up to the mid-1970s; from a basis of a much higher GDP per capita *they improved their position by 20%* and achieved nearly 80% of the EU average by 1975. Then until the mid-1980s there was a decline of about 10% and GDP per capita fell back to 70% of the EU average. Since 1985, similarly to Portugal, Spain has also shown convergence in economic development, and by the second half of the 1990s the country had again reached a position around 80%, already attained two decades before.

The changes in Ireland's position are unique from the aspect of economic convergence. Until the mid-1980s its GDP per capita remained around 60–65% of the EU average. From the second half of the decade an extremely fast catching up process started, and the country's relative development level compared with the EU15 average has grown from 65% in 1985 to 119% within a decade and a half.

3. COMPONENTS OF THE EU'S REGIONAL POLICY

The original version of the Treaty of Rome did not yet mention the regional policy of the Community, though on the basis of the treaty it was considered the task of the Community to facilitate the harmonious development of economic activities, steady and balanced growth, and improvement of the standard of living within the EU (Article 2). The original version of the Treaty of Rome touched upon regional aspects only in a few articles: regarding the agricultural policy, and in the articles on transport and on state subsidies. The Treaty of Rome also had at its disposal financial resources that had a certain regional impact: these included the European Social Fund and the European Investment Bank.

As early as 1957 it did not seem necessary to establish a joint regional policy, on the assumption that the integration process and the general economic upswing would result in equalizing developmental differences. Anyway, each of the member countries had its own regional policy at the time, so the EU considered it its duty merely to ensure that the national policies did not contradict the aims and joint policies of the Community.

Only gradually did it become obvious that *economic integration could aggravate the situation of the originally backward and peripheral regions,* and that it was necessary to handle these problems at community level also. The *WERNER plan* of 1970 on the establishment of monetary union, the first round of enlargement and the severe economic crisis all focused the Union's attention on the importance of regional policy.

Thus at the Paris summit of the heads of state and heads of government in 1972, the decision on setting up the European Regional Development Fund (the ERDF) was taken, which made it possible for the Fund to start its operation in 1975. Its establishment represented the first acknowledgement of the need for a Community-level regional policy.

Two other funds were also set up under the Treaty of Rome and serve the EU's regional policy. One is the European Social Fund (ESF), set up in 1960; the other is the Guidance Section of the European Agricultural Guidance and Guarantee Fund (EAGGF). The main purpose of the European Social Fund is to promote employment, and to increase the geographical and professional mobility of working people. At first the Fund concentrated on the area of re-training, then from the mid-1970s the focus of attention shifted to dealing with unemployment, which had started to increase in the wake of the decline of traditional industries. Their primary concern was training the young and the long-term unemployed. The Guidance Section of the agrarian fund supports the modernisation of agriculture and the development of new production methods. The three so-called structural funds were supplemented in 1993 with the Financial Instrument for Fisheries Guidance (FIFG), which supports the restructuring of the fishing industry and related branches (Council Regulation, 31 July 1993).

Also in 1993 the Cohesion Fund created on the basis of the Maastricht Treaty began operating, with the aim of helping low-income member states to catch up more quickly (Council Regulations, 1 April 1993 and 16 May 1994).

Originally, the aim in establishing the Cohesion Fund had been to enable the less developed member countries to meet the criteria specified for participation in economic and monetary union.

The Cohesion Fund is not one of the structural funds, since it has its own regulations, and unlike the structural funds, it supports countries and not regions. It provides subsidies for investments relating to construction of the trans-European networks. Besides the structural funds and the Cohesion Fund, the activity of the European Investment Bank also serves the EU's regional policy.

It can well be observed how the area of the existing structural policies has broadened as the number of EU member states has grown and as integration has deepened, since both processes have resulted in an increase in regional problems, while the nature of these has also changed. In terms of the regional policy the decisive moment was the enactment of the Single European Act. As it was obvious that the single internal market might cause serious hardships to the weaker member states, the Treaty of Rome was supplemented with articles on economic and social cohesion. In this way, *regional policy was included among the joint policies; it aims to counterbalance the possible negative effects of the internal market and to increase economic and social cohesion.*

In the interest of the efficiency of regional policy it became important to improve coordination of the activities of the different funds, and to make the handling of the problems in different regions more program-oriented, instead of supporting individual independent projects. As a result of the Commission's comprehensive reform proposal, in June and December of 1988 the Council adopted the legal regulations relating to the operation of the structural funds, which took effect in 1989. The reform served as a basis for the subsidizing programs for the period 1989–1993. Acting on the experience gathered in these years, in July 1993 the Council approved modifications for the period 1994–1999. These were the regulations they applied in deciding on the allocation of subsidies.

Another round of comprehensive changes was heralded by the document entitled Agenda 2000, published on July 16, 1997, in which the EU published its plans for the period 2000–2006 (European Commission: Agenda 2000, 1997). This document also included propositions for transforming regional policy. The decision on Agenda 2000 was taken by the European Council at its session held in Berlin, on March 24–25, 1999. This finalized the operational goals and the budget of regional policy for the period 2000–2006. The major project areas are the following.

1. Support for backward regions facing the most severe difficulties in terms of revenues, employment, the system of production and the infrastructure.

2. Support for regions facing structural difficulties because of economic and social restructuring. This includes regions undergoing changes in industry and services, declining rural regions, regions dependent on the fishing industry that are in crisis and urban regions facing hardships.

3. Support for the adaptation and modernisation of systems of education, training and employment.

Following the reform of 1988, subsidies are granted on the basis of *four common principles*:

– the first principle is *concentration,* i.e. in the most important areas the resources provided by the different funds must be used jointly; resources must not be dissipated;

– the second principle is the *program-oriented* approach, i.e. the planning of medium-term regional development programs, rather than independent projects;

– the third principle is *partnership,* i.e. responsibility for the preparation of the programs, the decisions and the implementation are divided between the EU Commission, national governments and local authorities;

– the fourth principle is *additionality (co-financing, contribution)*, i.e. subsidies granted by the EU can only be additional, complementary, they are not meant to replace national support. National governments, regional and local authorities and the private sector must also share in financing.

These four principles can also be supplemented by the principles of *subsidiarity and transparency, which refer to the operation of the Union as a whole.* Subsidiarity means that decisions must be made at the lowest possible level, where the most information is available, and where the most effective decision can be made. In the case of regional policy this must be accompanied by the decentralisation of resources and decision-making competences. Transparency means that the whole programming process must be verifiable, and, more specifically, it must be possible to scrutinize the utilization of the subsidies.

4. EXPENDITURE ON SUBSIDIES

The amount of expenditure on regional policy has had ever-increasing weight in the EU budget since the late 1980s. Between 1988 and 1992 the amounts spent on so-called structural operations increased – in terms of 1988 prices – from ECU 7.8 bn to ECU 13.5 bn, that is, they nearly doubled (European Commission: The Community Budget, 1989). Between 1989 and 1993, a total of ECU 63 bn – at 1989 prices – was spent on regional policy objectives; this amount was equivalent to ECU 71.36 bn at current prices. In the period between 1989 and 1993, of the five goals it was the first one, support for the most backward regions, which received nearly 65% of the structural funds' expenditure. Of all the funds, half of the expenditure on subsidies came from the European Regional Development Fund, while one third of the total expenditure came from the European Social Fund (Europäische Kommission: Die Durchführung der Strukturfondsreform in 1993).

In this period the four least developed countries received 34.18 bn ECUs in subsidies, at current prices, for infrastructure investments, for strengthening the bases of production (for the modernization of agriculture, industrial restructuring and other regional and local developments), for developing human resources, for developments relating to environmental protection and other technical assistance. This was further supplemented with 1.56 bn ECUs worth of subsidies.

In compliance with the decision of December 1992 of the Council of Europe in Edinburgh, the amount of subsidies paid out from the structural funds had to be increased between 1993 and 1999 from near 20 bn to over 27 bn ECUs, which meant an increase from 29% to 32% of the common budget. This was supplemented by the Cohesion Fund specifically intended to support the four countries with the lowest income levels. The Cohesion Fund was set up in 1993 with 1.5 bn ECUs, which increased from year to year so that by 1999 it provided €2.6 bn in subsidies. In the period between 1994 and 1999 the EU spent a total of about 143 bn ECUs, at 1994 prices, on subsidizing backward regions and regions facing structural difficulties.

Between 1994 and 1999, of the four least developed countries, Greece received 13.98 bn ECUs worth of subsidies, topped up with another 1 bn ECUs from the Community Initiatives, so altogether the country received a total of 15 bn ECUs in subsidies. Portugal also received 13.98 bn ECUs, to which Community Initiatives added another 1.4 bn ECUs, so the country was given a total of 15.4 bn ECUs. Spain received 32.7 bn ECUs including Community Initiatives, whereas Ireland was granted a total of 5.9 bn ECUs. *Over the period 1994–1999 the four countries received 69 bn ECUs' worth of subsidies including those from Community Initiatives, which meant the doubling of the support given between 1989 and 1993.*

The size of the support per capita also shows considerable growth. Between 1989 and 1993 the subsidies per capita granted under the first goal amounted to ECU 150 in Greece, ECU 253 in Ireland, ECU 171 in Portugal and ECU 91 in Spain. Between 1994 and 1999 the figure for Greece grew to ECU 255, for Ireland to ECU 262, for Portugal to ECU 235 and for Spain to ECU 188.

On the basis of the compromise reached at the Berlin summit, in the period 2000–2006 €213 bn can be spent on purposes of regional development in the current 15 member states: of this, €195 bn is provided from the structural funds, while €18 bn comes from the Cohesion Fund. For the new entrants, in theory €39.58 bn is available. *So in the period 2000–2006 the member countries of the enlarged EU will be able to use €252.59 bn for financing regional development programs.* By the end of the period the new members' share in the expenditure on regional development programs ought to be near 30%.

On the whole it can be stated that though over the last decade and a half expenditure on the structural funds has been gradually growing, even this cannot be considered significant help. Even through doubling the amounts available, *in the period of the completion of the internal market, i.e. between 1989 and 1993, the EU expended a mere 0.24% of its GDP (ECU 63 bn) on regional development.* This amount can be regarded as modest, especially since the CECCHINI report (CECCHINI 1988) calculated on a gain in prosperity of ECU 216 bn resulting from the single market. The subsidies, on average, amounted to 0.43% of the Union's GDP for 1994–1999, in accordance with the Edinburgh decision of the Council of Europe. For the period 2000–2006, the Berlin summit *determined the ratio between the structural funds and the union's GDP at 0.46%.* This means that the ratio of the amount to be spent on subsidies compared with the union's GDP will continue to be rather low. This reflects a continuing low degree of solidarity and self-sacrifice, although experience has shown that the greater proportion of the amounts from structural funds subsidies flows toward the developed regions in the form of purchases of finished products, machinery and investment goods. For this reason, increasing the level of subsidies would be beneficial for the developed regions also.

5. THE EFFECTS OF SUBSIDIES IN HELPING COUNTRIES CATCH UP

The EU expects the subsidies from the structural funds to have the effect of strengthening economic and social cohesion. Owing to this effect, the economic and social structure of the subsidized regions should be transformed. The subsidies, as factors in short-term development, have an impact on the position of the given region and launch endogenous and exogenous development that will result in the formation of long-term developmental factors. These factors will lead to a reduction in unemployment, a rise in income levels and an improvement in living conditions.

The primary goal of the subsidies spent on the development of human resources is to broaden the education and the skills of those supported, strengthening these skills and widening their applicability. This means that finding a job will become easier and the danger of being left out of work will be reduced. Subsidizing human resources will also influence enterprises: a special training program, for example, can be linked with the opening of a new plant. As a general, indirect effect, companies can also benefit from the advantages arising from improvement of the employability and the productivity of manpower. All these effects, combined, can result in improvement of the region's competitiveness and a decrease in unemployment.

Subsidizing enterprises may contribute to creating competitive advantages. Subsidies may also occur in the field of physical as well as of immaterial investment. Supporting an increase in production capacities contributes to cutting investment costs, which, together with the subsidies designed to increase productivity, leads to reducing production costs. This will enhance the company's cost-competitiveness.

Subsidies in the area of immaterial investment also increase the competitiveness of enterprises. The support given for developing marketing activities, for example, can directly be seen in the gaining of entry to new markets, and it can also be an indication of success if the given company is better able to stand up to increasing competition, thanks to subsidies spent on innovation. Indirect advantages for enterprises can also arise from the strengthened regional economic environment, which ensures better external conditions for companies owing to subsidies granted to research centres, innovation parks and conference centres.

The effect of subsidies provided for infrastructural development is shown indirectly, and affects the local population and enterprises alike. The effects are multiple. First, certain investments (e.g. the construction of a new port, a motorway or an energy network) *reduce production costs*; secondly, there are investments that *eliminate certain factors that hamper production* (e.g. the building of a water system enables farms to develop, an airport may contribute to boosting tourism, etc.); thirdly, infrastructural investments *improve the economic environment* (e.g. the establishment of a telecommunications network may help develop new contacts between local enterprises). Infrastructural investments also create more favourable conditions for already-established economic activities, while at the same time they increase the attractiveness of the region for new investors as well.

The macroeconomic effects of the subsidies have proved to be far-reaching. In the three least developed member countries and Ireland, the ratio of the subsidies from the structural funds compared with GDP reached a significant value in the period 1989–1999. The contribution of the subsidies from the structural funds and the Cohesion Fund to the annual investment rates of the given countries represented a major share over the past two periods. Approximately 15% of the investments in Greece and Portugal, close to 10% in Ireland and nearly 7% in Spain were completed in the support period that ended in 1999. For the current support period the share of investments is forecast at 12% for Greece and Portugal, over 5% for Spain and about 3% for Ireland.

Table 2. The share of subsidies from the structural funds and the Cohesion Fund in investments (as % of investments)

Country	1989–1993	1994–1999	2000–2006
Greece	11.8	14.6	12.37
Ireland	15.0	9.6	2.6
Spain	2.9	6.7	5.5
Portugal	12.4	14.2	11.4
EU4	5.5	8.9	6.9

Source: European Commission: Unity, solidarity, diversity for Europe, its people and its territory. Second Report on Economic and Social Cohesion. Luxembourg 2001.

According to the calculations of the EU Commission there is evidence of significant growth in GDP and a considerable reduction in unemployment compared with the period before subsidizing was commenced, owing to the regional policy subsidies. In the period 1989–1999 Greece reached a GDP level 9.9% higher than in the time before the subsidies; the corresponding figure for Portugal is 8.5%, for Ireland 3.7% and for Spain 3.1%. Unemployment in Greece decreased by 6.2%, in Portugal by 4%, in Spain by 1.6% and in Ireland by 0.4%, in consequence of the subsidies. For the period 2000–2006 the expected growth surplus is 7.3% for Greece, 7.8% for Portugal, 3.4% for Spain and 2.8% for Ireland. The subsidies are also expected to have the effect of lowering unemployment rates.

Table 3. Effects of Community subsidies compared with the situation without subsidies (compared with 1989 and 2000, as %)

	Greece		Portugal		Spain		Ireland	
Year	Increase in GDP	Decrease in unemployment	Increase in GDP	Decrease in unemployment	Increase in GDP	Decrease in unemployment	Increase in GDP	Decrease in unemployment
1989	4.1	3.2	5.8	3.6	0.8	0.5	2.2	1.4
1993	4.1	2.9	7.4	4.1	1.5	0.8	3.2	1.0
1999	9.9	6.2	8.5	4.0	3.1	1.6	3.7	0.4
2006	7.3	3.2	7.8	2.8	3.4	1.7	2.8	0.4

Source: European Commission: Unity, solidarity, diversity for Europe, its people and its territory. Second Report on Economic and Social Cohesion. Luxembourg 2001.

6. THE EU'S EASTERN ENLARGEMENT AND REGIONAL POLICY

From the point of view of the extension of regional policy subsidies to new members, the document entitled Agenda 2000 prepared by the Commission, and the session of the Council of Europe in Berlin that closed the debate on it, were of decisive importance. The EU's budget for 2000–2006 was approved at the Berlin summit of March 24–25, 1999. This meant that the minimum reforms necessary for enlargement had finally gone through in agricultural policy and regional policy, the two areas most affected by the financing of enlargement. It also became clear that *enlargement can be financed within the existing framework, i.e. it will not be necessary to raise the budget ceiling of 1.27% of the union's GDP in the future.*

Quite naturally, one of the most critical areas of enlargement for the EU, besides agricultural policy, was the extension of regional policy, since it has always been obvious that, *because of their low development levels, the future members will all be entitled to subsidies granted in accordance with the first goal.* Their considerable backwardness compared with the EU's average development, which is likely to remain a lasting problem in the long-term, even if dynamic economic growth is sustained, raises several questions in terms of regional policy and the enlargement process as a whole. *The problems are partly caused by the increasing burden on the joint budget, and partly by the endangering of the interests of the former beneficiaries, and the opposite interests of the net contributors.*

The two fundamental problems required strategic answers, partly because in 1999 the second period of the programs included in the Community Support Funds came to an end and for the period beginning from 2000 a new budget had to be drawn, in which the regional policy support for the following period had to be decided upon. This strategic decision was made at the Berlin summit in March 1999.

The support system intended for the prospective new members can be divided into two parts. One group of subsidies is represented by the pre-accession forms of aid, while the other group is made up of the subsidies that can be used only after the country has become an EU member. In line with the Berlin summit decisions, in the period left before their accession, the EU is to provide subsidies for the Central and East European countries from several sources. Until the end of 1999, candidates for membership can receive subsidies only through the PHARE program set up in

July 1989, but *from 2000 onwards two new pre-accession funds started their operation:* ISPA and SAPARD.

Both funds aim to support programs that make it possible for institutions to learn about the procedures customary in applying for EU subsidies, and to learn the appropriate methods. ISPA promotes investments in environment protection and infrastructure, while SAPARD is designed to help restructuring in agriculture and the development of rural areas. Every country will be entitled to apply for these subsidies until it has joined the EU. After their accession they will become entitled to subsidies from the structural funds and the Cohesion Fund.

The PHARE program has undergone continual modification since the decision about it was taken in Copenhagen, and supports preparing countries for accession has been given ever-increasing emphasis. Originally, PHARE was created *to support the transformation of the countries.* A strategic change was brought by the decisions of the Essen session of the Council of Europe, inasmuch as from that time on, PHARE was devoted to *preparation for accession* and it was also important that they applied a method of financing similar to the logic of the structural funds. Within the PHARE program a decision was made about increasing the ratio of subsidies for infrastructure investments: the 15% upper limit determined in Copenhagen was raised to 25%, i.e. a quarter of all subsidies was allowed to be used for such purposes. To promote cross-border cooperation, a decision was made about joint utilization of the resources of the PHARE program and some of the resources of the INTERREG II program, about supporting border crossings, the development of motorway and railway networks linking the countries, and about assisting environment protection programs.

The PHARE program has been further modified since the beginning of the accession talks. The number one priority became support for the individual countries in their preparation for accession in the areas determined in the documents constituting the Accession Partnership. In compliance with the above, the PHARE program is focused on two basic areas:

– one major task is to help public administration in the candidate countries to become able to adopt and apply the acquis communautaire (PHARE is helping national and regional institutions to acquaint themselves with the objectives and procedural techniques of the EU and also to become able to apply these methods);

– the other major task is to help individual branches of the economy and infrastructure development through mobilizing the necessary amount of investment.

The ISPA (Instrument for Structural Policies for Pre-Accession) has a range of activities to promote that is largely identical with the programs supported by the Cohesion Fund. On the one hand it supports programs related to environment protection, to make the country able to meet the requirements of the Community's legal standards. On the other hand it promotes the transport infrastructure to help link national networks with one another and with the trans-European networks. Subsidies received under the ISPA may only finance not more than 85% of the expenditure of the given program.

The other new program providing help in the pre-accession period is SAPARD (Special Accession Programme for Agriculture and Rural Development). It is intended to subsidize programs improving market efficiency, quality control and hygienic standards as well as initiatives aimed at creating jobs. The EU's contribution must not exceed 75% of the total program expenditure.

In the pre-accession period candidate countries have access to €3.12 bn yearly from the budget accepted at the Berlin session of the Council of Europe. Of this, the support provided by the PHARE program amounts to an annual €1.56 bn, the subsidies available from SAPARD are €520 m., while subsidies from ISPA come to €1.04 bn. For the period 2000–2006 this amounts to a total of €21.84 bn in subsidies.

At the Berlin summit the amounts available for the new members after accession were also approved. The approved budget still expected enlargement in 2002, so between 2002 and 2006 the new members can spend €39.58 bn on purposes of regional development, which provides for the major part of expenditure related to enlargement. Within the budget accepted for 2002, of the total of €6.45 bn available for the new members, subsidies from the structural funds and the Cohesion Fund would have been €3.75 bn. This support increases by about €2 bn per year, and by 2006, the end of the period, it will have reached €12.08 bn. At that time the total expenditure spent on the new members will have been €16.78 bn, in theory. Of the total expenditure of € 58.07 bn planned for the whole period, €39.58 bn will be spent on regional subsidies, which is over two thirds of the whole amount spent on the new members.

The decision of the Council of Europe emphasizes that subsidies relating to enlargement must not be used for any other purposes, and that items of expenditure allocated for the current 15 member states and amounts allocated for pre-accession support cannot be re-grouped for the new members. Should the accession of the new members involve a need for extra expenditure, the Council can only approve modifications to the budget approved in Berlin by a qualified majority. Nonetheless, the approved budget contains several ambiguities, since it is not clear what exactly is going to happen to the amounts scheduled for particular years if only some of the candidates join the Union. Will the countries that have already joined be able to use the whole amount approved for the given year or only a part of it? What will happen to the amount that has not been used? Since it cannot be regrouped, will it have to be carried over to the following year? It was also unclear how many countries will be involved in the enlargement, and when.

On the basis of the country reports published in 2001, the Commission suggests enlargement by as many as 10 countries in 2004. In the light of this the Berlin budget can be analysed in several ways, since at that time there were plans only for the most prepared of the six countries of the first round – i.e. the countries that had already started accession negotiations – to join the Union in 2002. Since then the target date of 2002 has been changed to 2004 and the number of candidates has also increased. If the amounts included and left in the budget are accumulated, there might be sufficient support available for the new members and they might be gradually able to reach the level of support received by the less developed current members.

In line with the original proposal of the Commission, the stipulation concerning the upper limit of subsidies to be claimed from the EU was also approved. Under this rule, *the current as well as the future members must adhere to the principle that transfers received from the structural funds and the Cohesion Fund may not exceed 4% of the given country's GDP.* This regulation actually sanctioned the situation that has developed with the main current beneficiaries and made this ratio the maximum of the subsidies provided. Part of the reason for this was certainly the wish to avert possibly very high GDP-dependent claims for subsidies by the future members. It may be misleading to make comparisons between the candidate countries and the experience of the less developed member states, as, *for several reasons, the absorption capacity of the Central and East European countries may be bigger* than that of the peripheral countries of the EU was earlier (Inotai 1997). Factors of the difference may be the following:

- their higher level of general education;
- their more favourable geographical location;
- their more flexible capacity for social and institutional adaptation.

It should be underlined that becoming integrated into the EU's regional policy also requires several internal changes from the new members. Being 'entitled' does not necessarily mean that the new members will be able to draw the subsidies from the structural funds without any prior preparations. These preparations require serious changes in the domestic regional development policies of the candidate countries. They have to be aware of the principles of operation of the EU's regional policy and must be able to ensure that those principles are followed, for which significant institutional reforms will be needed.

REFERENCES

Cecchini, P. (1988) *The European Challenge*. Wildwood House, Aldershot.

Council Regulation (EEC) No. 2080/93, OJ No. L 193, 31 July 1993.

Council Regulation (EEC) No. 792/93, OJ No. L 79, 1 April 1993.; Council Regulation (EC) No. 1164/1994 of 16 May 1994 establishing a Cohesion Fund.

Council Regulation (EEC) No. 2052/88, OJ No. L 185, 15. July 1988., Council Regulation (EEC) No. 4253/88, OJ No. L 374, 31 December 1988., Council Regulation (EEC) No. 4254/88, OJ No. L 374, 31 December 1988.

Council Regulation (EEC) No. 4255/88, OJ No. L 374, 31 December 1988., Council Regulation (EEC) No. 4256/88, OJ No. L 374, 31 December 1988.

Council Regulation (EEC) No. 2080/93, OJ No. L 193, 31 July 1993., Council Regulation (EEC) No. 2081/93, OJ No. L 193, 31 July 1993., Council Regulation (EEC) No. 2082/93, OJ No. L 193, 31 July 1993., Council Regulation (EEC) No. 2083/93, OJ No. L 193, 31 July 1993., Council Regulation (EEC) No. 2084/93, OJ No. L 193, 31 July 1993., Council Regulation (EEC) No. 2085/93, OJ No. L 374, 31 July 1993.

European Commission: *Unity, solidarity, diversity for Europe, its people and its territory. Second Report on Economic and Social Cohesion*. Luxembourg, 2001.

European Commission: *Agenda 2000. For a Stronger and Wider Union*. DOC/97/6. Strasbourg, 15 July 1997.

European Commission: *The Community Budget: Facts in Figures*. 101. Luxembourg, 1989.

Europäische Kommission: *Die Durchführung der Strukturfondsreform in 1993*. Fünfter Jahresbericht. Luxemburg, 1995.

European Commission: *The Europe Agreements and Beyond: A Strategy to Prepare the Countries of Central and Eastern Europe for Accession.* COM (94) 361, 1994

European Commission DG VI: *Fact Sheets, Special Accession Programme for Agriculture and Rural Development.* Brussels , 1999.

European Commission: *Proposal for a Council Regulation (EC) Establishing an Instrument for Structural Policies for Pre-Accession.* 98/0091 (CNS), COM(1998) 138 final, Official Journal C 164, 29 May 1998.

European Commission DG VI: *Fact Sheets, Special Accession Programme for Agriculture and Rural Development.* Brussels, 1999.

INOTAI, A. (1997) *The Costs and Benefits of Eastern Enlargement of the European Union.* Hungarian Academy of Sciences, Institute for World Economics, Working Papers No. 87.

VI.

THE INTEGRATION PERFORMANCE OF THE EU COUNTRIES

By

ÁKOS KENGYEL–TIBOR PALÁNKAI

Of the regional integration groupings that have developed worldwide, the *EU has undoubtedly proved to be the most successful and the most advanced.* Over the four and a half decades since the enactment of the Treaty of Rome, this organization has gone through important phases of integration: it has implemented a customs union, the common market, the single internal market and monetary union. Since March 1, 2002, in the euro-zone, which includes 12 member states, the only legal tender has been the euro. Social support for integration has become increasingly widespread in the few past decades. Integration has been accompanied by significant economic and political advantages, and today it is seen as desirable by the people of the continent. Differences of opinion exist mainly as to the pace and the depth of integration.

49% of the population in the member states consider the country's EU membership a good thing, 39% are not able to judge, and 12% deem it a bad thing. The ratio of those who approve of membership is the highest in Ireland, Luxembourg and Holland (78%, 77% and 73% respectively), while Sweden has the highest ratio (33%) of citizens rejecting membership, and disapproval can also be considered high in Britain, Austria and Denmark (23%). The ratio of those considering membership bad is the lowest in Ireland, Luxembourg, Portugal, Spain, Italy and Holland, between 3% and 5% (European Commission – EUROSTAT 2000: 39).

1. INTEGRATION IN TRADE AND PRODUCTION

Integration has had a great impact on the forms and structure of cooperation between the member countries as well as on the development of their national economies. The turnover of foreign trade in the EU member states has grown relatively fast in the past few decades. Exports of goods and services, on an annual average and at constant prices, grew by 7.9% in 1961–70, 5.6% in 1971–1980 and 4.5% in 1981–2000. This means that export in the period grew about 1.5–2 times faster than GDP. *The economies of the member states have been considerably internationalized in the past 40 years,* and an outstanding role in that has been played by the integration.

Between 1958 and 2002, the ratio of export of goods and services within GDP rose from 20% to 40% (the ratio is similar for import), and this means that *the EU countries are largely dependent on their foreign trade.* The ratio of the export of goods and services within GDP in 2002 amounted to 124% in Luxembourg, 94% in Belgium, 92% in Ireland, 68% in Holland, 53% in Austria, 52% in Sweden, 46% in Denmark, 45% in Finland, 38% in Germany, 33% in Portugal and Spain, 32% in France, 30% in Italy, 29% in the UK and 25% in Greece. The corresponding ratios for the US and Japan are around 12% (European Commission 2001: 184–185). With the launch of the euro, after the former 'internal' trade had really become domestic trade, structural openness to foreign trade fell to 20%. The evidence of figures proves that *integration into the world economy depends not just on the size of a country, but also on its level of development. This determinate correlation, however, is also valid inversely, i.e. a high degree of dependence on foreign trade is a condition of development.* The development of recent decades shows that taking advantage of the benefits derived from the international division of labour has become a vital, indispensable source of growth and efficiency.

Trade among the EU countries has grown especially fast. The ratio of internal export and import of goods within the GDP has nearly trebled between 1958 and 2002 (from 7% to nearly 19%), which has led to a high degree of integration and interdependence among the member countries. If, in accordance with the dependence theories, we accept 10% as the minimum level of dependence, then *by the late 1970s the member states of the EU had crossed the threshold of interdependence in their internal relations (Table 1).*

Table 1. Foreign trade as % of GDP (EU15)

Items	1960	1970	1980	1990	2000	2002
Total export	19.6	21.8	27.3	28.2	35.6	39.1
Total import	19.2	21.5	28.7	27.5	34.9	38.5
Internal export	7.7	10.0	13.3	14.5	16.9	18.8
Internal import	7.9	10.1	13.2	14.6	16.3	18.2

Source: European Commission: 2001 Broad Economic Policy Guidelines. European Economy No. 72.

Interdependence has been further deepened by cooperation in technology and production and by capital relations. The rapid transnationalization of the corporate spheres has become an important factor of integration and interdependence. *The infrastructure of integration has gradually been constructed* (transport, telecommunications, the financial system, etc.). As a result of the rapid expansion of relations among the member states, the foundations of integration were laid by the 1970s and the process became increasingly irreversible. Withdrawal from the integration process would have had such harmful consequences for a country that it could not be considered as an option. What remained to be disputed could only be the direction and the pace of further integration.

In the period between 1958 and the turn of Millennium, *the development of integration in trade and production, on the basis of world economic and internal conditions, can be divided into five stages:*

– the first stage lasts until the early 1970s (1973) and ends with the first oil price explosion;

– the second stage is the period between the early 1970s and the early 1980s, in which the cyclical and structural crisis caused disturbances in the integration process as well;

– the stage of the 1980s was characterized by the resumption and consolidation of integration processes, in respect not so much of quantitative as of qualitative changes;

– in the stage beginning from the early 1990s, the political and economic transformation of Eastern Europe, the enactment of measures regarding the single internal market and the Maastricht decisions of December 1991 led to the deepening of the integration process, and this stage closed with the adoption of the euro;

– after the period 1999–2002, in every respect a new era will begin in the economic development of the EU.

The important stages in the development of the integration by and large coincide with the decisive turning points in its deepening and expansion.

With the liberalization of trade, between 1958 and 1973, within the customs union, internal trade among the member states grew very dynamically. While in this period the expansion of total trade (at constant prices) was about 8% annually, the annual growth of internal trade reached 12% (GDP grew by almost 5% annually). The ratio of internal trade within total foreign trade between 1958 and 1973 grew from less than one third to more than half, and internal deliveries exceeded 10% both in production output (export) and in internal consumption (import) (OECD, Economic Outlook 1977).

The elimination of customs tariffs enabled the potential (static) comparative advantages to be utilized in large measure, which made the member countries' economies even more closely interwoven. There have been several empirical studies analysing the effects of the EU's customs union: though they pointed out a strong correlation between the establishment of the union and the expansion of trade, their findings concerning the gains were rather contradictory. In the development of trade several factors must have played a part, but there was a rough consensus that in 1970 about 30% of trade in internal manufacturing industry could be ascribed to the creation of trade, i.e. the replacement of costlier domestic products by imports (MÜLLER and OWEN 1989).

Contrary to the initial worries, it had a positive effect that the advantages of the division of labour resulting from the customs union were directly perceptible, and the negative effects were more moderate than expected. "The nature of the growth of the trade within the Community in the 1960s consolidated industrial support. Protectionists had feared that whole sectors of industry would be competed out of existence in their own country. But trade in fact expanded on different lines. It was predominantly intra-sectoral trade, with each member state's exports and imports both growing in each sector. This was the consequence of the dynamic effect of greater specialization within each sector, and of larger scale in the production of these specialized products than would have been possible in the protected national markets. It was easier to adjust to this kind of change, because most people could continue to work in the same sector and same place as before" (PINDER 1991: 63). Intra-sectoral specialization has led to a qualitatively new situation of interdependence and interwovenness.

The world economic disturbances of the 1970s had contradictory effects on the process of integration. Parallel with the deceleration of the dynamism of economic development, the pace of expansion of trade slackened. The factors exerting a significant negative influence on the division of labour among the member countries were the oil price explosions and the world economic recessions (1974–75 and 1980–83). In the wake of the decline, in 1973–75, internal trade decreased by an annual 2%, while external trade increased by 3.7%.

The crisis mainly disturbed internal trade. Between 1973 and 1975, the proportion of internal trade in total export fell back from 54% to 50%, while in import it fell from 52% to 49%. With the revival of business activity beginning from 1975 internal trade within the EU regained its relatively greater dynamism. Between 1975 and 1979, the volume of the EU's internal trade grew annually by 8.7% and its external trade by 5.8%. During the recession from 1980 the phenomena seen in the period 1973–75 were repeated. In 1979–81 the volume of internal trade showed a 2.2% decrease, while external trade expanded by 4.4%. Thus the ratio of internal trade in 1982 was below the level of interdependence achieved by 1973.

The decline in the ratio of internal trade after 1973 explains why this period is sometimes referred to as a time of disintegration. The change in the ratio and structure of trade had various causes. One of them was undoubtedly the repeated oil price explosions. Only the oil-producing countries were able to raise their share in the EU's trade in those years. The oil price explosions had a considerable effect on both import and export. Though the volume of oil imported decreased, the oil bills shot up, while increased effective demand also made it easier to raise exports in this area as well. *If we disregard the relations with oil exporters and leave them out of the general flow of foreign trade, it is really impossible to prove a higher degree of disintegration.* Besides the above, another major role in the decrease in the ratio of internal trade was played by the gradual worsening of European economic competitiveness. This resulted in powerful import penetration, especially in industries characterized by dynamic demand, while on the export side the striving after global integration by the leading European companies had a major influence on proportions.

It can be seen that the long-term integrative effects of the customs union and the common market did not cease to exist, though the recession periods caused ruptures in this process. Under normal economic circumstances integration went on, but the dynamism of the process decreased. Interdependence within the community increased also in this period, in production output as well as in internal consumption, the ratio of internal trade grew from a level of around 10% in the early 1970s to 13% by the early 1980s. A higher degree of expansion was achieved in trade in consumer goods and agricultural products. Empirical analyses based on the assumptions of dynamic customs union theories also forecast gains for this period. According to some research findings, the reduction of costs arising from the customs union in 1980 reached 3–6% of the Six's GDP (OWEN 1983).

From the early 1980s on, the process of integration revived again. By the early 1990s the ratio of internal trade within the total amounted to about 60%. Though the dynamism of foreign trade had decreased by the 1980s, it must be noted that the growth of GDP was also gradually slowing down. The trend of internationalization was not broken; on the contrary, it showed relative strengthening. Between 1958 and 1973 the growth of trade in the EU countries was 7.9%, which was 1.6% higher than the annual growth (4.8%) of GDP. In 1984–2001 the growth of the EU's foreign trade slowed down to an annual 5.4%, but in the same period the growth of GDP was also only 2.7%. So the dynamism of foreign trade was twice that of GDP, which means that internationalization strengthened. The proportions changed similarly in the internal trade of the integration.

The development of world economic positions is well reflected by the changes in trade with the two world economic power centres, the US and Japan, that have occurred in recent decades (European Commission DG Trade 2002a). The value of exports from the US grew from €50.7 bn in 1980 to €89 bn in 1990, and to €194 bn in 2001, while the EU's exports grew from €29.4 bn in 1980 to €82 bn in 1990 and to €238 bn in 2001. So the foreign trade balance shifted from a deficit to a significant surplus. Meanwhile, the US share in the EU's total imports remained basically unchanged, around 20%. On the contrary, an increasing proportion of the EU's export trade is conducted with the US: from 15% in 1980, with a 5% increase per decade, by 2001 it was nearing 25% of the EU's exports.

Imports from Japan grew from €15.4 bn in 1980 to €53 bn in 1990 and to €75 bn in 2001. The EU's exports increased from €5.2 bn in 1980 to €24 bn in 1990 and €45 bn in 2001, but even so there is a tremendous foreign trade deficit on the part of the EU. In 2001 the EU's deficit reached €30 bn, which accounted for nearly two thirds of Japan's world economic surplus of 44 bn. There is especially great inequality in trade in machinery, equipment and transport vehicles.

2. THE FLOW OF FACTORS AND THE INTEGRATION PROCESSES

Flows of factors are important carriers of integration processes and preconditions of more efficient resource allocation. The way closer micro-integration takes place is through the interdependence of capital. The establishment of the common market, the framework for the free flow of capital and labour, had a relatively limited impact on the movement of factors until the 1970s. *The movement of capital was not significant,* while the relatively noticeable *movement of labour* was restricted to workers with lower qualifications, and the labour force typically came from countries outside the EU. Within the union the major source of labour was southern Italy and the non-member countries of the Mediterranean basin.

Labour from abroad in 1974 amounted to 9% within the total number of workers in West Germany and France, but only a small part of this (one third in West Germany and less than one sixth in France) from the member countries (OECD 1977). Following 1974, the ratio of foreign workers in most member countries decreased (by 1985 the decrease in West Germany was from a former level of 9% to 6.9%, and in France to 6.4%). In 1975 there were 2.1 m. and in France 1.9 m. foreign workers. By 1989 this number had fallen to less than 1.7 m. in West Germany and 1.2 m. in France. In 1989, besides the 480 thousand EU citizens working in West Germany, there were nearly 1.2 m. who had come from outside the Union.

Until the early 1970s, *American direct private capital investment played a decisive role* in the community's capital flows. From 1950–58, the total of American direct private investments (without profits reinvested) amounted to an annual average of $63 m. in the then six EU member states. This amount rose to a yearly average of $837 m. in the period 1963–66. At the beginning of the 1970s yearly investments by American companies in the then member states of the EU already exceeded $2 bn. In 1957–1973, the rate of American direct private capital investments in the common market grew from less than $1.6 bn to nearly $19.3 bn, which is more than a seventeen-fold increase. In 1950, only 5.4% of American foreign private capital was invested in the EU countries. This proportion grew to 6.6% by 1957 and 18% by 1973. Including in the survey Great Britain, Ireland and Denmark, which joined the EU only in 1973, then the amount of American private working capital active in the Nine exceeded $31 bn, that is, nearly 30% of all American capital investment abroad.

From the 1970s onwards, *capital flows within the union* received a new impulse. As early as the late 1960s, long before their accession, the large British corporations had increasingly begun to orientate themselves towards the EU, which gradually became their main investment target (as opposed to the British Commonwealth). From the late 1960s companies from West Germany began larger-scale expansion abroad. By the mid-1970s West Germany became a net exporter in working capital investment, and a considerable proportion of its investment went to the EU countries. By this time the large West German corporations had strengthened and to an ever greater extent they had their own independent market aspirations.

The crisis also gave rise to the advancement of integration, so the assumption that integration can only proceed in boom conditions was not borne out by reality. By the 1970s the corporations of Western Europe had in many respects strengthened and by that time they had become prepared to take better advantage of the integration opportunities provided by the common market. *From the 1970s West European companies followed the example of their American and Japanese rivals and became more and more transnationalized, in line with the requirements of new technologies and the world economy.*

From the 1970s new tendencies emerged in both the global and the European processes of capital flow and interdependence. The most significant changes occurred, above all, in the relationship between American, Japanese and European capital. *The inflow of American capital slowed down from the early 1970s and the export of European capital intensified.*

American working capital investments abroad between 1975 and 1979 amounted to $16 bn annually, while the countries of the EU invested only an annual $14 bn abroad. These proportions changed to $23 bn and $60 bn respectively by1985–89, and in 1990 the EU countries' foreign investment was nearly three times more ($97.5 bn) than that of the US ($33.4 bn). After 1985 the Japanese also beat the Americans, with $48 bn of foreign investment in 1990. The data for capital inflow show a similar picture. In 1990 the amount of foreign capital invested in the US was $37 bn, and in the EU close to $86 bn Foreign investment targeting Japan remained marginal.

The EU acquired a leading role in both directions of capital flow. In 1990 44% of total foreign investment came from the EU and 48% of total foreign direct investment targeted the EU. Capital flow between America and Europe became a two-way road. Formerly, a chief incentive for American capital export had been that the dollar was overvalued. With the devaluations of the dollar after 1971 this was no longer valid, and the appreciation of some of the European currencies initiated contrary processes. Other factors playing a part were the changes in currency parities, the reduction of labour cost differences, the attraction of the huge American market and the advanced technology and the relatively low American energy costs. Many think that the growing political unrest in Western Europe from the end of 1960s also contributed to the same effect: large companies judged that the relationship between labour and capital was more favourable in the US.

From the 1970s the Atlantic orientation of the European integration process continued to gain in importance, while the balance of power between European and American companies became more equal. The flow of capital toward the US accelerated particularly from the early 1980s, when capital export was surpassed by a vast capital import surplus. A large proportion of European working capital investment went to the EU member states, consequently the Community became a net investor in the US in terms of working capital stock.

The situation took a different turn in 1983, when compared with the $78.9 bn American working capital investment in the EU, the union's direct working capital investment in the US reached $82.2 bn. In 1986 Great Britain had the largest capital stock ($54.4 bn), then came Holland ($42.9 bn), and West Germany ($17.4 bn). In 1986 about 60% of the working capital in the US came from the EU countries (11% from Japan and only 9% from Canada). Compared with this, the American working capital stock in the EU in 1986 was only $99.6 bn. In 1993 nearly half of the $240 bn worth of American foreign investment, and about 40% of the profits, were in Western Europe. Estimates indicate that about 60% of foreign capital in the US is from Western Europe. European companies mainly tried to acquire corporate stakes in the US, which resulted in the situation that in spite of their relatively large investments, their positions in terms of influence and control remained weak. They took full control only of smaller and less significant American companies and were not able to prevail over larger American corporations.

From the 1980s the Japanese also had an important role in foreign investment targeting the EU. In the early 1980s the Japanese capital stock invested in the EU was minimal. By 1986 the total of direct capital investment from Japan reached $14.5 bn, and according to estimates in early 1987 there were about 220 Japanese companies working in the EU. The number of their employees, however, was only around 75,000, which was less than the number of IBM's employees. By 1990 the direct working capital stock from Japan reached $42 bn, nearing a quarter of the amount of American investments. On the other hand, three quarters of Japanese EU investments were concentrated in only three countries, Great Britain (37.6%), Holland (24%) and Luxembourg (12.8%), mainly in the banking and insurance sector. In 1990 8.2% of the Japanese capital stock was in Germany and 6.9% in France. The appreciation of the yen, as well as the melting away of the comparative advantages in labour costs, which were important in Asian capital exports, and market expansion considerations also played a part in Japanese capital investments. Apart from saving on shipping costs, adaptation to local needs is easier in proximity to the markets. The Japanese were also driven by considerations such as that they would have a chance of obtaining vital orders in the telecommunications sector only if they were 'on the spot'.

From the mid-1980s, the single market established in 1992 played an important part in the acceleration of investment in the EU. The large transnational companies did not exclude the danger of a 'Fortress Europe' and to be on the safe side, did their best to get inside the walls. The danger of protectionism on the part of the EU, especially the dumping procedures, also prompted non-EU countries to do the same.

By the turn of the Millennium, foreign direct investment from the US in the EU rose from €60.7 bn in 1998 to €120.3 bn in 2000. In the year 2000, nearly 70% of direct capital investment flowing into the EU came from the US. The American capital stock in the EU in 2000 was worth €561 bn, and represented more than 62% of foreign capital stock in the Union. *The amount of capital transferred from the EU to the US considerably exceeded the value of direct investment by the US in the EU:* the size of the annual direct investment in 1998 was €133.4 bn, in 1999 €196.8 bn, and *in 2000 €172 bn.* In 2000 the European capital stock in the United States exceeded €794.5 bn, which represented 51% of the EU's total investment outside the Union (European Commission DG Trade 2002a). Thus the Atlantic ties of the integration have become very close, and the amount of European capital invested in the US significantly exceeds the American capital stock present in the EU.

In comparison with all this, *by the turn of the Millennium the inflow of Japanese capital and the Union's capital export to Japan amounted to almost zero.* Because of the crisis in the economy and the financial sector, Japanese expansion came to a halt from the 1990s; what is more, the volume of investment even decreased slightly. In 1998 there was barely more than

€1 bn of capital investment arriving in the EU, which in 1999 was followed by a withdrawal of capital worth more than €3 bn, and even in 2000 only €1.4 bn came to the EU from Japan. The Union's capital export grew from €700 m. in 1998 to €8.5 bn in 1999 and €7.9 bn in 2000. The Japanese capital stock in the EU was €35 bn, accounting for only 4% of the total foreign capital stock in the Union. Capital investment in Japan accounts for 2% of the EU's annual capital export, and also of the total capital invested outside the EU.

By the turn of the Millennium, the EU had stabilized its position on the world market as a net capital exporter, though capital export worth €202 bn in 2001 was a 37% decline on the record € 322 bn in the previous year. The net capital export record of €164 bn, accounting for 1.9% of the EU's GDP, was followed in 2001 by only €105 bn of capital export, worth only 1.2% of GDP (European Commission DG Trade 2002b). The US remained the EU's chief partner in 2001 as well, receiving nearly half of the EU's investment outside the Union and having a 55% share among investors in the Union from outside the EU. In 2001, Germany was the largest investor among the EU countries, with €60 bn worth of investments. Germany was followed by Belgium/Luxembourg with €40 bn, then came Holland with €36 bn. Belgium/Luxembourg was the leader in capital flow into the EU with €30 bn, followed by Holland with €28 bn and Great Britain with €23 bn. In net investment Germany came first with €51 bn in net capital export, then came France with €26 bn and Spain with €12 bn. In net capital inflow Great Britain was the leader with €18 bn.

3. THE DEVELOPMENT OF MICROINTEGRATION PROCESSES

The qualitative deepening of the integration process cannot be examined in its complexity without analysing the cooperation within the corporate sphere. In spite of the liberalization of the flow of factors of production in the 1960s, the microintegration processes in this area started to work slowly and in contrary directions. Integration, as we have seen, only proceeded through the channels of trade. Until the early 1970s microintegration rarely took the form of capital mergers or joint ventures, and it was dominated mainly by looser forms of cooperation in production.

On the basis of the common market, competition sharpened, and this resulted in changes in the market environment, which required adaptation from all participants. Competition forced companies, especially in the highly competitive sectors, to apply advanced technology and larger-scale production and to rationalize production. In the 1960s the concentration and centralization of production speeded up, and especially in the second half of the decade a wave of centralization swept through several countries. The merger 'fever' was typical not only of the EU countries, but the effects of competition on the common market were important anyway. *Until the late 1970s the process mainly took place between national producers, while the expected Community mergers and interdependence did not occur.*

At this time the common market tended to promote the internal integration of national industries instead of that of the Community, and the industrial structure of the European countries for the most part retained its national character. "But the most important amalgamations of all – the cross-frontier ones – have barely begun; Community firms co-operate across the frontiers through manufacturing and sales agreements in the normal commercial way and banks and insurance firms conduct their intra-Community affairs in the time-honoured but slow-moving ways. Apart from the Agfa-Gewaert joint German–Belgian operation in the photographic components business, there have been no complete trans-frontier mergers of any size – certainly not of the size needed to compete successfully on an international scale" (DE LA MAHOTIÉRE 1970: 83).

Under the motivating influence of the common market framework, as we have seen, from the early 1960s the EU became the main target of American investment. After 1958 more than 3,000 new American companies settled in Western Europe, and leading American corporations acquired stakes, shares, and occasionally control over parts of the European economy. Large British companies also increased their investment in the countries of the continent from the second half of the 1960s. So until the beginning of the 1970s the European microintegration processes, direct production cooperations and corporate mergers alike were dominated by extra-community, mainly American partners. It can be seen as symbolic that within the period, the French carmaker Simca and Germany's Opel finally merged under the auspices of the American Chrysler firm. The transnationalisation of capital and the corporate sphere started, but these companies were, for the most part, American. Though several European companies had subsidiaries in a number of countries (Philips, Siemens, Volkswagen, Fiat, etc.), there were only sporadic examples for transnational corporate mergers between West European companies.

Up to the early 1970s, the customs union and the common market entailed, simultaneously with the internal reconstruction of European industry, an increase in the number of companies with foreign, chiefly American participation. *American investment and cooperation with European companies resulted in an extensive modernization process.* The American presence sharpened the competition in European markets, which forced adaptation. For some companies and industries this had inconvenient consequences, but at the same time it contributed to the modernization of European industry. The 'Atlantic' nature of microintegration from the beginning signalled the close linkage between regional and global integration.

From the early 1970s the changing economic conditions had contrary effects on microintegration processes. In many respects, the crisis had a negative effect, mainly in the short-term, on microintegration. The cyclical disturbances and the slow-down of investment, and especially its stagnation or decline in times of recession, was not favourable for production cooperation either. Sales opportunities in the market worsened, the rationalization and reduction of production upset traditional cooperation relations and investment opportunities grew narrower.

At the same time the crisis forced increased technological and structural adaptation on the part of companies and focused attention on the requirements of effective corporate organization and business administration. Basically this also strengthened the constraints towards integration. *West European companies increasingly utilized the expansion of international cooperation in production and the different forms on integration cooperation as a means of cost-cutting and increasing efficiency.* Striving for lower costs in manufacturing industry resulted in new cooperation agreements. This tendency became general in the automobile industry, in which several joint ventures were set up for producing and assembling parts, spreading development costs and utilizing the benefits of serial volumes. Similar processes began in the electronics industry.

From the 1970s the structural crisis and the new wave of the technological revolution began to have strong reciprocal effects on one another. The energy crisis had a stimulating effect, for example, on the development of microelectronics and biotechnology; technological innovations enabled substantial savings in materials, energy and labour. Telecommunications and electronics promoted scientific business administration, while rapid product-innovation became an important factor in market expansion and retention. Technological development and the need to adapt had an increased effect on widening international corporate cooperation. Relations among EU companies gradually expanded from the 1970s and microintegration became ever more powerful.

Regional integration in Europe from the 1970s developed in dynamic interrelation with the global integration processes of the world economy. From the 1970s an important development was the beginning of the transnationalization of the European corporate sphere. By the 1980s, with the restructuring of capital and production relations, the former one-way character of the transnationalization process (the spread of American corporations toward Western Europe and other countries) ceased to exist. Though expansion was strongly concentrated on certain countries (Ireland, the UK, West Germany), the endeavour to create foreign production capacities characterized the whole industrialized world, and penetration into the so-called newly industrializing world became intense. A new development from the 1970s was that the relative isolation of the American economy came to an end.

Another important development from the 1970s was the appearance of Japanese companies in Western Europe, which in many respects influenced the integration processes. The major direction of the expansion was towards the electronics industry and automobile production. The Japanese achieved spectacular successes in exporting VCRs, and flooded especially the West European markets. European producers were, in the short-term, unable to adapt, and exerted great pressure on their governments to protect their markets with protectionist measures.

An agreement voluntarily restricting exports for several products (VCRs and cars) signed between countries of the EU and Japan fixed the amount of Japanese exports and minimum prices. The minimum prices temporarily improved Japanese profits, but it was clear that they would not be able to keep their market positions through merely exporting goods. Leading Japanese companies established assembly plants and occasionally joint ventures with West European firms in ever larger numbers. The main paths of penetration were Great Britain, (mainly Scotland and Wales), Ireland and West Germany, from which, as countries of the common market, they had free access to the major part of the European continent.

The Japanese penetration, though its quantity did not pose a serious danger from the aspect of control over European industry, still, as it was concentrated on a few 'sensitive' areas like electronics and the automobile industry, squeezed out local production capacities and temporarily worsened the trade balance. The import aspects of the investments were sometimes significant (because of the investment goods or the supply of spare parts), and the boom in exports only took place later. The Japanese for the most part built new plants (70% of the investments in Great Britain were of this kind) and only to a lesser extent did they buy shares or set up joint ventures.

The number of Japanese firms in manufacturing industry working in Western Europe grew from 189 to 728 between 1985 and 1994. By the 1990s all the Japanese carmakers had subsidiaries in Europe, with capacities reaching a total of 1.2 m. cars. According to estimates, by the end of the decade Japanese companies had acquired 16–20% of the West European auto market. Similar developments occurred in other areas as well, and the Japanese semiconductor, television and copier industries virtually settled in the EU. As European parts and materials are 15–20% more expensive than those made by Asian, mainly Japanese, suppliers, the manufacturing companies also encouraged their traditional suppliers to make investments in the EU.

The Japanese companies brought advanced technology and management and organization methods and proved able to produce the 'Japanese miracle' with European workers as well. Many believed that with their direct competitive effect they had positively influenced the adaptation of European industry. The 'Japanization' of European industry meant the spread of the 'just in time' method of inventory control and an increased awareness of the importance of quality control, while closer links were established with parts suppliers and more 'cooperative' employee-management relations became dominant. Leading European companies formed direct research and production relations with their Japanese partners (ICL-Fujitsu, Honda–Rover, Matsushita–Grundig and Bosch), and took advantage of the cheaper Japanese suppliers. European companies like Bull, Siemens and Olivetti have been increasingly buying from Japanese suppliers. As the Japanese economy fell into deep crisis, by the turn of Millennium the role of Japanese companies gradually diminished.

From the 1980s an important new development from the point of view of integration processes was *the extremely rapid expansion and increasing transnationalization of money and credit markets.* Integration has been manifested partly in the increasingly blurred dividing lines between the traditional forms of banking and capital market specialization (commercial and investment banks, savings banks, security-market operations, etc.). The different financial institutions have to a large extent penetrated each other's territories, and in close interdependence with other activities, the number and the variety of players in the money market have increased.

Over the past two decades we have experienced an unprecedented increase in international financing, which experts define as the 'globalization of finance', in the sense that compared with the macroeconomic value of the 'real economy', there has been a great increase in international transactions. In the case of the EU, the liberalization that occurred as part of the creation of the single market had a great impact on the merging process taking place in the market for financial services. This liberalization resulted in the sharpening of competition among money and credit institutions. The changes that started in the securities markets were accelerated by the launching of economic and monetary union: with the introduction of the single currency, close cooperation between the European stock markets began.

REFERENCES

European Commission – EUROSTAT (2000) *A Community of Fifteen: key figures.* Office for Official Publications of the European Communities. Luxembourg.

European Commission. DG. Trade (2002a) Bilateral Trade Relations. Brussels.

DE LA MAHOTIÉRE, S. (1970) *Towards One Europe.* Pelican, Middlesex.

MÜLLER, J. and OWEN, N. (1989) *The effects of trade on plant size.* The European Internal Market. Oxford University Press, Oxford.

OWEN, N. (1983) *Economies of Scale, Competitiveness and Trade Patterns within the European Community.* Clarendon, Oxford.

PINDER, J. (1991) *European Community.* Oxford University Press, Oxford.

VII.

THE MEMBER COUNTRIES' MACROECONOMIC PERFORMANCE

By

ÁKOS KENGYEL–TIBOR PALÁNKAI

1. PATTERN OF ECONOMIC DEVELOPMENT

The development of the EU can be divided, on the basis of its macroeconomic performance, into *five fairly clearly distinguishable stages*. Accordingly, since 1958 breaking points can be identified in the 1970s (1973), the 1980s (1983), the beginning of the 1990s (1991), and the period 1999–2002, with the introduction of the euro. At the same time, within these periods various smaller and bigger fractures can be observed in the trends of economic growth, unemployment and inflation (*Tables 1, 2* and *3*).

Table 1. Trends in economic growth (annual % change in GDP)

Country	1961–1973	1974–1983	1984–1989	1990–2001	2002*
Belgium	4.9	1.8	2.5	2.1	3.1
Denmark	4.3	1.5	2.4	2.3	2.4
Germany	4.4	1.6	2.6	1.9	2.6
Greece	7.7	2.5	2.3	2.3	4.8
Spain	7.2	1.7	3.8	2.6	3.3
France	5.4	2.2	2.5	1.7	2.8
Ireland	4.4	3.8	3.1	7.0	7.1
Italy	5.3	2.9	3.1	1.6	2.7
Luxembourg	3.5	2.6	4.5	5.8	5.5
Holland	4.8	1.6	2.5	2.9	3.1
Austria	4.8	2.3	2.2	2.3	2.6
Portugal	6.9	2.5	3.3	2.6	2.6
Finland	5.2	2.7	3.5	2.2	3.6
Sweden	4.6	1.5	2.7	1.7	3.0
Great Britain	3.2	1.1	3.5	2.2	3.0
EU 15	4.8	1.9	2.9	2.1	2.9
USA	3.8	2.3	4.3	3.4	3.0
Japan	9.7	3.8	4.5	1.3	1.3

* Forecast.

Source: European Commission: 2001 Broad Economic Policy Guidelines. European Economy No. 72, 2001.

Table 2. Trends in unemployment (as % of the workforce)

Country	1961–1973	1974–1983	1984–1989	1990–2001	2002*
Belgium	2.0	7.3	10.9	8.7	6.1
Denmark	1.0	6.1	6.9	7.1	4.5
Germany	0.8	3.7	6.4	8.1	7.1
Greece	4.2	3.2	7.5	9.5	9.9
Spain	2.8	9.4	20.1	19.6	11.9
France	1.8	5.7	10.0	11.3	7.8
Ireland	5.4	9.7	17.4	11.1	3.5
Italy	5.3	6.9	10.2	10.7	9.3
Luxembourg	0.0	2.0	2.5	2.5	1.8
Holland	1.1	7.1	10.2	5.4	2.4
Austria	2.2	1.9	3.6	3.9	3.2
Portugal	2.5	6.6	7.5	5.6	5.1
Finland	1.8	4.6	5.1	12.5	8.4
Sweden	1.6	1.8	2.1	7.7	5.0
Great Britain	2.0	6.1	10.0	8.1	5.1
EU15	2.2	6.0	10.2	9.9	7.2
USA	4.9	7.1	6.4	5.6	4.7
Japan	1.3	2.0	2.6	3.3	4.8

* Forecast.

Source: European Commission: 2001 Broad Economic Policy Guidelines. European Economy. No. 72, 2001.

Table 3. Trends in consumer prices (annual average change, %)

Country	1961–1973	1974–1983	1984–1989	1990–2001	2002*
Belgium	3.7	7.8	3.2	2.0	1.9
Denmark	6.6	10.5	4.7	2.4	2.5
Germany	3.6	4.8	1.2	2.0	0.9
Greece	3.5	17.3	17.3	9.4	2.7
Spain	6.6	16.6	5.9	4.1	2.5
France	4.8	11.5	4.4	1.5	1.6
Ireland	6.3	15.2		3.7	5.2
Italy	4.9	17.1	7.1	3.9	2.4
Luxembourg	4.1	6.5	2.5	2.5	3.3
Holland	5.0	6.4	1.2	2.1	2.9
Austria	4.2	6.9	4.1	2.1	1.1
Portugal	3.9	21.9	14.1	5.7	2.7
Finland	5.7	13.9	7.4	1.9	1.2
Sweden	4.7	10.3	8.7	2.2	2.1
Great Britain	4.9	13.4	5.0	3.1	2.5
EU15	4.7	11.8	4.9	2.8	2.0
USA	3.1	7.7	3.8	2.1	2.0
Japan	6.0	7.3	1.0	0.2	0.5

* Forecast.

Source: European Commission: 2001 Broad Economic Policy Guidelines. European Economy No. 72, 2001.

1.1. THE 'GOLDEN AGE' OF ECONOMIC DEVELOPMENT

Up to the beginning of the 1970s , economic growth in the EU countries was relatively rapid and well-balanced. Their *average annual GDP growth rate* (in real terms) *of almost 5%* corresponded more or less to the OECD countries' average; it could not compete with Japan's growth rate of around 10%, but their performance was slightly better than that of the US and the other countries of Europe (OECD 1977). In the EU countries, in spite of seasonal fluctuations and regional problems there was *virtually full employment* until the beginning of the 1970s (about 2%). Employment steadily grew, and integration (the free movement of labour) contributed to reducing unemployment (e.g. in southern Italy). The general level of unemployment in the EU was half that of the US (about 5%), and only a few developed countries' performance was better than that of the EU.

With regard to *inflation* the EU figure was slightly higher than the average for the OECD countries, and its gradual acceleration, particularly from the mid-1960s, was largely due to international factors (disturbances in the international monetary system). As in the other industrially developed countries, up to the beginning of the 1970s the main factors in favourable development were rapid technical modernization, dynamic investment activity and personal consumption, radical transformation of the structure of the economy and of consumption, and active and relatively effective conjuncture policy on the part of the states.

Within the framework of market integration there was better exploitation of the advantages of the international division of labour, and *the development of the common market structures helped to improve the member countries' macroeconomic performance and vice versa.* "The causality between trade and growth is arguably not only one-way, as it is usually implied. The rapid elimination of intra-EEC tariffs and quantitative restrictions between 1958 and 1968 was made possible largely because of the favourable macroeconomic environment, characterized by high rates of growth and low unemployment. Increased exposure to international trade brings with it adjustment costs for both labour and capital. They are much more easily absorbed in time of rapid growth, thus minimizing the resistance from potential losers. This points to a possible virtuous circle: the favourable macroeconomic environment of the late 1950s and the 1960s, attributable to a combination of different factors, created the conditions which permitted the signing of the Treaty of Rome and the successful implementation of its trade provisions. Liberalization then led to more trade and this, in turn, contributed to the remarkable growth rates of this period" (TSOUKALIS 1991: 27).

1.2. THE EUROPEAN ECONOMY IN CRISIS

After 1973 fundamental changes took place in the EU countries' economic performance. As in the other industrially developed countries, the EU got into *a structural crisis,* and because of their dependence (60%) on external sources of energy, chiefly oil imports (over 90%), the unfavourable external influences were even more perceptible. After 1973 economic growth slowed down, and because of the oil-price explosions the member countries' economy suffered a recession in 1974–75, and again in 1980–83. The rate of growth of investment and productivity lessened, and the member countries' competitiveness decreased.

From the second half of the 1970s, *long-term slowing-down tendencies in economic growth* became increasingly noticeable (as a result of costlier energy sources and infrastructural investments, the decline in consumer demand as the market for durable goods became saturated, the growing predominance of services in the economic structure, etc.), and cyclical uncertainty was difficult to eliminate. Other contributing factors were *the internal structural changes and the inflexibilities resulting from the expansion of the welfare state.* In addition to the loss of cheap energy, European companies had to cope with escalating wage costs. This was partly due to the gradual exhaustion of both domestic and imported labour sources, and the intensifying political struggle for a bigger share of income. The latter reflected the collapse of the political consensus on which the economic miracle of the 1950s and 1960s had been based.

The result was an increase in the proportion of wages and payments at the expense of profits, with negative effects on investment. "The real increase in wages and salaries, which regularly exceeded the growth rates in productivity, was one important factor behind the deterioration of the business climate in Western Europe. Another factor was, according to those theories, the rigidities created in the labour-market through job security legislation and the growth of the welfare state" (TSOUKALIS 1991: 35). *Thus in this period no country succeeded in combining rapid growth with the curbing of inflation* and stabilization of the balance of payments, and as a result growth-restricting (monetarist) economic policies were indispensable.

The EU countries' performance in respect of *inflation* was relatively poor, especially in certain countries. The inflationary processes had already begun to accelerate in the second half of the 1960s (in 1970 the consumer price level rose by 7% in the EU), and with the oil-price explosion inflation took double-digits. As in the other developed countries, in the EU the acceleration of inflation was partly due to the untenability of the former state system of economic regulation (excessive state expenditure due to Keynesian economic policy, the disturbances in the international monetary system and the structural crisis in the world economy, and especially the energy crisis). In the EU the peak year for inflation was 1974, with an average rise in consumer prices of 15% in the member countries; inflation was not brought down below 10% until after 1983 (except in 1978, when the EU average inflation rate was 9.2%).

Particularly as a result of the first oil-price explosion inflation reached record levels in several countries, peaking at 23.5% in Portugal and Greece, which were not yet EU members, 21.4% in Italy, 15.1% in France, 15% in Denmark, and 23.6% in Britain in 1975. At the same time in 1973–75 it remained at about 9–10% in Holland, and in West Germany the 1975 peak was just a 7.5% increase in consumer prices. In 1980 inflation again shot up in the EU to 13.6%. The effect of severe anti-inflation measures began to be felt only from the mid-1980s.

Unemployment grew steadily in the EU countries from the early 1970s, and climbed from 2.6% in 1973 to 10.7% in 1985. Over this 12-year period it rose higher every year, not responding to cyclical fluctuations. It was a reflection of the *stagflation phenomena* of the 1970s and 1980s, that as a result of the structural crisis, the traditional interrelations between investment, output, prices and employment collapsed.

The growth of unemployment was principally due not to the deterioration of employment conditions, since the number of those in employment decreased by only just over 1% in the 10 years between 1974 and 1983. The main reason was that the economy had lost its former dynamism, and in the existing structure was no longer able to absorb the large number of people entering the labour market (owing to the post-war baby boom). In the 1970s the move of population from agriculture to industry (partly to the cities) came to an end, *labour-saving technological advances were applied, and international competition forced European industry and economy to make more rational use of manpower.*

After 1973 *the balance of trade and payments* of the industrially developed countries deteriorated considerably. Between 1974 and 1983, with the exception of one or two years, the balance of payments of the OECD and EU countries showed a deficit. The deficit was particularly big in 1974, 1976 and 1980–82. In comparison with their levels of unemployment and inflation, greater polarization was observable among the EU countries in terms of their balance of payments. While France and Italy in 1973–1975 had a considerable balance of payments deficit, West Germany and the Benelux countries managed to maintain a balance of payments surplus. One major cause of the balance problems was the big increase in oil bills, which, despite a reduction of nearly 4% in oil import from 1973 to 1974, rose from $11.8 bn to $31.5 bn. There was also an internal reason for the deterioration of the balance of payments; Germany's favourable position was due to its significant internal trade surplus with Italy, France and Great Britain. Between 1979 and 1982 most of the member countries showed a balance of payments deficit, and this applied to West Germany as well (in 1979–81). By contrast, in 1980–82 Great Britain's due to its self-sufficiency in oil realized a substantial surplus.

In 1973–75 the Community suffered a 14% loss in its *terms of trade*, and in 1979–81 a loss of 7%. With some fluctuation, France's terms of trade deteriorated between 1973 and 1984 by 25.5%, Spain's by 25%, Portugal's by 21.5%, West Germany's by 15.5%, and those of Italy and Greece by 15%. At the same time, between 1974 and 1983 the UK, as a producer and exporter of oil and natural gas, gained an improvement of its terms of trade 19%, and those of Holland, an exporter of gas, stayed more or less on the same level throughout the period.

1.3. THE RESTORATION OF ECONOMIC STABILITY

From the beginning of the 1980s there was a certain improvement in the economic performance of the EU countries, and their economies stabilized between 1984 and 1989 (European Commission 1991). At the same time, in many respects the EU developed in a less favourable way than its main competitors in the world economy. Factors at company, national and Community level all played a part in the process. Especially from the 1980s onwards the company sphere made great efforts to adapt: production bases and product structures were modernized, and significant organization and rationalization measures were taken in the interest of improving competitiveness. National governments gave more determined support to the adaptation process, and every government took drastic steps to reduce inflation and the deficit in the state sector.

From the mid-1980s the announcement of the program of the single internal market had a beneficial effect on development in the EU. After 1985 the fall in oil prices was a positive external factor. *After 1983 relatively moderate recovery was experienced in the EU: between 1983 and 1987 growth in the real economy did not reach the level of 3% in any year* (on average it was 2.4%). The upswing after 1983 which was fairly prolonged in the US and Japan did not take place in the EU; in the period 1983–89 in both these countries average annual growth was above 4%. In the majority of EU countries the recovery was limited to 1988 and 1989 (4% and 3%), and in 1990 real growth slowed again to 2.8%.

The most noticeable development in the period after 1983 was the control of the inflationary processes. Between 1974 and 1984 the level of inflation in the EU was 10.6% on average. Between 1985 and 1991 it was successfully brought down to 4.6%, and in the three most favourable years of this period, 1986–1988 (3.6% annually) they returned to the level of the early 1960s. The plunge in oil prices undoubtedly played a part in this. Really spectacular performance was achieved by West Germany and Holland between 1984 and 1988, with a level of inflation of around 2%, which can be regarded as virtually inflation-free growth (they were exceptionally successful, actually producing negative inflation: consumer prices in Germany fell by 0.2% in 1986, and in Holland by 0.9% in 1987). After 1983 the French government carried out a radical economic policy which resulted in the stabilization of inflation at about 3% after 1986. After 1986 inflation in Italy stood at 5–6%, a significant reduction from the 1974–83 average of 17%.

In contrast to all this, *there was no real improvement in the employment situation.* The unemployment level of over 10% that characterized the mid-1980s was reduced somewhat only by the recovery of 1988–89 (to 9.7% in 1988, and to 8.4% by 1990). During this period unemployment was exceptionally high in Spain (20.1% between 1984 and 1989) and Ireland (17.4%), while in the same years in Portugal, West Germany, Denmark and Greece the level was typically around just 6–7%. There was little reliable evidence for a correlation between low inflation and high unemployment, or *vice versa*.

After 1983 there was an improvement in the EU countries' balance of payments. With regard to the balance of external trade the situation of the member countries remained strongly polarized: in contrast to the surpluses amassed by Germany and the Benelux countries, chronic balance of payments problems were experienced by Italy, Greece and the UK. These problems were both internal and external in origin. In the great majority of the member countries the terms of trade improved significantly after 1984 (by 16% in Germany, 20% in Spain, 12% in France and 18% in Italy between 1984 and 1991).

1.4. NEW TENDENCIES AND EFFORTS IN THE 1990s

The period that began in the early 1990s started with negative processes as far as economic growth and unemployment were concerned. From 1991, Europe's economy fell into recession, intensified by the 'transition crisis' in the CEE countries, and made worse by the unexpectedly high costs of Germany's unification. The persistence of structural problems, and the Maastricht decisions relating to monetary integration (monetary restrictions) meant that the EU's macroeconomic performance continued to be moderate. From the 1990s it became increasingly clear that unlike the US, *the EU was incapable of exploiting the dynamizing effects of the 'new economy'.*

In most of the member countries the slowing-down became obvious from 1991 and lasted until 1993. GDP growth slowed to 1.7% for 1991, 1.2% for 1992 and –0.4% for 1993. Among the leading countries only Great Britain saw a recovery beginning in 1993 (1.8%), while in the majority of the member countries GDP declined. *After 1994 recovery started* in most of the countries, but the rate of growth has remained relatively low, stabilizing at about 2.5% annually (European Commission 2001).

After 1990 unemployment rose again, from 8.2% to 10.7% in 1993, peaking at 11.1% in 1994, and remained around that level. Only from *1998 was it brought just below 10% again* and has since steadily fallen in every member country; it reached 8.3% in 2000 and could fall to around 7% in coming years. In the first half of the 1990s there were huge differences in the unemployment situation of the member countries: in the worst year, 1994, for example, the rate was 24.1% in Spain, 16.6% in Finland and 15.6% in Ireland while at the time it was just 3.8% in Austria, 6.9% in Portugal and 7.1% in Holland. Some countries managed to bring it down to around 3% by early 2000s (Ireland, Netherlands or Austria).

In the area of inflation, the tendency that began in the previous period continued, and further spectacular improvement took place. The rise in consumer prices fell below 3% for 1994, and with a level of 1.5% in 1999 and 2000 we are really justified in calling this *inflation-free development.* Though it has not been possible to maintain the *target level of 2% inflation* set when the euro was introduced, no significant increase in consumer prices has taken place. Particularly spectacular improvement has been seen in Greece, where from a level of 20% in 1990–91 the rate of inflation was reduced to 9.8% by 1995 and since 1999 has remained below 3%.

The international financial crisis of 1998 *had no real impact* on the macroeconomic performance of the EU economies. A certain slowing of economic growth rates (e.g. in Germany and Italy) was rather the result of internal factors, while in respect of other indices (inflation and the balance of payments), improvement continued. The crisis-stricken countries of the Far East and Latin America, and also Russia, being marginal partners of the EU, did not materially influence the economic situation of the EU countries.

It was a favourable circumstance that in this period oil prices fell to a historically low level, which helped to slow the rate of inflation. In addition, economic policies, with a view to the launch of EMU and participation in the euro zone, concentrated all their efforts on inflation reduction and budget-balancing. In connection with the single internal market established in 1992 certain measures aimed at structural improvement and enhanced efficiency had their effect, protecting the real economy to some extent against the consequences of the external financial crisis.

Certain general characteristics of development in the 1990s seem to be becoming long-term ones, and may determine development in the period ahead:

1. Long-term growth in the EU countries has slowed to about 2.5%, which is well below its growth performance in earlier periods and that of its main competitors. An acceleration of economic growth can only be achieved through more dynamic development of the new economy.

2. In the countries of the Union rates of investment have steadily declined, from a level of 23% (in GDP terms) in the 1960s and 1970s to 20% in the 1980s, dipping below 19% after 1991. This is 10% less than the proportion in Japan, which is about 30%. From the beginning of the 1990s long-term nominal interest rates were about 20–25% higher than those in the US, and almost double the level of interest rates in Japan. Though they have come down, the situation at the beginning of the 2000s was the same. Compared with the low American interest rates (around 1.5%), the level in the EU (about 3%) is a significant disadvantage.

3. In the EU countries, in comparison with the other developed countries, the relation between economic growth and job creation has been relatively weak. Between 1970 and 1992 there was hardly any difference in growth between the EU and the US, yet five times more jobs were created in the US. Structural unemployment is relatively high. In the period between 1991 and 1994, 4 million jobs disappeared in the EU, and the number of unemployed reached 17 million. Between 1991 and 1994 the average rate of employment fell by 4% in the Union, while in the four years between 1995 and 1998 growth in employment was less than 2%. Job creation accelerated only from the end of 1990s.

4. The EU countries' economic structure did not adapt sufficiently to global challenges. The Union's competitiveness deteriorated, especially in comparison with the US. It lost export market share, and was slow in developing new products and bringing scientific results to the market.

There is often talk in the EU about *the need for a so-called new European model of sustainable development* (European Commission 1993). This would suppose significant modification of micro- and macroeconomic strategies and policies. The EU has to adapt to the challenges of the new technological revolution, which involves far-reaching changes in technologies, employment and skills requirements. *The economy is becoming increasingly knowledge-based;* the possession and acquisition of information is a decisive factor in success. The world of multimedia is about to introduce changes so radical that their significance can only be compared to that of the first industrial revolution. Special attention must be paid to the development and application of new techniques, particularly the construction of the so-called European 'information highway' (information technologies, audiovisual technologies, etc.), which will form the arteries of the economy of the future. The e-Europe program was one attempt to formulate these aims.

All this demands gradual, systematic change in economic policies, especially in the areas of indirect taxation, fiscal regulation, the internal market and international trade and cooperation. At sectoral level *economic policy and environmental considerations must be harmonized* in the areas of energy utilization, transport, agriculture and industry. The ultimate aim of the new model of economic development is to harmonize the economic frameworks with sustainable growth, greater competitiveness, a high level of employment and a healthier environment, in a society in which everyone can take an active part.

The reasons of past failures of economic policies have been mainly of a structural nature, and will not be easy to eliminate them in the future either. With the creation of the euro-zone, the EU finds itself in a new situation.

REFERENCES

European Commission (1991) *European Economy.* December 1991. Brussels.

European Commission (1993) *Growth, Competitiveness, Employment. The Challenges and Ways Forward into the 21st Century.* White Paper, Commission of the European Communities. Bulletin. Supplement 6/93.

European Commission – EUROSTAT (2000) *A Community of Fifteen: key figures.* Office for Official Publications of the European Communities. Luxembourg.

European Commission (2000) *2001 Broad Economic Policy Guidelines.* European Economy No. 72.

European Commission DG Trade (2002a) Bilateral Trade Relations. Brussels.

European Commission DG Trade (2002b) Multilateral Issues. Trade and Investment. Brussels.

DE LA MAHOTIÈRE, S. (1970) *Towards One Europe.* Pelican, London.

MÜLLER, J. and OWEN, N. (1989) *The Effect on Trade of Plant Size. The European Internal Market.* Oxford University Press, Oxford.

OECD (1977) *Economic Outlook.* No. 22, December 1977. OECD, Paris.

OWEN, J. (1983) *Economies of Scale. Competitiveness and Trade Pattern in the European Community.* Clarendon Press, Oxford.

PINDER, J. (1991) *The Building of a Union.* Oxford University Press, Oxford.

TSOUKALIS, L. (1991) *The New European Economy.* Oxford University Press, Oxford.

VIII.

THE EU'S FOREIGN TRADE RELATIONS

BY

MÁRK BATÓ–TIBOR PALÁNKAI

1. THE FRAMEWORKS OF TRADE RELATIONS

The EU is the world's biggest trade and economic grouping: its trade with external countries accounts for about 1/5 of total world trade.

The EU countries are *structurally very open economies*. In 1998 the 15 countries' average import and export of goods and services amounted to approximately 40% of the members' GDP. Some highly developed small countries (Belgium, Holland and Ireland) are characterized by a particularly high degree of openness (50–70%), but the level of openness is considerable in the bigger countries (Germany, France, the UK and Italy) as well (25–30%). Understandably, structural openness correlates with the size and the level of development of the countries. The opening of these economies was particularly marked between the beginning of the 1970s and the mid-1980s. This relative openness, together with the internal integration processes indicates the important role of the international division of labour in these economies, which is a basic factor in their high level of development and efficiency of their economy. Foreign capital investment has played a crucial role in their openness.

Opinions are now divided regarding the *openness of the Union's trade policy*. The EU counts as an average region of the world in terms of customs tariff levels; only the protectionist common agricultural policy can be considered very strict. Since the Tokyo round, average tariffs on industrial products have been 4.7% in the EU, 4.4% in the US, and 2.8% in Japan. "It is a paradox of the present trade policy debate that where special measures such as VERs or anti-dumping duties are not applied, EC trade policy is actually very liberal. Even for Japan and the USA, which do not benefit from any trade concessions beyond the standard GATT obligations, the operational rates of tariff are low" (HOLMES and SMITH 1992: 192). Fears of a "fortress Europe" have basically been proved unfounded by the single European market created in 1992.

The EU has *intensive trade relations with countries all over the world.* About 85% of these relations in the sphere of trade are concentrated on industrially developed countries, and the situation is similar with regard to capital flows. The developing countries' share, which at the time when the Community was formed amounted to more than 1/4 of its trade, by the beginning of the 1990s had shrunk to around 12%. The CEE countries' share of Community trade was formerly small. With the association agreements, from the 1990s this situation has gradually changed. The 2–3% share in EU foreign trade that the 10 candidate countries had at the end of the 1980s had grown to 12–13% by the beginning of the 2000s. The candidate countries have thereby become strategic partners of the EU.

After 1999, with the introduction of the euro, the Union's trade with its internal partners became internal trade. Taking this into account, the following table shows the proportions of EU trade with external countries.

Table 1. The Union's foreign trade according to partners

Partners	EU export (€ bn)				EU import (€ bn)			
	1990	1997	1998	1999	1990	1997	1998	1999
	390.6	720.7	729.6	758.5	439.4	672.4	709.4	772.5
	Area's share in EU export (%)				Area's share in EU import (%)			
US	21.2	19.6	21.9	23.8	20.8	20.5	21.3	20.3
Japan	6.3	5.0	4.3	4.6	11.7	8.9	9.2	9.1
EFTA	15.3	10.8	11.5	11.4	13.3	12.0	11.3	10.5
CEE	6.2	12.1	13.5	13.1	5.4	9.0	10.1	10.3
CIS	:	4.7	4.0	2.7	:	4.7	3.9	3.6
Africa	11.9	7.2	8.0	7.4	11.6	8.4	7.4	7.0
Latin America	4.3	6.3	6.7	5.9	6.2	5.2	4.9	4.7
Dynamic Asian Economies	7.9	10.8	8.2	7.9	8.2	10.1	10.8	10.7
China	1.5	2.3	2.4	2.5	2.6	5.6	5.9	6.4
Middle East	7.9	7.1	6.8	6.3	6.0	4.5	3.7	4.0
Oceania	2.6	2.3	2.2	2.2	1.6	1.4	1.5	1.3
ACP	4.5	2.8	3.1	2.8	4.8	3.4	3.0	2.8
Mediterranean area	12.4	11.6	11.9	11.2	10.1	8.5	8.0	7.9
ASEAN	4.4	6.3	4.2	3.8	4.0	6.9	7.2	6.3
OPEC	9.6	7.2	6.6	5.9	10.6	7.8	6.1	6.2
NAFTA	24.9	22.6	25.2	27.3	23.8	22.9	23.6	22.7

Source: Eurostat, Comext and IMF, DOTS.

In terms of its trade balance the EU has produced an uneven performance over the past decade, and it appears to be especially vulnerable to the effects of recessions and disturbances in the world economy. The trade balance is particularly sensitive with regard to certain developed partners and the oil-exporting countries.

Table 2. The Union's foreign trade balance according to partners

Partners	€ bn				as % total trade*			
	1990	1997	1998	1999	1990	1997	1998	1999
	390.6	720.7	729.6	758.5	439.4	672.4	709.4	772.5
	–48.9	48.4	20.2	–14.0	–5.9	3.5	1.4	–0.9
US	–8.7	3.4	9.3	23.5	–5.0	1.2	3.0	7.0
Japan	–26.9	–23.7	–34.1	–35.4	–35.5	–24.7	–35.2	–33.8
EFTA	1.1	–2.4	3.6	4.9	0.9	–1.5	2.2	2.9
CEE	0.5	26.7	26.7	20.4	1.0	18.1	15.7	11.4
CIS	:	1.7	1.0	–7.4	:	2.6	1.8	–15.2
Africa	–4.5	–4.7	5.4	1.6	–4.6	–4.3	4.9	1.5
Latin America	–10.1	10.5	13.6	8.6	–23.0	13.2	16.2	10.6
Dynamic Asian Economies	–5.2	9.5	–16.9	–22.1	–7.8	6.5	–12.3	–15.5
China	–5.6	–21.0	–24.4	–30.2	–32.4	–38.9	–41.3	–44.2
Middle East	4.5	21.1	22.8	17.1	7.9	26.0	30.1	21.7
Oceania	2.9	7.3	5.3	7.1	16.7	28.5	20.1	26.4
ACP	–3.6	–2.6	1.2	0.2	–9.3	–6.0	2.7	0.5
Mediterranean area	4.3	26.4	29.5	24.2	4.6	18.7	20.5	16.6
ASEAN	–0.4	–0.7	–20.7	–19.6	–1.1	–0.8	–25.5	–25.2
OPEC	–9.1	0.0	4.2	–3.0	–10.8	0.0	4.6	–3.3
NAFTA	–7.1	8.6	16.6	32.2	–3.5	2.7	4.7	8.4

* Import and export.

Source: Eurostat, Comext and IMF, DOTS.

In the past decade the balance of trade with the US has steadily improved. In terms of its trade balance the EU is in the worst position with regard to Japan and China. Surpluses have recently tended to arise particularly in trade with Central and Eastern Europe. The surplus achieved with the candidate countries has been of strategic importance for the EU's world trade position. The success of Hungary's transformation and structural modernization is shown by the fact that since 1997 it has had a trade surplus with the European Union.

2. THE COMMON COMMERCIAL POLICIES

The Treaty of Rome declared trade policy to be Community policy. The common commercial policy is the responsibility of the Commission, subject to the approval of the Council. This means that in commercial policy matters the Council can take decisions only on the initiative and recommendation of the Commission, and from the beginning has decided on a majority basis. Commission proposals can be rejected only by a unanimous vote of the Council. In the area of trade policy EU statutes and regulations are valid without the approval of the national parliaments. Thus, for example, the Commission can conclude trade agreements. (For this reason the trade policy part of Hungary's association did not require ratification by the national parliaments, and it was possible to put it into effect on March 1, 1992.) Under the provisions of the Single European Act, the Commission's trade and cooperation agreements require the majority approval of the European Parliament.

The common commercial policy has many components, and is based on certain trade policy instruments:

– common external tariffs, deriving from the customs union; they were completed by 1968;

– the application of certain preferential customs duties (e.g. GSP);

– the imposition of quantitative quotas on external partners (from the creation of the single European market in 1992, this sphere of jurisdiction, with the abolition of the national quantitative restrictions, finally came under the authority of the Union);

– the concluding of trade agreements with other countries or trade groupings (EFTA, ASEAN, Gulf states and Mediterranean agreements);

– representation of the Community and the member countries in international trade forums, where it conducts negotiations on behalf of the member states (GATT);

– the EU sets rules of procedure in connection with subventions, unfair competition and suppression of dumping (anti-dumping measures belong to the Commission's sphere of authority; national governments can initiate them only in cases of emergency, and they can be invalidated by the Commission);

– restrictions of a non-tariff nature.

"A common trade policy, moreover, is *desirable* in so far as it strengthens the bargaining power of the Community. Small member states in particular benefit from this: on their own they would be vulnerable to US and Japanese pressure" (MCALEESE 1990: 422).

One of the weaknesses of the common commercial policy has been that it did not cover non-tariff barriers, while they played a substantial role in trade relations. So it has been progressively diluted as tariffs have been reduced in the framework of GATT agreements.

3. TYPES OF EU TRADE RELATIONS

In practice, the EU's foreign trade relations are carried on within institutional or contractual frameworks. Its cooperation with various countries can be categorized under different type of trade policy system.

3.1. NON-DISCRIMINATORY SYSTEMS

These are typical mainly of relations with non-European developed countries (the US, Japan, Australia, etc.). In institutional terms these relations are covered by the GATT frameworks (WTO), and are based on *the most-favoured-nation principle*. This group of countries is also linked by OECD membership. *The principle of national treatment* also ensures freedom from discrimination.

As a result of the measures and liberalizations carried out within the GATT framework, the rules of the game have been established and barriers have gradually been dismantled. Tariffs on industrial products have come down from about 40% at the end of the 1940s to a level of around 5% (as a result of the Tokyo round). Thanks to the Uruguay round, trade in services and intellectual products is becoming better regulated. The protective and trade-distorting role of tariffs is becoming increasingly marginal. In the agricultural sphere, however, the EU continues to exercise strong protectionism. Despite the principle of equal treatment, its policy contains discriminatory elements.

The EU has particularly close trade relations with the United States. In the economic field the large volume of mutual capital investment represents a considerable degree of integration in the microsphere. From the political and security points of view this cooperation has close frameworks in NATO. Through relatively substantial trade and investment the EU has close ties with Japan as well. In addition to the trade deficit, capital investment is also asymmetrical: European investment in Japan is minimal. European microintegration has widespread Euro-Atlantic and indeed global extensions.

Non-discriminatory relations are in some cases regulated by cooperation agreements. Besides application of the most-favoured-nation clause, these can extend to financial and technical cooperation. The 1988 Gulf cooperation agreement (in which Bahrein, Kuwait, Oman, Qatar, Saudi Arabia and the United Arab Emirates took part) and the 1988 Trade and Cooperation Agreement between Hungary and the EC can be included in this category.

Non-discriminatory procedures are implemented by the various sectoral agreements, chiefly for certain sensitive products.

3.2. PREFERENTIAL SYSTEMS

Relations based on preferential agreements are characteristic in cooperation with mainly the Latin American and Asian developing countries, and the Mediterranean region. These are partly based on the *General System of Preferences* (GSP).

The EU applies the GSP fairly widely and liberally, and in some cases ties to political conditions. The GSP was initiated in 1971, and about 150 countries are its beneficiaries. Up to defined quotas industrial products are duty-free, and the Union's GSP extends to 40,000 items. Products are categorized as sensitive or non-sensitive. Special quotas are applied to the roughly 140 products classed as sensitive. Since 1986, countries with per capita income of $2,000 or more, and products that account for 20% or more of EU import (10% in the case of textiles), are excluded from the concessions. The EU also applies the GSP to about 400 agricultural products, but products covered by the Common Agricultural Policy are excluded.

At the same time, for the regulation of preferential trade the EU also has *bilateral trade agreements* with most countries. These give concessions on tariffs and volume quotas, and reciprocity is regulated by contract. More or less free access is allowed for industrial products, while restrictions are maintained for sensitive goods and agricultural produce.

Comprehensive application of preferential treatment characterizes the EU's Mediterranean policy and trade agreements. The Mediterranean countries, without exception, are either moderately developed or can be classed as developing (the majority of the southern countries of the basin).

In 1972 the EC approved its so-called *global Mediterranean policy*. In accordance with the original concept, the EC would replace its various partnership and trade agreements with the countries of the zone with a uniform partnership construction, in the framework of which it aimed at customs union and full membership for the northern countries of the basin (including Cyprus and Malta). The countries of the southern coast would form an industrial free trade area, and depending on their level of development would have been granted a longer period for counter-liberalization. The EC promised concessions on about 85% of the agricultural exports of the Mediterranean countries. The Mediterranean partnership agreement offered industrial, technical and financial cooperation and assistance, and would have sought solutions to the problems of the 3 million guest-workers employed in the EC.

The Southern EU member countries have particular interest in Mediterranean policy and relations, but problems stem from the fact that most of the Mediterranean countries are agricultural exporters, and their products compete with those of the EU's members in the region. The situation is similar with regard to financial assistance, and the problems of guest-workers. The success of the Mediterranean policy is largely dependent on a settlement in the Middle East.

In 1992 the EU announced its so-called *new Mediterranean policy*. The "Euro–Maghreb partnership" approved at the June 1992 summit in Lisbon offers the countries concerned wide-ranging free trade, and extends to political dialogue and technical, economic, financial and cultural co-operation. The new policy was to some extent a reaction to Morocco's application for membership. In 1987 it was easy to reject the application on the formal basis that Morocco was not a 'European country', but it could not be left entirely without a response. Problems are caused by the constant flood of emigrants from the countries of North Africa. On the other hand, investment is discouraged by the region's internal political and social instability (including the growth of Islamic extremism).

The more developed 'northern' countries of the Mediterranean basin (Greece, Spain and Portugal) became full members by the 1980s. The EC signed preferential trade agreements with Israel and Yugoslavia. At the beginning of the 1990s the only Mediterranean countries the EC had not entered contractual relations with were Albania and Libya. Yugoslavia's successor states and Albania now have partnership agreements or a good chance not just of association but of EU membership some time in the future.

A further important breakthrough in the Mediterranean policy was the process launched in 1995 at the *Barcelona conference*. The EU's foreign (trade) policy towards the Mediterranean countries became more uniform and thereby more transparent. The conference covered the Union's relations with the Maghreb countries (Algeria, Morocco and Tunisia), the Mashreq countries (Egypt, Lebanon, Jordan and Syria) and also with Israel.

Among the results of the Barcelona process mention must be made of the introduction of a new financial instrument, the MEDA with the aim of promoting economic and social structural change in the non-EU Mediterranean countries. *In the area of trade, asymmetrical liberalization* continued to dominate as a means of development, with gradual elimination of the existing restrictions. The declared aim as a result of this is the formation of a free trade zone by 2010. In the course of this asymmetrical liberalization the EU, of course, protects its own economy in sensitive areas (agriculture, textiles), often to the detriment of the aim of development. Further, traditional development policy means are also made use of, such as *rural development* and *support for professional training*.

The countries of Latin America and Asia also receive general preferences, but the trade agreements with them are of a 'non-preferential' nature.

The Cooperation and Partnership Agreements with the republics of the former Soviet Union can be regarded as preferential agreements. Most of the agreements signed came into force at the end of the 1990s.

3.3. FREE TRADE SYSTEMS

The EU's many partnerships based on free trade include unilateral and reciprocal agreements, partial ones and comprehensive ones. Reciprocal, comprehensive liberalization is achieved through full membership, which really became complete with the creation of the single European market. In the framework of the EU's association agreements, liberalization is partial mainly because agriculture is left out. The European Economic Area was based on reciprocal liberalization, and in some cases this is considered the only example of external free trade. Typical examples of asymmetrical liberalization are the Lomé Conventions, signed with 71 developing countries. Some classifications assign these to the category of 'preferential agreements', since the liberalization is unilateral and limited in duration. The CEE association agreements (the European Agreements) are asymmetrical in their liberalization process, but after implementation (for non-agricultural products) they become reciprocal.

The first association agreement concluded by the EC was with *Greece*. The agreement was signed on March 30, 1961, and came into force on November 1, 1962. The association agreement was for a period of 22 years, which meant that Greece ought to have become a full member of the EC by 1984. The essence of the association was trade liberalization, and Greece received financial assistance. Under the terms of the agreement Greece undertook to liberalize its import of EC goods, and adopt the EC's common external tariffs. The association agreement also prescribed the provision of a long-term, low-interest loan to Greece, through the European Investment Bank, of $125 million.

After the fascist military junta came to power in 1967 the association agreement was partially frozen, and it was revived only on November 1, 1974, after the defeat of the military junta. Industrial and technical co-operation was renewed, and financial assistance resumed. After this Greece presented its application for full membership, which meant bringing forward the 1984 deadline. Greece became a full member of the EC on January 1, 1981.

In September 1963 the EC signed an association agreement with *Turkey* that came into force on December 1, 1964. This time the aim was the formation of a customs union and Turkey's full membership of the common market. Because Turkey's situation was equivalent to that of a developing country, the association began with a 5-year preparation period. In this framework some Turkish goods were given preferential treatment by the EU, and the country received a loan, under favourable conditions, of EUA 175 million from the European Investment Bank. The aim was to achieve a national income level of $180 per capita.

The Turkish association entered the so-called transitional phase with the Ankara agreement of 1969. Under the terms of this the EC undertook an obligation to remove import duties at once for Turkish industrial products, with a few exceptions (textiles, refined oil products), and liberalization was even extended to some agricultural produce. Trade liberalization on the EU's part was carried out by September 1971. In return Turkey was obliged to abolish import duties on a proportion (about 55%)

of its imports from the EU over 12 years, and the remainder within 22 years. Turkey also had to abolish quantitative restrictions on common market goods over 22 years. In the course of the transition period Turkey received further loans from the European Investment Bank.

In 1987 Turkey submitted its application for membership. Not only did the Commission question the country's 'Europeanness', but for various political reasons (concern about human rights and the state of democracy) as well as economic ones the possibility of its admission in the near future was rejected. In accordance with the association agreement, from 1995 Turkey entered into customs union with the EU.

As a result of the enlargements of the 1990s, and ever closer relations with Central and Eastern Europe, the need to reconsider EU-Turkish relations grew more and more pressing. Positive experience gained in the course of the operation of the customs union also encouraged the forging of closer cooperation. Mainly because of its considerable political and human rights deficit the country could not be treated similarly to the other applicants for admission. For these reasons it has still not been possible to begin accession negotiations.

The EC's association agreements with *Malta* from April 1, 1971 and with *Cyprus* from January 1, 1973 are still in force. They are broadly similar in content; both are based on the principle of 'one-sided liberalization'. Both agreements have as their long-term aim the creation of a customs union with the EU, and full membership. Malta's membership is formally problem-free, but since the country earlier withdrew its application, for a while the question did not feature on the agenda. Membership for Cyprus is made difficult by the conflict between Greece and Turkey, but on the basis of the talks that began in 1998 it is one of the countries with a chance in the coming round of enlargement. In 1999 Malta also joined the group of countries engaged in accession negotiations.

3.4. RELATIONS WITH EFTA AND THE EUROPEAN ECONOMIC AREA

The European Free Trade Association (EFTA) was originally set up in 1960 by seven countries of Western Europe (Austria, Denmark, Great Britain, Norway, Portugal, Switzerland and Sweden) as an answer to the EEC. As a free trade zone, EFTA was a loose economic grouping, since with liberalized internal trade the member countries continued to pursue independent tariff and trade policies towards the outside world. The free trade agreements applied only to the industrial sphere, and with only a few exceptions did not extend to agricultural produce. EFTA was not formally a common market, and flows of capital and labour were not comprehensively deregulated. At the same time, liberalization of capital movements was guaranteed by the OECD agreements, and free movement of labour by other agreements (among the Scandinavian countries). EFTA did not aim at achieving economic and political union, and did not establish integration institutions.

From the outset EFTA was of a temporary nature. Great Britain, which launched the organization and played a leading role in it in view of its economic weight, applied for admission to the EC as early as 1961. True, it was admitted only 12 years later, on January 1, 1973, but the future of the Association became uncertain. In 1993, Ireland and Denmark also joined the EC. In a referendum, Norway said no to joining. Portugal joined the EC in 1986, while later EFTA was joined by Finland and Iceland.

In connection with the breakaway of Great Britain and Denmark, in the course of 1972 and 1973 the EC concluded industrial free trade agreements with all the EFTA member countries (with each country separately, not with EFTA). In accordance with these agreements tariff reductions took place gradually over four and a half years, and as a result *by July 1, 1977 industrial free trade was established between the EC and the EFTA countries.* In industry, after the accession of Greece (1981) and Spain (1986) to the EC, market liberalization frameworks embraced the whole of Western Europe.

The basis of the free trade agreements was the EFTA countries' traditional close dependence on and cooperation with the EC. As early as the beginning of the 1970s almost 60% of EFTA's import was from the EC, and nearly 50% of its export went to EC countries. Inter-company contacts were traditionally close, and in the 1970s and 1980s, with the acceleration of the transnationalization processes, they expanded even further.

Despite the close integration of their real economies, right until the 1990s the present EFTA countries for several reasons strove to preserve their independence, and did not join the EC. Several countries (Austria, Finland, Switzerland and Sweden) renounced full membership in order to maintain their neutrality in a Community which, with the exception of Ireland, consisted of NATO members. Like Norway, a number of other countries (especially Switzerland) remained outside in order to safeguard their national sovereignty. In the case of other countries, structural weaknesses in their economy or fear for certain industries (fishing, in the case of Norway and Iceland) made them think twice about joining the integration. Switzerland, as a financial centre, wanted to preserve its special position in the international money markets, which participation in the monetary union would have put in doubt. By the 1990s, with the approach of the deadline for the establishment of the single European market in 1992, the question of closer cooperation between the two organizations was more seriously considered. It was also given urgency by the revolutionary changes in Central and Eastern Europe. After a long, hard process of bargaining and compromise, on October 22, 1991 the treaty establishing the European Economic Area (EEA) was signed by the EC and EFTA, but because of certain difficulties it came into force only on January 1, 1994, with 17 members (the EU plus Austria, Sweden, Norway, Finland and Iceland). In a referendum the people of Switzerland vetoed participation in the EEA.

The main points and measures in the treaty were as follows:

1. From 1993 within the EEA the movement of goods became completely free. This extended the 1992 single European market to the whole EEA. Regional free trade did not mean customs union; the EFTA countries continued to apply their differing national external tariffs. This was favourable from the point of view of outsiders, because instead of the EU's average 4.7% industrial external tariffs, the average EFTA tariff was just 2.3%. As a result it was necessary to retain the rule of origin (this was applied in connection with the free trade agreements as well). Border controls were not abolished between the EU and the EFTA countries either. The EFTA countries were not obliged to take part in the tax harmonization planned in the framework of the single European market.

2. There were separate regulations for trade in foodstuffs, coal and steel, as well as energy and fisheries products. The EFTA countries did not join in the common agricultural policy, to which they would have been net financial contributors.

3. From 1993 the citizens of the Area could freely take up residence, work and do business within the bloc. Professional qualifications were mutually recognized. Switzerland was originally allowed a 5-year grace period in which to alter its strict immigration rules and adopt the treaty.

4. Capital movements were completely liberalized, but the EFTA countries were given the possibility of retaining certain restrictions relating to direct investments and the purchase of real estate.

5. The EFTA countries adopted the EU regulations with regard to corporation law, environment protection, education, research and development, consumer protection and social policy. EFTA applies the EU competition regulations in antitrust matters, with regard to abuse of a dominant position, state procurement, mergers and state subventions. Fulfilling the EU regulations generally does not cause problems for EFTA, since in EFTA the level of support given to producers amounts on average to 2% of industrial output, whereas the corresponding figure in the EU is 6% (*The Economist*, October 26, 1991).

The establishment of the EEA involved 150 measures; two of these, fishing and transit routes, caused more disagreement between the EU and EFTA. The post-1973 treaties had established free trade in industrial products, and the EEA extended it to a wide range of services.

From the point of view of the fate of the agreement, it was a decisive development that most of the EFTA members (Austria, Sweden and Finland) became full members of the EU from 1995. As early as 1989, Austria had submitted its application for membership, and after 1991 its example was followed by Sweden, Finland and Norway. Only in the case of Iceland, which largely depends on its fishing industry, are there marked conflicts of interest; and it is uncertain when Switzerland may change its negative viewpoint. In 1994 in referenda the Austrians, Finns and Swedes said yes to joining, while the Norwegians rejected full membership for the second time since 1972. With the 1995 enlargement the importance of EFTA (Switzerland, Norway and Iceland) and therefore of the EEA became marginalized.

3.5. DISCRIMINATORY SYSTEMS

In the past, discriminatory treatment was applied by the EU in the case of the former socialist countries.

The main forms of discrimination are:

– special discriminating tariffs (in addition to GATT treatment);

– special quantitative restrictions (after Hungary became a GATT member in 1973, about 2000 such restrictions were retained);

– special, rigorous application of dumping procedures;

– control and prohibition of the transfer of advanced technologies on the COCOM lists (in practice, together with NATO and the other developed countries);

– the imposition of an embargo, usually for political reasons and with other developed countries (against the Soviet Union because of Afghanistan, and against Poland because of the 1981 MARSHALL Law).

From the end of the 1970s the EU implemented a so-called common commercial policy with regard to the then socialist countries, which chiefly meant that the member countries' former trade agreements lost their validity, and new trade agreements could only be concluded with the EU Commission. In the circumstances of the Cold War the socialist countries rejected EC 'recognition' (in the diplomatic sense), which also meant the rejection of the common commercial policy. As a result a peculiar ex lex situation developed, in which relations were governed partly by tacit adherence to some of the former agreements, and partly by the obligations of membership of international institutions (GATT, UNCTAD, etc.).

The discriminatory measures served to counterbalance the protectionist and discriminatory nature of centrally planned economies (CPEs) and state trading countries (STCs).

Because of the nature of central planning, it distorts market and trade relations:

– the choice of trading partners is based not on efficiency and other economic considerations but often on political ones, which are discriminatory and arbitrary;

– planned foreign trade severely restricts consumers' freedom of choice;

– the targets for production and foreign trade can be regarded as virtually quantitative quotas or restrictions;

– price-fixing, the wide range of subsidies, and the various forms of disguised taxes can be interpreted in practice as equivalent to tariffs and other trade barriers of a tariff nature;

– artificially low wages and other input prices severely distort cost conditions.

'Normalization' of relations with the then socialist countries began in the second half of the 1980s. As a result of the revolutionary events their character and frameworks changed with lightning speed. Between 1987 and 1991 Hungary changed over from its discriminatory system directly to a free trade (partnership) system (skipping the non-discriminatory and preferential systems – PHARE).

Discriminatory systems today are mostly applied on an individual basis in the case of the so-called least-favoured socialist or developing countries (Cuba, North Korea, Iraq and Libya).

4. ASSOCIATIONS WITH FORMER COLONIES

When the Treaty of Rome was signed, the members declared their former – mostly African – colonies associated territories. After the countries concerned gained their independence, in July 1963 a new association agreement (the Yaounde Convention), was signed; it was joined by the majority of the former associated colonies of the member countries (except for Guinea), and was subsequently renewed several times.

The EC's association agreements with African countries commenced with continued liberalization of trade (relations dated back to colonial times), and trade expansion. Free trade with those countries was only partially achieved; as in the case of agreements with other less developed countries, it was not reciprocal. Within the association framework the African countries, as developing countries, were allowed to retain their tariffs and quotas on imports from the EC countries; indeed, they could make them more restrictive, or they could reintroduce restrictions that had earlier been lifted. The association agreements allowed this in the interest of economic development, the protection of industry, standard-of-living policy considerations, and the increasing of budgetary revenues. Under the terms of the agreements the associated countries also received financial assistance and credits.

The Treaty of Rome provided for the establishment of the *European Development Fund,* the purpose of which was to give assistance to the associated territories and countries. The financial resources of the Fund were provided by the member countries, in accordance with appropriate quotas; these were raised in their own national currencies and paid into the common budget. The assistance provided by the Fund contributed chiefly to the financing of infrastructure and agricultural investments.

In1968 the EC signed an association agreement with the East African Community. The so-called *Arusha Agreement* was valid only until June 30,

1969. Parallel with the Yaounde Convention, the countries of East Africa signed a new agreement under which the second Arusha Agreement also expired on January 31, 1975.

In connection with the 1973 enlargement of the EC the question of expansion of the association agreements was brought up. From 1975, with the expiry of these agreements, the EC offered the possibility of association to the majority of the developing countries of the British Commonwealth as well. From the outset the Asian countries of the Commonwealth (India, Pakistan, Malaya, Sri Lanka and Singapore) were excluded from the possibility of association. Negotiations concerning the new treaty began in July 1973. After hard and lengthy bargaining, the agreement was concluded on February 1, 1975 between the EC and 46 African, Caribbean and Pacific (ACP) developing countries, and on February 28 was embodied in the *Lomé Convention* signed in the capital of Togo. (The developing countries objected to their relations being described as association, so the term 'convention' was used instead.) After ratification, the convention came into force in April 1976. The trade agreements had been valid since August 1975.

The Lomé Conventions were fixed-term associations, concluded at first for just 5 years. The Second Lomé Convention came into force on March 1, 1980 for a further 5-year period. This time 58 developing countries joined the Convention (in 1980 it had 61 participants). The Third Lomé Convention was signed for the period 1985–1989, and the Fourth Lomé Convention was valid for a 10-year term (1990–2000). By 1994 the number of participating countries had risen to 70.[1] The majority of the ACP countries are backward countries with small populations. In this group Nigeria is in a special position: it is a major oil-producing country, its population (close to 100 million) alone represents a quarter of the total population of the Lomé countries, and its trade a third of their total. The

[1] The Lomé Convention was signed by the following countries: *a)* The countries of the Yaounde Agreement: Burundi, Cameroon, the Central African Republic, Chad, the People's Republic of Congo, Benin, Gabon, the Ivory Coast, Mali, Mauritania, the Republic of Madagascar, Mauritius, Niger, Rwanda, Senegal, Somalia, Togo, Upper Volta (Burkina Faso) and Zaire. *b)* The countries of the Arusha Agreement: Kenya, Tanzania and Uganda (British Commonwealth countries). *c)* Other countries of the British Commonwealth: Botswana, Gambia, Ghana, Lesotho, Malawi, Nigeria, Sierra Leone, Swaziland, Zambia, the Bahamas, Barbados, Grenada, Guyana, Jamaica, Trinidad and Tobago, Fiji, Tonga and Western Samoa. *d)* Other countries: Ethiopia, Equatorial Guinea, Guinea, Guinea-Bissau, Liberia, Sudan, Angola, Antigua, Barbuda, Belize, the Dominican Republic, Mozambique, Namibia, Haiti, the Comoro Islands, the Cape Verde Islands, Papua-New Guinea, Sao Tomé and Principe, the Seychelles, Surinam, Djibouti, Dominica, the Solomon Islands, Tuvalu, St. Lucia, Kiribati, St. Vincent, Grenadine, New Hebrides (Vanuatu) and Zimbabwe.

highest per capita income is to be found in the Bahamas ($7,150 in 1985), Trinidad and Tobago ($6,010) and Barbados ($4,680). Altogether just 15 countries had a per capita income above $1,000; the majority belong to the so-called least-developed category; they include the Sahel countries, which suffer the most from famine.

4.1. THE MAIN MEASURES OF THE LOMÉ CONVENTIONS

The First Lomé Convention differed from its predecessors not only in its scope and form but also in its content. In the new agreement, compared with earlier ones, broad liberalization of trade was implemented. The Convention ensured free access to EC markets for the greater proportion of the exports of the ACP countries, and only certification of origin was demanded of them. Industrial goods enjoyed complete liberalization. With the exception of about 4% of EU imports, tariffs on agricultural produce were more or less abolished, but in the case of some products that came under Common Market agricultural regulations the import levies were retained, partially or wholly, with regard to the ACP countries. For certain agricultural products (beef, rum, bananas and sugar – about 40 in all), special agreements were signed. For EC companies the ACP countries guaranteed investment and settlement 'on a non-discriminatory basis'.

Compared with earlier agreements, an important new feature of the trade agreements was that the developing countries managed to secure *the abolition of the principle of reciprocity*. Thus the ACP countries were not burdened by any mutual liberalization obligations with regard to goods originating from the EC; in this matter they could decide on the basis of their own economic interests. They stipulated, however, that EC goods should not be given less favourable treatment (under the 'most-favoured nation' clause) than imports from other developed countries.

In the Second Lomé Convention trade liberalization was extended to 99% of the exports of the ACP countries, and the products affected by the common agricultural policy also received preferential treatment. Several countries received concessions for exports of vegetables, and the main exporters of beef (Kenya, Swaziland, Madagascar and Botswana) were granted an annual quota of 30 thousand tons. The regulations relating to certification of origin were more flexibly applied in the case of the least developed countries. The specification of 60% local (ACP) content applicable until the Third Lomé Convention was reduced to 45% (of the product's added value).

A new element in the Lomé Conventions was the *export-income stabilizing system* (STABEX). Its purpose was mainly to support the 'less developed, island or inland' developing countries (of the original 46, 34 fell into this category) which exported mainly just a few raw materials or agricultural products, and were vulnerable to wide fluctuations in their export income. Originally the export-income stabilizing system applied to 12 products (bananas, cocoa, coffee, coconuts, cotton, peanuts, undressed hides, sisal, tea, wood, palm products and iron ore), but under the Fourth Lomé Convention 48 products were given support. The STABEX system extended to every major agricultural product exported by the ACP countries. The STABEX support fund was gradually increased.

In accordance with the STABEX financing regulations, if income from these products fell below the average for the preceding 4 years, the ACP countries were entitled to financial support. This export-income guarantee took the form of direct financial assistance; thus it did not aim at price stabilization or direct market intervention. Every ACP country could benefit from the system, but with the exception of the 24 countries designated as the 'least developed', the others were obliged to repay any support received, if their export income rose above the average for the previous 4 years. This was abolished by the Fourth Convention. The grants were received by the governments.

In the Second Lomé Convention a new element was the so-called *MINEX* (or SYSMIN), created to support mining products. This system of support covered copper, cobalt, manganese, phosphates, bauxite, aluminium, tin and iron ore, the last-mentioned being transferred from the STABEX list. Later, uranium and gold were also included in the system. In the MINEX system it was not reduced income but reduced production that was the condition of support. A country became entitled to claim if on average in the previous 4 years a given mineral accounted for at least 15% of export (10% in the case of the least developed countries), and the drop in production or export capacity amounted to 10%. Under the terms of the Fourth Convention, any country where export income from these products amounted to 20% was entitled to assistance. Compensation took the form of loans on favourable conditions (repayment over 40 years, 1% interest, and a 10-year moratorium on repayment) to finance programs aimed at maintaining capacity. In addition, the EIB provided guaranteed loans to assist mining development in the ACP countries. By means of these loans they sought to encourage and guarantee private capital investments.

Within the framework of the Lomé Conventions the ACP countries received various kinds of financial assistance from the European Development Fund. These countries did not succeed in increasing the assistance substantially in subsequent Conventions. The increase in assistance was not proportionate to the growth in the number of participants, and the increase in inflation. In the course of time steps were taken to speed up the distribution of grants and make it more flexible. The expectations that the Lomé Conventions would be like the MARSHALL Plan or a sort of New Deal were not fulfilled. This was particularly the case in view of the fact that in the 1980s many of the Convention countries fell deeply into debt.

The Lomé Conventions did not substantially alter the world economy position or the structural problems of the developing countries taking part. "In economic terms, the Lomé Conventions have also faced criticism over their inability to deal effectively with the debt crisis of developing states, to empower ACP members to diversify and strengthen their economic activities by lessening their dependency on primary exports and more generally to prevent marginalization of developing states in the international economic system" (ARCHER and BUTLER 1992: 130).

In the given world economic situation, few of the ACP countries possessed really saleable products (like Nigeria's oil); most of the Convention signatories lost ground in the EC markets. The monocultural nature of trade remained unchanged: in the case of the majority of the ACP countries, one product accounted for more than one-third of export income. Just four products (oil, coffee, copper and cocoa) traditionally accounted for more than 50% of EC imports. Trade between the EC and the ACP countries was similarly concentrated in certain countries. Almost half of EC imports came from just 3 countries (Nigeria, Zaire and the Ivory Coast), and a significant proportion of EC exports to these countries, year in, year out, depended on Nigeria's export income.

Not only the size of their market share but also the ACP countries' balance of trade developed unfavourably. After the 1970s the ACP countries' trade surplus changed to a deficit, and the deficit was especially serious, if imports of oil products to the EC are disregarded. The value of the manufacturing industry trade conventions in favour of the developing countries was greatly reduced by the fact that they continued to be formal and were not related to actual trade flows. The Lomé Convention concessions relating to manufacturing industry products were devalued by the general preferences as well, and the EU's other free trade and association agreements. The Conventions' trade policy concessions have thus gradually crumbled away.

4.2. THE COTONOU AGREEMENT

In 2000, when the Fourth Lomé Convention ran out, international conditions were very different from those that had characterized the world economy at the beginning, in 1990. These changes and the above-mentioned experience gained in the course of the Conventions made it necessary to review relations between the EU and the ACP countries. In 2000 in Cotonou, the capital of Benin, a treaty was signed laying new foundations for relations between the two groups of countries. After ratification, the agreement was to come into force in 2002. The treaty rested on five pillars, that is, five priorities:

– *political dialogue to be pursued*

The aim of intensive political consultations is to avoid crises arising because of breaches of democracy, the rule of law and human rights. Particular attention is paid, in the carrying out of public functions, to promotion of 'good governance' and especially the elimination of the corruption that greatly reduces the effectiveness of development programs. A concrete program for achieving the latter aim is to be worked out.

– *involvement of civil society*

A change compared to the Lomé Conventions that is significant in every respect is the emphasis on the role of the civil sphere in relations. This pillar reflects a very important phenomenon of the last decade, the strengthening of the civil sector, which could contribute greatly to the success of development policy.

– *reduction of poverty*

This is the main aim of the new partnership, for which and through which the various sub-areas of cooperation must be coordinated.

– *the plan for a new trade system*

A system that will further liberalize trade between the ACP countries and the EU is to be established by 2008.

– *reform of the system of financial assistance*
Rationalization and simplification of the EDF and the programs relating to it.

Not only reform but the ensuring of continuity is very important, as is consistent handling of initiatives launched earlier, taking into account the interests of both parties. There has also been significant improvement with regard to the financial background. In addition to utilizing fund allocations not already drawn, the EU has supplemented them with a substantial amount of new resources for the coming period. This amounts to 25 billion euros for the period 2000–2007, which will enable grants to be substantially increased.

Table 3. Amounts of financial assistance in the Cotonou Agreement

Types of financial assistance	Assistance (in millions of euros)
Grants	10,000
Regional grants	1,300
Risk fund	2,200
9th EDF total	*13,500*
Left over from earlier EDF	9,900
EIB loans	1,700
Total	25,100

The agreement is valid for a period of 20 years, and is to be supplemented by four financial protocols to be signed at five-year intervals. A Council of Ministers consisting of representatives of the EU and ACP countries is to meet at least once a year, and if need be, adapt the agreement to changing circumstances.

The establishment of *a trade regime aimed at development* is based on application of the great amount of experience gained from the Lomé Conventions. The trade policy followed during the period of the Conventions did not achieve its aims: the developing countries did not improve their position in the world economy. For this reason the Cotonou Agreement set as its aim the establishment of a new trade system, which after an 8-year transition period would come into force in 2008 at the latest. During the transition period the former system would continue to operate.

Starting from 2000, the Community has been implementing gradual liberalization of elements of its import from the least developed countries, with the exception of sugar, beef and veal. This coincides with the Community's general policy towards the least developed countries, which aims at complete liberalization of its import from these countries by 2005. In addition, free trade negotiations are to be started with the ACP countries by 2008 at the latest, which must be followed by a long transition period of at least twelve years.

In contrast to trade regulation, *reform of financial assistance* is already familiar. This has been based on the experience gained in the course of the operation of the EDF. The operation of the various instruments of the Fund has shown significant differences, and they have not been harmonized. This has meant unnecessary difficulties for claimants and assessors alike, and has been reflected in their level of success. Program types are at least standardized at country level with regard to their operating mechanisms, and individual concrete programs are also assessed country by country, which makes for more successful coordination. A further important basic principle is the assignment of decisions to the lowest possible level, and evaluation of them according to their results. If need be, non-state organizations or individuals are also drawn into the financial support system. The aim is to activate local capacities, which are continuously evaluated by the Union on the basis of their performance.

The new program distinguishes two channels of EDF support. One conveys grants to the beneficiaries; the other supplies risk capital and loans to the private sector in the target countries. The plan specifies 10 billion euros for the first sub-program, in addition to which amount another 1.3 billion is available for regional programs with similar aims.

The beneficiaries receive their grants on a country-by-country basis, and have more freedom than formerly to use them as they see fit. The grants may be used to finance support for agriculture, sectoral programs, debt relief, supplementary support in the event of a sudden drop in export income, and indeed, in special cases, humanitarian assistance. There are no grants that are tied to specific, exclusive aims, and the new system provides the possibility of reallocation and modification of grant amounts if necessary. Coordination of these grants is carried out by the Commission together with the ACP recipients, through continuous assessment and review of the programs. The beneficiaries of the sums set aside for regional programs are the regions to be formed by the ACP countries, which will also have the possibility of concluding new trade agreements with the Union.

Investment activity is the other main component of the new support program, and is supervised by the European Investment Bank. The EU has allocated 2.2 billion euros to this program. It is important that according to the plans the program should become self-supporting in the long-term, that is, claims, which it is hoped will increase, should be covered by repayments.

The main aim of the sub-program is to support viable enterprises particularly in the private sector, but in justified cases a publicly-owned company may also be a beneficiary. In so doing the program assists privatization, promotes the development of the local financial sector and the local capital market, and encourages foreign capital investment and the investment of savings. The Fund undertakes a role especially in areas where capital requirements cannot be met from other sources, and in the case mainly of high-risk investments in which the private sector and local financing institutions are unable to participate. Support may take the form of a loan, share purchase or guarantee. Its aim of promoting the involvement of private capital through its operation is an important one.

There may be a possibility of interest-rate support, for specific social or environmental purposes. In addition to this allocation the EIB intends to activate its own resources in the ACP countries, which will mean a supplementary amount of 1.7 billion euros for the period 2000–2005.

Evaluation of countries takes place on the basis of two criteria: needs and performance. The former category includes per capita income, the level of debt and the degree of export dependence, while in the latter such aspects are examined as the country's achievements in the areas of institutional reform, utilization of resources and cooperation with the Community.

The STABEX and SYSMIN systems familiar from the Lomé Conventions have also undergone important changes. The allocation no longer contains sums set aside separately for these purposes; if need be, application can be made for support from the long-term grant budget. A further condition that has been formulated is that such support can be granted only if the worsened situation endangers the stability of the economy. The governments continue to be the beneficiaries.

Compared with the Lomé Conventions, here it is a matter not so much of reform of content but rather of the development of the operating mechanism, since in the past decades it has been the badly-organized structure of the program that has chiefly hindered the implementation of promising development aims.

The single European market may be beneficial for the ACP countries (in terms of prosperity and trade creation), but could also have many negative effects (trade diversion or increasing competition). There is concern about the increasing competition from the CEE countries (in textiles, and semi-processed goods), and their role in 'diverting' financial assistance and private investment. It is important to emphasize that the stabilization and modernization of Central and Eastern Europe should not take place at the expense of the poor developing countries. At the same time, only a strong and consolidated CEE will be capable of helping to solve the problems of the developing world.

REFERENCES

ARCHER, C. and F. BUTLER (1992) *The European Community*. Pinter Publishers, London.

HOLMES, P. and A. SMITH (1992) The EC, the USA and Japan: the trilateral relationship in the world context. D. A. DYKER (ed.), *The European Economy*. Longman, London.

MCALEESE, D. (1990) External trade policy. In A. M. EL-AGRAA (ed.), *Economics of the European Community*. Philip Allan, New York.

IX.

CENTRAL AND EASTERN EUROPE AND THE EUROPEAN UNION

1. ASSOCIATION AGREEMENTS BETWEEN CENTRAL AND EASTERN EUROPE AND THE EUROPEAN UNION

1.1. FROM 'EAST-WEST' RELATIONS TO ASSOCIATION

Up to the end of the 1980s, as far as the Central and East European region was concerned, internal economic relations within Europe were determined by the confrontation between the 'two systems'. Relations between the CMEA/COMECON countries and the EC were characterized by discrimination and lack of mutual recognition. In the centrally planned economies (CPEs) the state trading companies (STCs) were by their nature discriminatory, and in response the industrially developed countries applied discriminatory trade policies. In case of the EC, for Hungary, a GATT member from 1973, this meant that the most-favoured nation clause was only partially recognized, and for certain products (about 2000 in all), in addition to fixed quotas special tariffs and duties were imposed. The forms of discrimination applied to the COMECON countries showed fairly wide differences, depending on the internal planning system, GATT membership, and political considerations. Poland, Hungary and Romania were GATT members, while Bulgaria and the Soviet Union were not. Alone among the COMECON countries, Romania had a trade agreement with the EC, signed in 1980, based on partial liberalization. Yugoslavia had a particularly favourable trade agreement with the EC.

Against the COMECON countries dumping procedures were applied with special rigour, and their domestic prices were not recognized as reference prices. The COCOM high technology lists applied to Hungary too. Several COMECON countries were the object of embargoes from time to time (e.g. the Soviet Union because of Afghanistan, and Poland because of the 1981 state of emergency).

Relations between the EC and COMECON were largely unaffected by the détente that took place in the 1970s as a result of Helsinki. The COMECON countries did not accept the EC's common commercial policy, which placed relations under the jurisdiction of the Commission in Brussels. They also refused to grant the Brussels Commission diplomatic recognition. Changes began in the COMECON countries' policy after the death of Brezhnev in 1982, but real steps towards normalization were taken only after 1985, when Gorbachev came to power.

As early as the early 1980s, Hungary took steps to normalize relations with the EC. On Hungary's part real negotiations with the EC began in June 1987, and a so-called *trade and cooperation agreement* was signed on September 26, 1988. In the EC system of relations this was a new construction, and Hungary was the first country with which the EC signed such an agreement. Later, similar agreements were concluded with the other former socialist countries. Within the framework of the trade and cooperation agreement, the main result for Hungary was the gradual removal of the discriminatory 'special' quantitative restrictions formerly applied against it, which it was planned to implement in three stages (from January 1989, and January 1993) by December 31, 1995. Under the terms of the agreement Hungary received similar treatment to other industrial states (the US and Japan) i.e. *full application of the most-favoured-nation principle,* and passed from a discriminatory system to a non-discriminatory one. Approval of the agreement was an expression of the EC's recognition of Hungary's market economy reforms.

From 1989, as a result of the revolutionary changes taking place, the normalization and development of relations accelerated. At the Paris summit of the leading industrial powers on July 14, 1989 the decision was taken to launch the PHARE program (Pologne, Hongrie, Aide à la Reconstruction Economique), which was approved by all the OECD countries (G24). The EC Commission was asked to coordinate and direct the program, which gradually passed entirely into the jurisdiction of the EC.

Within the framework of the PHARE *financial assistance,* Hungary was granted a 3-year bridging loan of 1 billion ECUs to stabilize its balance of payments. PHARE offered the possibility of bilateral loans and assistance. From April 1990 the PHARE program was gradually extended to other countries (with the exception of certain former Yugoslav republics). After the European Agreements were signed, PHARE was incorporated in association constructions. Later for the CIS countries the so-called TACIS program (Technical Assistance to the Commonwealth of Independent States – and Georgia) was launched.

Trade policy measures were linked with PHARE: in the framework of these, as early as from January 1, 1990 (instead of December 31, 1995) a most-favoured-nation treatment was implemented, and discriminatory quotas were abolished. In addition, Hungary benefited from so-called general preferences (GSP) accorded to a proportion of its products, and thus joined the *category of preferentially treated countries.*

The possibility of association with the CEE countries arose as early as the autumn of 1989. Officially it was the April 1990 Dublin summit of the EC Council that recommended *association* to the CEE countries, on the basis of Article 238 of the Treaty of Rome. The offer of association was made at that time to 'all the countries of Central and Eastern Europe'. Because of the great differences among the countries of the region, formal negotiations were begun on December 19, 1990 only with Czechoslovakia, Poland and Hungary. In the course of 1990 the mandate for association was worked out, and the term 'Europe Agreements' was introduced, to emphasize the extraordinary importance and special nature of these. The negotiations were completed in November 1991, and the three agreements were *signed on December 16, 1991.*

The trade policy part of the three agreements (the Interim Agreement) was valid from March 1, 1992; the other parts, after the ratification processes, came into force with regard to Hungary and Poland on February 1, 1994. After 1992, because of the separation of the Czech and Slovak Republics, the association agreement was renegotiated.

Later, in 1993, the EU signed similar agreements with Bulgaria and Romania, in 1995 with the Baltic states (Estonia, Lithuania and Latvia), and in 1996 with Slovenia. Among the former Yugoslav republics, the EU signed a Stability and Cooperation Agreement with Macedonia and Croatia. In the future the EU hopes to integrate the Balkan countries, as well.

In their nature and the main points of association the Europe Agreements are very similar, but there are certain differences in view of the special characteristics and problems of individual countries. Like other traditional associations, they aim to establish a free trade zone, and in the long-term they have committed themselves to the 'four freedoms' (liberalization of flows of goods, services, labour and capital). The Agreements undertake concrete obligations with regard to only two of the four freedoms (movement of goods and capital), and not fully for them either, since agriculture is left out; whereas for the other two (flows of services and labour) they have set liberalization as only a long-term aim. Free trade in agricultural products has not materialized, but the associated countries have gradually been given substantial reductions in quotas and tariffs.

In Hungary's case, in the area of trade in goods – with the exception of agricultural products – *the aim was to establish a completely free trade zone by December 31, 2000.* The situation is similar with the other countries, but for example in Poland duties on cars could be retained until January 1, 2002. This means *a free flow of goods, without customs tariff burdens, other financial costs or quantitative restrictions.* Restrictions are temporarily retained with regard to industrial sectors that have traditionally been the subject of special regulations (metallurgy and textiles).

In the framework of the Europe Agreements, liberalization of trade is carried out reciprocally. The free trade zone thus created, however, is *asymmetrically* formed. The association treaty specified a maximum *transition period* of ten years, in two successive steps, each theoretically lasting for five years.

'Asymmetrical' liberalization meant that Hungary, for example, was granted *a 4–5-year postponement* of its removal of trade restrictions. Hungary began lifting *quantitative restrictions* only on January 1, 1995, and had to complete their removal by December 31, 2000. For imports of agricultural products Hungary eases restrictions within fixed quantitative limits, particularly in the case of products that have up till now played an important role in the Hungarian market.

The associate countries were entitled to protect new or restructuring industrial sectors up to December 31, 2000 by unilaterally introducing market protection measures in the form of tariff increases (in the case of structural reorganization or social tensions, to protect infant industries, or from balance of payments considerations). The measures could not affect more than 15% of import, and tariffs higher than 25% could not be applied. Dumping procedures are allowed by the association rules, and it is only necessary to inform the Association Council.

In the case of *direct capital investments,* repatriation of profits and capital was immediately guaranteed, though in Hungary this had in practice been going on since 1986 in the legal framework relating to joint ventures. A gradual changeover to the free flow of capital prescribed by the Community regulations must be implemented. Existing restrictions could not be made more severe by the addition of new ones, and the EU acknowledged Hungary's right to restrict capital transfers by individuals and companies. This was gradually eased, with the introduction of convertibility, up to 1996. By 1995–96 convertibility had been achieved in all the associate countries. With regard to *freedom to take up residence and to set up a business,* the Agreements generally prescribed what was called 'national' treatment. The majority of the countries achieved complete convertibility of their currency by the beginning of the 2000s (in Hungary's case, 2001).

With regard to *trade in services,* the parties' stated aim was liberalization, but the necessary future decisions were left to the Association Council. The possibilities of liberalization of the service sphere were outlined in the 1995 White Paper.

Liberalization measures relating to *the movement of labour* were left to the bilateral treaties to be concluded with the member countries. Free movement of labour was therefore merely a theoretical possibility, and it was clear that no real opening-up could be expected on the part of the EU until the high level of unemployment (about 10%) had been substantially reduced. The Agreement does, however, guarantee the entitlement of workers from the associate countries to non-discriminatory social treatment. Hungary has bilateral agreements of this kind only with Germany and Austria.

Real liberalization with regard to services and mobility of labour can be expected with full membership.

Compared with earlier forms of association, the Europe Agreements are characterized by many *new features.* On the one hand they introduce new elements into association, and on the other hand in some areas they are narrower than earlier ones.

1.2. THE MAIN ELEMENTS AND NEW FEATURES OF THE EUROPE AGREEMENTS

One new aspect was that intensive political consultations and cooperation between the EU and the associate countries was designated as an aim. *Political dialogue and cooperation* is based on common values and aspirations (integration into the community of democratic nations, consideration of the interests of the other partners, increased security and stability in Europe). This affected broad areas of economy, society, culture, etc., of associated countries. These countries aimed at increased integration into Europe.

The agreements emphasize the importance of *political transformation*: commitment to pluralist democracy, the rule of law, human rights, basic freedoms, a multi-party system, free and democratic elections, a market economy and the principle of social justice. From the second round of association, particularly in the renegotiated Slovak agreement, and then in those with Bulgaria and Romania, certain *political conditions* were included in the aims. These included the implementation of minority rights.

In broad areas association specifies *harmonization measures*, which enable Hungary to adapt gradually to EU norms, regulations and legal prescriptions (on consumer protection, competition, the environment, standards, etc.). In this way associated countries are adjusting partially to the single market measures, particularly in areas directly affecting trade. Liberalization of services also demands wide-ranging law harmonization.

As far as *financial assistance* is concerned, association involves the undertaking of only a vague obligation: in practice this is assigned to the PHARE framework. Compared with other association agreements this was a serious omission, since the majority of them (the Lomé Conventions and Mediterranean agreements) undertook concrete obligations with regard to assistance. No financial protocols were attached to the Europe Agreements. As the Hungarian agreement states, the rules of financial cooperation "enable the Community to take part, in the form of grants and loans, in programs aimed at promoting the development of the Hungarian infrastructure, stabilization and the transformation of the economic structure". The grants received in the framework of PHARE have indeed contributed to the process of transformation, stabilization and modernization.

The association agreements do not contain specific *monetary prescriptions* either (with the exception of financial support for currency convertibility). In the light of the Maastricht decisions relating to EMU, however, the importance of financial performance and cooperation has increased, not only for members but also for the associate countries.

The associate countries simultaneously *concluded free trade agreements with the EFTA countries, as well;* these agreements came into force on

October 1, 1993. When Austria, Sweden and Finland joined the EU in 1995, the EFTA agreements became much less important, since they really only affected trade with Switzerland and Norway.

1.3. THE RESULTS OF THE EUROPE AGREEMENTS

The association agreements have had many positive effects on the development, transformation and modernization of the CEE countries.

1. Most of the CEE countries are small, with an open structure, and heavily dependent on foreign trade. After the collapse of COMECON the CEE countries were in a difficult situation, and understandably tried to *reorient their trade* towards the western countries. The *EU was the main partner in this.* After 1989–90 the proportion of all these countries' trade with the EU increased considerably, and in the case of the Visegrád countries in just a few years it had risen spectacularly, from the former level of 20–25% to around 50%, thereby reaching the proportions characteristic of the European integration in the 1970s (about 50% of total trade). In practice the EU proved capable of replacing the declining COMECON trade relations, and the importance of this for stabilization and modernization cannot be over-emphasized.

It must be underlined that between 1989 and 1992 the CEE countries effectually redirected their trade to the EU markets, that is, in reality the radical change in relations *took place before the association agreements came into force* (on March 1, 1992, in the area of trade).

Although the transformational crisis caused a temporary decline in trade as well (Hungary's export to the EU, for example, decreased by 20% in 1993), from 1994 with the recovery trade expansion accelerated again, and played a large part in speeding up the economic growth of the region. It is also a fact that *the real dynamizing effects of liberalization* soon faded out, since tariffs, as factors hindering trade, disappeared. Thus the growth of trade now tended increasingly to depend on *long-term structural modernization,* though it was in fact free trade that created the necessary competitive environment in the long-term. By the beginning of the 2000s the EU gradually gained 60–70% of the associate countries' foreign trade. Thus *in little more than a decade trade integration had developed to the high level characteristic of the EU member countries.*

2. The association agreements *improved the region's international position and reputation* both *in international forums* and among *foreign capital in-*

vestors. Obviously the associations served as a condition of later membership of the OECD and NATO, and had a beneficial effect on the reputation of the countries of the region in the international economic institutions (the IMF, the EBRD and the World Bank). At the same time, from the point of view of foreign investment association could be regarded merely as a *favourable framework condition,* and many other factors and considerations could have a decisive influence. Western companies almost entirely invested in Central Europe; so far, more than 90% of *foreign direct investment* in the CEE region (counting the former Soviet Union as well) has been concentrated in Hungary (40% in this country alone), the Czech Republic and Poland. Yet these are the three countries where wage costs are the highest, and from the investment point of view cost savings derive mainly from the region's comparative wage-cost advantages. In the choice of where to invest, many other factors are taken into account, including the state of the infrastructure, the level of development of the capital and money markets, the security and predictability of legal regulation and economic policy, and the stability of social and political relations. Thus it is no accident that although wage costs are very low in Bulgaria and Romania, foreign capital has hesitated to invest in these countries.

Thus association is a necessary but not a sufficient condition from the point of view of foreign investment. Obviously, without association the roughly 22 billion dollars' worth of foreign operating capital would not have come to Hungary. The fact that it came here instead of going to other associate countries depended on many other advantages. And the fact that it came has enabled Hungary to exploit the advantages of association. This is shown by the fact that about 70% of Hungary's industrial export derives from the transnational companies operating here. These correlations are even more valid in connection with full membership.

3. The countries of Central and Eastern Europe hope for *long-term modernization of their economies through their integration with Western Europe.* Association has undoubtedly had wide-ranging modernizing effects already, but these have by no means been unequivocal, and will really develop only with full membership.

After the rapid industrialization of the 1950s and 1960s, from the 1970s the CEE countries increasingly lagged behind in the world economy. Many factors contributed to this. In addition to the deficiencies of the system (lack of interest in innovation and technological modernization, wasteful use of resources, etc.), Hungary's situation was made worse from the end of the 1970s by severe restrictive policies. Because of financial difficulties and restrictions, investment declined or remained at a low level, so that there could simply be no question of the large-scale reconstruction and development that had been going on for the last two decades in the developed countries. The loans taken up in the 1970s were used partially for development, but poor choices of targets and sectors, a lack of accompanying innovation and the squandering of resources meant that they did not represent a real inflow of capital. The result was that the country gradually fell deeper into debt. Its failure to keep up with the world economy, together with the crisis, were important factors in the change in the system.

At the beginning of the 1990s, therefore, the CEE countries were faced with the complex task of *structural modernization*. It had become necessary to change and renew production capacities and technologies. In order to reduce the relatively high energy and materials intensiveness of production, it was decided to transform the economic structure, taking into account the need to increase competitiveness on the world market. Modernization of the direct infrastructure at both micro- and macrolevel could no longer be postponed. There were problems in most countries of repairing damage to the environment, which was far more badly polluted than had earlier been estimated.

Modernization requires *four important factors*:

- the adoption and application of up-to-date technology;
- dynamic markets;
- development resources (capital); and
- a skilled, highly-motivated workforce.

Central and Eastern Europe possessed only the last of these, more or less, and technology and capital had to be obtained from external sources.

From the point of view of structural modernization the EU, as a developed economic zone with a population of 380 million, acted as a *natural 'centre of gravity' or 'modernization anchor'* for the CEE countries, which hope that integration will enable them to break out of their centuries-old peripheral situation. The majority of the EU members are highly developed countries characterized by a modern industrial structure, developed financial markets and banking and services spheres, and a continental-level infrastructure network. The average level of development of the EU countries is about 2–4 times higher than that of the CEE countries (in per capita GDP terms).

Europe – especially the EU – *possesses the technologies necessary for modernization of the economies of Central and Eastern Europe.* This applies equally to European companies which are integral parts of the global economy, and to the transnational companies from outside Europe that operate in the EU countries.

At the same time, the EU only partially fulfils the requirement for *dynamic markets,* which are important from the point of view of modernization. Since the 1970s the economy of the EU countries has slowed down, and it appears to be capable in the long-term of producing a growth rate of only 2.5–3%. This is just half the growth achieved in the 1960s, and lags behind that of many regions of the world economy such as the United States and particularly China and other developing countries. In other respects as well the EU's relative macroeconomic performance has deteriorated. This is a disadvantage, and a limiting factor from the point of view of association and especially of full membership (high unemployment – free movement of labour; budget deficit – resource transfers).

Nevertheless the dynamic expansion of export in recent years has proved that the EU economy has many segments that are capable of absorbing goods from the CEE countries, and where these can count on favourable market positions in the long-term as well. In the development of the East European region there are enormous opportunities for development and investment, which should have wide-ranging stimulating effects on the whole European economy. "At present there are about 400 million people living in the central and eastern part of Europe. There would be demand, since the population is poorly supplied with cars, consumer electronics and agricultural machinery. So there is no doubt that the most fruitful markets of the coming decades will be in Europe"(NYE JR. 1993).

For successful modernization, not only dynamic external markets but *adequate net transfers of resources* are needed, in the form of both private investment and official grants. The process of trade liberalization is generally accompanied by trade and balance of payments deficits and growing debt resulting from this. From the point of view of resource transfers, the *debt problems* of some of the countries of the region must be highlighted.

Undoubtedly with regard to technological and structural modernization private capital investments on a commercial ground are of fundamental importance. This is proved by the case of Hungary, where considerable foreign capital investment has had many-sided modernizing effects. At the same time, with particular regard to the undeveloped nature of the region's infrastructure there is a great need for inter-state resource transfers. This was recognized from the outset, and as early as 1989 recommendations were made concerning the possibility of 'MARSHALL Plan' to be given to the CEE countries. These proposals were rejected and were not implemented later either. On the one hand, the developed western countries did not have *the necessary surpluses and financial reserves* for this purpose, and on the other hand the threat of the collapse of the Soviet Union *weakened their strategic interest* in the consolidation of Central and Eastern Europe (at least it was weaker than in the case of America's interest in Western Europe after the war, or in 1990 at the time of the Gulf War).

It was not by chance, therefore, that whereas all earlier associations, especially in the case of the developing countries, had offered some form of assistance, *the financial obligations undertaken in the Europe Agreements were very modest.* In the PHARE framework, between 1990 and 2000 Hungary received 1 billion ECUs (100 million ECUs a year) in financial support, and more than 1 billion ECUs from the European Investment Bank (EIB) and the EBRD for infrastructure investments and the support of small enterprises. These transfers represented less than 0.5% of Hungary's GDP, and only one-tenth of the support given to Greece and Portugal. It was only a fraction of the amount received by Germany's eastern Länder. The countries of the region can expect bigger sums for infrastructure development only once they have become full members. One source of problems is the fact that, *like Central and Eastern Europe, the EU is struggling with a restructuring crisis.* It is another matter, how different its crisis is in its nature and depth.

4. The association agreements placed great emphasis on promoting the process of *transformation* in CEE. This transformation proceeded very dynamically after 1990, with regard to both *privatization* and *the development of market institutions*. The transformation process was strengthened particularly by the fact that this later became a criterion (one of the Copenhagen criteria) for full membership.

5. There have been considerable changes in the *'dependence asymmetries'* in trade between the EU and the associate countries. In 1989 the CEE associates accounted for only 2.7–2.9% of the EU's foreign trade, which meant that these countries were *marginal partners*. Asymmetries

still remain, but by the beginning of the 2000s the 60–70% proportion of the associate countries' trade that was carried on with the EU accounted for over 13% of the EU's trade. If we accept the minimum dependence threshold of 10% postulated by the dependence theories, then the EU has become dependent on the 10 CEE associate countries' markets. In 1997 Hungary contributed a 1.7% share of EU import and received 1.9% of EU export. Because of the asymmetries in relations, the levels of dependence vary from one country to another. For example, after Germany Hungary is Austria's second biggest trade partner. At the same time, with the exception of Germany, Austria and Italy, for the EU countries CEE is still a marginal partner. This motivates interest in enlargement in different ways.

1.4. THE DEFICIENCIES OF THE ASSOCIATION AGREEMENTS

In connection with the Europe Agreements *some deficiencies and drawbacks* of the CEE associations must be pointed out.

1. The CEE associations formulated in 1990–91 reflected the *optimism of the beginning of the 1990s*, when rapid, favourable growth was predicted not only for the East but for the whole continent. In 1990 a Commission report stated that after the introduction of the proposed free market reforms the Central and East European region would emerge from the recession and after 1992–93 would be able to show 5–6% annual growth (*Financial Times*, May 15, 1990). Many believed that the 1992 measures, with the opening of the markets of the associate countries, would have a powerful stimulating effect on the whole European economy.

Economic development in the associate countries of Central and Eastern Europe in the first few years after association was much more unfavourable than had been expected in 1990–91, during the negotiations. Both sides had *seriously underestimated the difficulties of consolidation and transformation,* which undoubtedly explain but do not justify the modest results of association.

One unfavourable circumstance was that, parallel with the transformation crisis in CEE and to no small extent because of it, in the period 1991–93 *the economy of the EU countries also went into recession.* In such circumstances it was not surprising that the EU in this period was not capable of *contributing* to the *stabilization of the economy* of the CEE countries *and initiating processes of growth.*

There was justifiable anxiety that the rapid liberalization due to association obligations could deprive the CEE countries of the ability to *protect their economies effectively against harmful external competition*. Because of transformation, privatization and the radical reorganization of company structures, the structures of production and other activities changed; considerable reconstruction was needed, and new markets and relations had to be developed. In broad areas of the economy, *new enterprises had to face the problems of 'infant industry'*. These proved more serious than the parties had thought at the time of the negotiations. This raised questions such as the inadequacy of the 4–5-year postponement and the narrowness of the scope for protection provided by the association agreements. The Hungarian economy managed to get over the structural shock quickly, thanks to foreign capital investments. In some other countries this was a long-drawn-out process.

2. The years of association that have elapsed up till now indicate that in reality the agreements *offered better export expansion opportunities to the EU than to the associate countries*. Up to 1990 the EU had a trade deficit with the East which fluctuated between 2.5 billion ECUs (in 1984) and 0.6 billion ECUs (in 1989). Then the balance tipped from a deficit of about 1 billion ECUs in 1990 to EU surpluses of 1.4 billion ECUs in 1991, 2.5 billion ECUs in 1992, and almost 5.6 billion ECUs in 1993 (the year of deepest crisis). In the years after association this surplus grew, and *between 1992 and 1999 the EU achieved a surplus of more than 100 billion ECUs altogether* in trade with the 10 associate countries. This was not at all surprising, since the earlier experience of the associations also indicated that liberalization in the long-term has a negative effect on the less developed countries' trade balance. What was surprising was rather the size of the effect. At the same time Hungary, alone among the associate countries, managed to reverse the deterioration of its trade balance, and in 1997 achieved a surplus of $250 m., followed in 1998 by a surplus of $302 m. The main source of the surplus was its trade with Germany; in 1998 Hungary's surplus with Germany was $1,170 m. In this process the positive modernizing and export-expanding effects of foreign capital investment can be seen.

It must be added that despite the balance deficit, trade integration is a positive-sum game for the associate countries as well, because without their export to the EU these countries would hardly have been able to stimulate their economies.

3. The association agreements with their 'asymmetrical' liberalization timetable recognized the developmental disadvantages of the CEE coun-

tries. At the same time, however, in practice they did not take account of the *trade 'asymmetries'* that developed in them to the detriment of the CEE countries.

3.1. To open up its markets the EC/EU did actually abolish the tariffs that hindered trade, but the average level of these was no higher than 3–5%. Such a level of tariffs does not in itself really hinder trade, and their removal does not represent a real trade advantage. By contrast, Hungary's average level of tariffs was about 13% in 1991; although over the years this has been reduced to an average of 8%, it still has a considerable protective effect. Thus in spite of the few years' postponement the associate countries have given more than they have received in return. In view of the EU's big trade surplus, in the circumstances the delay on its part in liberalizing certain 'sensitive' goods (steel, textiles) with regard to which the associate countries had considerable surplus export capacity was particularly unjustified.

3.2. In the association framework, while Hungary undertook to liberalize about 90% of its import, reciprocal liberalization extended to only 75% of its export to the EU, in view of its position as an agricultural exporter. Taking account of the other trade restrictions, this 'asymmetry' operated to the detriment of Hungary. This is indicated by the fact that for these reasons, among others, the proportion of agricultural products in Hungary's export has decreased in ten years from 20% to 7%.

3.3. Within the agricultural sector itself as well, the conditions of market access are asymmetrical. In comparison with the protectionist system of the common agricultural policy, Hungary has provided much more favourable market access conditions for EU agricultural products. Especially at the beginning of the 1990s the level of agricultural protection on certain products (beef, wheat) was over 100%, while the Hungarian level of protection was just 21–26%. Later, the EU agricultural trade concessions were substantially extended.

Hungary is also at a disadvantage compared with the EU in the so-called 'subsidy competition'. This puts Hungarian agricultural products at a disadvantage not only on external markets but often on the internal Hungarian market as well. Apart from subsidized export, the EU has the advantage of being able to bring some goods to the Hungarian market more cheaply than Hungarian domestic prices.

On the basis of all these, the unfavourable development of Eastern Europe's agricultural trade with the EU is not surprising. *The associate countries*, especially since the Europe Agreements came into force, *have actually changed from net exporters to net importers of agricultural products, the only exception to this being Hungary.* Growth in Hungarian exports has been accompanied by an increase in imports from the EU, and the former good trade balance has worsened in relative terms.

Table 1. Agricultural trade between Hungary and the EU between 1988 and 2001 (in millions of ECUs/euros)

Year	Hungarian export (X)	Hungarian import (M)	Balance	X/M
1988	615	90	525	6.79
1989	762	114	648	6.68
1990	854	128	726	6.67
1991	1169	173	996	6.75
1992	1108	230	878	4.82
1993	878	347	531	2.53
1994	997	467	530	2.13
1995	1257	468	789	2.69
1996	1300	405	895	3.21
1997	1157	458	699	2.52
1998	1210	494	716	2.45
1999	922	296	626	3.11
2000	1141	504	637	2.26
2001	1361	594	767	2.29

Source: PÉTER HALMAI (1993: 154); data from EUROSTAT and the Ministry of Agriculture and Rural Development.

3.4. Difficulty was caused by the CEE *associate countries' undeveloped trade policy system* (their lack of industry protection, consumer protection and other non-tariff instruments), and the hasty *one-sided liberalization* that took place at the beginning of the 1990s. As a result, while the liberalization provided by association in many sectors barely improved access to the EU for Hungarian products, EU goods had free entry. "It can safely be said that the most important practical experience gained from the association agreement is that successful cooperation cannot be established with an institutionally sound and sophisticated integrational grouping unless the associate country possesses an equally sound and sophisticated institutional system" (RÁCZ 1994: 6).

4. The *asymmetry of relations* in CEE–EU trade has been partly an obstacle created by the association agreement, and partly an opportunity. Roughly half of Hungary's trade with the EU is transacted with Germany alone. In 1997, of Hungary's export 52.3% went to Germany, 16% to

Austria and 8.6% to Italy. Just these three countries accounted for about three-quarters of Hungary's export (76.9%), and two-thirds of its import (66.3%). Similar proportions were typical of the other 'Visegrád countries', as well. The relatively modest proportion transacted with the other 12 EU countries is on the one hand a source of differences in interests, but at the same time there is the potential for increasing trade by expanding relations.

2. SUB-REGIONAL COOPERATION AND INTEGRATION

The EU is the most comprehensive organizational framework and form of pan-European integration. With economic and monetary union it has become a globally and historically unique experiment in regional integration among sovereign states. The EU *is structured with sub-regional groupings* from inside (Benelux) and outside (Nordec). Of these, some came into being to counterbalance the EC (e.g. EFTA), but most were supplementary in nature.

Up till now integration on the European continent has been concentrated mainly in Western Europe. *The EU forms its centre of gravity,* and from the 1980s onwards the north and south perimeter areas of the continent have joined in the process.

Experience has shown that sub-regional integrations do not conflict with pan-European integration: on the contrary, they can form organic parts of it. This applies to cooperation within Central Europe as well, and it is no accident that such experiments have been actively supported by the EU.

Efforts at sub-regional cooperation *in the Central European region* have been observable since the 1970s.

One of the first steps in Central European cooperation was the *Alps–Adria Community,* in which the participants were regions of four countries. The community was a sub-regional group formed by provinces or counties of the various countries on a multilateral basis for purposes of cross-border cooperation. The community consisted of 5 counties of Hungary, 4 provinces of Austria and 5 of Italy, Bavaria from Germany and the (then) Yugoslav republics of Slovenia and Croatia. The Swiss canton of Tessin had observer status. Cooperation was largely limited to cultural, tourism, environmental and certain economic affairs (cross-border trade, employment and communications).

At intergovernmental level cooperation among the four countries began in 1988, despite their differing obligations and orientations at the time (Hungary: the Warsaw Pact and COMECON; Italy: NATO and the EC; Yugoslavia: non-aligned; Austria: neutral, and EFTA), and before long was extended to Czechoslovakia and Poland (it was called the Pentagonale, then the Hexagonale, and for a short time 'the Poligonale' was suggested because of the large number of countries involved). The main areas of cooperation were the economy, tourism, and the environment, but these acquired an increasingly political character. In 1992 it changed into the so-called *Central European Initiative,* and these countries held intensive political consultations in many fields. Since 1994 17 countries of the region (Austria, Bosnia–Hercegovina, the Czech Republic, Croatia, Poland, Macedonia, Hungary, Italy, Slovakia and Slovenia, etc.) have taken part. The heads of government meet annually, and the foreign ministers every six months.

The leaders of Hungary, Czechoslovakia and Poland, signed a declaration at Visegrád on February 15, 1991, on the subject of cooperation. (In 1335 the Visegrad Congress took place, between Charles I, King of Hungary, King Casimir III of Poland, and the Czech King John.) The cooperation of the *Visegrad Three* was an answer in the course of 1991 to the growing uncertainty in the Soviet Union. Later, as the *Four* (separation of Czech Republic and Slovakia), they recognized that it offered the possibility of improving their positions in the talks then in progress with the EU. In April 1992 the four countries established the Central European Cooperation Committee, as their consultative forum.

On December 21, 1992 the economic ministers of the four countries (the Czech Republic, Hungary, Poland and Slovakia) signed an agreement in Krakow, Poland, dealing with the establishment *by 2001 of a free trade zone* (the Central European Free Trade Association – CEFTA). The member countries decided to carry out accelerated liberalization.

The agreement, based on bilateral treaties, came into force on March 1, 1993. In this case liberalization took place in a symmetrical manner in three stages. Liberalization took effect at once for products on which trade restrictions had not been introduced after the collapse of COMECON. For Hungary, about 55% of its export to the Czech Republic and Slovakia became free, as did 50% of its export to Poland. Tariffs on 'normal' goods were reduced over 3–4 years, basically in the period between 1995 and January 1, 1997. Liberalization for 'sensitive' goods was carried out over 8 years, ending on January 1, 2001. The agreement applies to agricultural products, but like the association agreements does not aim at free trade. While agricultural import to Hungary from the organization is marginal, in Hungarian export to the other CEFTA countries the proportion of agricultural products (animal products, foodstuffs, drinks) is relatively large. This has given rise to many trade policy disputes in recent years.

The establishment of CEFTA was partly justified by the collapse of COMECON, and partly followed logically from the EU associations and other free trade agreements (e.g. EFTA). CEFTA later was extended to Bulgaria, Romania and Slovenia.

On September 12, 1993 in Tallin, Estonia, Latvia and Lithuania signed the Baltic Free Trade Agreement. *Many bilateral free trade agreements were signed* between former COMECON countries.

The association and free trade agreements were in fact based on *bilateral liberalization obligations.* The range of goods to be included in the free trade was determined bilaterally, on the basis of 'local or domestic content'. This meant, for example, in the case of cars that at least 60% local content (value added) was required, for the given product to be allowed into the EU markets, in the association framework. In the case of Hungary, in the local content both the Hungarian and the EU added value (components, services, etc.) were taken into account. Because of the nature of the agreements it was not possible to include Czech or Polish components in the calculations, even though the EU had separate similar association agreements with both the Czech Republic and Poland. In such circumstances the association and reciprocal free trade agreements did not really *add up to form a free trade zone,* in spite of the fact that for a given category of goods in all the relations trade had been liberalized. This situation gradually changed, with *the introduction from July 1, 1997 of the so-called pan-European cumulation.* With the possibility of reciprocal inclusion, cooperation improved, as did the conditions for foreign capital investments in the region.

There are *many arguments* in favour of maintaining and developing Central European cooperation:

– cooperation can help to strengthen these countries' newly-gained independence and the consolidation of their democratic systems;

– it may help in the handling of ethnic and national conflicts (e.g. the document on the protection of minorities worked out in the Central European Initiative);

– it may contribute to the development of more balanced regional and pan-European power relations;
– it will help the process of economic and political transformation in the former socialist countries;
– it could be a security-enhancing factor in the face of internal and external threats;
– it could act as a 'bridge' in developing cross-border cooperation; and
– instead of seeking separate accession to the EU, these countries could improve their chances and negotiating positions by acting jointly in the matter.

Apart from looser forms of cooperation, there is little likelihood of any closer integration, any economic or political sub-regional bloc being established in Central Europe in the foreseeable future, and its viability would be questionable. *The intensity of economic cooperation* among the countries of the region is low, and the necessary conditions for *economic cohesion* are largely *missing*. In recent decades their economies have developed 'in parallel structures' and mutual trade has not developed nearly as much as it might have done. Direct company and capital relations (microintegrations), which are vitally important for any integration, have not developed sufficiently, and have begun to emerge only in the last few years.

External dependencies are similar, *and every one of these countries needs help* in catching up in the world economy. Problems they all share are a *lack of capital*, which has to be obtained from outside, *a shortage of energy*, which up till now they have been able to obtain only from the former Soviet Union, and *high technology*, which likewise they cannot get from one another, but only from the developed West.

The necessary *political cohesion has not yet become strong enough*, and they continue to be divided by ethnic disputes and nationality problems. It is widely accepted that the historical lack of self-confidence of the new nation states is a serious political and emotional obstacle in the way of any sub-regional integration.

There is a lack of a generally used and accepted common language (like, for example, German in the Austro–Hungarian Monarchy), which is important from the point of view of regional communication and cohesion.

It must be emphasized *that Central European cooperation cannot substitute but only supplement participation in the pan-European integration*. With the marginalization of EFTA no alternative of the kind now exists within Europe, and with countries or groupings outside Europe it would be totally unrealistic.

3. CENTRAL AND EASTERN EUROPE ON THE WAY TO FULL MEMBERSHIP

3.1. THE START OF NEGOTIATIONS ON FULL MEMBERSHIP (ANTECEDENTS AND CONDITIONS)

In Athens on April 1, 1994 Hungary as the first of the countries of the CEE region submitted its application for accession to the current president of the EU Council. A few days later Poland did the same. Romania, Slovakia, Bulgaria and the Baltic states followed, submitting their applications in 1995. In 1996 the Czech Republic and Slovenia announced their intention of joining the EU.

At first the EU tried to exclude the CEE countries from the possibility of full membership. In 1991 in the association agreements, despite strong pressure from the CEE countries the EU was willing to undertake only a vague and uncertain obligation with regard to their *future full membership*. According to the Europe Agreement: "We are aware that it is Hungary's ultimate aim to become a member of the Community, and this association, in the opinion of the Parties, will assist in the attainment of that aim." Thus the agreement merely records Hungary's intention, while there is no mention of that of the EU.

The unresponsive behaviour of the EU towards the region was due above all to *conflicting political and strategic interests.* It had been characteristic of earlier accessions without exception that with regard to conflicting economic interests, strategic and political considerations had tipped the balance in favour of a positive decision. With the end of the Cold War and the collapse of the Soviet Union its interest in stabilizing external security and internal democratic structures, and the urgency of this, declined or evaporated. Indeed, in the EU for some reason it was actually felt that by joining, the region could become a 'threat' to security and stability. The EU was palpably unwilling to commit itself to stabilizing this uncertain region burdened with national, ethnic, social and political conflicts and to guaranteeing its security. Many were of the opinion that with Eastward enlargement the EU would 'import' security threats and jeopardize the process of deepening integration. The situation changed only at the end of the 1990s, when with the culmination of the Yugoslav crisis it became clear that the security of the continent could be consolidated only by admitting the eastern regions to closer integration with the EU. Intensive expansion of economic relations strengthened the interests of both sides in integration.

In September 1992 the governments of the 'Visegrád Four' submitted a joint request to the Union that by 1996 their development be assessed from the point of view of determining the conditions of full membership. The discussion of EU Commission's report entitled "Towards closer association with the countries of Central and Eastern Europe" took place at its Edinburgh meeting on December 11–12, 1992, but a decision in the matter was taken only at the Copenhagen summit of June 1993. The EU *officially undertook the obligation to admit the associate countries that were signatories of the Europe Agreements to full membership in the future. The strategic importance* of these decisions, from the point of view of consolidating democracy in the region, increasing security and attracting an inflow of foreign capital, cannot be overestimated.

The Copenhagen summit defined the *membership criteria* for the countries of Central and Eastern Europe:

– democracy, the rule of law, and stability of the institutions guaranteeing human and minority rights;

– a functioning market economy, capable of withstanding the keen competition typical in the Union and the pressure of market forces;

– fulfilment of the obligations of membership and acceptance of the aim of political as well as economic and monetary union.

A new aspect of the Copenhagen decisions was that the EU *now for the first time* formulated *concrete accession criteria* for the applicants. (Apart from the condition that in accordance with the Treaty of Rome a Union member had to be a 'European country'.) Up to then, membership maturity had been examined only from a political point of view, and was in fact made dependent on the state of political democracy. In some cases (for example, those of Portugal and Spain) the decision was really motivated by right- or left-wing threats to political democracy. So far, economic criteria had not been defined for applicants.

On July 18, 1994 the Council of Ministers debated the Union's working document dealing with the CEE countries, which was presented at the

Essen summit of December 1994. They examined further possibilities of developing 'structured relations' with EU institutions (for example, the inviting of heads of state of the CEE countries to some summit meetings), expansion of the internal market, law harmonization and financial co-operation.

On the basis of the Commission's recommendation, at the June 1995 Cannes summit the Council approved a 'White Paper' in which proposals were formulated for the applicant CEE countries with regard to their gradual adaptation to the 1992 program of the single internal market and their integration into it (law harmonization, application of standards, etc.).

From the beginning the CEE associates urged *the setting of a date for the start of accession negotiations*. At first the EU undertook such an obligation only in respect of the Mediterranean enlargements. At the summit in Lisbon in June 1992 the Council decided that accession talks with Cyprus and Malta, which had applied in 1990, should begin not more than six months after the conclusion of the 1996 Intergovernmental Conference. This meant that the EU gave priority to a certain extent to its 'southern' enlargement compared with its eastern expansion. Later, in 1996 Malta withdrew, but the priority remained in practice. Greece in particular made it clear that eastward enlargement could not take place without the admission of Cyprus to the EU.

From the point of view of the accession of the CEE countries, an important development was the decision taken by the Council at its Madrid meeting in December 1995 to start accession negotiations with the 10 CEE associate countries, as in the case of the Cyprus–Malta formula, 'not more than six months' after the conclusion of the 1996 Intergovernmental Conference. Though the promise was expressed in a conditional manner, the CEE countries did succeed in obtaining what they had so urgently requested

In the spring of 1996 the EU sent the 12 candidates an Avis containing its questions in order to assess the readiness of these countries, particularly with regard to their adaptation to the EU's legal system. On the basis of their answers and the Commission's analyses, in July 1997 'country reports' were issued, and the 'Agenda 2000' document, which outlines the EU's strategy and aims with regard to the prospective members.

The Amsterdam summit of June 1997 had made it clear that on the basis of their preparedness and fulfilment of the membership criteria the EU did not regard it as possible for all the CEE candidates to join at the same time, but in a first round it intended to negotiate seriously with just Cyprus and 5 of the CEE associate countries. The five 'first-round' CEE countries were designated at the December 1997 Luxembourg summit: they consisted of the Czech Republic, Estonia, Poland, Hungary and Slovenia. According to the compromise formula on March 30, 1998 the enlargement process was formally initiated with a meeting of the foreign ministers of the 15 member states together with those of the 11 candidate countries (10 CEE countries + Cyprus), but from March 31, 1998 the talks were continued with only the designated six countries. After *screening, real accession negotiations with Hungary got under way on November 10, 1998.*

At its April 1999 meeting in Berlin the Council approved Agenda 2000, which fixed the budget target figures for the period 2000–2006. By assuming the admission of new members in 2002, for the first time it officially indicated an accession date. At the same time, only six countries were included in the first round of enlargement planned for 2002.

The December 1999 Council meeting in Helsinki can be regarded as a turning-point, because enlargement was now declared unequivocally to be its number one strategic commitment. The accession talks were extended to include the 'second-round' countries as well (Bulgaria, Latvia, Lithuania, Romania and Slovakia + Malta). In evaluating the candidates the principle of individual assessment is applied, according to which membership can be granted depending on how the candidates fulfil the requirements and thereby achieve their goal (the Regatta principle).

Enlargement as a strategic priority was confirmed by the December 2000 Council meeting in Nice. The Treaty of Nice decided on certain institutional measures made necessary by enlargement (majority voting, the number of seats in the European Parliament, etc.) and fixed the timetable of further negotiations (the Road Map). It expects that the negotiations could be concluded by the end of 2002, and the first accessions could take place on January 1, 2004. Thus it is possible that the newly admitted countries' citizens might take part in the European parliamentary elections due to be held in the summer of 2004.

The Council meeting in Göteborg in April 2001 confirmed the accession timetable, and formulated the aim of participation in the 2004 parliamentary elections.

The 2001 Council meeting in Laken emphasized the irreversibility of enlargement by designating as a realistic aim the conclusion of the accession negotiations by the end of 2002. Though the candidates must be judged on their merits, it does name the 10 countries that have a realistic chance of becoming full members in 2004. Among the candidates only Bulgaria and Romania are indicated as likely to be able to join only later (around 2007).

3.2. THE NEW MEMBERS' "FITNESS" (MATURITY) FOR INTEGRATION

We can best obtain some indication of the CEE candidates' readiness for integration, or integration maturity, from analysis of their fulfilment of the so-called Copenhagen membership criteria. It is largely on this basis that the EU forms its standpoints and the conclusions drawn from its reviews.

The majority of the candidate countries fulfil the political criteria for membership, and this is recognized by their EU partners. Parliamentary democracy and the institutions that ensure the rule of law have been consolidated, and political conflicts are solved in accordance with the rules of democracy. In Hungary the main political trends (socialists, liberals, conservative Christian parties, Greens, etc.) are adequately represented and the balance among them that is necessary for stability has evolved. Freedom of the media is guaranteed, and civil society is gradually developing. The situation is broadly similar in the other Central European countries (the Czech Republic, Poland and Slovenia). In most of the countries deficiencies are to be found chiefly in the protection of minority rights (Roma population). From the point of view of security, it is an important requirement that stable, normal relations with the neighbouring countries should be established.

A great challenge and danger to democracy is the deterioration of public security, the criminalization of the economy and society, and large-scale corruption. This is the number one concern in every candidate country. The EU lays great emphasis on the proper and efficient functioning of institutions, which cannot be achieved without consolidation and development of the legal system. Enormous tasks are involved in law harmonization.

From the point of view of integration maturity, in the case of the CEE candidates *their level of economic development* is of particularly great importance. The new would-be member countries are all only moderately or poorly developed, so the question of development levels is a crucial one. True, Eastward enlargement is a political question, so there is no mention of whether there is a minimum level of development that would exclude the membership of any country below it. On the other hand, since claims in connection with the Structural Funds are determined on the basis of per capita income, obviously this indirectly carries great weight in the actual assessment.

The majority of the candidate countries *formally* fulfil, more or less, the requirement of a 'functioning market economy', and among them Hungary leads in transformation with regard to several parameters. About 97% of prices have been liberalized, free market-access is assured, foreign trade has been liberalized, the Hungarian forint has been convertible since 1996 (fully since 2001), interest rates and exchange rates reflect market conditions, privatization has not merely been completed but has been accompanied by widespread company restructuring unique in the region, and the capital and money markets are expanding and being modernized. Market-conform forms of taxation have been consolidated (for example, the VAT-type turnover tax introduced in 1987), and stabilization of the Hungarian economy has been successfully achieved. It is worth mentioning that introduction of a VAT-type turnover tax took place only at the beginning of the 1990s in the other CEE countries, while in Slovenia the changeover was carried out 10 years later than in Hungary. Experience has proved that after it is launched, several years are necessary for VAT consolidation. Economic legislation now approximates more closely to European norms.

In spite of divergences it can be added that all this applies *in fact to the 8 'first-round' countries* of the region, and in the areas where they lag behind, they are capable of catching up before accession. At the same time it must be remembered that these countries are joining a functioning 'single internal market', which means that they will not just have to be generally satisfactory but will have to adjust concretely to the rules of that "internal" market.

Complete transformation will of course require more time. Further modernization of the banking sector is important, as is a reform of the public services sphere and public finance, and no less essential is the suppression of the black or grey economy, the excessive scale of which, in addition to its criminalizing and demoralizing effects, is a serious burden from the point of view of the efficient functioning of the economy and the rational investment and fair redistribution of incomes. The modern market infrastructures are still undeveloped (credit cards, forms of money, the logistical structures of participation in global networks).

A perfectly 'functioning market economy' in reality is not fully achieved even of the most highly developed countries. For the candidate countries, a 'functioning market economy' as a criterion of integration maturity means that they can exploit the advantages offered by integration, and will not find themselves in a worse situation than if they had not joined. If complete construction of the elements of a real market economy is not carried out, there will be a danger that the economy will remain at a sub-optimal level, resources will be inefficiently utilized, there will be a constant loss of resources, the country will not find partners, and modernization of the economy will not take place. This has been clearly confirmed in recent years by the example of other countries.

The ability to "withstand the pressure of market competition", as a criterion, in fact sets the *requirement of competitiveness* on the part of prospective new members. Competitiveness is an important condition from the point of view of exploitation of the advantages of integration. Withstanding 'the pressure of market competition', as it was described in Copenhagen, expressed concern about the ability to meet the tough demands of Union competition. And now another anxiety is frequently voiced. Will the Union, and especially its less developed members and their industries, be able to stand the pressure of competition from the countries of Central and Eastern Europe?

As to "meeting of competitive pressures", it must be emphasized that these countries, as a result of association, have already opened their markets on a great extent to future integration partners. In many respects with full membership the competitive conditions will not be worse but will rather improve.

– With full membership liberalization will extend to agriculture as well, in which Hungary at least has surplus capacity. As a participant in the common agricultural policy Hungary could receive income transfers.

– With full membership, 'asymmetry' with regard to non-tariff, informal trade barriers will disappear, and associate's goods will have access on more favourable terms to EU markets.

– In becoming part of the single market associates will be able to make use of their cost advantages in many service sectors, especially where apart from lower costs they can offer services capable of competing in quality with the EU (health, technical design, education, etc.).

– With full membership the possibilities of protection will be reduced, but there will be greater chances of compensation, particularly in the form of budget transfers.

4. THE EU'S 'RECEPTIVENESS' (ABSORPTION CAPACITIES) AND ITS INTERESTS

Eastward enlargement demands reforms in the EU countries as well that will bring qualitative changes. In fact, whether they be institutional or structural reforms, they point in the same direction as in the case of the deepening of integration. The latest enlargements, certainly, were able to take place without the consistent implementation of radical reforms. In 1995 the accession of the three new members did not involve significant changes in market competition, since they did not alter the order of magnitude of the EU's dimensions, and on the basis of earlier agreements trade with these countries had already been liberalized since the end of the 1970s. In the framework of the European Economic Area these countries gradually became incorporated in the single internal market. As overall net contributors, even if on a small scale, they did not 'jeopardize' the EU budget.

The situation is very different with the Eastern enlargement now in progress. On the one side, the last three countries to join basically had to become incorporated in a common market type of integration. By contrast, those joining in the next wave will be entering economic and monetary union. Whereas the previous three new members were prepared for EMU, those taking part in the Eastern enlargement face a difficult adaptation process.

On the other side, the EU is not capable either of carrying out further enlargement without consistent implementation of the reforms described above. So European integration has reached a decisive, critical stage at the turn of the millennium. With regard to both deepening and expansion the basic decisions have been taken. Depending on the reforms to be carried out, implementation is the task of the coming years, and will decisively determine the development and fate of the whole process of European integration.

Oddly enough, the Copenhagen membership criteria prescribe that as one of the conditions of enlargement, the EU *must be capable of 'absorbing the new members'*. This makes reform an urgent necessity in three areas:

- institutions;
- the Common Agricultural Policy; and
- the budget.

Concerning institutional reform, it is an obvious requirement that after enlargement, with the increased number of members the various institutions' ability to function must be maintained. With 15 member countries at present, the EU institutions already have difficulty in operating. With 25–27 members, clearly the situation will become impossible. Therefore institutional reform is one of the conditions of Eastern enlargement. The decisions taken in Amsterdam and Nice in fact made the minimum institutional changes that were absolutely essential for the admission of the present 10 candidates. It is clear that the effective functioning of the Union in the future will require further reforms, the main direction of which was in many respects outlined at the Convention preparing for the next IGC.

From the point of view of the 'absorption capacity' of the EU, the other critical question is that of *reform of the Common Agricultural Policy*. Enlargement to the east will increase the EU's agricultural production capacity by one-third, and will double the size of its farming population. Without reform of the CAP this would lead to enormous over-production, and would place intolerable burdens on the agricultural budget (European Commission DG for Agriculture 2002). Resistance to reform is a barrier to enlargement, but at the same time enlargement may be forcing the acceleration of reform.

The admission of the new members will certainly be a big challenge to the present member countries' producers, while in the candidate countries the relative weight of agriculture is coupled with considerable backwardness. Enlargement therefore means a huge market not just for the EU's agricultural products but for companies manufacturing agricultural and food products. The technological backwardness of the new members in this area is particularly great.

For the *agriculture* of the candidate countries *the most critical question is competitiveness*. The *apparent competitiveness* of the countries preparing for accession is due at present to their low production costs, but when they join the EU these costs will rise considerably:

– *compliance with EU regulations* will have the effect of raising costs (standards, animal and plant hygiene regulations, environmental regulations, food safety norms);

– *increased prices for land* will have a significant effect on production costs. Since at present the market for land is just developing, there are no real land prices;

– the acquisition of new means of production, modernization of the machine park and the *carrying out of the necessary investments* all contribute to increasing costs. Labour costs are at present extremely low: Union membership will be accompanied by wage rises.

Thus after they join, the new members' comparative advantages will not be either substantial or lasting, and the present members' fears cannot be regarded as really justified. It must be added that since the regime changes, in all the CEE countries without exception an extremely *fragmented land-ownership structure* has developed. In most cases this structure is not at all suitable for efficient agricultural production, and very small farms will not be able to qualify for many Union supports. The critical problem of agriculture in the candidate countries is *under-capitalization,* and no breakthrough can be expected in this area in the short-term. Budget transfers will not be sufficient to change this; the land laws limit foreign capital investment, and domestic farmers' capacity for accumulation and borrowing is unable to counterbalance this.

While the increase in costs that membership entails will reduce competitiveness, on the other hand *the changed conditions of market access will create new opportunities for the countries joining.* In the present framework the association agreements grant only certain concessions in the area of agricultural products, but accession will enable unhindered access to the common agricultural market. At the same time, access will obviously be possible only within the framework of production quotas, so it is very important what size of quotas are agreed on during the accession negotiations.

It is important that *the new members should enjoy the same competition conditions* as the present member countries. Thus the aim is complete participation in the Common Agricultural Policy. The main point at issue in the accession talks is after how long a transition period this should take place.

From the point of view of the full membership of the CEE countries, the other critical obstacle is the question of *financial transfers.* The less developed EU members such as Spain, Portugal and Greece are afraid that the economic assistance they have been receiving up to now from the integrating Community will in future go to Central and Eastern Europe. The more developed countries, on the other hand, do not want to undertake further payment burdens.

The *budgetary conditions of accession* for the CEE countries were fairly concretely outlined by Agenda 2000 for the period of 2000–2006. In the budget approved in Berlin in March 1999, enlargement by the addition of the 5+1 'first-round' countries is envisaged as taking place from 2002. From January 1, 2000 the so-called *pre-accession funds* were established: they include the Instrument for Structural Policies for Pre-Accession (*ISPA*), the Community Support Regulation for Pre-Accession Measures for Agriculture and Rural Development (*SAPARD*), and also PHARE. In 1995 the CEE countries received about 1.2 billion ECUs from the EU budget, and for the period between 1995 and 1999 6.5 billion ECUs were allocated for this purpose. According to Agenda 2000, from 2000 in the framework of pre-accession support the 10 candidate countries will receive annually €1.04 bn from the ISPA, €520 m. from SAPARD, and €1.56 bn from PHARE. The transfers have thereby more than doubled.

Meanwhile, the earliest date for enlargement has changed to 2004, and 10 countries are preparing to join. The total allocation of €58.160 m. prescribed for the new members remains unchanged, and although four more countries than were planned for (with a total population of little more than 10 million) will be joining, this amount is judged to be enough for the period up to 2006. Of the planned budget €45.390 m. will be provided by the 15 present members' contributions and €12.770 m. from contributions paid by the new member countries. All this, of course, limits the scope for compromise in the talks on budget transfers.

Table 2. Allocation of resources available for enlargement, according to the EU–21 formula (in millions of euros)

Types of resources	2002	2003	2004	2005	2006
Total resources	6 450	9 030	11 610	14 200	16 780
New members' contributions	2 310	2 320	2 720	2 760	2 570
EU–15 contributions	4 140	6 710	8 890	11 440	14 210
Distribution of expenditure					
Agriculture	1 600	2 030	2 450	2 930	3 400
Structural policies	3 750	5 830	7 920	10 000	12 080
Internal policies	730	760	790	820	850
Administration	370	410	450	450	450

Source: Agenda 2000. March 1999, Berlin.

According to Agenda 2000, transfers to the new member countries from the structural funds *cannot exceed 4% of their GDP.* The obtaining of grants from the structural funds depends partly on the co-financing resources that can be mobilized, and partly on the candidates' ability to work out acceptable projects that make efficient use of resources. As far as co-financing is concerned, according to estimates, *the Hungarian budget may be largely suitable for the receiving of grants*. A lot of effort is needed, however, both from points of view of working out competitive projects, and also professional training. The resources, particularly from the structural funds, are not automatically available, and even among the older member countries there are large differences in absorption rates.

Although Central and Eastern Europe is poor in terms of capital and modern technology, in the last few years a *surplus labour* has accumulated. After the earlier full employment, economic transformation was accompanied by a high level of unemployment, and it was impossible to predict the level at which it might in the future be consolidated. Before 1972 the EC integration still played a stabilizing part in European markets, particularly with the great demand for unskilled labour. Since then this has radically changed and because of the high level of unemployment it was no accident that in the Europe Agreements the EU accepted in principle the free movement of people, but avoided any kind of concrete commitment or measure. Fears of a huge 'flood of refugees' from the East to the West have proved unfounded, but in connection with accession several EU countries (Austria, Germany, etc.) have strong reservations about mobility of labour. This was expressed in these countries' insistence on a 5–7-year transition period.

All the same, *human resources must be treated as an exceptionally important factor of production*, and indeed unemployment underlines this. It is a fact that only about 8% of the potential workforce in the EU is unemployed, but there is a shortage of well-educated intellectual workers, engineers, technicians and researchers. According to estimates about 2 million of the unemployed are out of work because of their low level of skills, and 3 million owing to regional causes. This means that associate's level of *education and training is of greater strategic importance*, and will be a key factor in its competitiveness in terms both of market competition and the exploitation of the possibilities of the single market. Enlargement is a challenge for the new members as well, since it is not in their interest that the better part of their skilled labour should leave the country. In the long-term even the expanded Union will show a demographic deficit, and because of this, better utilization of labour and the possibility of its free flow will become even more important.

From the 1990s the integration of the EU countries *was expected to develop in the economy at differing speeds* (this applied particularly to EMU). A Europe of 'multiple speeds' or 'varying geometry' does not conflict with the interests of the prospective members, since over-rapid integration might force adaptation measures that would be difficult to accept, socially and politically. Thus they might for a long time be kept out of the integration. The faster progress of the 'hard core' would of course be relative, meaning merely that they would sooner attain their goal (EMU). Actually it is the new members that will have to progress most quickly, if they want to catch up. 'Multiple-speed' integration should not mean that some countries become second-class members.

With earlier enlargements, the incorporation of the new member countries into the different policies of the EC/EU took place after *a longer or shorter transition period*. With regard to the transition period, the standpoints and interests of the EU and the accession countries are contradictory. Agenda 2000 indicated *immediate accession, without any transition period or grace period* (the 'big bang' solution) in most areas. This follows logically from the desire for rapid expansion of the single internal market, which is in the EU's fundamental interest, while grace periods would involve unforeseeable difficulties. The retention of border controls is disadvantageous for both sides. It is in the CEE countries' interest to join quickly and fully at once, because thus they can avoid acquiring second-class status (which could be important with regard to their participation in decision-making), and in this way they hope to maximize the budget transfers to them as soon as possible. The beneficial effects of membership can thus be obtained most quickly.

Nevertheless, Agenda 2000 does in many areas implicitly count on certain transition periods. This is particularly clear on the basis of the 2000–2006 budget targets. The budget transfers are basically conceived in terms of the Pre-Accession Strategy, and the consequences of full membership are not comprehensively counted on until 2006. This certainly applies to the compensatory payments connected with the agricultural policy, and to the participation in EMU. In relation to the land question and the free movement of labour, the transition period is expected to be 5 years, but may be as long as 7 years. Obviously, in certain sectors a longer period is required for adapting and fitting in.

Not only the countries of the region have an interest in 'Eastern enlargement'. In spite of all the difficulties and dangers, enlargement serves the interests of the EU and in fact of the whole of Europe. It aims at increasing security in Central and Eastern Europe and consolidating its newly established democracy, and this is not just a one-sided interest but a mutual one. With bigger markets the EU countries should gain market advantages that will amply compensate for their extra budgetary burdens. Enlargement should produce constraints towards modernization and structural improvement that will increase the continent's competitiveness in global markets. A peaceful, prosperous Europe may be a guarantee of a more stable world order.

REFERENCES

Agenda 2000. March 1999, Berlin.

Communication on "The Europe Agreements and Beyond: A Strategy to Prepare the Countries of CEE for Accession". Commission of the EU, July 27, 1994.

Europe Agreements.

European Commission DG for Agriculture (2002): Analysis of the Impact on Agricultural Markets and Incomes of EU Enlargement to the CEEcs. Brussels, March 2002.

HALMAI, P. (1993) *A közös agrárpolitika rendszere és reformja. Az Európai Közösség és Magyarország az 1990-es évek közepén* (The Common Agricultural Policy system and its reform. The European Community and Hungary in the mid-1990s). Aiula, Budapest.

NYE, JOSEPH. S., JR. (1993) *Merre tart az európai gazdaság 2000-ig?* (Where is the EC heading by 2000?) HVG, January 2.

RÁCZ, M. (1994) Magyarország útja az EK-ba, külső és belső meghatározottságok (Hungary's Road to EC, External and Internal Determinations). Thesis V. Hungarian Academy of Sciences, World Economic Institute. Budapest. May.